MW00845588

Mastering Access 365

An Easy Guide to Building Efficient Databases for Managing Your Data

Nathan George

Mastering Access 365: An Easy Guide to Building Efficient Databases for Managing Your Data

Disclaimer: Every effort has been made in the preparation of this book to ensure the accuracy of the information presented. However, the information contained in this book is sold without warranty, either express or implied. Neither the author nor publishers will be held liable for any damages caused or alleged to have been caused directly or indirectly by this book.

Published 2022.

Published by GTech Publishing.

ISBN: 978-1-915476-00-5

Contents

Introduction

Welcome to Mastering Access 365, the latest version of the most powerful desktop database application available today. In choosing this book, you're probably aware that Microsoft Access can help you manage your data in ways that other desktop applications can't. If you're using Access for business or personal data management, and you need a guide to get you up and running very quickly, then you've come to the right place.

Access occupies a unique position in the data management space. It is currently the best tool that bridges the gap between spreadsheet solutions like Excel and more complex enterprise solutions like SQL Server. In managing your data, if you've hit the limit of what you can do with a spreadsheet application, and a database server is currently not a viable option for you, then Access is the perfect tool for you. Access can help you create efficient and robust database solutions to manage your data faster and easier than any desktop database management system available today.

This book provides you with all the tools you need to build working databases from the ground up to manage your data. By the time you finish reading this book, you'll have all the knowledge required to create normalized tables, table relationships, queries, forms, and reports that provide efficient solutions for your data.

This book is concise, using clear and practical examples to demonstrate how to use the various features in Access to create database solutions.

Access Versions

Access 365 is the version of Access that comes with a Microsoft 365 subscription, while Access 2021 is the latest 'one-time purchase' version of Access that comes with Office 2021.

Over the last few years, Microsoft has adopted a regular release cycle where new features are released for Microsoft 365 products throughout the year. Conversely, the one-time purchase version of Office gets new features only when a new version of Office is released, approximately every 2-3 years. Security updates and bug fixes are released equally to all versions.

This book covers the latest version of Access in Microsoft 365 (2022 update) as well as Access 2021.

Who Is This Book For?

Mastering Access 365 is for you if you want to learn how to create database applications using Access quickly. You don't need to have any prior experience of Access, as this book starts with database basics and progresses through the various components of Access. If you're a beginner or an intermediate user, this book will enhance your skills in Access.

You also do not need any programming experience to use this book as we do not go into Access programming. Access VBA (Visual Basic for Applications) is a vast subject requiring a dedicated volume. However, it has fallen out of favor in recent years, and Microsoft recommends avoiding using VBA in shared databases for security considerations. The good news is that Access is so feature-rich that you can build complex and fully functional Access applications without writing a single line of code.

How To Use This Book

You can use this book as a step-by-step training guide or a reference manual that you come back to from time to time. If you're new to Access, you should start at the beginning of the book and read the chapters in sequential order.

If you're already familiar with Access, you can go directly to the chapters that cover the topics you want to learn. Although the chapters have been organized logically, the book has been designed to enable you to read each topic as a standalone tutorial if you're already familiar with prerequisite topics covered in previous chapters.

Assumptions

When writing this book, the software assumptions are that you already have Microsoft 365 or Access 2021 installed on your computer and are working on the Windows 10 or 11 platform.

If you're using an earlier version of Access, for example, Access 2016 or Access 2019, you can still use this book because many core features of Access remain the same. Note, however, that some menus and dialog boxes may be slightly different.

Practice Files

This book comes with downloadable Access files with the sample data used in the examples in the book. The sample files should save you time recreating the sample data if you want to practice as you follow the examples in the book. All examples are fully detailed in the book, and these files have been provided to save you some typing, so they're optional.

You can practice by changing the data to view different results. Please note that practice files have only been included for chapters where new Access objects have been created or the examples use a sizable amount of sample data. You can download the files with the following link:

https://www.excelbytes.com/mastering-access-365-dl/

Notes:

- Type the URL in your Internet browser's address bar, and press Enter to go to the download page. **If you encounter an error, please double-check that you have entered all characters in the URL correctly**.

- The files have been zipped into one download. Windows 10 (or Windows 11) comes with the functionality to unzip files. If your OS does not have this functionality, you'll need to get a piece of software like WinZip or WinRAR to unzip the file.

- The practice files are Access (.accdb) files. You would need to have Access (2007 and above) installed on your computer to open and use these files. You can use Excel or Google Sheets to open the included Excel files. Windows 10 and 11 come with the functionality to unzip files, but if your OS does not have this feature, you will need to get a piece of software like WinZip or WinRAR to unzip the file.

- If you have any problems downloading these files, please contact me at **support@excelbytes.com**. Include the title of this book in your email, and the practice files will be emailed directly to you.

Part 1

Introduction to Access

In Part 1

This part of the book introduces you to relational databases, database concepts and terms, and an overview of what you can do with Access. Chapter 2 gets you started in creating a new database, and in chapter 3, you get to explore and familiarize yourself with the Access interface and working environment.

Contents at a Glance

Chapter 1: Introduction to Databases

A database is any organized collection of data, which does not necessarily have to be computerized. For example, a manual filing system with cabinets and folders containing documents in some organized fashion is a manual database. Before computer systems became common, records were mostly stored using index cards organized in alphanumeric order for easy information storage and retrieval. An Access database is simply a computerized version of these manual filing and retrieval systems.

What is a Relational Database?

A relational database management system (RDBMS) stores its data using a relational table structure. A relational table structure organizes data in tables made up of rows and columns. Tables are linked by related fields called keys. Keys are used to uniquely identify records as well as link records between different tables.

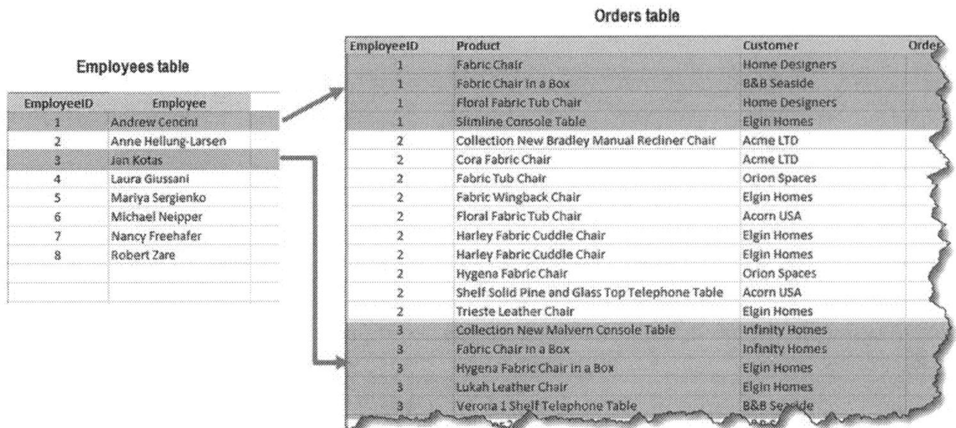

Employees table

EmployeeID	Employee
1	Andrew Cencini
2	Anne Hellung-Larsen
3	Jan Kotas
4	Laura Giussani
5	Mariya Sergienko
6	Michael Neipper
7	Nancy Freehafer
8	Robert Zare

Orders table

EmployeeID	Product	Customer	Orde
1	Fabric Chair	Home Designers	
1	Fabric Chair in a Box	B&B Seaside	
1	Floral Fabric Tub Chair	Home Designers	
1	Slimline Console Table	Elgin Homes	
2	Collection New Bradley Manual Recliner Chair	Acme LTD	
2	Cora Fabric Chair	Acme LTD	
2	Fabric Tub Chair	Orion Spaces	
2	Fabric Wingback Chair	Elgin Homes	
2	Floral Fabric Tub Chair	Acorn USA	
2	Harley Fabric Cuddle Chair	Elgin Homes	
2	Harley Fabric Cuddle Chair	Elgin Homes	
2	Hygena Fabric Chair	Orion Spaces	
2	Shelf Solid Pine and Glass Top Telephone Table	Acorn USA	
2	Trieste Leather Chair	Elgin Homes	
3	Collection New Malvern Console Table	Infinity Homes	
3	Fabric Chair in a Box	Infinity Homes	
3	Hygena Fabric Chair in a Box	Elgin Homes	
3	Lukah Leather Chair	Elgin Homes	
3	Verona 1 Shelf Telephone Table	B&B Seaside	

Example of a one-to-many relationship that avoids data duplication

As you can see from the image above, each order is linked to the employee that processed it. However, we only need to store employee information once in our system and use the employee key (EmployeeID) to establish the link between the two tables.

Below are some benefits of organizing your data in different related tables:

- **More efficient data storage**

  In a relational data structure, you enter your data only once. This can save a lot of space, especially when you have a lot of data.

- **Greater accuracy and data integrity**

  When you enter data more than once, you risk introducing errors. For example, let's say we were entering customer names and addresses directly into records. If you make a mistake with the customer's name in one or more of the entries, it means you will not find all the records for that customer when you perform a search for records linked to that customer. Also, when you make a mistake or need to make a change, you only need to do it in one place.

- **Best way to capture transactions**

  The relational table structure is the best way to capture more complex data, such as transactions. Transactions can have one main record and several related records. For instance, you can have one customer order that includes several items, making up several order lines. If you were to capture this with a spreadsheet, it would mean entering the customer details multiple times. This uses up more storage space, and repetition can introduce errors in your data.

Database Concepts and Terms

Before we delve into creating a database, you need to be familiar with some basic terms and concepts of databases that we'll be using throughout this book.

- **Tables**
  In Access, a table is a container for your data. Each table contains information about a single entity, for example, employees, customers, or products. The data in the table are organized into rows and columns. Each table in Access is an entity. As you organize your data into tables, you should think of how the tables represent the physical entities for which you want to store information and how the entities relate to each other.

- **Records and fields**
  After creating your table, your table will have columns and rows, and you can view this as a datasheet in Access. The rows in a datasheet are also called records, and the columns are fields. The first row of every table contains the names of the fields in the table. Each row in your table is a record. Each record is an instance of the entity the table represents. A column (or field) in each row represents the smallest possible unit in the database. A field could be the first name, last name, or the customer's phone number in your table. As you design a database, the fields in your table represent columns.

- **Primary key**
  A primary key is a unique identifier for each record. For example, in a table with data for several customers, you may have customers with the same first name and surname. Therefore, we need a method to uniquely identify each customer record in the database. The primary key can be numeric or alphanumeric.

- **Foreign key**
  A foreign key is placing the primary key of one table in another table to link related records between both tables. A common example of using a foreign key is organizing customer and order records. Instead of saving full customer details with each order, you place customer details in a separate table and only add the customer key with related orders as a foreign key.

- **Parent-Child table relationships**
  One of the benefits of using a relational database is to avoid repeating data. You can create relationships between two tables using a foreign key. For the example used above to describe a foreign key, the Customers and Orders tables will be linked in a parent-child relationship because the two tables have a one-to-many relationship.

What You Can Do with Access

Access 2021 is a powerful relational database management system (RDBMS) geared for the desktop. Access occupies a unique position between flat-file systems like spreadsheets and database servers like SQL Server and Oracle regarding data management. You may be reading this book because your data has become too complex for a spreadsheet, but a database server is not suitable for your current situation. Access is currently the best tool for you if you are in this position.

Once upon a time, Access was the tool of choice for the rapid development of small corporate databases. However, Access eventually became a victim of its success regarding ease of use. Corporate IT departments felt Access made it too easy for employees to create complex databases critical to core business functions without any central oversight. Hence there was a general shift to centralized database servers and web-based client applications, almost like a return to the days of mainframes and dumb terminals. However, now we have database servers like SQL Server and Oracle on network servers. Database servers offer a higher level of security than Access but often require dedicated database administrators.

Since this shift, though, there is still a sizable demand for small, rapidly developed database applications to manage data more complex than a spreadsheet can handle. Therefore, Access still has a significant role in the data management space.

Build Business and Personal Databases

As mentioned earlier, despite its age, Access is still currently the best tool in the market if you want to quickly create a solution for a small business or personal database. Access can handle multiple tables and hundreds of thousands of records up to 2 GBs of data.

- **Forms:** As well as a database management system (DBMS), Access provides rapid application development tools that enable you to create front-end applications that allow users to interact with the database.

- **Reports:** Access has many tools to create all kinds of reports. You can create reports for print or on-screen display. The reporting tools allow you to calculate running totals, group, sort, and filter data. These rapid application development tools are not found in database servers. For example, suppose you store your data in SQL Server. In that case, you may need to develop a front-end application using a programming language like Visual Studio to interact with the database to enter and modify records. Access provides all these tools in one package, which is the beauty of Access.

- **Queries:** Access has a graphical user interface, also known as Query by Example (QBE), that makes it quick and easy to create queries. When you have hundreds of thousands of records, the ability to create queries to sort, filter, and group your data is very important. These queries also make it easy to create reports that pull data from different tables.

- **Macros and Visual Basic for Applications:** You can create robust working databases without the need for programming. But macros and Visual Basic for Applications (VBA) offer additional options if you wish to extend the functionality of your database.

- **Multiuser:** An Access database can theoretically have up to 255 concurrent users. This multi-user capability makes Access superior to a tool like Excel as a data management tool in a multi-user environment.

- **Connectivity to other applications:** Access has built-in tools that make it easy to import and export data to other applications like Excel, text files, SharePoint, SQL Server, and Oracle. This compatibility makes Access an ideal solution if you want more database functionality than Excel can provide and intend to migrate your data to a database server like SQL Server one day.

Data Transformation

Access is excellent as a data transformation tool because it has many features that allow you to easily transfer data to and from a wide range of applications. You can bring data into Access, run queries to transform the data, and export the transformed data back to the source application. For example, Access is great for carrying out batch updates, removing duplicate rows, and splitting data into different tables.

Chapter 2: Getting Started with Access

To get started with Access, you need to create a new blank database or open an existing one. There are several ways you can open an existing Access database or create a new blank database. We will go through the various option in this chapter.

In this chapter, we will cover how to:

- Create a new blank database.
- Open an existing database from File Explorer.
- Open an existing database from Access.
- Create a new database from one of the database templates.
- Open an existing database in a different open mode.

Creating a New Database

There are several ways you can create a new database in Access. We'll go through the three methods below.

Creating a Blank Database from Access

To create a new blank database:

1. Click Start (or press the Windows key on your keyboard to display the start menu.

2. Click Access (Access should be listed in the group of applications under A)

   The Access Home screen is displayed.

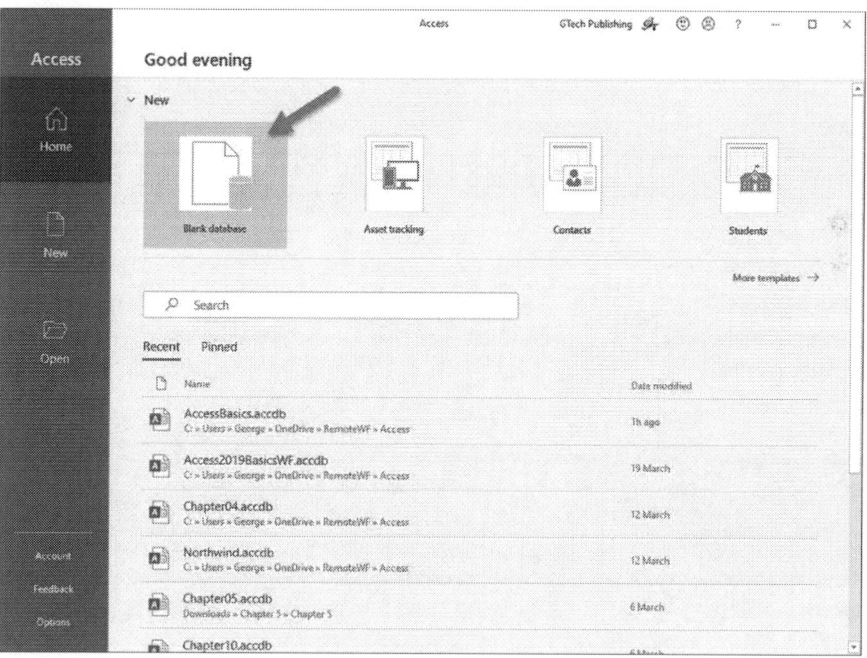

Access home screen

3. Click **Blank database**.

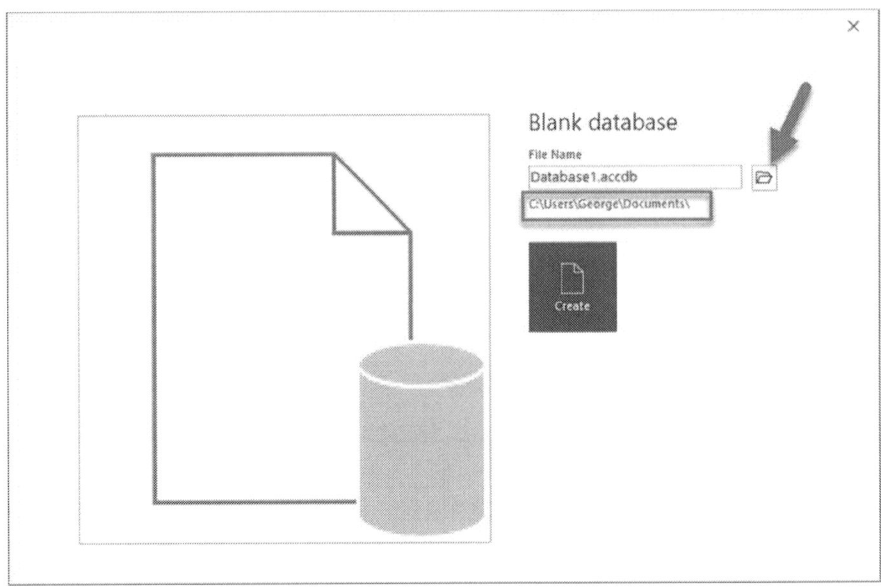

4. The default file location will be your Documents folder on your C: drive. Click the folder icon and select a new location from the **File New Database** dialog box to change the folder location.

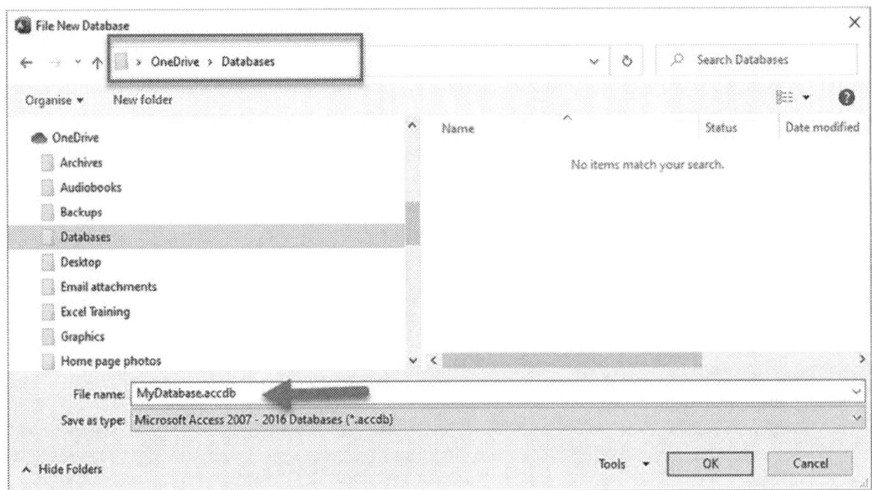

5. In the File New Database dialog box, navigate to the folder where you want to save the database.

6. In the **File name** field, enter the name of your database.

7. Click **OK**.

Access takes you back to the previous dialog box, where you'll notice that the file name and location have been changed to the values you entered.

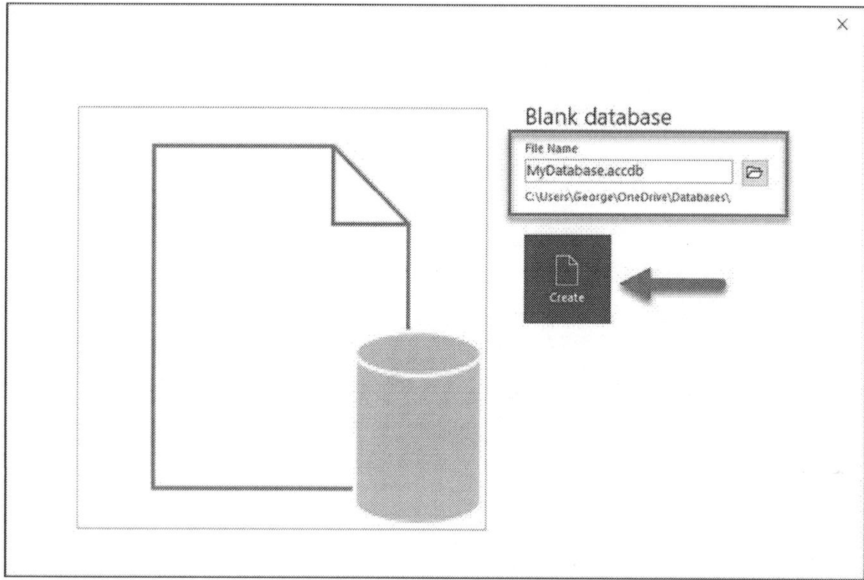

8. Click the **Create** button to create the new database.

Creating a Blank Database Using File Explorer

One of the first things you need to do to create a new blank database in Access is select the database's directory. Navigating to the correct folder through the New Database dialog box can sometimes be confusing. One quick way to create a new Access database is to do it in File Explorer.

To create a new Access database using File Explorerin Windows), do the following:

1. In File Explorer, navigate to the folder where you want to create the Access database.

2. Right-click any blank area on the right pane of the File Explorer window and select **New** > **Microsoft Access Database** from the pop-up menu.

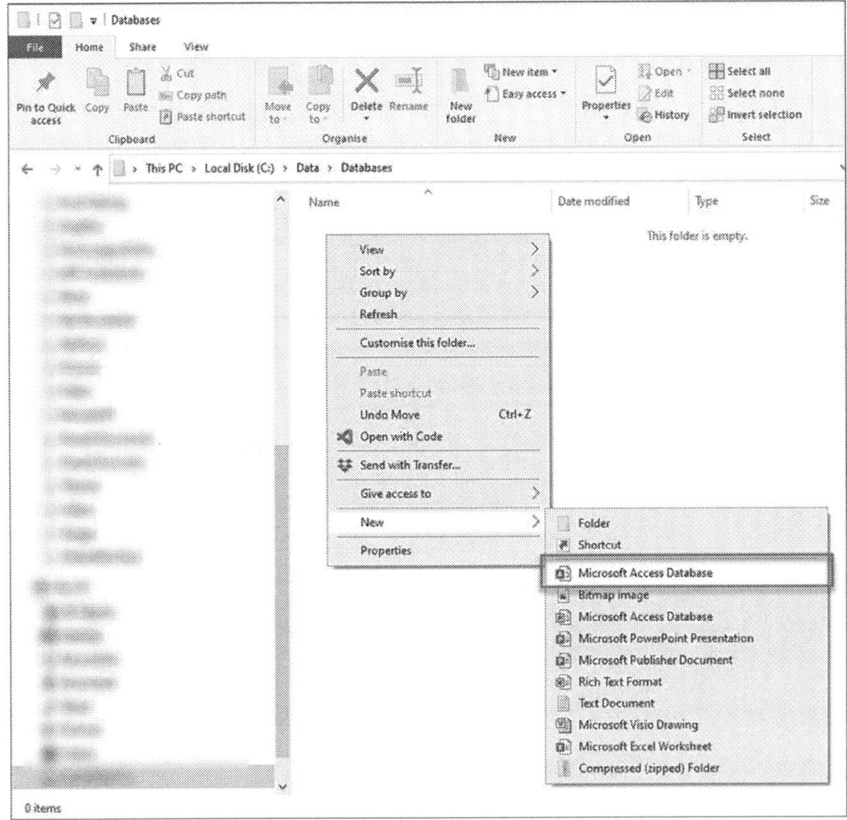

Create a new database in File Explorer

3. Windows creates a new database file in the folder and selects the default name, enabling you to type over it.

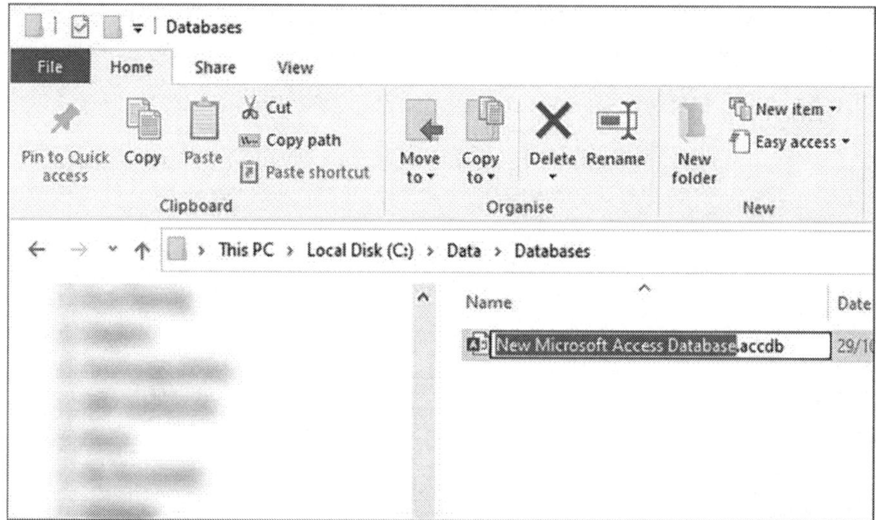

4. Type in the name for your database file and press **Enter**.

5. To open and use the database, double-click the file in File Explorer.

That's it. You now have a new blank database created in the location you want it.

Create a New Database from a Template

To create a new database from a template, after launching Access, click **New** on the menu on the left of the screen to display the **New** dialog box.

You'll notice a couple of Access database templates that you can use as a starting basis for your database. You can select one of the categories listed under **Suggested searches** to filter the list. These categories include **Business**, **Logs**, **Industry**, **Lists**, **Personal**, and **Contacts**.

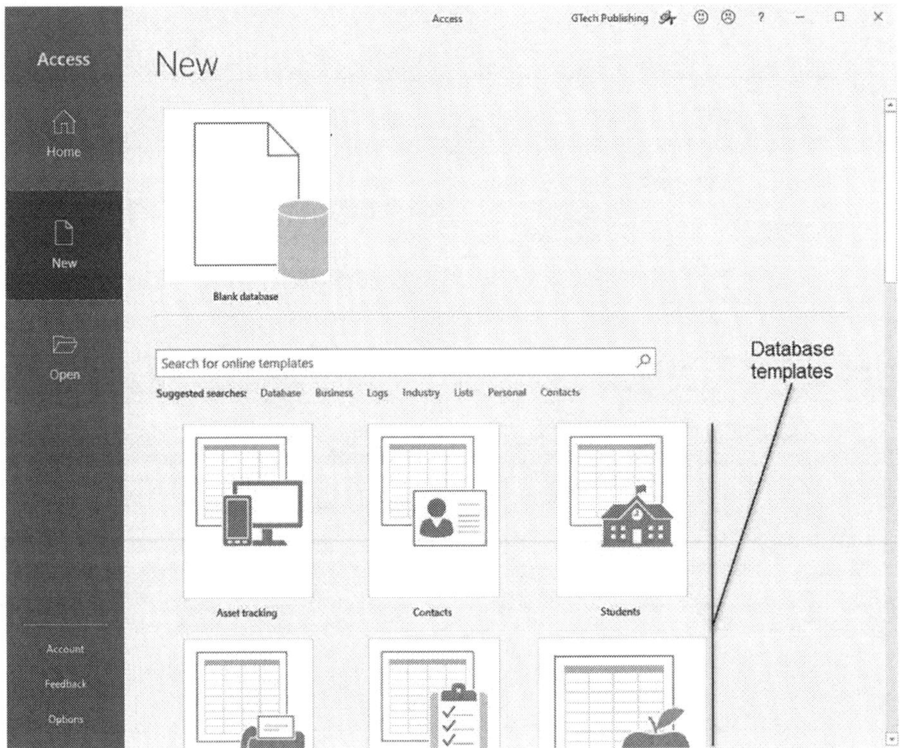

Access database templates

1. Click the template that's the best match for the type of database you want to create. For example, if you want to create a contacts list, select Contacts.

   The next dialog box has a brief description of the template, which gives you an idea of how suitable the template is for your requirements.

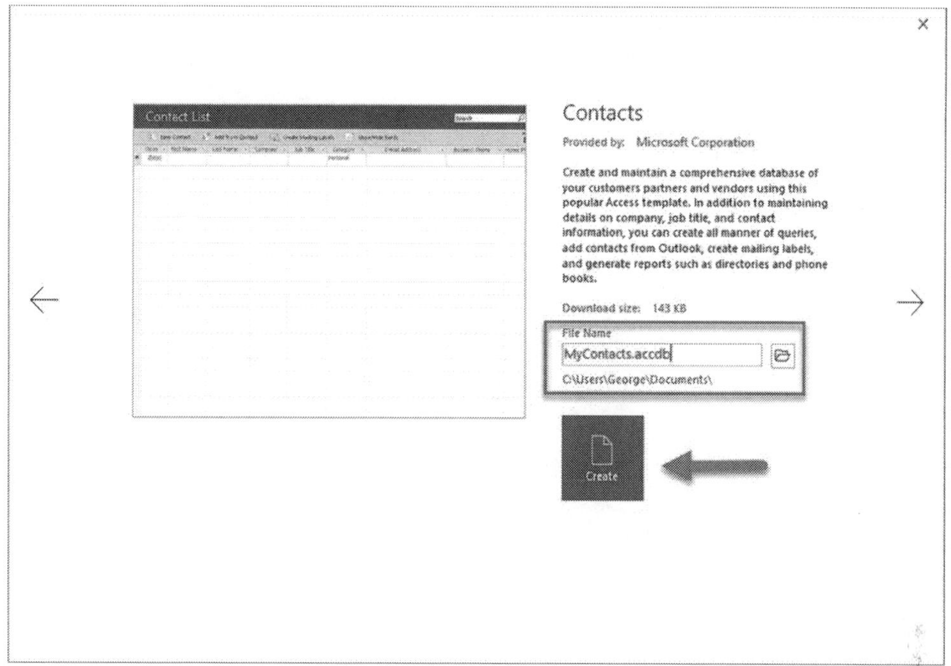

Note You can view descriptions for the other templates by clicking the right arrow (to go forward) and the left arrow (to go back).

2. Enter the file name. Click the folder icon to change the directory if you want to save the database in a different location from the default.

3. Click **Create** to create the database.

Note As this database has a macro to display a welcome screen, you'll get a security warning just under the Ribbon telling you that some content was disabled. Click the **Enable Content** button to start using the database.

Open an Existing Database

There are two ways you can open an existing Access database. You can open the Access file from within Access or open it directly from File Explorer.

Open an Access Database from File Explorer

If Access 365 is installed on your computer, all files with the **.accdb** file extension will be associated with Access. Hence, when you double-click the file, Windows opens it in Access.

To open an Access database in a File Explorer directory, navigate to the folder containing the Access database you want to open and double-click the file.

Open a Database from Within Access

Launch Access (or if Access is already open, click **File** to display the Backstage view).

On the left side of the start page, click **Open** to go to the Open pane of the Backstage view.

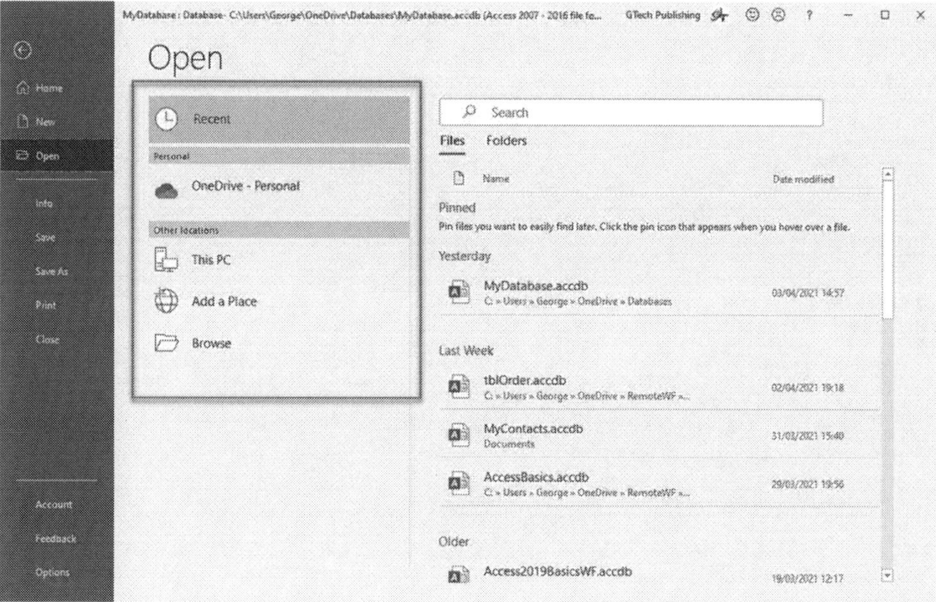

On the left side of the screen, you'll see the following options:

- **Recent**: This option shows a list of files and folders you've recently opened. To open a database you've recently opened, click Recent, and then on the list on the right, locate and double-click the database to open it.

- **OneDrive**: You will see this option if you're using OneDrive on your Windows account. This option displays a list of folders on OneDrive from where you can navigate to the database you want to open and double-click it.

- **This PC**: This option displays a list of databases in the last folder in which you saved an Access database. If you haven't previously saved an Access database on this installation of Access, this option takes you to your default Windows Documents folder.

- **Add a Place**: You can use this option to add OneDrive locations. For example, if you have OneDrive for Business, you can use this option to add it to your list of locations.

- **Browse**: This option opens the Open dialog box where you can navigate to the drive or folder containing the database you want to open. The File Open dialog box also allows you to open Access in various modes.

Open an Access database in a Different Open Mode

1. In the Backstage view, in the Open area, click **Browse** to show the **Open** dialog box. Then navigate to the folder that contains your database.

2. When you find the database, you have several options for opening it:

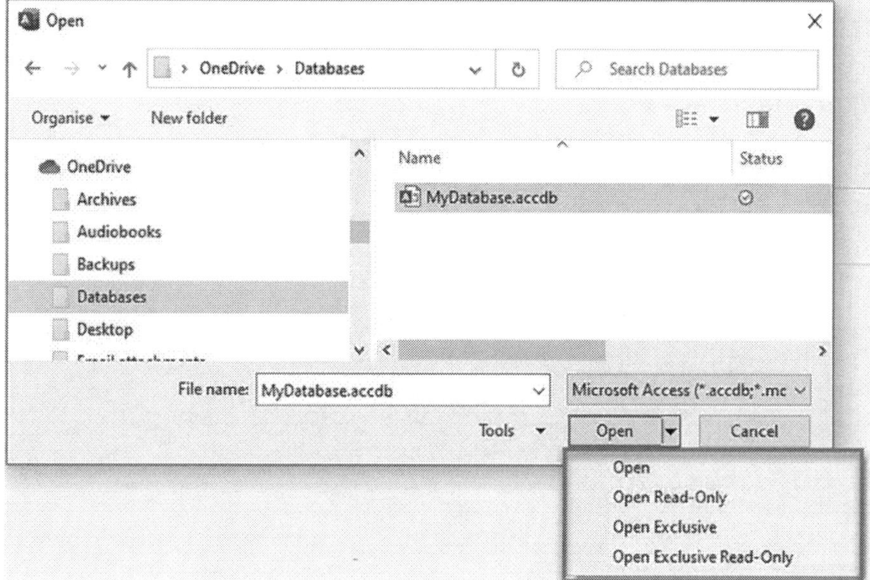

Access database open options

- **Open:** Double-click the database or select the database and click the **Open** button to open the database in the default open mode.

Note The *Default open mode* can be set in **Access Options** > **Client Settings** > **Advanced**. This option is set to 'Shared' for a default installation of Access, meaning other users can also read and write to the database in a multi-user environment.

- **Open Read-Only**: To open the database in read-only mode, click the arrow next to the Open button, then select **Open Read-Only** on the drop-down menu. This mode enables you to view but not edit data. Opening the database in this mode will not affect other users' access.

- **Open Exclusive**: Click the arrow next to the Open button and select **Open Exclusive** on the menu. When you open the database in Exclusive mode, anyone else who tries to open the database will receive a "file already in use" message.

- **Open Exclusive Read-Only**: To open the database as exclusive but read-only, click the arrow next to the Open button and select Open Exclusive Read-Only from the menu. With this option, you get read-only access. Other users can still open the database, but they are limited to read-only access.

If the list of recently used files is not displayed, configure it in Access Options (if it is not set):

1. On Backstage view, click **Options**.
2. In the Access Options dialog box, click **Client Settings**.
3. Scroll down and under **Display**, enter a number in the **Show this number of Recent Databases** box.
4. Click **OK** to save and exit Access Options.

Open Multiple Databases Simultaneously

In a single instance of Access, you can have only one database open at a time, meaning you can't open more than one database within the same Access window. However, you can open multiple instances of Access simultaneously, and each could have a database open.

To open more than one Access database, for example, to have two Access databases open at the same time:

- Find the first database using File Explorer and double-click the file to open it in a new Access window. Repeat the process for the second database.
- Start Access and open the first Access database within Access, and then start a new instance of Access and open the second database.

Each instance of Access runs in a separate window. Thus, if you have more than one instance running, you can tile the windows to view them simultaneously.

Note The number of Access instances you can run simultaneously depends primarily on your computer's memory capacity. Available memory depends on how much RAM your computer has and how many applications are using it simultaneously.

How to Open Access 97 Files

Files created with Access 97 are not compatible with Access 2021. If you try to open an Access 97 MDB file with Access 2021, you will get the following error message:

"Cannot Open a database created with a previous version of your application."

To work around this issue, you'll need to open the database with Access 2003 and save it as an ACCDB file.

Follow the steps below to open an Access 97 database:

1. Open the Access 97 database in Access 2003.
2. On the **Tools** menu, click **Database Utilities** > **Convert Database** > **Access 2002-2003 file format**.
3. Enter a name for the database, and then click **Save**.
4. Close Access 2003.
5. Open the database in Access 2021.
6. Click the **File** button to go to the Backstage View.
7. Click **Save As**, select **Access Database (*.accdb),** and then click the **Save As** button on the page.
8. Click **Save** in the Save As dialog box.

You can also open Access 97 databases with Access 2007 or Access 2010. However, in those versions, the Database Enhancement Wizard will appear to help you to convert the database to the ACCDB format.

Note Access allows you to directly open a database in a different file format. For example, you can open Paradox, dBASE, Microsoft Exchange, Excel files from Access.

Closing an Access Database

To close Access, click the close button (x) on the top right of the window. If you have any unsaved design objects, Access will prompt you to save them first.

To close an Access database instance without closing the Access window:

On the Ribbon, click **File** > **Close**.

Access closes the active database, leaving an empty window.

To open another database from Access, click **File** > **Open**.

Chapter 3: Understanding the Access Interface

If you're new to Access, the user interface may initially look confusing and too busy. But don't worry, it gets familiar very quickly as you use the application. Like other Microsoft 365 applications, the Ribbon is mostly contextual, meaning, Access often only shows the tabs and commands that are relevant to the task you're currently performing.

In this chapter, we will cover:

- The Ribbon, including the (standard and contextual) tabs and commands.
- How to use the Navigation Pane to work with Access objects.
- Overview of the menu options in the Backstage view.
- How to enable and customize the Quick Access Toolbar.
- How to customize the tabs and commands to the Ribbon.
- An overview of the object types you can create in Access.
- How to use the Navigation Pane to rename, copy, or delete an Access object.

The Access Ribbon

The Access interface is displayed after you create a new database (or open an existing one). See the image below.

At the top of the screen, you have the **Ribbon**. On the left side of the screen, you have the **Navigation Pane**, and on the right of the screen, you have the **Work area**.

This chapter will cover the Navigation Pane, the Ribbon, and the backstage view.

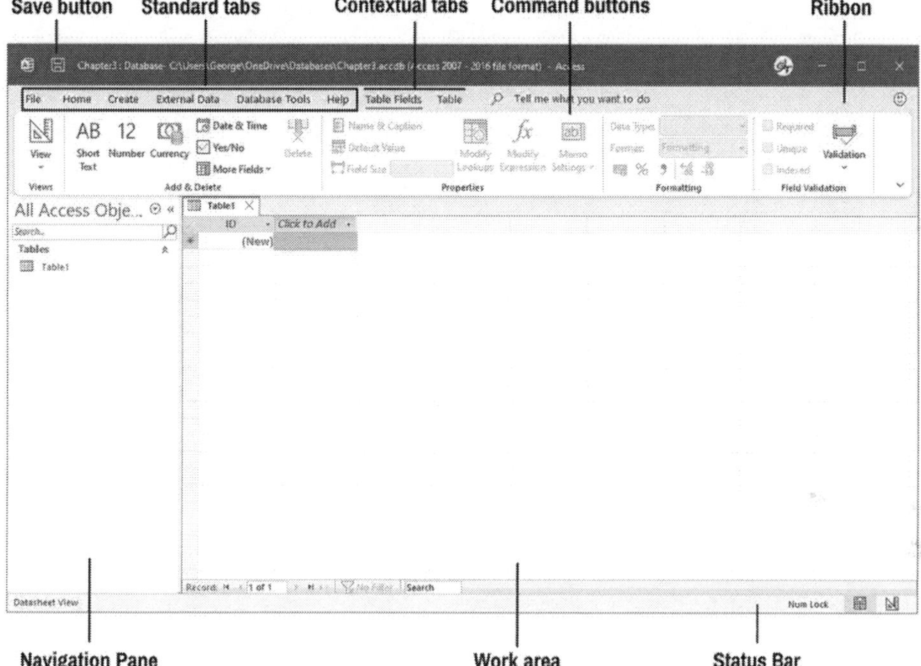

The Ribbon is the top part of the Access window that includes the tabs and the command buttons. The Ribbon was introduced in Access 2007 in place of the old menus and toolbars to create a uniform look across all Office applications.

Standard Tabs:

- **File**: When you click the File tab, Access takes you to the Backstage view. The Backstage view contains several menu options to do with creating, opening, saving, and configuring databases. We will explore the Backstage view later in this chapter.
- **Home**: The Home tab contains the most frequently used commands. Here, you'll find general commands that are more frequently used when working with Access. The Home tab contains commands used for text formatting, finding records, copying & pasting, sorting & filtering.
- **Create**: The Create tab contains commands to create and design various Access objects. This is where you have the commands to create tables, queries, forms, reports, and macros.
- **External Data**: This tab provides commands that enable you to connect to other data sources. In this tab, you can export or import data to/from file formats like Excel and CSV files (comma separated values), databases like Access, SQL Server, Azure, ODBC data sources, and web services like SharePoint.
- **Database Tools**: This tab contains commands that relate to the inner workings of an Access database. On this tab, you will find commands that enable you to compact & repair databases, create macros, create table relationships, analyze and tune the performance of your database, and move your database to different files like a backend Access database or a SharePoint server.

Contextual Tabs:

In addition to the standard tabs described above, Access has contextual tabs specific to the type of Access object you are working with. These contextual tabs only show up when working with a particular object. For example, when working in the table design view, you will see a new tab named **Table Design**. Sometimes you can have several contextual tabs added to the Ribbon, depending on the task you're performing.

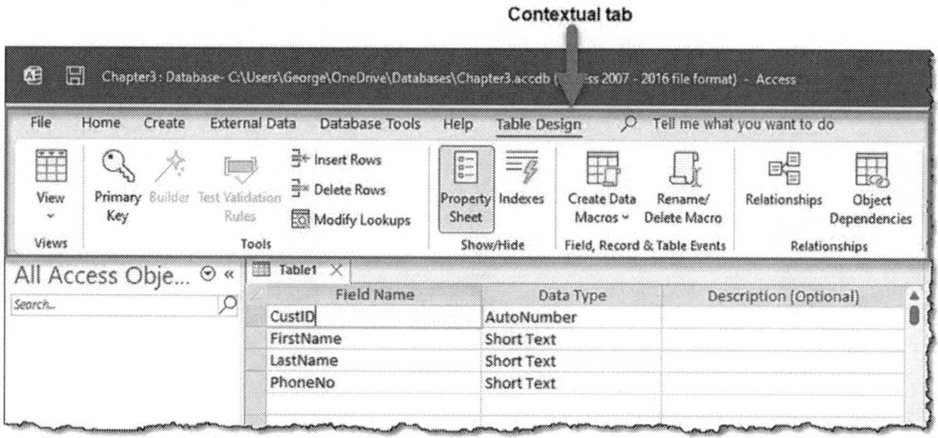

Tabs and commands appear and disappear on the Ribbon as you work with Access because you're given just what you need for the task you're performing.

Dialog Box Launcher

In some groups on the Ribbon, you'll have a dialog box launcher - a small arrow on the lower-right edge of the group. You can click this arrow to open a dialog box with additional commands and information for that group.

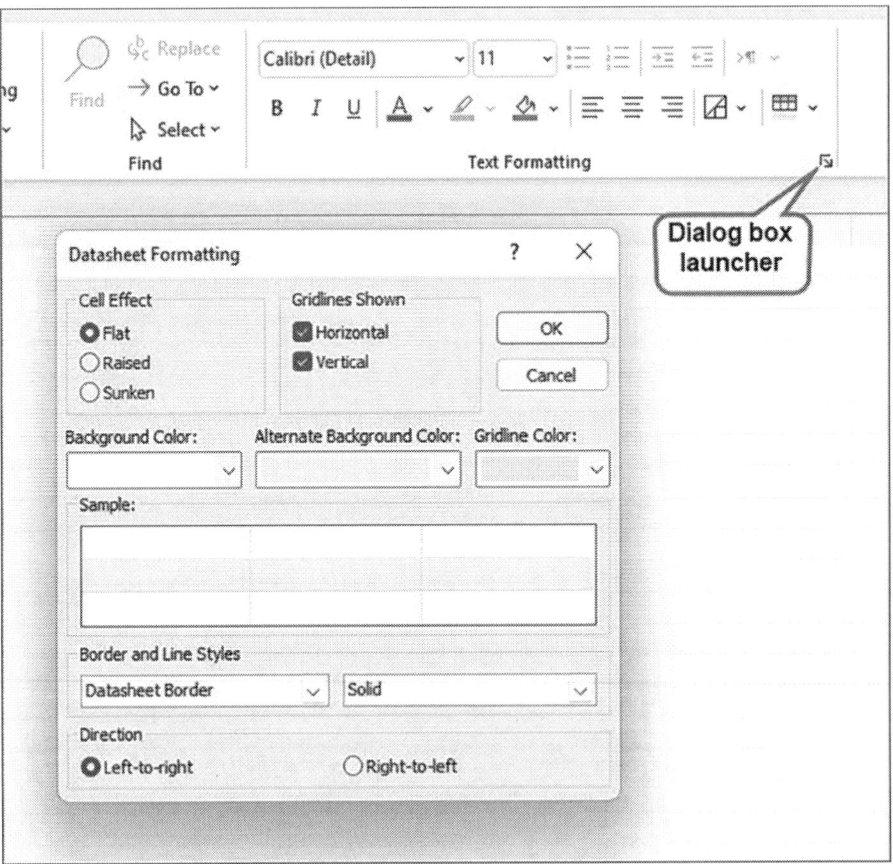

Some command buttons on the Ribbon also have an arrow pointing down, indicating a menu of additional options you can select.

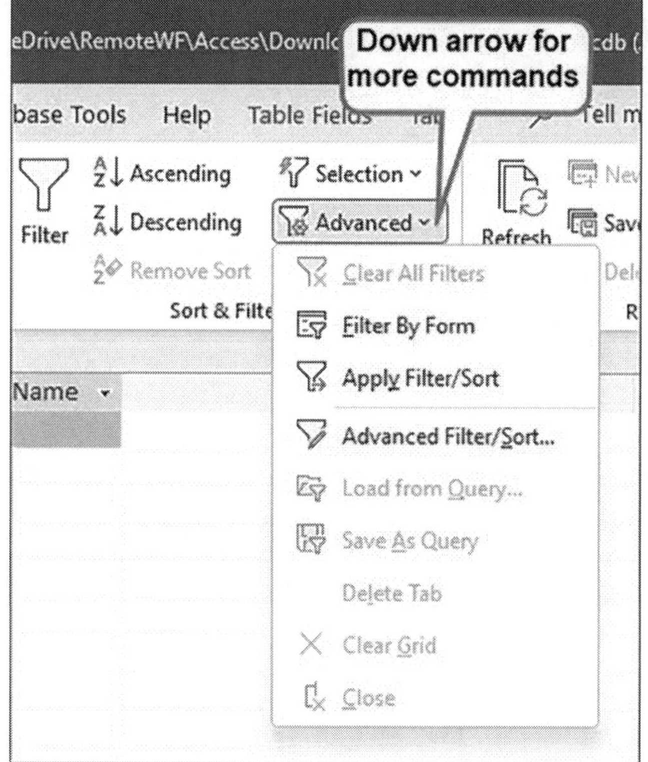
eDrive\RemoteWF\Access\Downlc
Down arrow for more commands
base Tools
Help
Table Fields
Tell m
Filter
Ascending
Descending
Remove Sort
Sort & Filte
Selection
Advanced
Refresh
Clear All Filters
Filter By Form
Apply Filter/Sort
Advanced Filter/Sort...
Load from Query...
Save As Query
Delete Tab
Clear Grid
Close
Name

The Backstage View

When you click on the **File** tab on the Ribbon, Access takes you to the Backstage view. The Backstage view offers a series of menu options and commands to manage the current database and configure general Access settings. The Back button takes you back to the Access workspace.

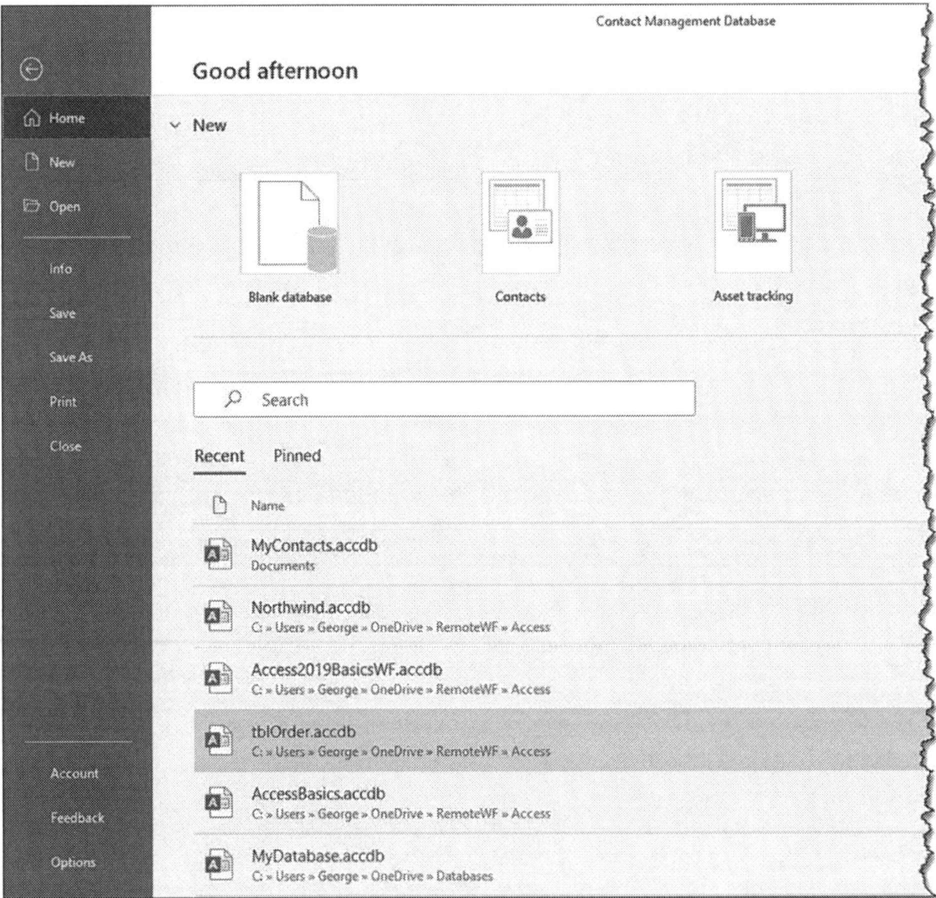

An overview of the menu options in the Backstage view:

- **Info**: This option enables you to view and edit various properties of the current database, compact & repair the database, and encrypt the database with a password.

- **New**: This option enables you to create a new blank database or create one from a predefined database template.

- **Open**: You can use this option to open an existing database, including viewing a list of recently opened databases.

- **Save**: This option takes you back to the Access workspace, where you can save individual Access objects.

- **Save As**: This menu option gives you various options to save or convert the current database. You can save the database with a different name, in which case, a copy of the database will be created. You can also convert the database to a different Access format, as it is an object, or save it as a PDF or XPS file.

- **Print**: You can use this option to:
    - **Quick Print**: Send the object directly to the default printer without making changes.
    - **Print**: Configure various printing options before printing.
    - **Print Preview**: Preview and change the pages you want to print.

- **Close**: This allows you to close the current database but leave Access open.

- **Account**: View and manage information relating to the current Office user. Most of the options and setting here affect all Microsoft 365 applications installed on the computer and not just Access. For example, changing the Office Theme here will change it for all Office applications on the machine.

- **Options**: Launches the Access Options dialog box, which contains a series of settings you can use to customize Access, for example, language, display, proofing, the Ribbon, the Quick Access Toolbar, and other settings.

- **Feedback**: This allows you to provide feedback and suggestions to Microsoft and to explore the feedback from others.

The Quick Access Toolbar

The Quick Access Toolbar is no longer displayed by default in Microsoft 365 because the most popular commands on the Quick Access Toolbar are now on the Ribbon by default. These commands are **Save**, **Undo**, and **Redo**.

You can skip this section if you seldom use the Quick Access Toolbar and don't need to display it.

To display the Quick Access Toolbar, right-click any blank area of the Ribbon and select **Show Quick Access Toolbar** from the pop-up menu.

Access will display the Quick Access Toolbar below the Ribbon by default. You can switch the toolbar to the top of the Ribbon by right-clicking anywhere on the bar and selecting **Show Quick Access Toolbar Above the Ribbon**.

Note If you hide and redisplay the Quick Access Toolbar, Access will remember where it was last positioned and display it there again.

The Quick Access Toolbar is a customizable toolbar with commands independent of the active tab on the Ribbon. The Quick Access Toolbar allows you to add commands you often use in Access.

To customize the Quick Access Toolbar, click its down arrow to display a drop-down menu.

Check items on the menu you want to add to the Quick Access Toolbar and uncheck those you want to remove.

To add commands to the Quick Access Toolbar that you can't find on the menu, do the following:

1. Click the **More Commands** menu option. Access will open the Quick Access Toolbar pane in Access Options.

2. In the drop-down list named **Choose commands from**, select **All Commands**.

3. From the list of commands on the left, select a command you would like to add to the Quick Access Toolbar and click the **Add** button to add it to the list on the right. Do this for every command you want to add to the list.

To change the order of the commands on the Quick Access Toolbar, select a command on the list on the right and use the up and down arrows (next to the list) to move it up or down.

4. Click the **OK** button when you are done.

Customizing the Ribbon

You can customize the Ribbon to your liking by adding or removing tabs and command buttons.

To customize the Ribbon, do the following:

Right-click anywhere on the Ribbon, below the tabs, and select **Customize the Ribbon** from the pop-up menu.

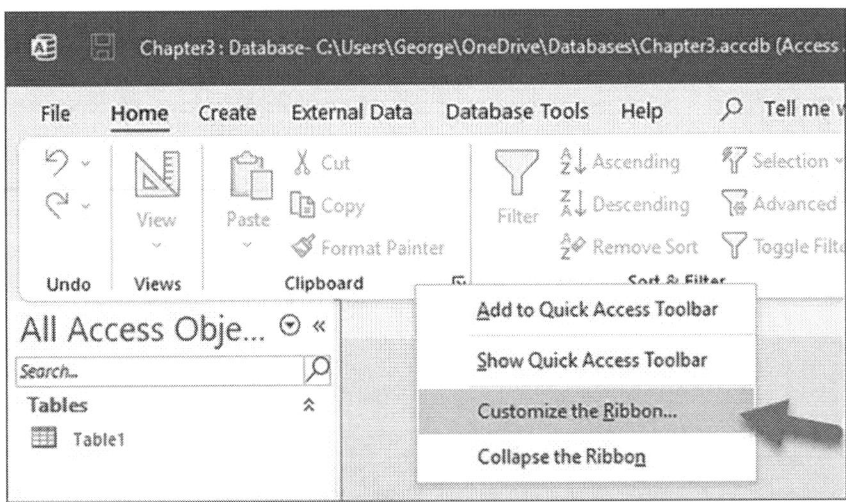

This will open the **Customize Ribbon** pane of the **Access Options** dialog box.

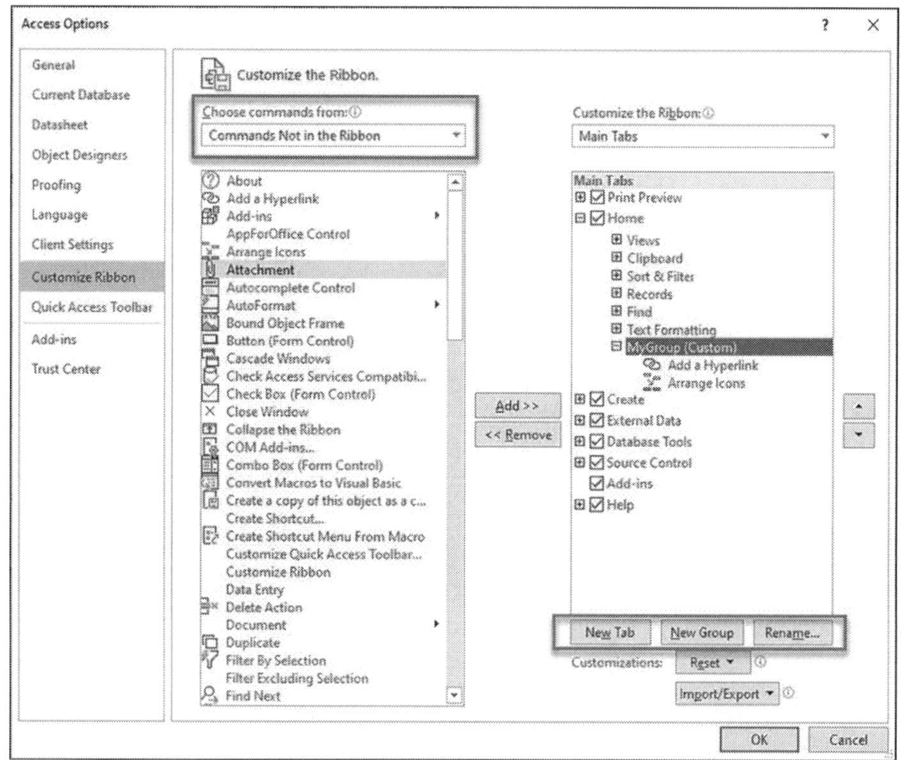

On the **Customize Ribbon** pane, you have two main list boxes. On the right, you have a list showing your current tabs - **Main Tabs**. On the left, you have the command buttons that you can add to the Ribbon.

To expand a group in the **Main Tabs** box, click on the plus sign (+) to the left of an item. To collapse a group, click on the minus sign (-).

To find commands that are not currently on the Ribbon, in the drop-down list named **Choose commands from**, select **Commands Not in the Ribbon**.

You will see a list of commands that are not on your Ribbon. This is useful as it filters out the commands already on your Ribbon.

Note You cannot add or remove the default commands on the Ribbon, but you can uncheck them on the list to prevent them from being displayed. Also, you cannot add command buttons to the default groups. You must create a new group to add a new command button.

To create a new tab:

Click on the **New Tab** button to create a new tab. Within the tab, you must create at least one group before you can add a command button from the list on the left side of the dialog box.

To create a custom group:

1. Select the tab in which you want to create the group. This could be one of the default tabs or the new one you've created.

2. Click on the **New Group** button (located at the bottom of the dialog box, under the Main Tabs box). This will create a new group within the currently selected tab.

3. Select the new group and click **Rename** to give it your preferred name.

   You now have a custom group in which you can add commands.

To add commands to your custom group:

1. Select your custom group in the list on the right side of the dialog box.

2. Select the new command button you want to add from the list on the left side of the dialog box.

3. Click on the **Add** button to add the command to the new custom group.

4. If you want to remove a command from your custom group, select the command on the right box and click **Remove**.

5. Click **OK** to confirm the change.

When you view the customized tab on the Ribbon, you'll see your new group and the command buttons you've added.

The Navigation Pane

The Navigation Pane on the left of the window is your primary navigation tool when working with Access. The Navigation Pane shows the tables, forms, queries, reports, and macros that have been created in the database. Over the years, the Access Navigation Pane has become more feature-rich, allowing you to display the objects in different views and combinations.

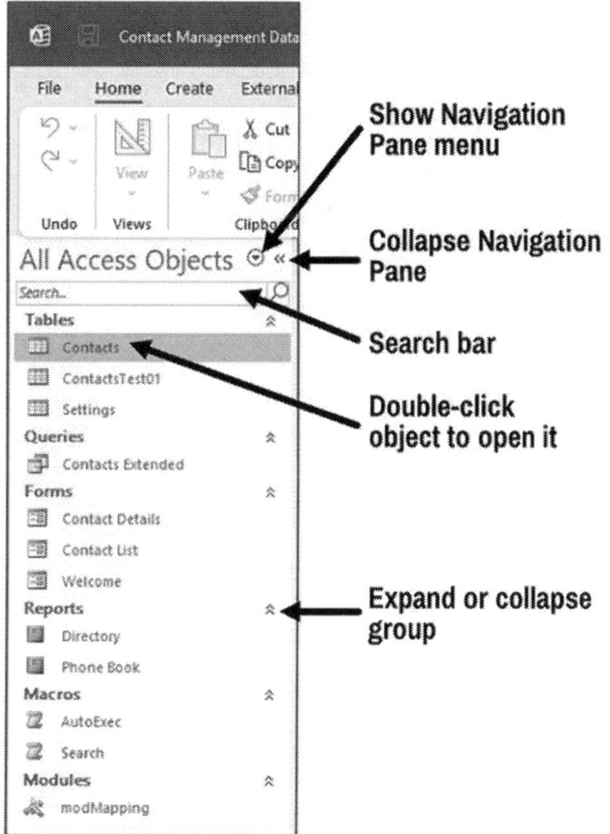

The Navigation Pane

To see the options available for displaying objects in the Navigation Pane, click the drop-down list on the Navigation Pane's title bar. As you can see from the image below, the navigation options are divided into two categories:

- Navigate To Category
- Filter By Group

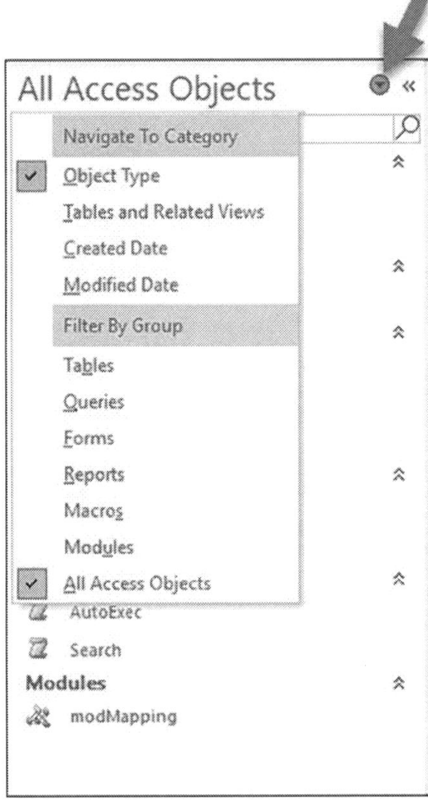

The filter options available under Filter by Group are dependent on the option selected in Navigate To Category. To choose what Access objects to display and how to display them, select an option under Navigating To Category and then an option under Filter By Group.

Navigate To Category options:

- **Custom**: The custom option creates a new group in the Navigation Pane called Group 1 by default. You can drag and drop objects into this group hence allowing you to arrange and view various functionally related objects you've created like tables, queries, forms, and reports in one custom group. The items added to a custom group still appear under their various object types when you switch back to listing the objects by object type. When you select custom in Navigate To Category, the Filter by Group category will list all the custom groups you've created in the Navigation Pane for the current database.

- **Object Type**: The Object Type option is the default when you install Access. With Object Type selected, you will have the following options under Filter By Group - Tables, Queries, Forms, Reports, and All Access Objects. This list allows you to display only some object types or all Access Objects. This is useful when you have created a lot of Access objects, and you want to reduce clutter by displaying just some objects. For example, if you want to display just the queries you've created, select **Queries** on the list. To display all objects again, select **All Access Objects**.

- **Tables and Related Views**: This option shows you all the tables in your database and the queries related to them grouped together. This is useful when you want to know the queries related to each table in your database.

- **Created Date**: This option groups the database objects by the date they were created. Grouping by date is useful if you want to know when an object was created or if you're searching for an object based on its created date. When you select Created Date, you will get the following options depending on the objects in your database and when they were created.

    - Today
    - Yesterday
    - Last Week
    - Two Weeks Ago
    - Older

Note You will only get filter options that correspond to the dates of the objects in the database. For example, if all the objects created were more than a month ago, you'll only see filters for Older and All Dates.

- **Modified Date**: This option groups the database objects by the date they were last modified. This option is useful if you want to know when an object was last modified or if you're searching for an object based on its modified date. When you select Modified Date, you will get the following options depending on the objects in your database and when they were created.

- Today
- Yesterday
- Last Week
- Two Weeks Ago
- Older

Like the options for Created Date, you will get filter options that correspond to the modified dates of the objects in your database. For example, if the objects in your database were created over a year ago, the only options you will see are Older and All Dates.

Organizing Access Objects

As you work with Access, you'll often need to organize your database by renaming, copying, and deleting objects. You can perform these actions in the Navigation Pane.

Rename an Access Object

To rename an Access object in the Navigation Pane, do the following:

1. Ensure the object you want to rename is not open. If the object is open, close it.
2. Right-click the object you want to rename in the Navigation Pane and select **Rename** from the pop-up menu.
3. Type in the new name and press **Enter**.

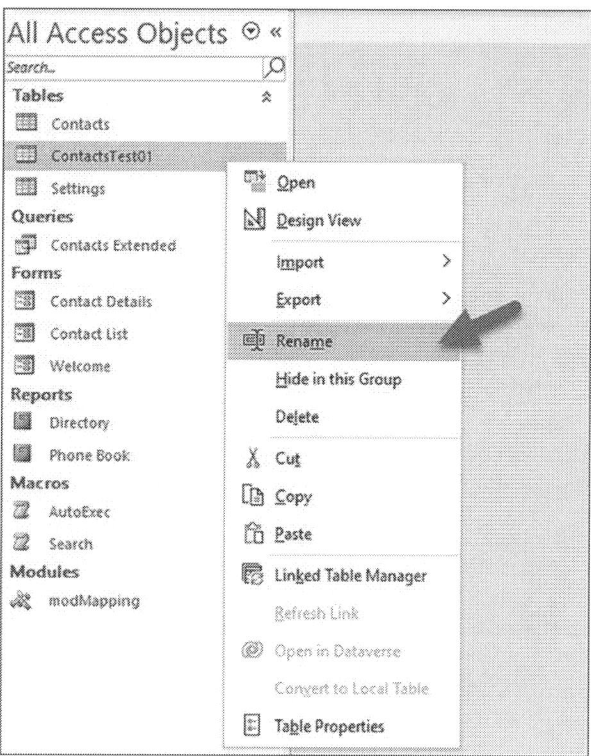

Delete an Access Object

⚠ **Important** When you delete an Access object, you cannot Undo the deletion. So, ensure your database is backed up before you delete any object that you may want to restore if necessary.

To delete an Access object in the Navigation Pane, do the following:

1. Ensure the object you want to delete is not open. If the object is open, close it.
2. Right-click the object you want to delete in the Navigation Pane and select **Delete** from the pop-up menu.
3. At the prompt, click **Yes** to confirm the deletion.

Make a Copy of an Access Object

To duplicate an object in the Navigation Pane, do the following:

1. Right-click the object in the Navigation Pane and select **Copy** from the pop-up menu.
2. Right-click the blank space at the bottom of the Navigation Pane and select **Paste** from the pop-up menu.

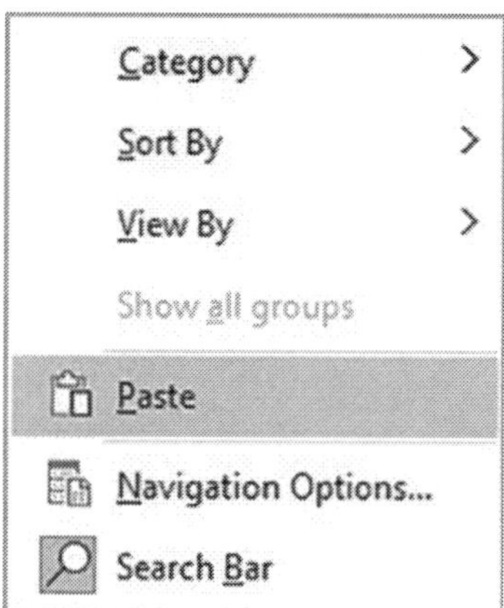

3. Access will display a dialog box where you can enter a name for the object you're about to paste. Enter a unique name for the object and click **OK**.

Note The dialog box displayed at this stage will vary, depending on the object you're copying and pasting.

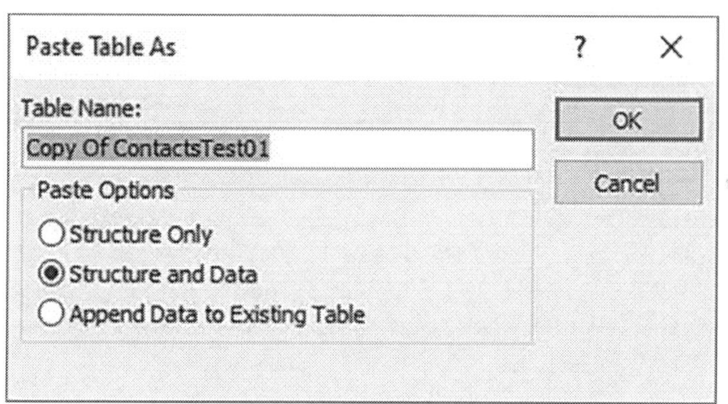

An Overview of Access Objects

Access provides six types of database objects that you'll find grouped in the Navigation Pane when created. These objects enable you to take full advantage of your data. In this chapter, we will look at the role of each object.

Tables

Access tables are the first objects you will create after you create your database, and most of the other objects you'll create will be based on your tables. Tables have rows and columns like spreadsheets, but each table stores information specific to an entity. Most databases require more than one table.

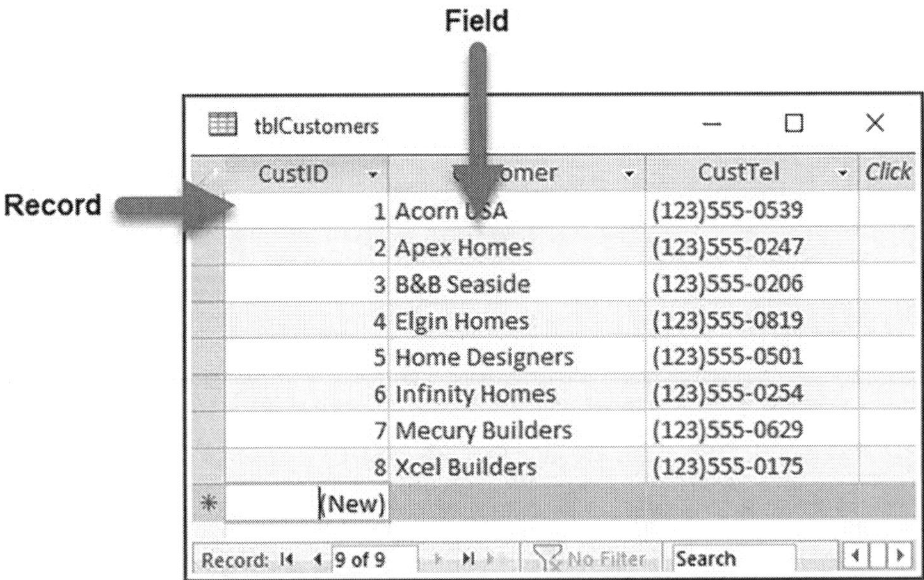

A row in a table is called a record, and a column is called a field. A record contains all the information for an entity, for example, a customer or an order. A field is the smallest piece of information about an entity, for example, a customer's telephone number.

Queries

Queries are tools that you can use to ask questions about your data or carry out actions that transform the data. For instance, you may want to determine how many orders were placed in the last quarter or pull up a particular client's records. You can create a query that filters the orders database based on the criteria you've provided to display the results for your question. As databases often have multiple tables with related data, queries are used to pull related information together to display in forms or reports.

Queries can also be used to perform actions on your database tables like adding, deleting, and updating records.

There are many types of queries in Access, but the two basic types you'll often use are:

- **Select queries**: Used to retrieve data from one or more tables.
- **Action queries**: Used to change data in the database like adding, updating, and deleting data. Action queries can be used to carry out batch updates.

Forms

Forms provide a user interface that enables you to interact with the data in your database and other objects. For example, in a corporate environment, most end-users will only interact with the database through forms. So, forms are the front-end objects that bring everything together in a user-friendly way. Forms provide an interface that users can use to add, edit, or delete data from a database without directly accessing the tables or queries.

Reports

Reports enable you to present your data in different views and formats. For example, you can create a report that groups your transactions by year and month. Access reports can be used to summarize your data in the same way pivot tables can be used in Excel. You can create groups, subgroups, running totals, or filter data using different criteria. You can also use reports to generate mailing labels based on addresses in a table. Reports are mostly powered by queries and provide a user-friendly interface to your queries.

Macros

Macros enable you to automate tasks and add functionality to your forms and reports. Most of the forms you will create in Access will have buttons that you will click to perform a command. Macros power the OnClick events of these buttons. For example, you could have a form with a command button to open another form, open a report, or run a query. Access provides an interface that makes it easy to create macros without programming skills.

Modules

Modules are VBA subroutines that you manually write to automate tasks and processes in Access. You need Access/VBA programming skills to create the procedure, declarations, and statements in Access modules. As VBA programming is outside the scope of this book, we will not be covering modules in this book.

Getting Help in Access

To get help in Access, click on the **Help** command button on the Help tab on the Ribbon. Access displays the Help pane on the right side of the window. You can use Help to find any topic for which you want help.

Tip

To quickly display the help pane, press the **F1** shortcut key.

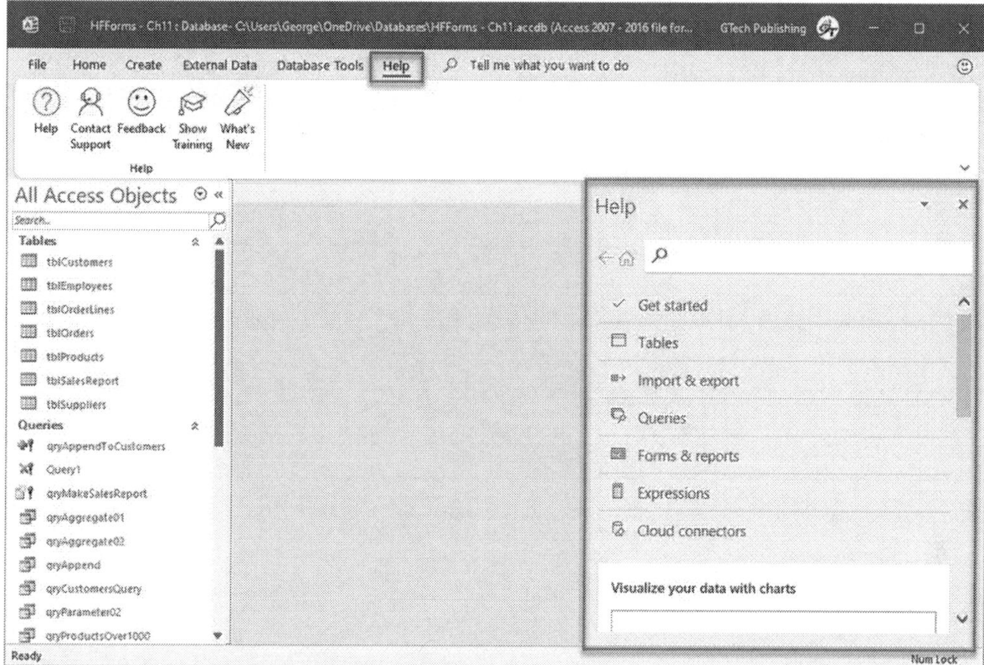

Tell Me Help Feature

Another way to get help in Access is to use the **Tell Me** help feature (Alt+Q). Tell Me provides a text field on the Ribbon named **Tell me what you want to do** where you can enter words or phrases regarding actions you wish to perform or a topic for which you want help. The help provided by this feature is contextual, meaning it gives suggestions based on the Access object or window that's currently active.

Depending on the topic or how direct your question is, Tell Me will either list the steps needed to complete the task, take you to the appropriate screen, or display helpful information related to the topic in the Help pane.

When you click **Tell me what you want to do**, a search box is displayed. Enter a search term to display a drop-down list of options related to your search. When you click an option on the list, Access will automatically take you to the appropriate tab or dialog box where you can perform the task. If there is no related dialog box, Access displays the Help pane with information related to your search term.

Dialog Box Contextual Help

Another way to get contextual help in Access is to click the question mark on the top-right of the dialog box for which you want help (if a question mark is present).

Clicking this button will take you to the Microsoft Access online help page for that feature. The webpage will often have detailed descriptions for all the options on the dialog box, including step-by-step instructions for how to perform the tasks you can perform using the dialog box.

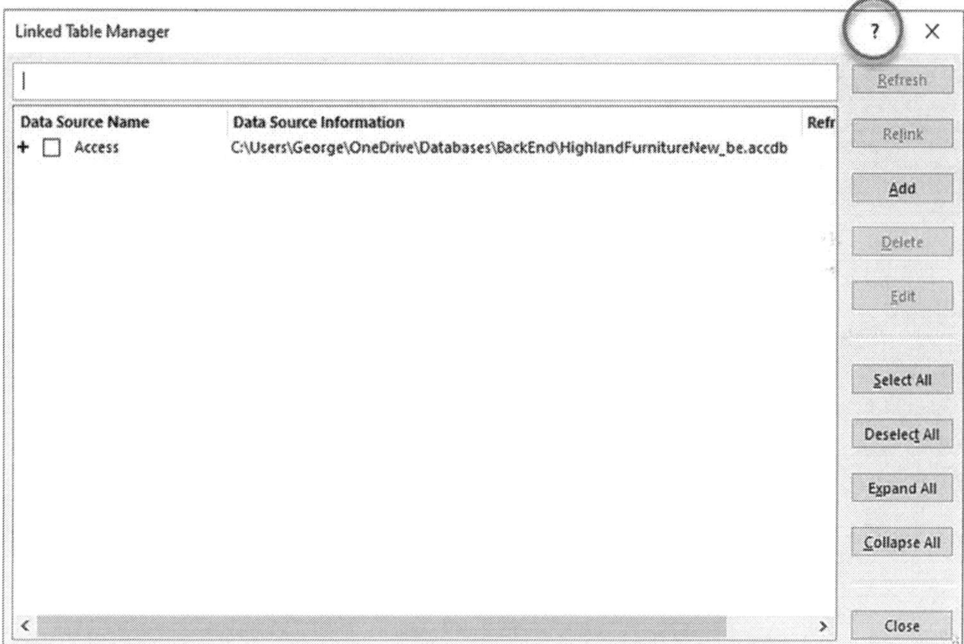

Part 2

Planning Your Database

In Part 2

Part 2 of this book involves an important and necessary stage before creating a database, planning your data. The topics in this part give you the skills to identify the data items in your systems that you need to store in your database based on your data and processing requirements. You learn how to normalize your data design to create a robust data structure that promotes data integrity. This part also introduces the case study used in illustrating most of the examples in this book.

Contents at a Glance

Chapter 4: The Five-Step Design Plan

Before you start creating a database in Access, you want to first plan the design of the database. You can do this manually on paper or use supporting tools like OneNote, Word, or Excel (if you have other Microsoft 365 applications installed on your computer). The more effort you put into getting your data design right before creating your tables in Access, the better your database will be.

In this chapter, we will cover:

- The fundamental principles to a good database design.
- An overview of the case study we'll use to create the examples in this book.
- Five key steps you need to go through in planning your database.

Fundamental Principles

There are two fundamental principles to a good database design:

1. **Avoid data duplication**: You want to avoid data duplication or redundant data in your system. The primary aim of a relational database system is to avoid duplication as it can waste disk space and cause data integrity issues.

2. **Capture all vital information**: As much as possible, ensure every piece of data that needs to be stored in the system is captured at the design stage. If the design omits vital information, it introduces problems down the line. For example, suppose an important piece of information required in a report was not captured in the data design, and this omission was only discovered when the database has gone into production use. That would mean redesigning several parts of the database to include the missing information.

Highland Furniture Case Study

To illustrate the process of information gathering and planning, we can use a case study of a fictional furniture company called Highland Furniture. Highland Furniture is a small and exclusive furniture house that sells high-end furniture to businesses like builders, property developers, hotels, office spaces, etc.

Highland Furniture currently uses an Excel spreadsheet to record its sales data and to generate monthly reports. As the sales data has grown, the spreadsheet is becoming too cumbersome, and many issues have developed. For example, data duplication has become a serious problem. Information for the same customer is being entered multiple times in different records, sometimes with spelling mistakes, making reports from the system inaccurate.

Highland Furniture wants a small local database that enables them to:

1. Store customers, products, suppliers, and employee details without duplication.
2. Record orders that may include several items per order without data duplication.
3. Generate quick reports from the database like *sales per month* or a breakdown of *items sold per month.*
4. Export data to Excel to create summaries for meetings and presentations.

As we proceed through the chapters in this book, we'll be referring to examples from this database to illustrate the concepts.

Step 1: Determine the Purpose of Your Database

In this step, you want to write a summary of what your database will do. This is like a mission statement to define the project's scope that you can come back to from time to time to stay focused on the project's goal.

For example, if you're creating a database for a home-based business, your summary could look like this:

"The database keeps information on products, orders, and the revenue generated from sales. The goal is to generate reports and queries for how much profit each product generates monthly and the overall monthly revenue of the business."

If you're creating a payroll system for a small business, your summary may look like this:

"The payroll database maintains employee data, including salary, bonuses, and other remunerations. The goal is to record weekly employee pay, generate payment slips, and generate various payroll reports."

If you are creating an enterprise database for a larger business, then the mission statement could have several paragraphs summarizing the role of the database.

The point is to keep the scope of your database narrowly focused on a specific goal. If you leave the focus too vague, you could encounter what is referred to as "scope creep," i.e., when new requirements are constantly added to the project during the development phase.

Without a clearly defined mission statement, as you build the database, you may begin to see more things that seem like a good idea to add to the project. This scope creep could lead to a situation where the project becomes too complex, cumbersome, and far removed from the initial goal. Having a clearly defined scope enables you to know when you're straying away from the goal and when to refocus efforts on the requirements that matter.

Step 2: Find the Information to Store

In this step, you want to find the information your database will store and group them into subjects. For example, Products, Sales, Employees, Invoice, and so on.

- **Method 1: Examine Current Processes and Reports**

  The best way to identify what needs to go in your database is to look at your current processes (either manual or electronic) for which you want to build the database. You need to examine the outputs of your current system, like spreadsheets, other electronic documents, and paper documents. What data items are in those documents that are important to you?

  As you go through these documents, you need to list down all the data items that are important to your system and will be part of the new database. For example, if you currently use an Excel spreadsheet to capture your data, you want to list down all the columns that you'll add to your database.

  Look at any documents like invoices, purchase orders, or manual lists.

  Your current reports (electronic or paper-based) are a good place to start looking for what the system will capture:

  - Gather all current reports in your system, whether electronic or paper-based.
  - Identify any new data items you want the database to capture. If your current system does not meet your data needs, then there could be more information that you want to capture.

- **Method 2: Create Mock-ups of Reports and Documents You Would like to Generate from the Database**

  On some occasions, you may not have a current system in place, and the proposed database introduces a completely new system. Hence there will be no electronic or paper documents we can examine. In such a case, you can create quick mock-ups of the kind of reports you'd like to see generated from the database. These quick mock-ups will help identify what information is important to you and thus what you want to capture in your database.

For example, if you want a report that captures monthly *sales by city*, then you know you need to capture sales information at the city level. If you want a report that shows how much each employee has sold per month, then that means you would need to link sales data to employees.

A mock-up that shows the data items you want to see in a report can be done in Excel, Google Sheets, or Microsoft Word.

A mock-up of a report created in Excel might look like the example below:

	A	B	C	D	E	F	G	H
1	Employee	Product	Customer	Order Date	Ship City	Item Cost	No. of Items	Total Cost
2	Anne Hellung-Larsen	Cora Fabric Chair	Acme LTD	11/24/2020	Las Vegas	$475.00	20	$9,500.00
3	Jan Kotas	Lukah Leather Chair	Elgin Homes	05/13/2020	New York	$345.00	9	$3,105.00
4	Mariya Sergienko	Habitat Oken Console Table	Mecury Builders	04/28/2020	Las Vegas	$36.00	28	$1,008.00
5	Michael Neipper	Hygena Fabric Chair	Infinity Homes	11/06/2020	Portland	$407.00	23	$9,361.00
6	Anne Hellung-Larsen	Harley Fabric Cuddle Chair	Elgin Homes	07/16/2019	New York	$803.00	20	$16,060.00
7	Jan Kotas	Windsor 2 Seater Cuddle Chair	B&B Seaside	04/27/2020	Denver	$302.00	8	$2,416.00
8	Mariya Sergienko	Fabric Chair	B&B Seaside	06/26/2019	Los Angelas	$425.00	11	$4,675.00
9	Laura Giussani	Verona 1 Shelf Telephone Table	Home Designers	04/07/2020	Milwaukee	$282.00	8	$2,256.00
10	Anne Hellung-Larsen	Floral Fabric Tub Chair	Acorn USA	08/17/2020	Memphis	$158.00	2	$316.00
11	Jan Kotas	Fabric Chair in a Box	Infinity Homes	04/20/2020	Portland	$857.00	28	$23,996.00
12	Mariya Sergienko	Slimline Console Table	Apex Homes	11/01/2021	Chicago	$534.00	29	$15,486.00
13								
14								
15								

Output report mock-up

This mock-up example indicates that we need to capture the following information in our database:

- Employees
- Products
- Customers
- Orders

Step 3: Identify Your Entities/Tables

Once you have a list of the information you want to store in your database, determine the major subjects and group them into entities.

An **entity** is a subject for which you want to capture information in your database. For example, entities in your current system could be *Product*, *Customer*, *Order*, or *Employee*. Each entity will eventually represent a table in your Access database. A table stores multiple instances of an entity as records.

An **attribute** is the smallest unit of an entity. Attributes become fields when an entity is implemented as a table.

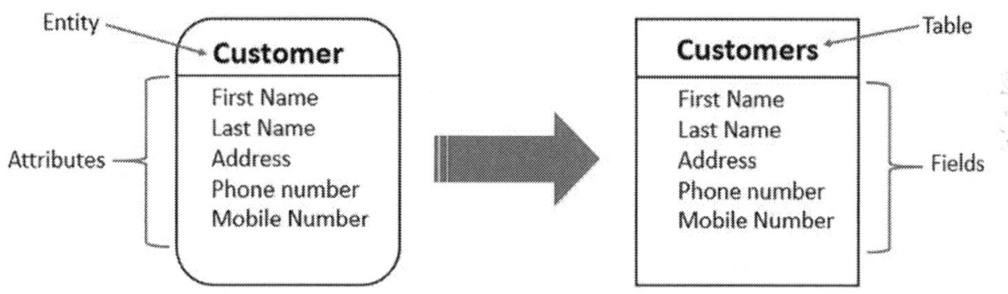

A table stores multiple instances of an entity as records

To identify your tables, think of data you want to store in terms of entities. When you focus on entities first, it gives you a clearer picture of the information you need to capture in your database. Thinking of your information in terms of tables from the onset can muddle the process of isolating entities because a table is more of an abstract concept while an entity is defined by certain characteristics.

We will properly define the fields for these entities at the next stage, so you don't need to worry about getting them exactly right at this stage.

It is OK if some data items are duplicated across different entities at this stage. The goal, for now, is to identify our top-level entities and how they're related. We will resolve any duplication issues and properly establish the links between the entities later using *normalization*.

To illustrate this with our Highland Furniture example, let's say we identified four main documents being used in the current system:

- A sales report (spreadsheet).
- A list of products (spreadsheet).
- A list of employees (spreadsheet).

The list of all the attributes identified from each document is shown below:

Sales report	Product list	Employee list
Order number	Product name	First name
Customer name	Price	Last name
Customer address	Quantity in stock	Job title
Employee name	Status	Address
Order date	Product category	Work phone number
Quantity		Mobile number
Description		Home phone number
Unit price		
Tax rate		
Tax amount		
Subtotal		
Discount percent		
Shipping cost		
Total amount		

We can identify four main entities from the list:

- Order (the sales report is a list of orders)
- Product
- Employee
- Customer

There is no customer list, but we see customer details included in the sales report.

We can now list the entities we've identified with their corresponding attributes. But the list is still an unrefined list of entities and attributes. We will refine and flesh out the attributes for each entity at the next stage.

The following are the top-level entities we've identified in the Highland Furniture system:

Order	Product
Order number	Product name
Customer	Price
Employee	Quantity in stock
Order date	Status
Quantity	Product category
Description	
Unit price	
Tax rate	
Tax amount	
Subtotal	
Discount percent	
Shipping cost	
Total amount	

Customer	Employee
Customer Name	First name
Customer address	Last name
Email	Job title
Phone number	Address
	Work phone number
	Mobile number
	Home phone number

Step 4: Identify Attributes/Fields

After identifying our entities, we need to review and refine the list of data items (or attributes) associated with each entity that we discovered in the previous stage.

If you have not done so already, group the discovered attributes under each entity.

For example, the Customers table might include Name, Salutation, Address, and Email address. Each customer in the table contains the same set of columns, so you store the same information for each customer.

Think of any additional attributes for each entity you want to store in the database. For example, you may want to capture additional data items not currently in your reports. Add them to the list under the associated entity.

Next, you want to break attributes into the smallest possible data items. For example, if one of your initial attributes is Address, you want to break that down into Street Address, City, State, and ZIP/Postal Code (if your customers are global, you may need more fields). That way, you can run reports and queries that group, sort, or filter records by City, State, or even ZIP code. This also enables you to do mailings in the proper format to generate mailing lists from your database if needed.

If one of your entities represents a person, for example, Customer or Employee, and you have a Name attribute, you need to break that down to First Name and Last Name (you can also include Middle Name if that data item is required in your system).

Just ensure that all the items are broken down to their smallest unit. After this, we are now ready to assign an identifier to each entity. The identifier will eventually become the primary key for the table.

To illustrate this concept with the Customer entity of the Highland Furniture database, we need to split up the Name and Address attributes. Also, we need to add some more attributes to better capture information about a customer.

For example, as Highland Furniture sells to individuals and businesses, we want to have field options for both. When we revise the attributes, we get the following list:

Customer		Customer
Name		Company Name
Address		Last Name
Email	→	First Name
Phone number		Email Address
		Job Title
		Business Phone
		Home Phone
		Mobile Phone
		Street Address
		City
		State
		ZIP Code
		Notes

Flesh out attributes to individual data items

We need to carry out the same process for other tables where attributes need to be fleshed out, for example, the Employee table.

Step 5: Specify Primary Keys

A primary key uniquely identifies each record in a table. For instance, you can have customers with the same first and last name. The way to separate those two records is to issue each customer with a unique customer ID. The customer ID is then used to create relationships with related records in other tables, for example, customer orders. If we were to use the customer's name as the identifier, we would not be able to separate customers with the same name.

Once we are happy with our entities and attributes, we want to identify the unique identifier for each entity. This will eventually be the primary key for that table.

Sometimes your current system already has a unique identifier for some entities. For example, you may already have unique identifiers for employees in the spreadsheet you currently use, and you want to use that in Access. Or perhaps you have a unique alphanumeric key for each of your products in your current system. For entities that already have a unique identifier, you can use that identifier as your primary key, or you may choose to use an auto-generated number.

The unique identifier will be the first attribute on the list of attributes for an entity. If you don't currently have a unique identifier, you can create an ID field that will be an AutoNumber data type in Access. An AutoNumber field is automatically incremented with each new record, so you don't have to worry about entering a unique ID for each new record.

For example, if we generate customer orders as part of our business processes and we want the database to auto-generate a new ID for each order, we will add an OrderID attribute to our Orders entity. When we create the table for Orders, we will assign the AutoNumber data type to that field. We will be covering this in detail later when we get to creating tables.

Every record in your system must have a primary key. Sometimes you may use more than one attribute for the primary key, especially when the table is acting as a bridge between two tables. This will be explained in more detail when we cover relationships between tables.

The primary key is a value that is set once and doesn't change. The key is used to establish links to related records in other tables, so any change to the key also changes in the tables being referenced.

For our Highland Furniture database example, we can now add keys to the four entities we've discovered. Keep in mind these entities have not been fully normalized. We'll cover normalization in the next chapter.

Highland Furniture top-level entities with primary keys underlined:

Order	**Product**
<u>OrderID</u>	<u>ProductID</u>
Customer	Product name
Employee	Price
Order date	Quantity in stock
Quantity	Status
Product name	Product category
Unit price	Picture
Tax rate	Supplier
Tax amount	
Subtotal	
Discount percent	
Shipping cost	
Total amount	

Customer	**Employee**
CustomerID	Employee ID
Company Name	First name
Last Name	Last name
First Name	Job title
Email Address	Address
Job Title	Work phone number
Business Phone	Mobile number
Home Phone	Home phone number
Mobile Phone	
Street Address	
City	
State	
ZIP Code	
Notes	

Chapter 5: Normalizing Your Data

Normalization is the process of refining groups of data items to produce tables that conform to specified standards for relational databases known as *normal forms*.

We start the process of normalization by converting our unnormalized tables (UNF) to First Normal Form (1NF). For a table to be in 1NF, all fields must be single-valued, and we must move any repeating groups into separate tables. Second and Third Normal Forms are achieved by moving all data items that are not directly related to the primary key into separate tables.

There are further normal forms that are only encountered in rare and complex data structures and hence, beyond the scope of this book. For most databases, by the time you achieve Third Normal Form (3NF), all the issues associated with unnormalized tables have been resolved.

If you started your data design process by separating the entities you identified in your system into their own tables, you wouldn't have to carry out too much normalization to get your tables to 3NF.

In this chapter, we will cover:

- The benefits of normalization and why it is important.
- The kind of update anomalies you might experience from unnormalized data.
- How to normalize your data – from First Normal Form (1NF) through Third Normal Form (3NF).

Benefits of Normalization

To see the benefits of normalization, we first need to look at an example of unnormalized data and the associated problems known as *update anomalies*.

Unnormalized Form (UNF)

The entities we identified earlier in this chapter for Highland Furniture have been partly normalized (because we focused on identifying and isolating the entities in the system). Hence, those entities are unsuitable for demonstrating the normal forms we will be discussing in this section.

To illustrate the problems with unnormalized data, let's look at the following example (image below). In the Customer Orders table below, each order can have one or more products. This has been represented by a single Product field in the table where several products and quantities can be entered.

An example of a table with multiple data items in a field:

tblCustomerOrders

OrderID	OrderDate	Customer	CustTel	Product
1	11/24/2020	Acme LTD	(123)555-0175	20 Cora Fabric Chair, 3 Console Table, 4 Tessa Fabric Chair
2	05/13/2020	Elgin Homes	(123)555-0819	9 Fabric Wingback Chair, 6 Lukah Leather Chair,
3	04/28/2020	Mecury Builders	(123)555-0629	28 Habitat Oken Console Table, 2 Floral Fabric Tub Chair
4	11/06/2020	Infinity Homes	(123)555-0254	23 Hygena Fabric Chair, 4 Floral Fabric Tub Chair
5	07/16/2019	Elgin Homes	(123)555-0819	20 Harley Fabric Cuddle Chair
6	04/27/2020	B&B Seaside	(123)555-0206	4 Ibstone Windsor Chair, 2 Seater Cuddle Chair
7	06/26/2019	B&B Seaside	(123)555-0206	5 Angel Accent Chair, 4 Slimline Console Table
8	04/07/2020	Home Designers	(123)555-0501	8 Verona 1 Shelf, 3 Telephone Table
9	08/17/2020	Acorn USA	(123)555-0539	2 Floral Fabric Tub Chair
10	04/20/2020	Infinity Homes	(123)555-0254	28 Fabric Chair in a Box
11	11/01/2021	Apex Homes	(123)555-0247	29 Slimline Console Table, 15 Oak Console Table
(New)				

Record: 1 of 11 Search

Unnormalized table (UNF)

Many of the records in this table contain multiple values in the Product field, separated by a comma. Hence, the table above violates the rules of normalization. Running queries against this table will be a nightmare. For example, if we wanted to run a summary report grouped by the Product field, it would be very difficult. If we wanted to tabulate how many products each customer has bought, it would be difficult and would require us to parse the data contained in the Product field.

A slight improvement of this table would be to create multiple pairs of fields for Product and Quantity (Product1/Qty1, Product2/Qty2, Product3/Qty3, and so on).

Each order can have one or more products so this is a repeating group.

tblCustomerOrders2

OrderII	OrderDate	Customer	CustTel	Product1	Qty	Product2	Qty	Product3	Qty	Cli
1	11/24/2020	Xcel Builders	(123)555-0175	Cora Fabric Chair	20	Console Table	3	Tessa Fabric Chair	4	
2	05/13/2020	Elgin Homes	(123)555-0819	Fabric Wingback Chair	9	Lukah Leather Chair	6			
3	04/28/2020	Mecury Builders	(123)555-0629	Habitat Oken Console Table	28	Floral Fabric Tub Chair	2			
4	11/06/2020	Infinity Homes	(123)555-0254	Hygena Fabric Chair	23	Floral Fabric Tub Chair	4			
5	07/16/2019	Elgin Homes	(123)555-0819	Harley Fabric Cuddle Chair	20					
6	04/27/2020	B&B Seaside	(123)555-0206	Ibstone Windsor Chair	4	Seater Cuddle Chair	2			
7	06/26/2019	B&B Seaside	(123)555-0206	Angel Accent Chair	5	Slimline Console Table	4			
8	04/07/2020	Home Designers	(123)555-0501	Verona 1 Shelf	8	Telephone Table	3			
9	08/17/2020	Acorn USA	(123)555-0539	Floral Fabric Tub Chair	2					
10	04/20/2020	Infinity Homes	(123)555-0254	Fabric Chair in a Box	28					
11	11/01/2021	Apex Homes	(123)555-0247	Slimline Console Table	29	Oak Console Table	15			
(New)										

Unnormalized table – repeating columns

The problem with this table, however, is that the maximum number of products that can be bought is a permanent feature of the table. Even if we anticipate the maximum number of products that can be bought per order and design our table with that number of fields, if a customer orders just one product, the other columns will sit empty in the table, which is very wasteful and inefficient. Also, querying this table to get the sales figure for a particular product would be very difficult.

Update Anomalies

Update anomalies is a general term used to describe the problems encountered when updating, inserting, and deleting data in an unnormalized table.

For the unnormalized table described above, we would encounter the following update anomalies:

- **Insertion anomalies**

  We can't add more than three products without having to change the design of the table. Also, we can't add new customers to the system without setting up an order.

- **Deletion anomalies**

  If we delete the last remaining order for a given customer, we will lose all information for that customer from our system.

- **Amendment anomalies**

  Let's say we want to change details for one of the customers, for example, their telephone number. That would mean we would need to amend every order for that customer in the system. This could be several records, which can introduce errors.

The goal of data normalization is that, by the time you get your data to Third Normal Form (3NF), you should have tables of closely associated attributes that are fully dependent on only the primary key. Apart from very rare data scenarios, a table in 3NF eliminates the issues with update anomalies described above.

Many of the problems encountered in flat file systems or poorly designed databases arise from failures to deal with these anomalies, particularly amendment anomalies, which would happen even if data items were duplicated in separate tables.

The major advantage of normalizing your data is that it becomes flexible and easier to expand. A well-normalized data structure enables you to add new fields without any adverse effects.

There are some disadvantages of normalization. The main one is that maintaining many related tables can be more complex than using a flat file. However, maintaining the data becomes easier once you have created the database. On rare occasions, you could include fields in a table that violates the rules of normalization if it significantly improves the performance of the database. This is known as denormalization.

First Normal Form (1NF)

For a table to be in First Normal Form, the cells of the table need to be single-valued, and there should be no repeating groups of data items.

To convert the unnormalized table **tblCustomerOrders2** to 1NF, we need to split the table in two and move the repeating group of fields to a new table named tblCustomerOrderLines. To maintain the relationships between the records in both tables, we need to place the primary key from tblCustomerOrders3 (OrderID) as a foreign key in tblCustomerOrderLines.

When we split the table up and move the repeating fields into another table, we get the following two tables:

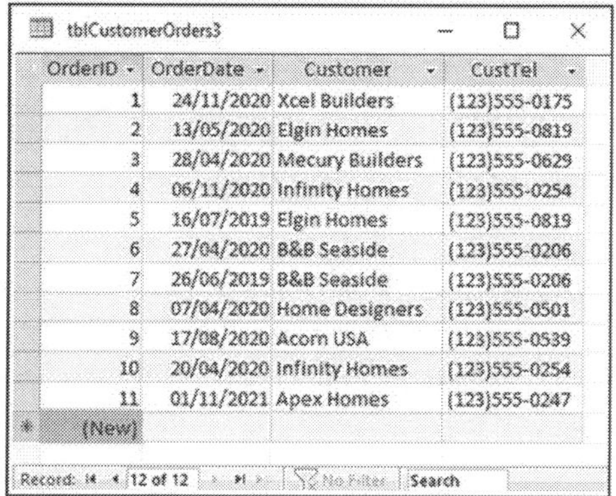

tblCustomerOrders3

OrderID	OrderDate	Customer	CustTel
1	24/11/2020	Xcel Builders	(123)555-0175
2	13/05/2020	Elgin Homes	(123)555-0819
3	28/04/2020	Mecury Builders	(123)555-0629
4	06/11/2020	Infinity Homes	(123)555-0254
5	16/07/2019	Elgin Homes	(123)555-0819
6	27/04/2020	B&B Seaside	(123)555-0206
7	26/06/2019	B&B Seaside	(123)555-0206
8	07/04/2020	Home Designers	(123)555-0501
9	17/08/2020	Acorn USA	(123)555-0539
10	20/04/2020	Infinity Homes	(123)555-0254
11	01/11/2021	Apex Homes	(123)555-0247
(New)			

Record: 12 of 12 No Filter Search

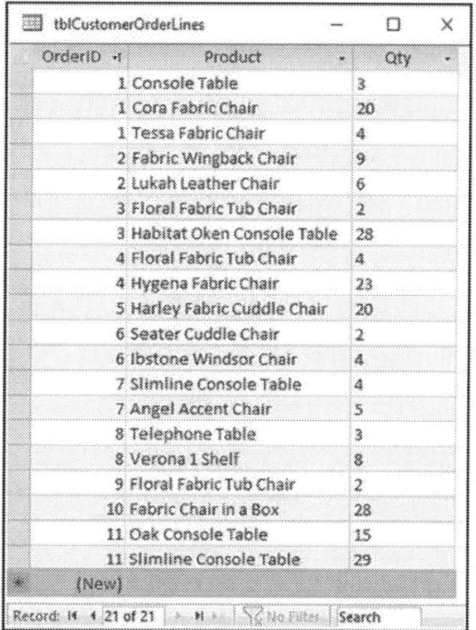

tblCustomerOrderLines

OrderID	Product	Qty
1	Console Table	3
1	Cora Fabric Chair	20
1	Tessa Fabric Chair	4
2	Fabric Wingback Chair	9
2	Lukah Leather Chair	6
3	Floral Fabric Tub Chair	2
3	Habitat Oken Console Table	28
4	Floral Fabric Tub Chair	4
4	Hygena Fabric Chair	23
5	Harley Fabric Cuddle Chair	20
6	Seater Cuddle Chair	2
6	Ibstone Windsor Chair	4
7	Slimline Console Table	4
7	Angel Accent Chair	5
8	Telephone Table	3
8	Verona 1 Shelf	8
9	Floral Fabric Tub Chair	2
10	Fabric Chair in a Box	28
11	Oak Console Table	15
11	Slimline Console Table	29
(New)		

Record: 21 of 21 No Filter Search

Tables in First Normal Form (1NF)

Both tables are now 1NF, but there are still issues with these tables. As you can see, there are several repeating values in the Customer, CustTel, and Product fields from both tables. This is an inefficient way to store and maintain data.

In a well-designed database, the only data duplication should be in key fields used to link tables. The data in key fields rarely change, so it is okay if the values are repeated. On the other hand, the data in non-key fields are more likely to change frequently, so we need to store them just once in the system.

As these tables are still susceptible to the update anomalies discussed earlier in this chapter, we need to refine them further. To continue the refinement process, we need to convert them to Second Normal Form (2NF).

Second Normal Form (2NF)

For a table to be in Second Normal Form, data items that are not fully dependent on the table's primary key should be moved into another table.

This rule is primarily for a table with a composite key (that is, where more than one attribute makes up the primary key). A table in 1NF with a single attribute as its primary key is already technically in 2NF.

In our example, tblCustomerOrderLines (image below) has three fields: OrderID, Product, and Qty. None of the fields acts as a unique identifier. The repeating values for the Product field indicate there is an issue with this table, and the Product field belongs to a different entity. For example, if the name of a particular piece of furniture changes, we will have to change it in several records. Also, we can't add a new piece of furniture to the database without a customer order.

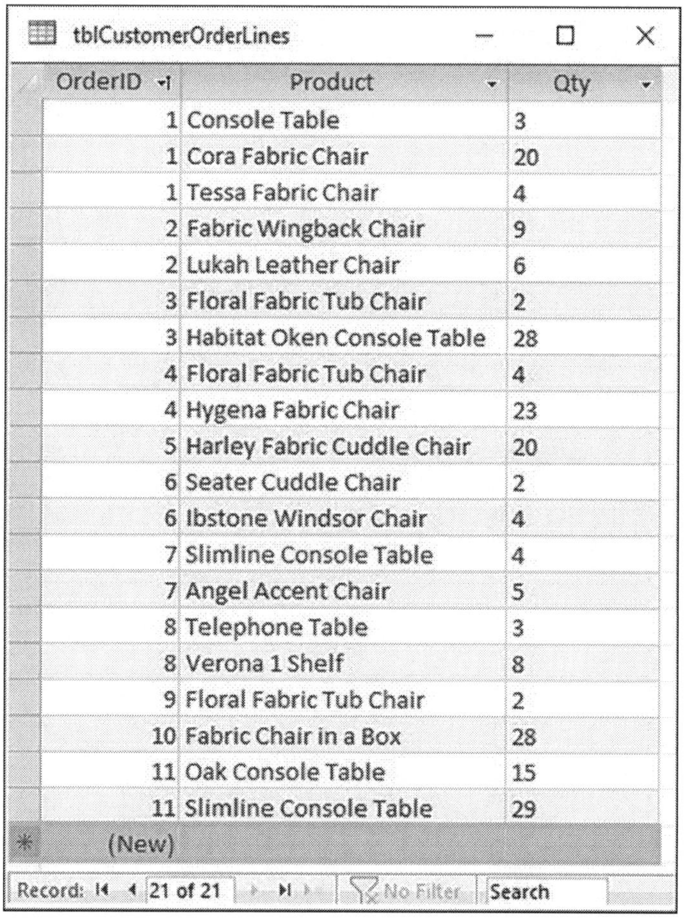

tblCustomerOrderLines

OrderID	Product	Qty
1	Console Table	3
1	Cora Fabric Chair	20
1	Tessa Fabric Chair	4
2	Fabric Wingback Chair	9
2	Lukah Leather Chair	6
3	Floral Fabric Tub Chair	2
3	Habitat Oken Console Table	28
4	Floral Fabric Tub Chair	4
4	Hygena Fabric Chair	23
5	Harley Fabric Cuddle Chair	20
6	Seater Cuddle Chair	2
6	Ibstone Windsor Chair	4
7	Slimline Console Table	4
7	Angel Accent Chair	5
8	Telephone Table	3
8	Verona 1 Shelf	8
9	Floral Fabric Tub Chair	2
10	Fabric Chair in a Box	28
11	Oak Console Table	15
11	Slimline Console Table	29
(New)		

Record: 21 of 21 No Filter Search

A table in First Normal Form (1NF) may still have issues

As we're still in the process of normalizing tblCustomerOrderLines, it doesn't have a primary key. But if we did have a primary key for this table in an ideal 1NF scenario, it would be a composite key made up of OrderID and a key field representing the product, for example, *ProdNo.*

OrderID	ProdNo	Product	Qty
1	1	Product 1	2
1	2	Product 2	6
1	3	Product 3	4

Thus, if we assume a reasonable primary key to apply to this table is (OrderID, ProdNo), we can see that the Product field is dependent only on part of the primary key, i.e., ProdNo. Therefore, we must move the Product field out of this table into its own table, **tblProducts**, and create a primary key for that table that we will name ProdNo.

To maintain the relationship to tblCustomerOrderLines, we insert ProdNo as a foreign key in tblCustomerOrderLines (for the purpose of this exercise, a new version of the table was created as tblCustomerOrderLines2). tblCustomerOrderLines2 now has a composite primary key made up of OrderID and ProdNo.

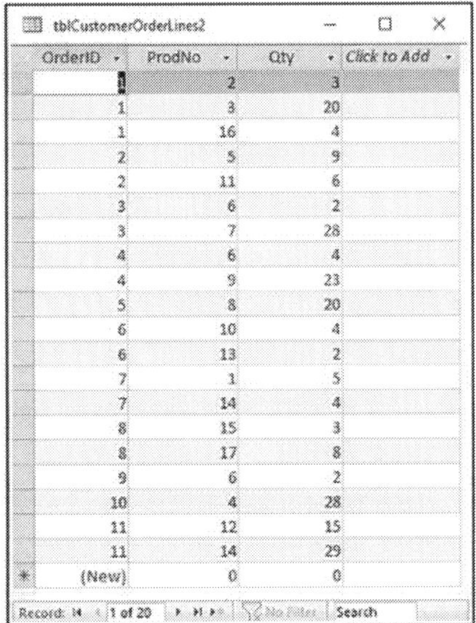

tblCustomerOrderLines2

OrderID	ProdNo	Qty	Click to Add
1	2	3	
1	3	20	
1	16	4	
2	5	9	
2	11	6	
3	6	2	
3	7	28	
4	6	4	
4	9	23	
5	8	20	
6	10	4	
6	13	2	
7	1	5	
7	14	4	
8	15	3	
8	17	8	
9	6	2	
10	4	28	
11	12	15	
11	14	29	
(New)	0	0	

Record: 1 of 20 No Filter Search

tblProducts

ProdNo	Product	Clic
1	Angel Accent Chair	
2	Console Table	
3	Cora Fabric Chair	
4	Fabric Chair in a Box	
5	Fabric Wingback Chair	
6	Floral Fabric Tub Chair	
7	Habitat Oken Console Table	
8	Harley Fabric Cuddle Chair	
9	Hygena Fabric Chair	
10	Ibstone Windsor Chair	
11	Lukah Leather Chair	
12	Oak Console Table	
13	Seater Cuddle Chair	
14	Slimline Console Table	
15	Telephone Table	
16	Tessa Fabric Chair	
17	Verona 1 Shelf	
(New)		

Record: 1 of 17 No Filter Search

Tables in Second Normal Form (2NF)

Both tables are now in second normal form. Each product is now only entered once in the database, and its primary key is inserted as a foreign key in other tables where a relationship needs to be established. The issues to do with update anomalies have now been eliminated from these two tables.

Third Normal Form (3NF)

A table is in Third Normal Form if, in addition to being in 2NF, no non-key fields are determined by the value of another non-candidate key field.

The table tblCustomerOrders3 that we created in 1NF is also in 2NF because it has only one field representing its primary key, OrderID. However, tblCustomerOrders3 is not in Third Normal Form (3NF) because we have a field in the table, CustTel, which is dependent directly on another non-key field, Customer, rather than the primary key OrderID.

tblCustomerOrders3

OrderID	OrderDate	Customer	CustTel
1	24/11/2020	Xcel Builders	(123)555-0175
2	13/05/2020	Elgin Homes	(123)555-0819
3	28/04/2020	Mecury Builders	(123)555-0629
4	06/11/2020	Infinity Homes	(123)555-0254
5	16/07/2019	Elgin Homes	(123)555-0819
6	27/04/2020	B&B Seaside	(123)555-0206
7	26/06/2019	B&B Seaside	(123)555-0206
8	07/04/2020	Home Designers	(123)555-0501
9	17/08/2020	Acorn USA	(123)555-0539
10	20/04/2020	Infinity Homes	(123)555-0254
11	01/11/2021	Apex Homes	(123)555-0247
(New)			

Record: 12 of 12 No Filter Search

A table in Second Normal Form (2NF)

The repeating values in the Customer and CustTel fields indicate this table is susceptible to the update anomalies mentioned earlier in this chapter.

For example, we would encounter the following update anomalies:

- If the name or telephone number of a customer changes, we will have to find and change the value in multiple records.
- We can't add a new customer to the system without creating a customer order.
- If we remove the last order for a customer, we lose all information for that customer.

Therefore, Customer and CustTel belong to a different entity, and we need to move them to a new table we'll name **tblCustomer** with a new primary key called CustID. We then insert CustID as a foreign key in the previous table (now named tblCustomerOrders4) to maintain the relationship between the records in both tables.

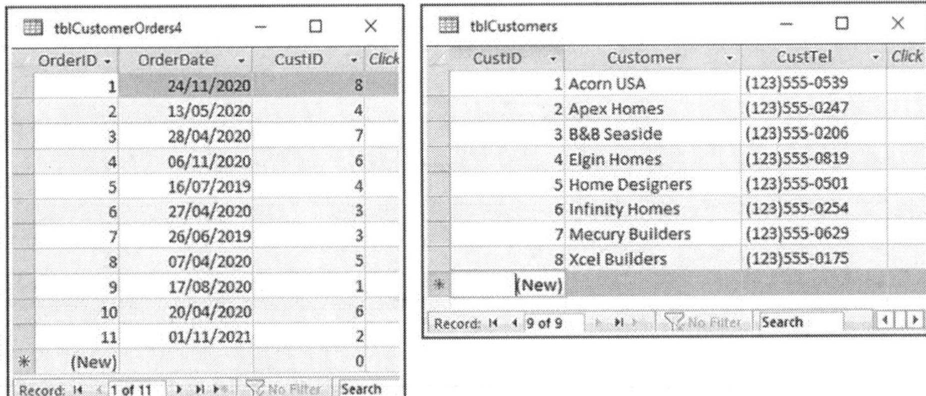

tblCustomerOrders4

OrderID	OrderDate	CustID
1	24/11/2020	8
2	13/05/2020	4
3	28/04/2020	7
4	06/11/2020	6
5	16/07/2019	4
6	27/04/2020	3
7	26/06/2019	3
8	07/04/2020	5
9	17/08/2020	1
10	20/04/2020	6
11	01/11/2021	2
(New)		0

tblCustomers

CustID	Customer	CustTel
1	Acorn USA	(123)555-0539
2	Apex Homes	(123)555-0247
3	B&B Seaside	(123)555-0206
4	Elgin Homes	(123)555-0819
5	Home Designers	(123)555-0501
6	Infinity Homes	(123)555-0254
7	Mecury Builders	(123)555-0629
8	Xcel Builders	(123)555-0175
(New)		

Tables in Third Normal Form (3NF)

With the tables split, both are now in 3NF, and this resolves the update anomaly issues inherent in tblCustomerOrders3.

With the tables in 3NF, we can now:

- Enter information for customers just once in our database.
- Create a new customer record without creating an order.
- If we delete the last order for a customer, we won't lose all information for that customer from our database.

Simple Normalization Guidelines

We've used an example in this chapter that enables us to illustrate the three main normal forms. However, depending on the structure of your data, you may not necessarily need to go through all three normal forms. For instance, you may convert your tables to 1NF and discover they're also 2NF compliant. In which case, you would proceed to 3NF if there is still some normalization to be done. On other occasions, you may only need to split your table into two for your data to be 3NF compliant.

It can be easy to get unnecessarily bogged down with the intricacies of normalization. Don't let the specifics of the normal forms bog you down if the nature of your data means you don't need to go through all three normal forms. The example we've used here is an idealized scenario to illustrate all three normal forms.

Just remember to follow these recommendations for normalizing your tables:

- Identify *entities* in your system and group related data items into their own tables.
- Move all repeating groups of data into their own table with their own primary key.
- To maintain a relationship between related records in two tables, place the *primary key* of the parent table as a *foreign key* in the child table.
- Ensure all fields in a table are dependent on the primary key only.

Highland Furniture - Normalized Tables

Using the rules of data normalization that we covered in the previous section, we can now revise the structure of the entities/tables for the Highland Furniture database.

Note that in the new normalized structure (see below), any repeating groups have been moved to their own table. Also, all calculated fields have been removed. We can use expressions and queries to perform any calculations required for displaying calculated data on forms and reports.

Order	OrderLines	Product
OrderID	OrderLineID	ProductID
CustomerID	OrderID	Product Name
EmployeeID	ProductID	Price
Order date	Quantity	Quantity in stock
Tax rate	Unit price	Discontinued
Shipping cost	Discount rate	Product category
		Picture

Supplier	Customer	Employee
SupplierID	CustomerID	EmployeeID
Supplier Name	Company Name	First Name
Contact Name	Last Name	Last Name
Email	First Name	Job Title
Address	Email Address	Work Phone
City	Job Title	Mobile Phone
State	Business Phone	Home Phone
ZipCode	Home Phone	Street
Phone	Mobile Phone	City
	Street	State
	City	ZIP Code
	State	Notes
	ZIP Code	
	Notes	

Part 3

Understanding Access Tables

In Part 3

In part 3 of this book, we focus on Access tables, which are the core building blocks of your database. You learn tools and techniques for translating the data structure created in Part 2 into physical Access tables. You create fields, define properties, and create relationships between related tables. You also learn how to work with data in Access tables using datasheets, including connecting to external sources to import and export data.

Contents at a Glance

Chapter 6: Creating Access Tables

Now that we've created and normalized our table design, it is time to create the table objects in Access. Before we start, though, it is important to go through the guidelines for naming Access tables. We also want to introduce consistency in our naming process by following a recommended naming convention for Access objects.

This chapter will cover the following:

- Guidelines for naming tables.
- Naming conventions for Access objects to enable consistency.
- Creating Access tables.
- Creating fields and setting data types.
- Setting field properties.
- Creating indexes.

Guidelines for Naming Tables

The following are guidelines and recommendations for naming Access tables:

- A table's name can be up to 64 characters.
- Access allows spaces in names, but it is best to avoid spaces to make it easier to reference table names in other objects like queries, forms, and VBA code.
- If you need to separate different words in names, use camel case. Capitalize the first letter of each word to differentiate the words, for example, CustomerNumber.
- Many special characters are not allowed. So, apart from underscores, avoid special characters altogether.
- Use letters, numbers, and underscores only.
- Use an underscore to separate words if you're unable to use camel case.

Naming Conventions

Adopting a uniform naming convention for your database objects is important for consistency and making maintenance easier. Access imposes very few restrictions for naming database objects. Hence, it can be easy to give different types of objects similar names that can make things confusing in the future.

For example, you could name a table, *Customers*, and also name a corresponding data entry form, *Customers*. However, at some point in the future, if you decide to write VBA subroutines for the database, you'll need to do extra work to differentiate the object names in your code.

A simple recommended naming convention to use is the Leszynski naming convention. You can read more about this naming convention here:

https://en.wikipedia.org/wiki/Leszynski_naming_convention

The Leszynski naming convention recommends a three-letter prefix for all Access objects, as shown in the table below. For example, you'll name a table tblCustomers instead of Customers, and an entry form for that table can be named frmCustomers to differentiate it from the table.

Access object	Prefix	Example
Table	tbl	tblEmployees
Form	frm	frmCustomers
Query	qry	qryOrdersByMonth
Report	rpt	rptOrdersByMonth
Macro	mcr	mcrShowSplashForm
Module	bas	basGlobalVariables

Another aspect of this naming convention is to use camel case for your names. This means you use capitalization to separate words instead of a space or an underscore, for instance, tblCustomerOrders instead of Customer Orders.

People generally find camel-case names easier to read and remember than names that are all lowercase or all uppercase. For example, tblCustomerOrders is more legible than tblcustomerorders or TBLCUSTOMERORDERS.

Note This naming convention is a recommendation and not mandatory in Access.

Creating a Table

Follow the steps below to create a table:

1. On the Ribbon, click the **Create** tab.

2. In the **Tables** group, click the **Table Design** button.

   This opens a new table in Design view. The Field Properties and Property Sheet are displayed. If you don't see the Property Sheet, click the **Property Sheet** button in the **Show/Hide** group (or press **F4**).

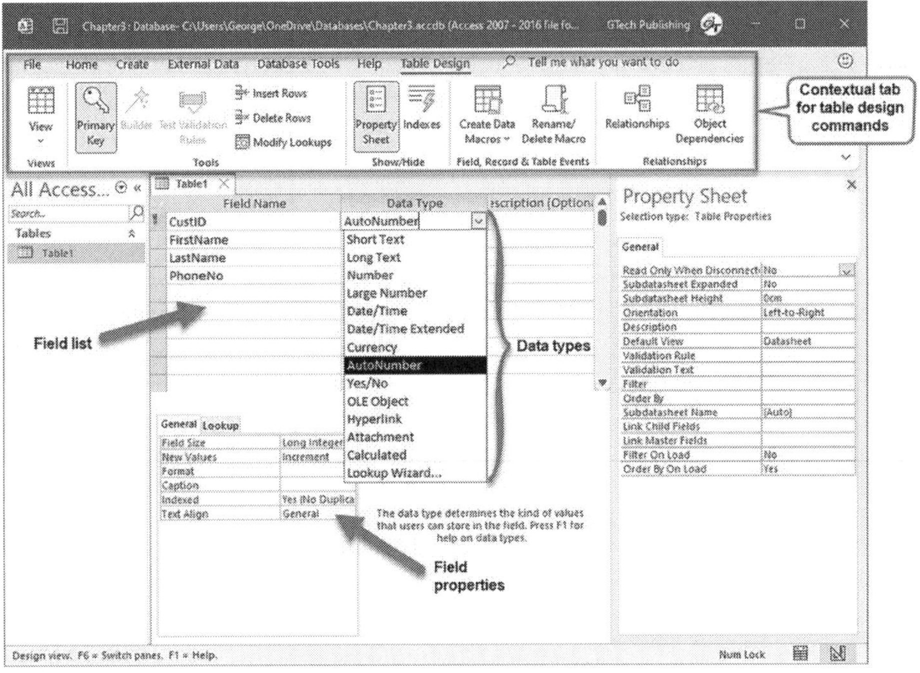

Note Access requires at least one field for you to be able to save the table. In the next section, we'll cover how to enter fields.

Creating Fields

Now that we've created and saved our table, we can create fields for the table. At this point, you should have already planned your data design and specified the field names for your table. If you haven't done this, please see chapter 4, Planning Your Database.

Guidelines for Naming Fields

The following are guidelines and recommendations for naming fields:

- A field name can be up to 64 characters.
- Avoid spaces in field names to make it easier to use them in other objects like queries, forms, and reports.
- If you need to separate words in field names, use camel case (that is, capitalize the first letter of each word to differentiate the words).
- Many special characters are not allowed, so avoid them altogether apart from underscores.
- Use letters, numbers, and underscores only.
- Use an underscore to separate words if you don't want to use camel case.

Data Types in Access

When creating fields in Access, you need to select a data type. The default data type is Short Text, and it lets you enter almost any kind of data. However, choosing the correct data type for a field improves the efficiency and accuracy of your database. Below is an overview of the data types available in Access.

Data Type	Usage	Size
Short Text	Alphanumeric characters	Up to 255 characters
Long Text	Alphanumeric characters	Up to 1GB of characters
Number	Numeric values	1, 2, 4, 8, or 16 bytes
Date/Time	Dates and times	8 bytes
Currency	Monetary values	8 bytes
AutoNumber	Automatic number increments	4 bytes
Yes/No	Boolean values: True/False (-1/0).	1 byte
OLE Object	Images, audio, or video	Up to about 2 GB
Attachment	Files like pictures, documents, spreadsheets, or charts	Up to about 2 GB
Hyperlink	A link to a web source	Up to 1GB of characters.
Calculated	An expression that uses data from one or more fields	It depends on the data type selected in the Result Type property
Lookup Wizard	Displays data from another table or a value list	This depends on the data type of the lookup field

Short Text

This data type can hold alphanumeric characters like letters, numbers, and punctuation. You use this data type for text values that will not be longer than 255 characters. This should be your default data type for a text field unless the field is for notes or comments. To conserve space, set the Field Size of the text to the number of characters you think will be the absolute maximum. For example, the field size of a first or last name field should not be more than 50.

Long Text

Use this data type only for fields that require more than 255 characters, like a field for comments or notes. This field can store up to 1 GB of text, but most Access controls that show text are limited to 64,000 characters.

Number

This is the data type you will use for most of your number fields. It enables you to store numeric values, and there are different field sizes from which you can choose. The table below shows an overview of the field sizes for the Number data type.

Field Size	Range	Digits	Size
Byte	0 to 255	3	1 byte
Integer	32,768 to +32,767	5	2 bytes
Long Integer	-2,147,483,648 to +2,147,483,647	10	4 bytes
Single	-3.4 x 1038 to +3.4 x 1038 and up to seven digits.	7	4 bytes
Double	-1.797 x 10308 to +1.797 x 10308 and up to 15 digits.	15	8 bytes
Decimal	-9.999... x 1027 to +9.999... x 1027	29	12 bytes

When choosing field sizes, always allow for more than you currently expect to store in the database as a contingency. Try to find a balance between allowing for contingencies and not going too far with large field sizes. Choosing unnecessary large field sizes can consume too much space and slow down your database as the field size is reserved for each data item, even if unused. For an integer field, a safe bet is to go with Long Integer to cover all scenarios. For decimal numbers, it's best to go with a Single. A Double is very large (8 bytes) and should be used only when necessary.

Tip To avoid incompatibility issues, use a Long Integer if you're creating a foreign key in a child table to relate to an AutoNumber primary key field in the parent table.

Date/Time

This is a field for dates. You can specify the date format you want in the field properties. Date fields make it easy to filter, sort, and calculate data using dates.

Currency

Stores monetary data with 4 decimal places of precision. Use this data type for financial values and when you don't want Access to round up numbers.

AutoNumber

The AutoNumber field generates a unique number when you create a new record. Use this data type to uniquely identify a record if you don't have a custom primary key. An AutoNumber field is equivalent to a Long Integer and occupies 4 bytes. This is more than enough for a primary key field.

Yes/No

This is a Boolean (true or false) field. In Access, you have three format options you can use for this field, Yes/No, True/False, and On/Off. Internally, Access uses -1 for true and 0 for false. Use this data type if you want to specify a Yes/No value for a status update in a record.

OLE Object

You can use this data type to store images, files like Word or Excel documents, video clips, and audio files. For example, you can use this data type to store an image in your database to go with a record.

In most cases, you should use the Attachment field introduced in Access .accdb versions. An OLE Object does not allow you to attach multiple files to a single record and supports fewer file types than an Attachment field.

Attachment

You can use this field to attach images, documents, audio, and video clips to a record. You can attach up to 2 GB per record. This is like how you can attach files to an email message. Attachment fields were introduced in Access 2007 and provide more flexibility and efficiency than OLE Object fields as you can attach multiple files per record, and they use less storage space.

Calculated

Enables you to store an expression in the field based on one or more fields from the same table.

A calculated field is technically against the rules of normalization, but there are scenarios, like in transient tables, when a calculated field can provide a more efficient solution than using a query. Just ensure you minimize the risk of a calculated field compromising the integrity of your data.

Lookup Wizard

The Lookup Wizard is not actually a data type. When you choose this option in the Data Type column, a wizard starts to help you define lookup values for the data type you want for the field. The Lookup Wizard can be used to create fields that enable the end-user to choose a value from a value list, another table, or a query. The user can select a meaningful name that's more easily recognized (instead of an ID), but the ID is what's stored in the table. The values are usually presented in a combo box (but you can also use a list box).

Tip Using the Lookup Wizard in a table for a foreign key field enables you to create a lookup list that becomes available throughout the application anywhere that field is used. This can save you a significant amount of time and effort down the line, especially when creating foreign key fields on forms, as you often would need a combo box (lookup list).

Note There are other data types like 'Large Number' that have been included in Access recently to support the integration with server platforms like SharePoint, Azure, and SQL Server. These are outside the scope of this book.

Create Table Fields and Set Data Types

Now that you're familiar with data types in Access, you can flesh out your data design to include data types. For each field in your table designs, you can add the data type and size (where applicable). You can use an application like Excel or Google Sheets for this. See the example below for the Customers table of the Highland Furniture application.

	A	B	C	D
1	tblCustomers			
2				
3	Field name	Data Type	Size	
4	CustomerID	AutoNumber	N/A	
5	CompanyName	Short Text	100	
6	LastName	Short Text	50	
7	FirstName	Short Text	50	
8	Email	Short Text	50	
9	JobTitle	Short Text	100	
10	BusinessPhone	Short Text	15	
11	HomePhone	Short Text	15	
12	MobilePhone	Short Text	15	
13	Street	Short Text	50	
14	City	Short Text	50	
15	State	Short Text	2	
16	ZIPCode	Short Text	10	
17	Notes	Long Text	N/A	
18				
19				

Sheet1

Ready

List of fields with datatypes in Excel

Continuing the table design from the previous section, we can now enter our field names.

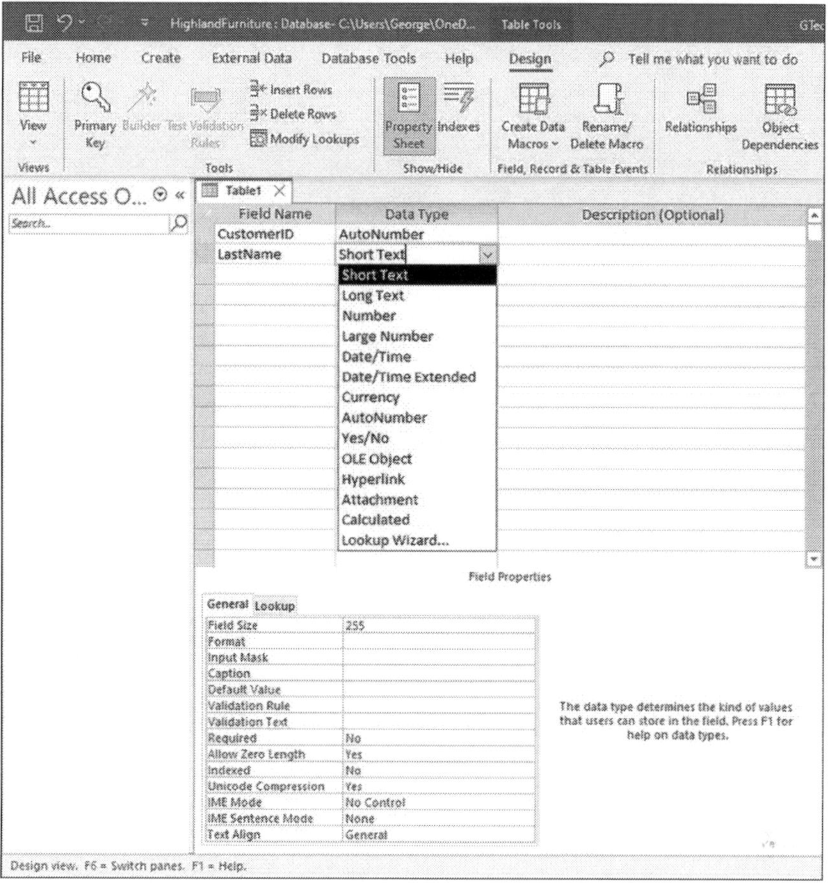

Follow the steps below to enter your table fields:

1. Place the cursor in the **Field Name** column in the row where you want to enter the field name.

2. Type the field name and click in the **Data Type** column (you can also press Enter or Tab to move to the Data Type column).

3. In the Data Type column, select the field's data type from the drop-down list.

4. You can add a description for the field in the **Description** column. This is optional but useful if you're designing a database that might be maintained by other people down the line.

5. Repeat the steps above for each field that belongs to your new table.

Press the **up/down** arrow keys on your keyboard to move between rows, or use the mouse to click on any row. To delete rows and rearrange fields, see Organizing Fields below.

6. To set the primary key, click on the field you've designated as the unique identifier for the table. This will be the ID field.

7. Next, click the **Primary Key** command button in the **Tools** group on the **Table Design** tab.

8. When done, select **File** > **Save**. Alternatively, you can click the **Save** button on the title bar (or press **Ctrl+S**).

9. At the **Save As** prompt, enter the name of the table and click **OK**.

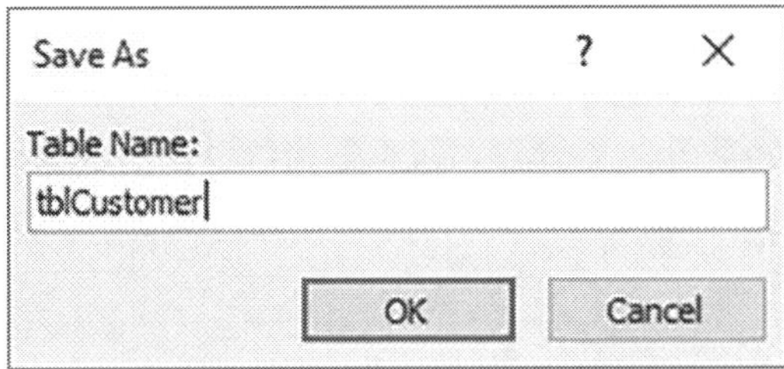

Organizing fields

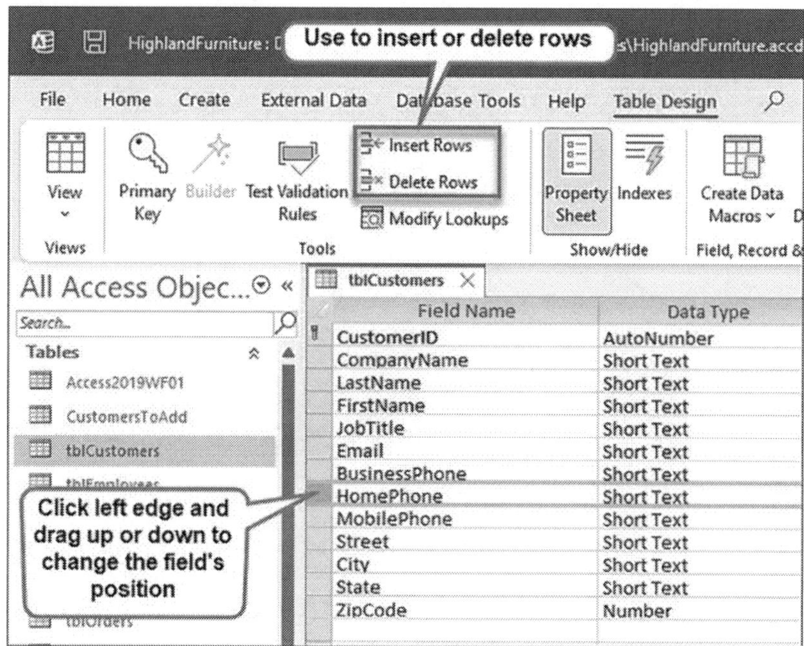

To organize your fields, you can:

- **Insert a field**: Use the **Insert Rows** command button in the **Tools** group of the **Table Design** tab to insert a row above the active/selected row.

- **Delete a field**: Use the **Delete Rows** button on the Table Design tab to delete the active row.

- **Reposition a field**: To move a row up or down with your mouse, do the following:
    1. First, select the whole row by clicking its left edge (row header).
    2. Click the left edge again and with your mouse and drag it up or down to the position you want it on the list of fields.

Field Properties

After you enter a field and select its data type in Access, you can set field properties that control its behavior. In most cases, the field properties are enforced throughout the database, which means you'll have consistency wherever the field is used, like in forms or queries.

Each data type has a different set of properties, but some field properties are shared. For example, the Number and Short Text data types have different sets of field properties but share some field properties like Field Size and Format.

When you enter a data type in the fields list, the field properties for that data type are displayed in the Fields Properties section at the bottom of the window. See the image below.

General Lookup

Field Size	255
Format	@
Input Mask	
Caption	
Default Value	
Validation Rule	
Validation Text	
Required	No
Allow Zero Length	Yes
Indexed	No
Unicode Compression	No
IME Mode	No Control
IME Sentence Mode	None
Text Align	General

Field properties for Short Text

Field properties enable you to set business rules and constraints for your data. For example, you can set a validation rule that limits the range of values a user can enter in a field.

There are many field properties you'll never need to change from their default values unless you're doing something quite advanced in Access. In this section, we'll focus on the field properties you're most likely to use.

Field Properties Overview

- **Field Size**: Used to set the maximum field size for data being stored as a Number, AutoNumber, or Short Text data type.
- **Format**: Changes the way the data appears when displayed or printed. Many types of formats can be applied to Access data. We'll cover these later in this chapter.
- **Decimal Places**: Specifies the number of decimal places to use when displaying data with decimal places.
- **New Values**: Specifies whether an AutoNumber field is incremented or given a random number.
- **Input Mask**: Used to specify a predefined format for data entry. Useful for phone numbers, dates, product IDs, zip codes, Social Security numbers, and other data where you want to restrict input to a particular format. Input Masks can be used on both Number and Text data types. Note that input masks can also be set on forms, i.e., at the point of data entry.
- **Caption**: When set, Access will use the Caption property instead of the field name on datasheets, forms, and reports bound to the table.
- **Default Value**: You can enter a default value here that is automatically assigned to a field when a new record is created.
- **Validation Rule**: You can use this property to set any business rules or constraints you have for a field. For example, you could set a constraint that says the data entered has to be between 5 and 10 for that field. You set this by entering an expression that must be true whenever you add or change the value in this field.
- **Validation Text**: If you've set a Validation Rule, you can enter text here that appears to the user whenever a value violates the rule.
- **Required**: Used to specify whether you must enter a value in the field.
- **Allow Zero Length**: This allows the entry of a zero-length string ("") if set to Yes. Applicable to Short Text, Long Text, and Hyperlink fields.
- **Indexed**: Use this to index a field. An index can be used to considerably speed up data access in a table. We'll cover table indexes later in this chapter.
- **Text Format**: Applies to the Long Text field. You've got the option of Plain Text or Rich Text, which stores text as HTML, enabling text formatting like bold, italics, font color, underline, etc.

- **Expression**: Applies to a Calculated field. Use this property to specify the expression used for the Calculated field.
- **Result Type**: Applies to a Calculated field. This specifies the data type used to store the return value generated by the Expression property for the Calculated data type.

Changing the Field Size

To change the field property of one of the fields of your table, for example, a Short Text field, do the following:

1. Open the table design view (if it's not currently open).

   Tip: To quickly open a table in Design view, right-click the table in the Navigation Pane and select **Design View** from the pop-up menu.

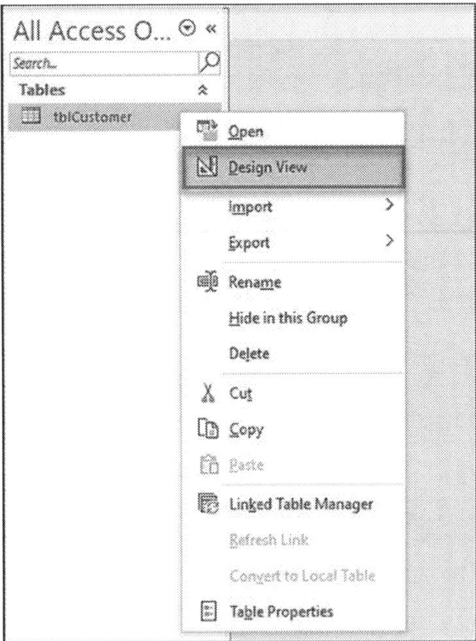

2. Click in the field name for which you want to change field properties. In our case, we're changing the LastName field size from 255 to 50.

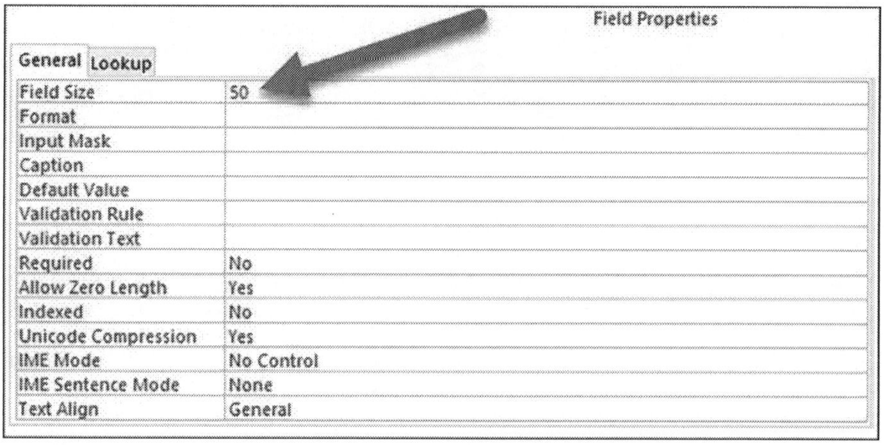

Field Properties

General | Lookup

Field Size	50
Format	
Input Mask	
Caption	
Default Value	
Validation Rule	
Validation Text	
Required	No
Allow Zero Length	Yes
Indexed	No
Unicode Compression	Yes
IME Mode	No Control
IME Sentence Mode	None
Text Align	General

3. Repeat steps 2 and 3 above for any other field property you want to change.

4. Click **Save**  (or type **Ctrl+S**) when done.

Setting Field Formats

The **Format** field property is used to specify how data in a table is formatted when displayed or printed. When you set a field's format at the table level, that format is used for that field in other objects throughout the application. Access provides a series of built-in format options you can select for most data types. The Region settings in the Control Panel will determine the built-in formats available to you.

For example, if the systems Region setting of your computer is set to 'United States', you'll get a dollar sign ($) for the Currency data type. If your computer's Region is set to 'United Kingdom', you'll get a pound sign (£) for the Currency data type.

Note that the Format property only affects the way a value is displayed and not how the value is stored in the database. Also, if a Format and an Input Mask are defined for the same field, the Format property takes precedence.

Number and Currency Formats

Built-In Number and Currency field formats

To set a number or currency field format, after entering your field name, select the Number or Currency data type in the fields list.

Click in the **Format** field property and select one of the built-in options from the dropdown list.

The built-in options you'll see will be dependent on your Region setting in your operating system Settings (or Control Panel).

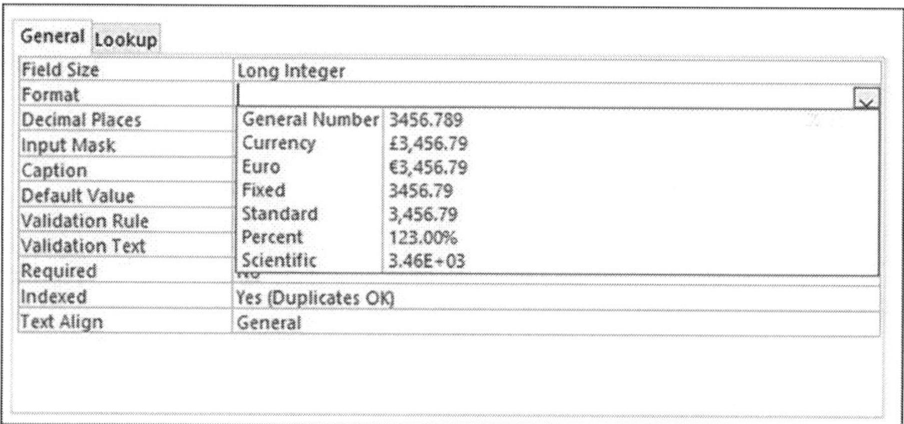

The built-in formats are as follows:

- **General Number**: Displayed as entered.
- **Currency**: Displays the number entered as currency based on the Region setting of your computer.
- **Euro**: Displays the number entered with the Euro currency sign.
- **Fixed**: Always display two digits to the right of the decimal point.
- **Standard**: Formatted with the thousands separator and two digits to the right of the decimal point.
- **Percent**: The value entered will be displayed as a percentage. For example, 0.4 will be displayed as 40%, and 3 will be displayed as 300%.
- **Scientific**: Formats the value in scientific notation.

Number format examples:

Format Type	Number Entered	Displayed as	Internal Format
General	123456.789	123456.789	#.###
Currency	123456.789	$123,456.79	$#,##0.00;($#,##0.00)
Euro	123456.789	€123,456.79	€#,##0.00;(€#,##0.00)
Fixed	123456.789	123456.79	#.##
Standard	12345	12,345.00	#,##0.00
Percent	.456	45.60%	#.##%
Scientific	123456.789	1.23E+05	0.00E+00

Notes:

- To use the Percent format for a Number field, ensure the Field Size property is Single. When you select the Number data type in the fields list, Access selects Long Integer as the default Field Size. You must change this to Single because a Percent field needs to be a floating-point number to display percentages correctly.
- You can use the Internal Format column in the table above as a basis for defining custom formats. For example, if your Region is set to the UK or an EU country, and you want to display currency values in dollars ($) in your database, you can simply enter the following custom format string: $#,##0.00;($#,##0.00).

Custom Number Formats

You can create a custom format if none of the built-in formats meet your requirements. You combine several symbols to create a format.

Global symbols you can use in any custom format:

Character	Description
Blank space	Inserts blank spaces.
! (exclamation point)	Forces characters to be displayed from left to right.
\ (backslash)	Forces Access to display the character immediately following the backslash. This is like surrounding a character with double quotation marks.
"Literal text"	Displays the text inside the quotes as literal text.
* (asterisk)	Fills an empty space with the character after the asterisk.
[color]	Displays the output using the color specified in the brackets. You can use one of the following colors: black, blue, cyan, green, magenta, red, yellow, or white.

Symbols you can use in Number and Currency fields formats:

Character	Description
# (hash sign)	Used as a placeholder to display a digit or a blank space if no value exists.
0 (zero)	Used as a placeholder for a number or zero (if a number is absent). For example, the format ####.00 will display 4567 as 4567.00.
$ (dollar sign)	Used to display the dollar sign character.
% (percent sign)	When placed as the last character in a format string, it multiplies the value by 100 and displays the result with a percent sign.
. (period)	Specifies the position of the decimal point in the number.
, (comma)	The thousands separator.
E+ or e+ E- or e-	Used to display numbers in scientific (exponential) notation. The plus sign is used for a positive exponent, and the minus sign is used for a negative exponent.

Example:

#,###.##;(#,###.##)[Red];0,000.00;"Empty"

This custom format displays:

- Positive values with two decimal places.
- Negative values in red, with two decimal places, and enclosed in parentheses.
- Zero values as zeros (0), with two decimal places.
- The word "Empty" in place of null values.

Date/Time Formats

Built-In Date/Time Formats

To set a date format for a field:

1. Enter the field name and select the Date/Time data type in the fields list.
2. Click the down arrow in the **Format** field property and select one of the built-in options from the dropdown list.

   The built-in options you'll see are dependent on the Region setting of your computer.

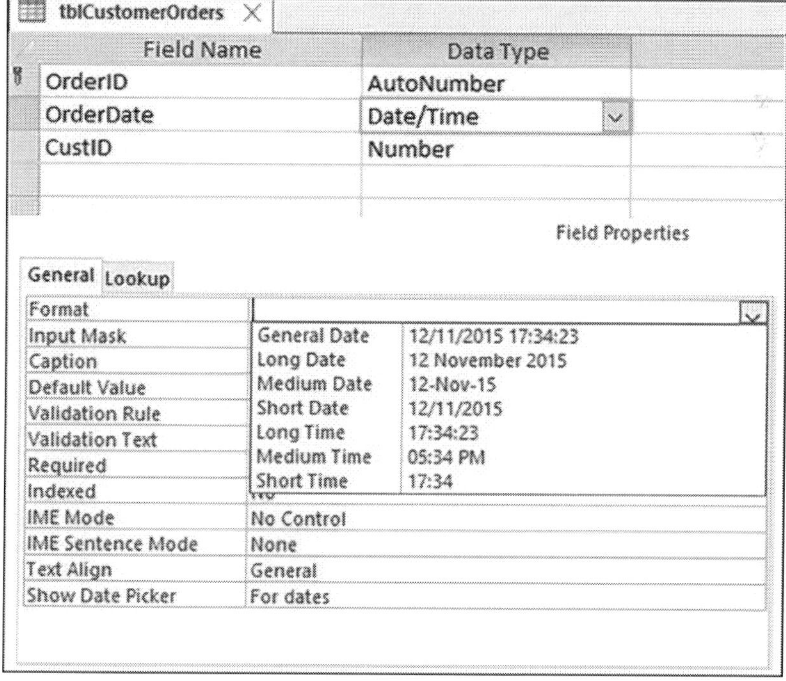

Custom Date/Time Formats

You can create custom date formats by constructing a specification string using the following characters:

Character	Description	Example
d	Shows the day as one or two digits (1-31).	2
dd	Shows the day using two digits (01-31).	02
ddd	Displays the day as a three-character abbreviation.	Tue, Wed, Thu
m	Displays the month using one or two digits (1-12).	4
mm	Shows the month using two digits (01-12).	04
mmm	Displays the month as a three-character abbreviation.	Sep, Oct, Nov
yy	Displays the year as two digits.	21
yyyy	Displays the year as four digits.	2021

Examples:

- **m/d/yy** will display *April 6, 2022,* as 4/6/22.
- **mm/dd/yyyy** will display *April 6, 2022* as 04/06/2022.

Text Field Formats

You can use the Format property to clarify the data contained in fields with Short Text and Long Text data types.

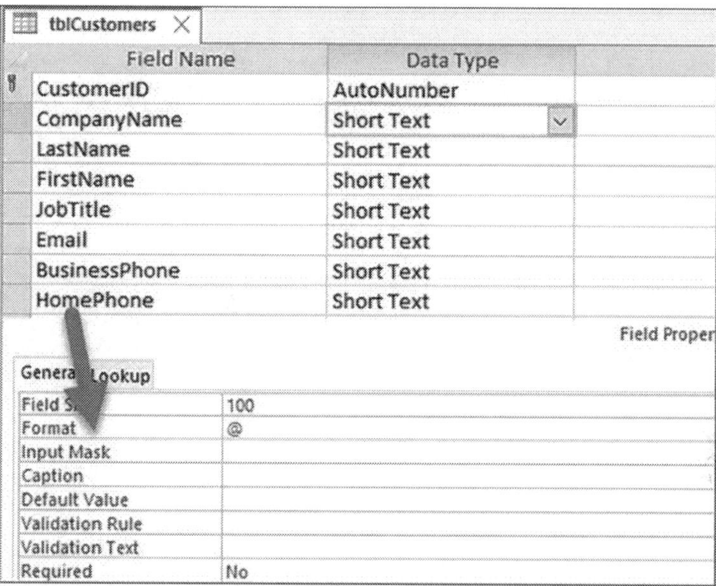

By default, Short Text and Long Text fields are displayed as plain text. However, you can use the symbols below to construct a format that changes the way text is displayed in a field.

Character	Display option
@	Display a character if there is one. Otherwise, show a space.
&	Display a character if there is one. Otherwise, do nothing.
<	Show all characters as lowercase.
>	Show all characters as uppercase.

You can have up to three sections in a custom text format separated by semicolons. The first section is for fields containing text, the second is for fields containing zero-length strings, and the third section is for fields containing null values.

For example:

@;"Empty";"Null"

The format above displays “Empty” when there is an empty string in the field and “Null” when the value in the field is Null. Otherwise, the text in the field is displayed:

Format examples:

Format	Data as entered	Displayed as
>	Jasmine Barker	JASMINE BARKER
<	JasmineBarker@Arcon.com	jasminebarker@arcon.com
@@-@@	PC01	PC-01
@;“Empty”	“”	Empty
@;“N/A”	Null	N/A

Yes/No Formats

A field using the Yes/No data type can display a Yes, No, True, False, On, or Off value depending on the format selected in the Format property for the field.

Access has three predefined formats you can select for the Yes/No field type:

- **Yes/No**: Displays Yes or No (default).
- **True/False**: Displays True or False.
- **On/Off**: Displays On or Off.

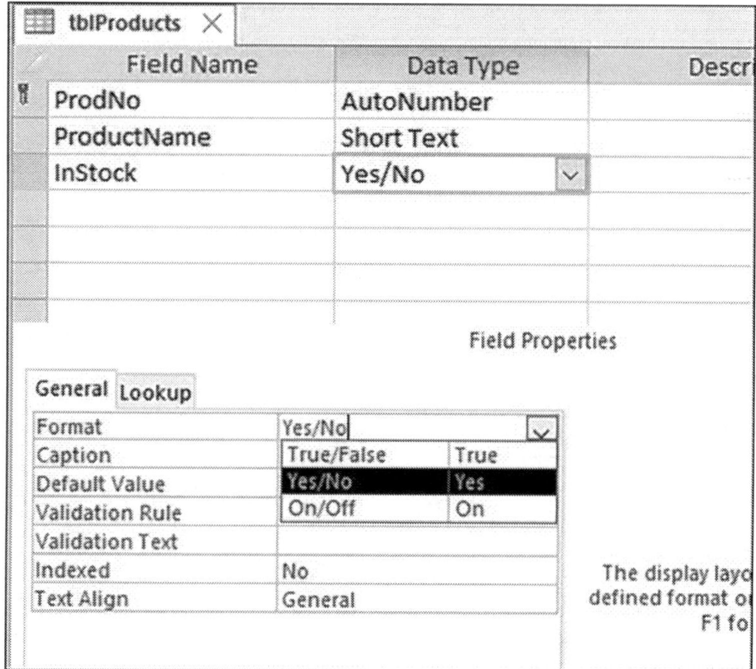

To select a format that's different from the default Yes/No:

1. With your table in Design view, in the fields list, click the field you want to change. If you're creating a new field, select the Yes/No data type.
2. In the Field Properties section, select the format you want from the **Format** dropdown list.

Tip Access uses a check box to display Yes/No fields by default. Checked = Yes, True, or On. Unchecked = No, False, or Off.

If you want to be able to type Yes, No, True, False, On, or Off in the field, click the **Lookup** tab in Field Properties and select **Combo Box** from the **Display Control** dropdown list.

Note that Access stores Yes/No values internally as **Yes = -1**, and **No = 0**. Normally, you would expect Yes = 1, and No = 0. So, remembering this is important when working in situations where the formatting is not applied to the data.

Entering Field Captions

Adding meaningful captions to your table fields can make creating forms and reports easier because the bound controls, like text boxes and combo boxes, will come with labels bearing the caption. So, you won't need to manually edit the labels on your form and report design.

In the example below, Access will use **In Stock** to label the **QtyInStock** field whenever you create any form or report bound to tblProducts.

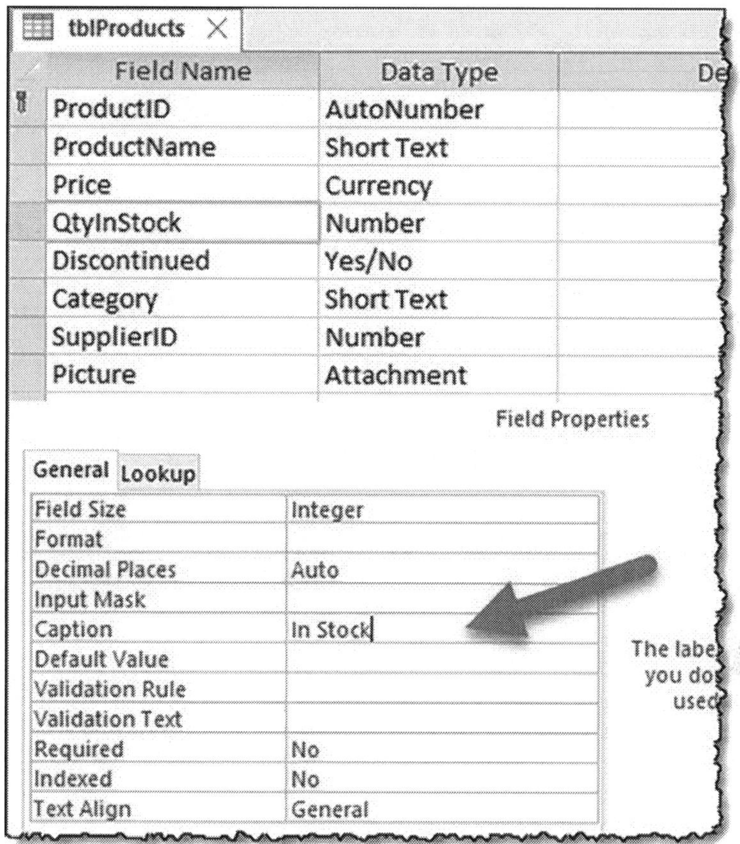
tblProducts
Field Name
Data Type
ProductID
AutoNumber
ProductName
Short Text
Price
Currency
QtyInStock
Number
Discontinued
Yes/No
Category
Short Text
SupplierID
Number
Picture
Attachment
Field Properties
General
Lookup
Field Size
Integer
Format
Decimal Places
Auto
Input Mask
Caption
In Stock
Default Value
Validation Rule
Validation Text
Required
No
Indexed
No
Text Align
General

If you leave the Caption property blank in this table, Access will use **QtyInStock** for any labels associated with that field on forms and reports. So, you'll need to edit the label to a more meaningful name. This can become repetitive and laborious if you're creating multiple objects bound to that table.

Taking a few minutes to add captions at the table level will save you loads of time and effort down the line when working with forms and reports.

Creating Input Masks

You can use an input mask to ensure data is entered in a field in a specific way. For example, in a date field, you use an input mask to ensure dates are entered in a chosen format like DD-MM-YYYY. You can use an input mask to ensure alphanumeric identifiers like FPN-40000 are entered correctly.

An input mask reduces the ability to enter invalid values. It ensures that when a user makes a mistake, the entry is rejected. This will increase the accuracy and integrity of your data.

Note that an input mask does not change how the value is stored in the database. The characters used to make up the mask are not stored as part of the value.

An input mask is made up of three parts, with the first part compulsory and the other two optional. You separate each part by a semicolon.

- **First part**: Required. This contains the mask characters or string, including placeholders and literal data like periods, hyphens, and parentheses.
- **Second part**: Optional. This part indicates whether the embedded mask characters are stored within the field. If you set this part to **0**, the characters are stored with the data, and if you set this part to **1**, the characters are displayed but not stored in the table. To save database space, you can set this part to **1**.
- **Third part**: Optional. This path specifies a single character or space that is used as a placeholder. Access uses an underscore by default. If you want to use a different character, enter it in this part of the mask.

You can use the following characters to create the input mask string:

Character	Explanation
0	A digit is required (0 to 9).
9	A digit is optional (0 to 9).
#	This represents an optional digit, including a space, a plus sign, or a minus sign. If omitted, Access enters a blank space.
L	A letter is required (a-z).
?	A letter is optional (a-z).
A	A letter or digit is required.
a	A letter or digit is optional.
&	A character or a space is required.
C	Any character or space is optional.
: (colon)	Date and time separator.
. (period)	Decimal placeholder.
, (comma)	Thousands separator.
/; -	Separator characters.
>	Coverts all characters to uppercase.
<	Converts all characters to lowercase.
!	The characters fill from left to right instead of from right to left.
\	Displays the characters immediately following the backslash as literal characters.
“”	Displays the characters in the quote literally.

You can use input masks for fields with Text, Number, Currency, and Date/Time data types.

Examples of input masks and how they display values:

Input mask	Value	Notes
(000) 000-0000	(502) 555-1288	All digits are required.
(999) 000-0000	(502) 555-1288 () 555-1288	The digits enclosed in the brackets are optional.
>LL00000-0000	PF14021-0776	A combination of required letters and digits converted to uppercase.
ISBN 000-0-0000000-0-0	ISBN 978-1-9162113-3-9	ISBN number with literal text followed by required characters.

To use one of the built-in input masks, do the following:

1. Open your table in Design view (if it's not in Design view already).
2. Click the field for which you want to add an input mask.
3. In the Field Properties section, on the General tab, click the Input Mask property box. The **Builder** button (three periods) appears on the right of the input box.
4. Click the Builder button to open the **Input Mask Wizard**.

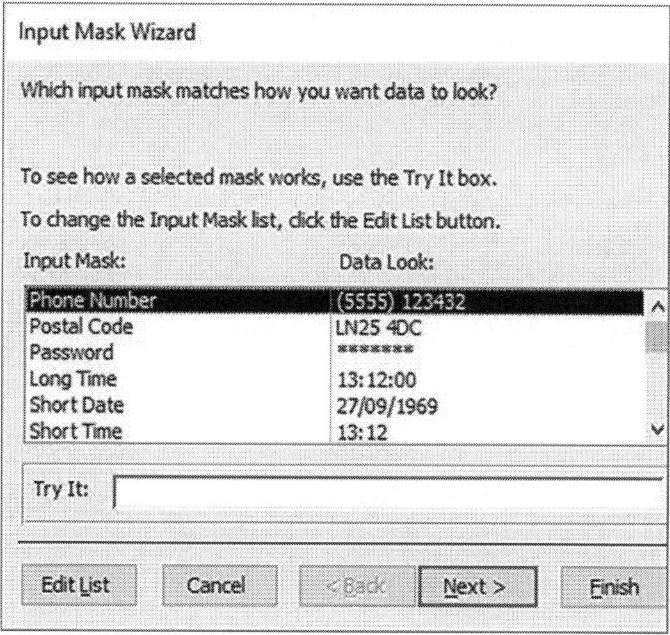

The Input Mask Wizard presents a list of options, showing you a sample for each option.

5. Select the type of mask that you want to add.
6. You can click in the **Try It** box and enter a value to test how the mask shows it.
7. To use the selected input mask, click Next.
8. In the following screens, choose the default options offered by the Wizard, unless you specifically what something different.
9. Click **Finish** when done.

The Wizard will insert the mask in the Input Mask property of the field.

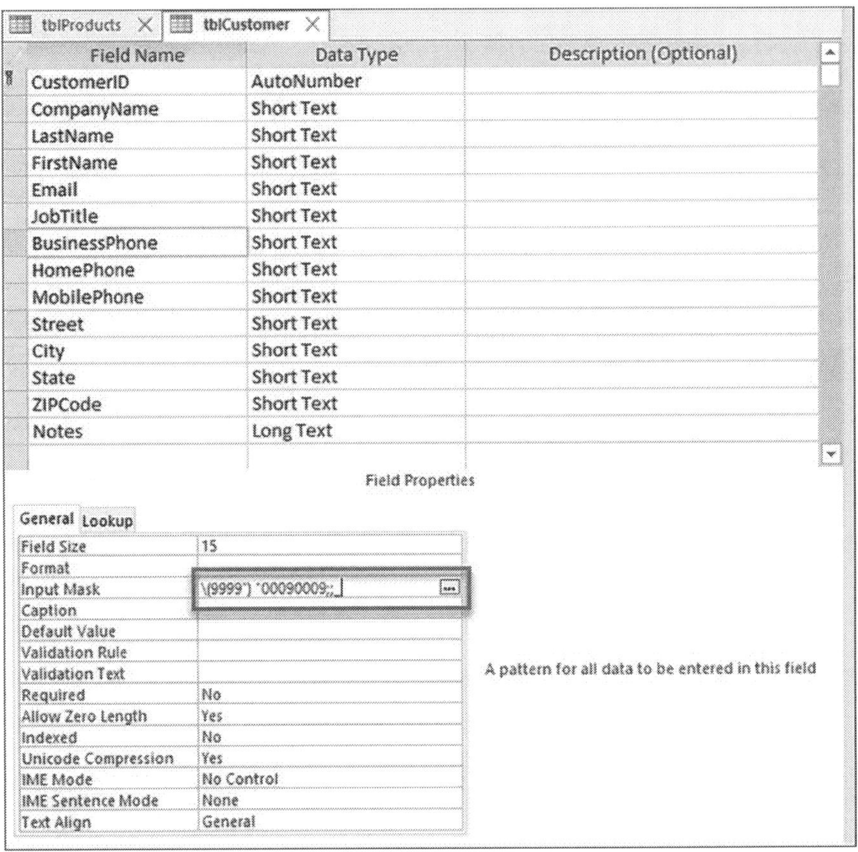
tblProducts
tblCustomer
Field Name
Data Type
Description (Optional)
CustomerID
AutoNumber
CompanyName
Short Text
LastName
Short Text
FirstName
Short Text
Email
Short Text
JobTitle
Short Text
BusinessPhone
Short Text
HomePhone
Short Text
MobilePhone
Short Text
Street
Short Text
City
Short Text
State
Short Text
ZIPCode
Short Text
Notes
Long Text
Field Properties
General
Lookup
Field Size
15
Format
Input Mask
\(9999") "00090009;;_
Caption
Default Value
Validation Rule
Validation Text
Required
No
Allow Zero Length
Yes
Indexed
No
Unicode Compression
Yes
IME Mode
No Control
IME Sentence Mode
None
Text Align
General
A pattern for all data to be entered in this field

Restricting Data Input with Validation Rules

Access allows you to insert validation field properties, which enables you to enforce business rules on your database. For instance, you may have a business rule that says a sales discount can only be between 5% and 10%. You can set this rule in the discount field property to ensure users are only able to enter values within that range.

To set a validation rule, you enter an expression in the **Validation Rule** property that evaluates to TRUE or FALSE. When a user enters data in that field, it triggers the test. If the expression evaluates to TRUE, the value is accepted. If the expression evaluates to FALSE, the value is rejected.

The **Validation Text** property enables you to specify the message that is displayed when an invalid entry is made.

Validation rules can also be set in data entry forms. However, the best way to prevent invalid entries in a field is to enforce the validation in the field's table properties. Validation rules work best for number, currency, and date fields.

The following table contains examples of the type of validation rules you're most likely to use:

Validation Rule	Description
<>0	The value cannot be zero.
>=0	Must be zero or greater.
> 0 AND <= 100	Must be greater than 0 and less than or equal to 100.
<=0 OR >= 10	Must be less than 0 or greater than 10.
BETWEEN 0 AND 100	Must be between 0 and 100.
<#01/01/2022#	The date must be before 2022.
>=#01/01/2022# AND <#01/01/2022#	The value must be a date in 2022.
<Date()	Must be earlier than today's date (current date on your computer).
>=Date()	Rejects dates from the past.
>= #1/1/2013# AND <= Date ()	Must be between January 1, 2013 and today.
>=0.05 And <=0.1	Must be between 5% and 10% (inclusive).

Validation rules with the **AND** operator mean the expressions on either side of the AND must be true for the validation rule to be met.

Validation rules with the **OR** operator mean just one of the expressions needs to be true for the validation rule to be met.

To enter a validation rule in a table field, follow the steps below:

1. In the Navigation Pane, right-click the table you want to work with and select Design view from the shortcut menu.

2. Click in the name of the field for which you want to set a validation rule.

3. Enter the validation rule.

Note You can click the Builder button in the field property box to open the Expression builder. The Expression builder provides help on operators and other elements you can use to compose an expression.

---

4. Next, you need to enter the validation text, so click in the Validation Text field and enter the message you want to be shown to the user if their entry is invalid. You want to keep the message short and simple. For example, the message could look like this: "The Price cannot be a negative value."

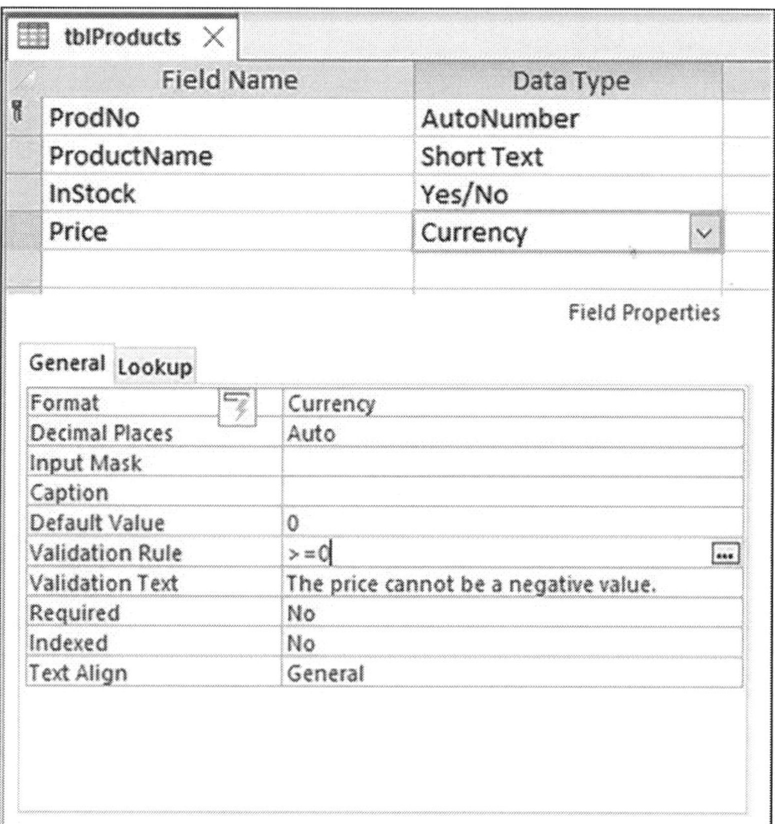

5. Click **Save** (or press **Ctrl+S**) when done.

6. **Test Validation Rules**. If you have existing data in the table, when you save the table with a new validation rule, Access will prompt you to run the validation rule against existing data. When prompted, follow the onscreen instructions to run the test.

   To run the test manually at any time when the table is open in Design view, click the **Test Validation Rules** button in the **Tools** group on the **Table Design** tab.

Creating a Lookup Field

A lookup field enables you to display a more meaningful value in place of a foreign key in a datasheet, form, or report. It also makes data entry easier by providing users with a list of possible values. Another advantage of a lookup field is that it reduces errors by restricting the values a user can enter.

For example, let's say you want to enter the customer for an order in the Orders table. However, all customer information is stored in the Customers table. Rather than having to figure out the ID for a particular customer, you can create a lookup field that displays a list of customer names from the Customers table. When a user selects a customer from the list, Access enters the customer's ID in the Orders table.

This feature can also be added at the form level using a combo box control. However, a benefit of placing the lookup field on the table is that the lookup list becomes available across the application for that field. Whenever you create a datasheet or form bound to that table, Access automatically creates a combo box for the lookup field.

Creating lookup fields for foreign keys in your table can save you a significant amount of time down the line when creating data entry forms. One of the advantages of Access is rapid application development, so take advantage of features like this to make creating forms faster and easier.

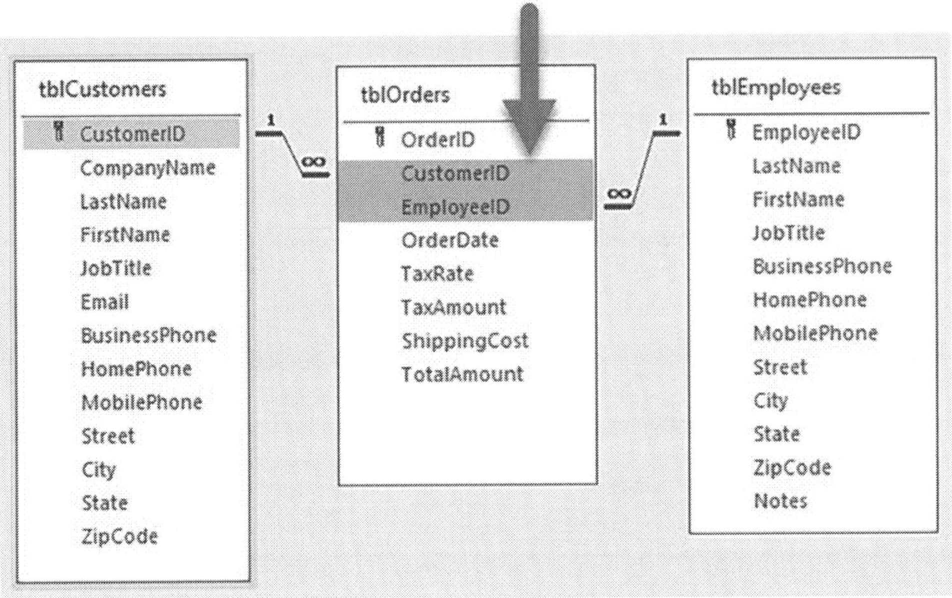

Manually Create a Lookup Field

To convert a field in a table to a lookup field, do the following:

1. Open the table in Design view.
2. In the **Field Name** column, click the name of the field for which you want to add a lookup list.
3. Under Field Properties, click the **Lookup** tab.
4. Set the **Display Control** property to **Combo Box**. This will display all the available properties for a combo box.
5. Ensure **Row Source Type** is set to **Table/Query** (this is the default).
6. In the **Row Source** property box, click the **Builder button** (with the ellipsis).

   This opens a Query Builder window.
7. In the **Add Tables** pane, double-click the table that contains the field(s) you want to display in the combo box. Access adds the table to the table/query pane (top). For our example, this will be the tblCustomers table.

8. There are several ways you can add fields to the query design grid (see figure below):

    - Double-click a field in the table in the top pane. Access will add the field in the next available column in the query design grid.
    - Select a field in the table in the top pane, and then drag and drop it on a column in the query design grid (see figure below).
    - To add several fields at the same time, hold down the **Ctrl** key, click the fields, and then drag and drop them on the query design grid.

    Add the ID field you want to store in the table and the field you want to display to the user in the query design grid. For our example, these would be the CustomerID and CompanyName.

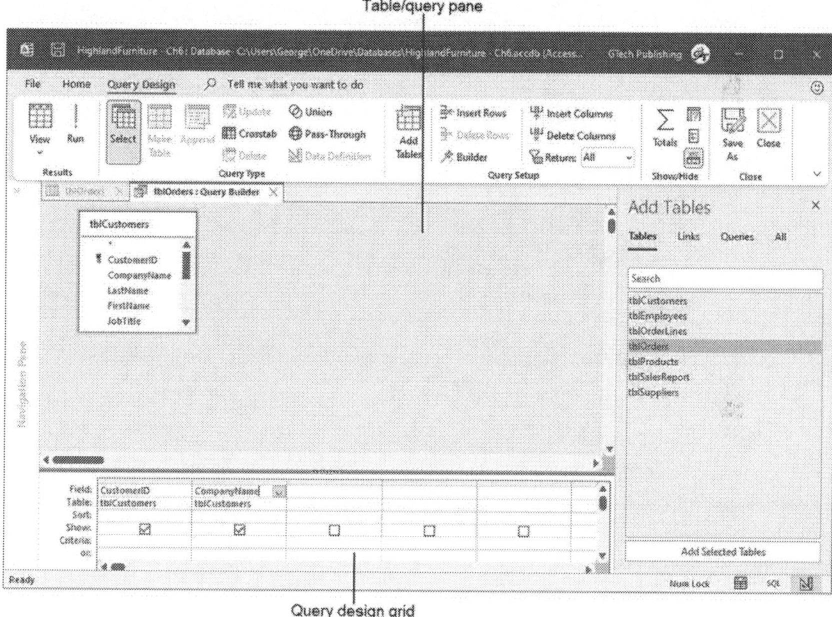

9. (Optional) You can view the results of the query by clicking the **View** button in the **Results** group of the **Query Design** tab. To return to the Query Builder, click the **Design View** button.
10. On the **Query Design** tab, in the **Close** group, click the **Close** button.

    Access will ask if you want to save the changes made to the SQL statement in the **Row Source** property of the control.

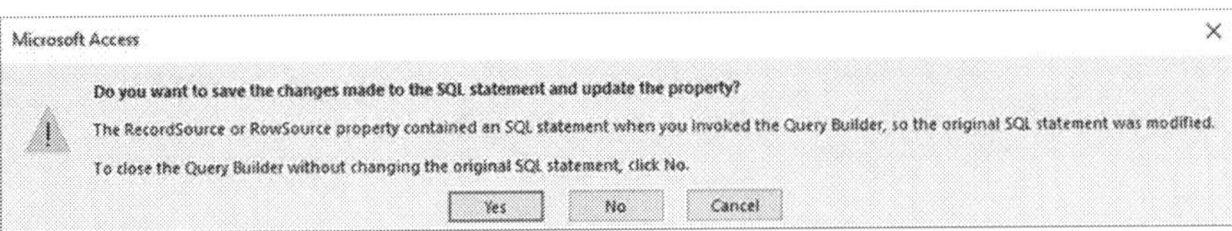

11. Click **Yes**.

    Access will enter the SELECT statement in the **Row Source** property (on the Lookup tab).

12. Ensure the **Bound Column** property is set to 1 (this means the first column of the dataset returned by Row Source is bound to the field).

13. Set the **Column Count** to 2, and the **Column Widths** to 0cm;6cm.

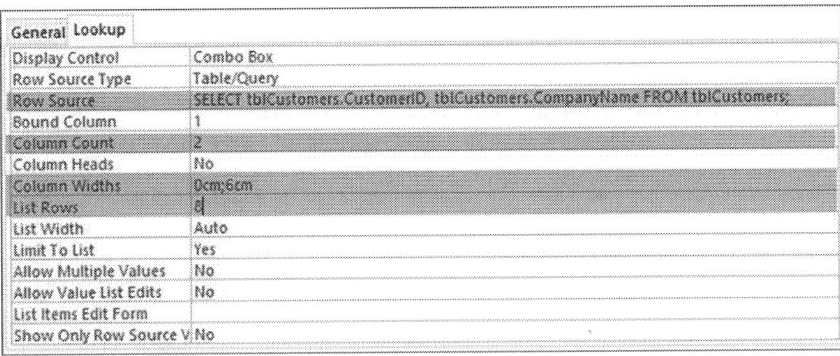

The **Column Count** and **Column Widths** values create two columns in the combo box. However, the first column (which is the ID field) is hidden from the user. We want to only display the value of the second column to the user, but Access stores the value in the first column. In our example, this will hide the CustomerID while displaying the CompanyName.

14. When done, click **Save** on the title bar (or press **Ctrl+S**).

You can view the table in Datasheet view and test the combo box.

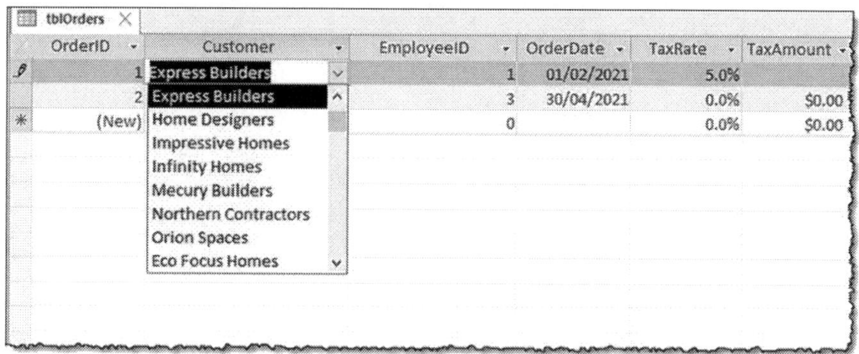

Creating a Lookup Field with the Lookup Wizard

You can add a lookup field to your table from scratch by selecting **Lookup Wizard** in the **Data Type** column. The Lookup Wizard creates three types of lists based on the options you selected in the wizard. You can create a lookup field from a table/query or a manual value list.

To create a new field with the Lookup Wizard, do the following:

1. Open the table in Design view.
2. Click in the **Field Name** column of the next available row, and then enter a field name for the lookup field.
3. Click in the **Data Type** column for that row and select **Lookup Wizard** from the drop-down list.
4. The wizard will guide you through the following steps:
   i. On the first page, ensure **I want the lookup field to get values from another table or query** is selected, and then click **Next**.
   ii. On the second page, select the table or query that contains the values you want to display in the combo box, and then click **Next**.
   iii. On the third page, select one or more fields (usually the ID field and another field you want to display in its place, like a name field), and then click **Next**.
   iv. On the fourth page, sort the field to be displayed in the combo box in Ascending order, and then click **Next**.
   v. On the fifth page, adjust the width of the column to ensure it fully displays all the values in the list, and then click **Next**.
   vi. On the sixth page, decide if you want to **Enable Data Integrity** between the two tables and whether you want to set **Cascade Deletes** or **Restrict Deletes** (see the chapter on Table Relationships for more on data integrity settings) and then click **Finish**.
5. When done, click **Save** on the title bar (or press **Ctrl+S**).

Setting Indexes

Access uses indexes to increase the speed of operations that fetch or sort data. An index uses a separate table, which is hidden, to reorder the records based on the indexed field. This makes accessing a particular record searched using that field faster than going through the whole table to find an item. Think of how a book index works. You use an index table, usually at the back of the book, to locate and go directly to the page with your desired topic rather than leafing through every page until you find the topic. A database index works in a similar way.

What Fields Should You Index?

There are pros and cons to using indexes. As indexes create separate tables which reorder the records for quick retrieval, it also comes with costs when inserting and updating records because the index tables must be updated too. While record retrieval can become considerably faster, too many indexes can slow down insert and update operations. Hence, you should carefully choose which fields you want to index. Only index fields that you expect will be used for searching, sorting, and creating joins in queries.

Note Access automatically indexes the primary key of a table, so you do not need to worry about setting manual indexes for primary keys.

You can have multiple-field indexes, just as you can have multiple-field primary keys. However, this can have a negative impact on performance. Thus, it is best to stick to single-field indexes unless you're a power user with advanced knowledge of indexes.

To set an index, you use the **Indexed** field property of the table. The table below lists the three available settings for the Indexed field property and their meaning.

Indexed property setting	Description
No	This field is not indexed (or delete the index if there is an existing one).
Yes (Duplicates OK)	Create an index on the field (the field can store non-unique values).
Yes (No Duplicates)	Create an index on a field (values in the field must be unique).

Choosing **Yes (No Duplicates)** means Access will not allow duplicate values to be entered in that field. There are scenarios where you may need such an index in a non-key field. For instance, you may want to index a field that stores unique serial numbers of products in your database, even if that is not the key field. Such a field is often used for performing searches.

Create a Single Field Index

To create a single-field index, follow the steps below:

1. Open the table in Design view (right-click the table name in the Navigation Pane and select **Design View** from the shortcut menu).
2. Click in the field that you want to index.
3. In the **Field Properties** area, ensure the **General** tab is selected.
4. Click the down arrow in the **Indexed** property and select **Yes (Duplicates OK)**.

   If you want to enter only unique values in the field, select **Yes (No Duplicates)**.
5. Click **Save** on the title bar (or press **Ctrl+S**) to save your changes.

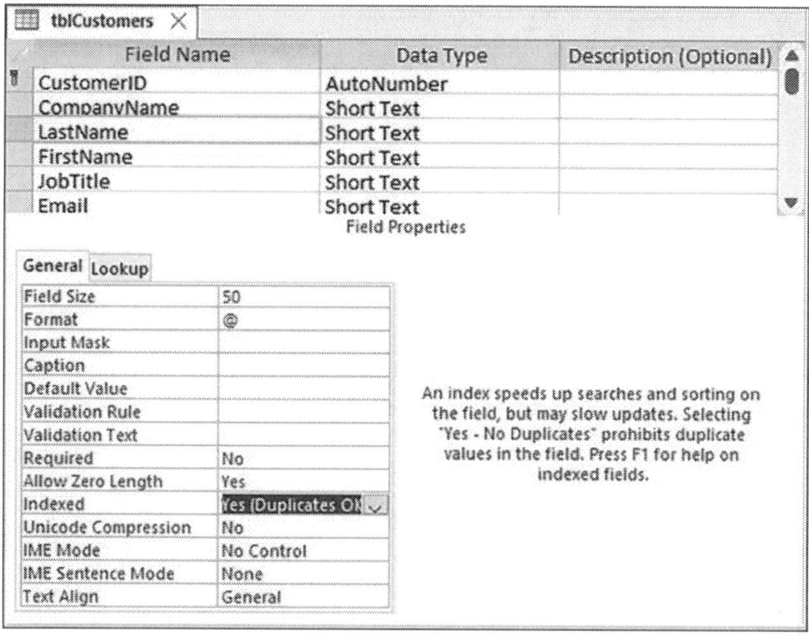

In the example above, the *LastName* field has been indexed because we expect to use the surname of customers often as a search term to find customer records in the Highland Furniture database.

How to Delete an Index

You can delete an index if you think it has become unnecessary or if it's having too much of a negative impact on performance. When you delete an index, you're simply removing the index table for that field and not the field itself.

To delete an index, do the following:

1. Open the table in Design view.
2. On the **Table Design** tab, in the **Show/Hide** group, click the **Indexes** button.

   Access displays the **Indexes** window for the active table. If necessary, resize the window so that the **Index Properties** section is shown at the bottom of the window.

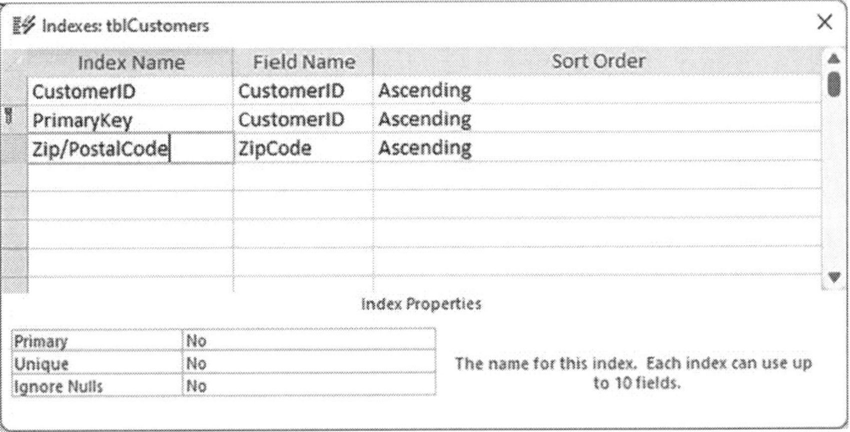

3. Click the row header to select the whole row containing the index that you want to delete, and then press **Delete** (on your keyboard).
4. Click **Save** on the title bar (or press **Ctrl+S**) to save your changes.
5. Close the Indexes window by clicking the close button (top-right of the window).

Note You can also view and edit indexes using the Indexes window. Simply follow steps 1 and 2 above to open the Indexes window. You can then view or edit the indexes and index properties that you want to edit.

Chapter 7: Defining Table Relationships

One of the benefits of relational databases is being able to isolate entities in their own tables for clarity and then linking related data across multiple tables using relationships. After establishing the relationships between your tables, you can start to create other database objects like queries, forms, and reports.

In this chapter, we will cover the following:

- The types of relationships you can create between tables.
- Resolving many-to-many relationships in your data design.
- Creating a one-to-many relationship in Access.
- Enforcing referential integrity rules between related tables.
- When to create a one-to-one relationship between tables.
- Editing a table relationship.
- Deleting a relationship if it is no longer required.
- How to print a hard copy of your table relationships.

Types of Relationships Between Tables

There are three types of relationships your tables can have:

One-to-One

This is when an item only appears once in each table. For example, an employee can only have one security ID. A one-to-one relationship may indicate that those fields should be in the same table. However, there are occasions when you may want to separate the items into different tables. For example, for security reasons, you may want to keep an employee security ID in a separate table from the table containing general employee data.

Another example is employees and allocated company cars. Even if each employee can only be allocated one company car, it would be best to store the car details in a separate table as the allocation of company cars can change over time.

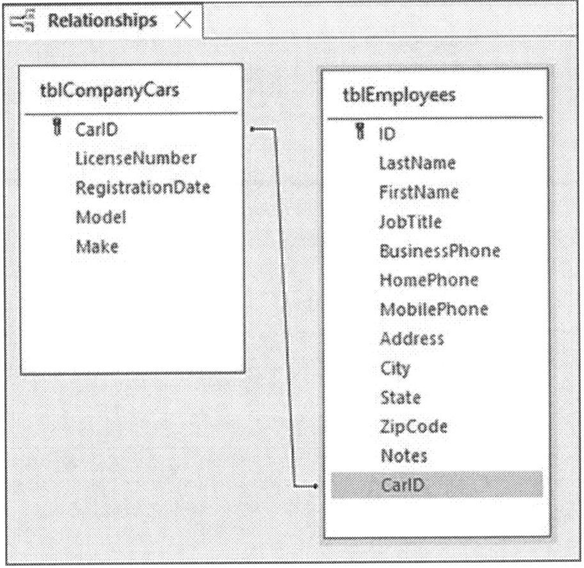

One-to-one relationship

One-to-Many

This is the most common type of relationship you'll find in a relational database. A one-to-many relationship means a record in one table can be related to multiple records in another table. For example, each customer can have one or more orders. The table with the 'one' is the parent table, and the table with the 'many' is a child table.

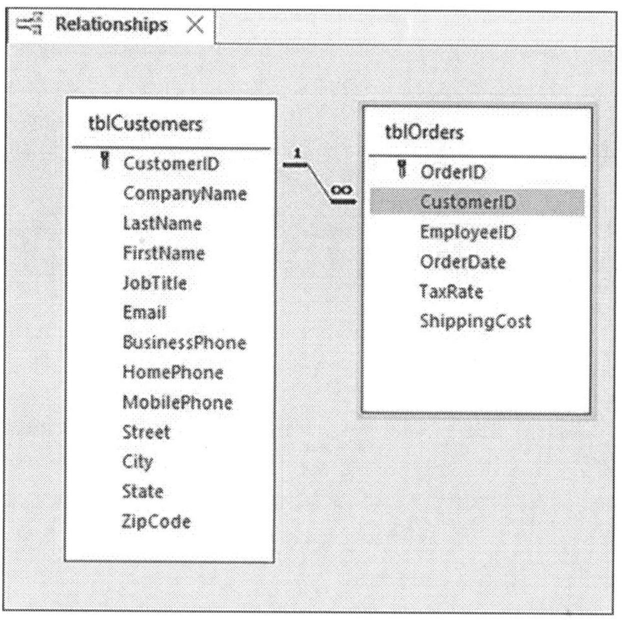

One-to-many relationship

The lines between the tables indicate a relationship. In the image above, tblCustomers is the parent table, and tblOrders is the child table. The line between the tables connects the primary key in the parent table to the foreign key in the child table.

In a one-to-many relationship, the infinity symbol (∞) denotes the *Many* side of the relationship, while number 1 denotes the *One* side.

A thick line connecting the tables means Enforce Referential Integrity is selected. Enforce Referential Integrity enforces the rule that you can't have records in the child table without a corresponding record in the parent table, which reduces the chances of invalid records in the child table.

Many-to-Many

This is when one or more items in one table can be related to one or more items in another table. For example, each order can have multiple products, and each product can have multiple orders. Many-to-many relationships are not ideal for relational databases as they introduce update anomalies. Therefore, these relationships are usually converted to one-to-many by using junction tables. We will discuss how to resolve these types of relationships in the next section.

Resolving a Many-to-Many Relationship

It is important to resolve all many-to-many relationships to one-to-many in a relational database. In Access, we need to create what is called a *junction* table that links both tables in a one-to-many relationship.

Note An **associative entity** (a table used to resolve many-to-many relationships) is colloquially known under many names depending on the database platform being used. In Access, they're generally referred to as **junction** tables. In SQL Server, they're generally referred to as **join** tables.

To illustrate a many-to-many relationship, let's say we have two tables, *Products,* and *Orders*. Each Product can have many Orders, and each Order can have multiple products. Therefore, we have a many-to-many relationship between these two tables.

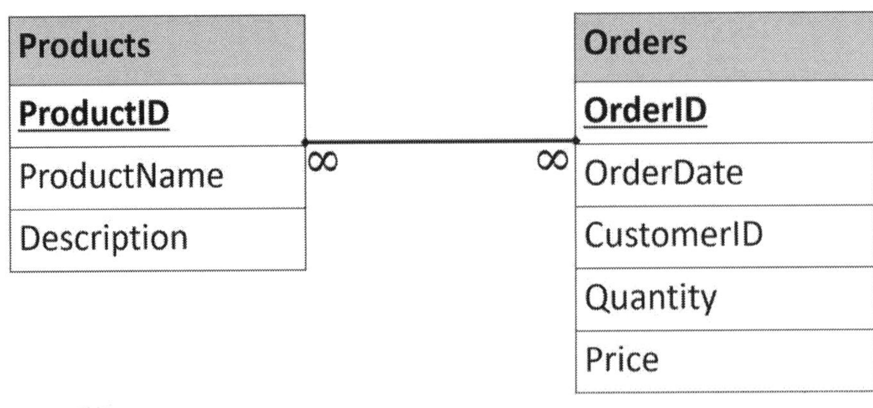

Many-to-many relationship

If we implement the database with a many-to-many relationship, it introduces the update anomalies we discussed in the chapter on normalization.

Follow the steps below to resolve a many-to-many relationship:

1. Create a new table to use as the junction table. For our example, the table is named OrderLines.
2. Create a copy of the primary key from both tables in the junction table as foreign keys. For example, OrderID and ProductID.
3. Move any other repeating data items into the junction table. In our example, we moved *Quantity* and *Price* from Orders into OrderLines.
4. You can either create a new Autonumber primary key field for the junction table or create a composite primary key made up of the foreign keys from the parent tables. In our example, we've set the primary key for the junction table using both the OrderID and ProductID fields from Orders and Products, respectively.
5. You can now create two one-to-many relationships linking all three tables.

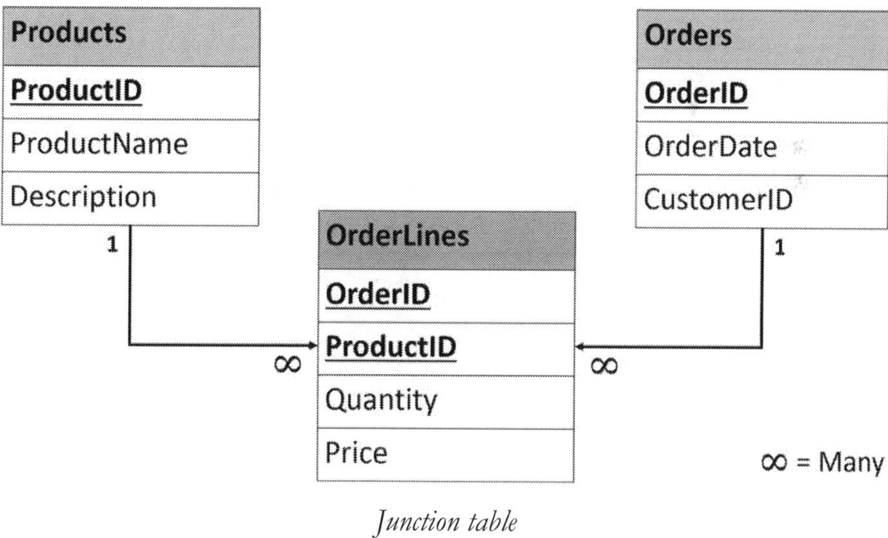

Junction table

Creating a One-To-Many Relationship in Access

Note For details on how to identify and specify your primary keys and foreign keys, see Chapter 4: The Five-Step Design Plan, and Chapter 5: Normalizing Your Data.

The most common relationship between tables in properly designed databases is a one-to-many relationship. In a one-to-many relationship, the primary key of the parent table is inserted in the child table as a foreign key.

In the relationship shown below, each customer in tblCustomers has a primary key called CustomerID. The primary key is indicated by the key symbol next to the field.

You can see that CustomerID also appears in tblOrders as a foreign key.

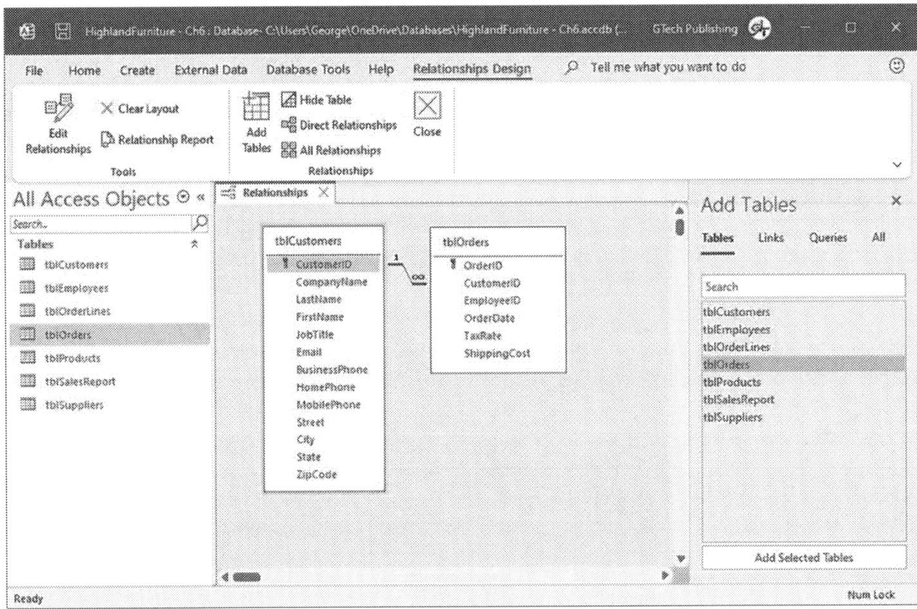

In this relationship, each customer can have multiple sales records in tblOrders, while each record in tblOrders can only be associated with one customer in tblCustomers.

In the Relationships window, the infinity symbol (∞) is used to represent **many** in the relationship, and one (1) is used to represent **one** in the relationship.

Once your tables have been created and normalized, you can begin to define relationships between the tables.

To create a relationship design, do the following:

1. Open the database for which you want to create a relationship design.
2. On the Ribbon, click the Database Tools tab, and then click the **Relationships** button in the Relationships group.

   Access opens the **Relationships** window. If the database has any relationships defined, you'll see them on the relationships pane. If no relationships exist, the relationships pane will be blank. On the right side of the window, you should see the **Add Tables** pane.

   Note If the Add Tables pane is not visible, click the **Add Tables** button in the **Relationships** group on the **Relationships Design** tab.

   ---

3. To add a table to the Relationships pane, double-click the table in the Add Table pane. Alternatively, select the table in the Add Table pane and drag it onto the Relationships pane. Do this for all tables you want to add to the diagram.

   Tip You can also drag tables from the Navigation Pane onto the Relationships pane.

   ---

4. To create a relationship between two tables, select the primary key in the parent table and drag it on top of the foreign key in the child table and then let go.

   For example, to create a relationship between **tblCustomers** and **tblOrders**, drag CustomerID from tblCustomers and drop it on CustomerID in tblOrders.

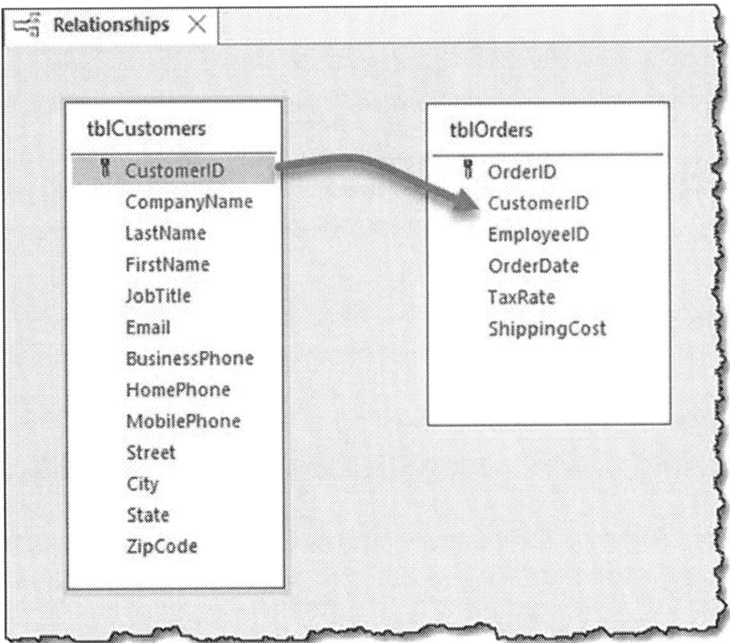

This will open the **Edit Relationships** dialog box. This dialog box shows the names of the tables and respective fields for which you're creating a relationship.

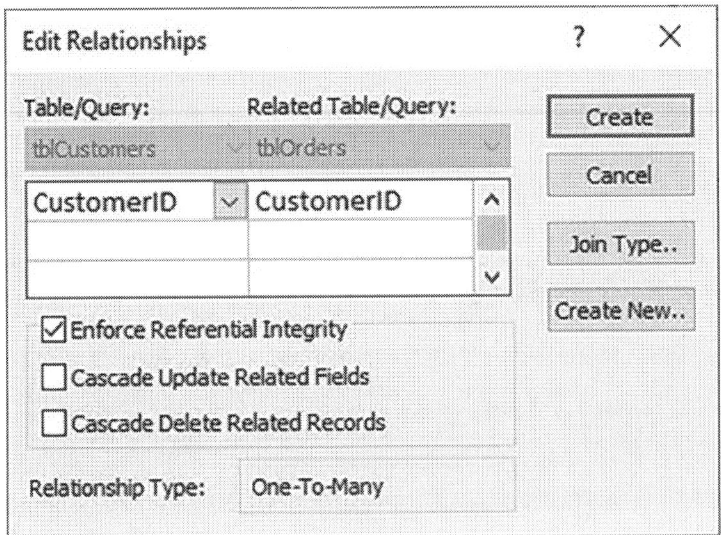

5. Select **Enforce Referential Integrity** in the Edit Relationships dialog box.

6. Ensure the field names are correct, and then click **Create**.

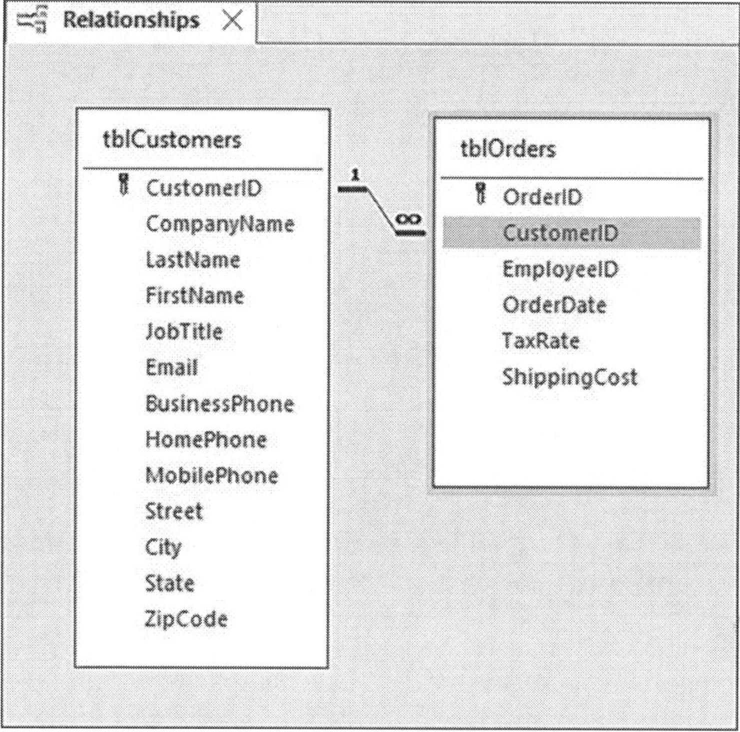

As shown in the image above, Access shows the new relationship in the Relationships pane. The line between the related fields indicates that the tables are related. With Enforce Referential Integrity selected, a 1 will be placed next to the parent in the relationship and an infinity symbol next to the child.

7. To create more relationships, repeat steps 3 to 6 above.

Note If a table is already in the relationship window, do not add the table again. Use the tables already in the window.

Enforcing Referential Integrity

You can use the three checkbox options on the **Edit Relationships** dialog box to change the way Access synchronizes your data between tables.

- **Enforce Referential Integrity**

  This option means a record cannot be inserted in the child table without a corresponding record in the parent table. Also, a record cannot be deleted from the parent table if there are related records in the child table.

- **Cascade Update Related Fields**

  Access acknowledges that you may sometimes want to change or delete records that are in a relationship. For example, when you delete a supplier from your Supplier table, you may also want to delete all the products they supply from your Products table. You may also want to change the primary key for a shipper because they changed their code, and you want the changes propagated through your database. For such cases, you want Access to update related records automatically.

  Select **Enforce Referential Integrity** and then **Cascade Update Related Fields** if you want Access to update related records as a result of a change.

- **Cascade Delete Related Records**

  Select Enforce Referential Integrity and Cascade Delete Related Records if you want Access to delete all related records in a child table when you delete a record from the parent table.

⚠ Important

Select **Cascade Delete Related Records** with caution as deleting related records may not be suitable in all cases. It depends on your business rules. There are often scenarios where you may not want to change or delete child records when the parent record is updated or deleted.

For example, suppose you have a one-to-many relationship between Employees and the orders they've processed in the Orders table. When an employee leaves the company, and you delete them from the database, you may not necessarily want to remove related orders from the Orders table. For cases like these, you would not select Cascade Delete Related Records.

When to Create a One-To-One Relationship

As mentioned earlier in this chapter, a one-to-one relationship may indicate that the related fields belong in the same table. However, there are occasions when a one-to-one relationship between two tables may be necessary. For example, you may have an Employee table with employee data, and you want to separate sensitive data like Social Security Numbers and other security info into a more secure table that's accessible to just a few people.

Another scenario is when you have two entities that are so different that it makes more sense to put them in separate tables. For instance, let's say we want to store details of company cars allocated to employees. Each employee can only be allocated one car at a time. If an employee leaves the company, the car could be assigned to a different employee. With a scenario like this, it would make more sense to store the details of company cars in a separate table rather than with employee records.

With cars and employees in different tables, we would have a one-to-one relationship between employees and company cars (as shown in the image below). In an example like this, tblCompanyCars is acting as a lookup table for tblEmployees.

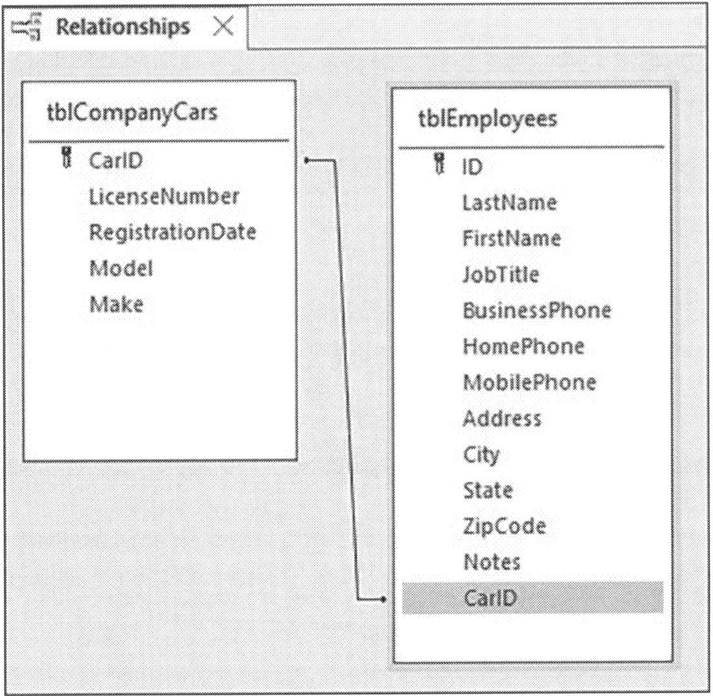

When one-to-one data requires two tables

To create a one-to-one relationship, follow the steps detailed above for creating a one-to-many relationship. That is, select the field in the table with the primary key and drag it over the field in the table with the foreign key.

On the **Edit Relationships** dialog box, you may choose to enable **Enforce Referential Integrity** but leave Cascade Update Related Fields and Cascade Delete Related Records unchecked.

In one-to-one relationships, we often do not want to cascade deletes. For instance, in our example (in the image below), if a company car is deleted from the database, we don't want any related employee record deleted, and vice versa.

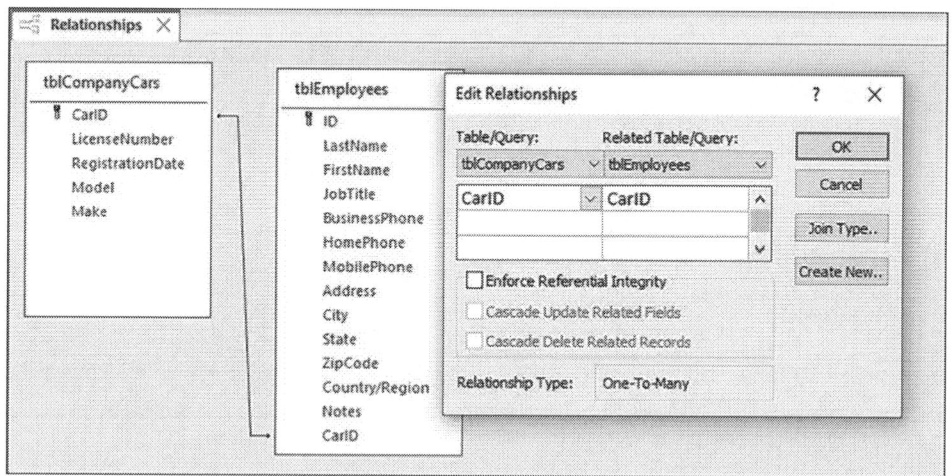

Editing a relationship

Note If you enable Enforce Referential Integrity, Access will show the relationship with a 1 and an affinity symbol (∞) even if it's a one-to-one relationship according to your business rules. Access always defines a one-to-many relationship, but your business rules will determine which ones are one-to-one for you.

Editing a Table Relationship

To edit a relationship between tables, do the following:

1. With your database open, select **Database Tools** > **Relationships**.

Note If you have created a relationship, but you can't see it in the relationships pane, it may be hidden. To display any hidden relationships, click **All Relationships** (in the **Relationships** group, on the **Relationships Design** tab).

---

2. Click on the connecting line (between the two tables), and it will appear thicker.

3. Right-click the connecting line and select **Edit Relationship** from the pop-up menu.

   Alternatively, you can click the **Edit Relationships** button, in the **Tools** group, on the **Relationships Design** tab.

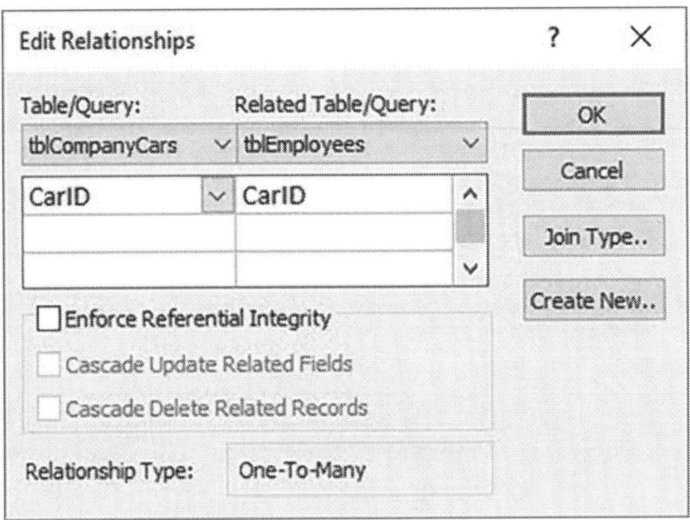

Table/Query is the parent table, and **Related Table/Query** is the child table. The table on the left is always the parent table (one), and the table on the right is the child table (many), even if they don't appear in this order in the relationships pane.

4. To change the fields that form the relationship, choose a different field below each table shown. In the example above, the CarID field in tblCompanyCars connects to the CarID field in tblEmployees.

5. To change the relationship shown in the Edit Relationship dialog box, select another table from the **Table/Query** drop-down list. Note that only tables that have been defined as part of a relationship in the relationship pane will appear on the list.

6. When done, click **OK** to confirm your changes.

Deleting a Table Relationship

To delete a relationship between two tables, first ensure both tables are not open in datasheet view or design view. If they are open, then close them as Access will not allow you to change the relationship if they're open.

To remove a table relationship, do the following:

1. On the Ribbon, select the **Database Tools** tab, and then click the **Relationships** button in the **Relationships** group.
2. Click the line connecting both tables to select it (when selected, the line should appear darker/thicker).
3. Right-click the connecting line and choose **Delete** from the pop-up menu. Alternatively, press the **Delete** key.
4. Access will prompt you to confirm the delete. Click **Yes**.
5. To remove any table from the relationships pane, right-click the table and select **Hide Table** from the pop-up menu.
6. To save your changes, click the **Save** button on the title bar (or press **Ctrl+S**).

Note When you delete a relationship, you also delete any referential integrity setting involved. Thus, Access will no longer prevent someone from creating an orphan record in a child table.

Arranging Your Relationships Diagram

If you're creating relationships between many tables, the Relationships window may look chaotic, with relationship lines crossing each other. Crossing relationship lines may make it challenging to figure out which tables are related to each other. To fix this issue, you can click and drag the title bar of each table to another part of the screen.

As much as possible, place a parent table to the left of a child table. Also, try to arrange the parent and child tables in such a way to prevent relationship lines from crossing each other.

After making changes to your relationships design, save your changes by clicking the **Save** button on the title bar (top left).

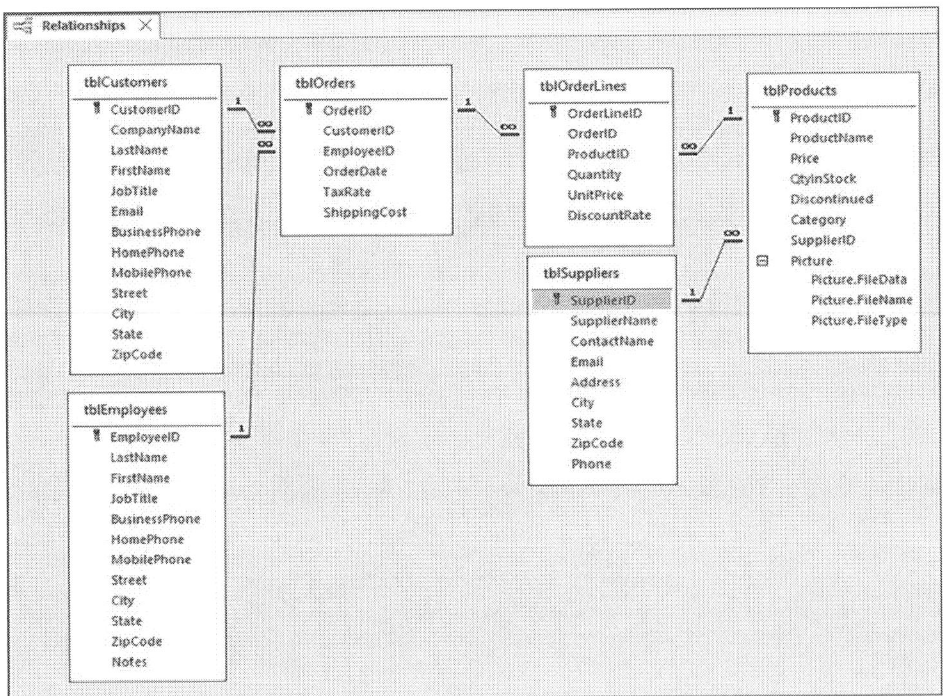

Printing Your Relationships Diagram

To generate a printable version of your table relationships, do the following:

1. With the **Relationships** window open, click the **Relationships Design** tab.

2. On the **Relationships Design** tab, in the **Tools** group, click the **Relationship Report** button.

   Access displays a printable version of your table relationships in a new window in print preview mode, with a Print Preview tab.

3. On the **Print Preview** tab, you can:
   - Select the paper size (the default is A4).
   - Adjust the page margins.
   - Set the Page Layout to Portrait or Landscape.
   - **Print** the relationships diagram.
   - Other commands on the toolbar allow you to export the report to different formats, including PDF, Word, or sending it as an email attachment.

4. When you're done, close the report to return to the Relationships window.

Chapter 8: Working with Data in Access Tables

In Access, there are several ways you can interact with your data. One way you can interact with your data is by using a table datasheet. You can use a datasheet to work with records as well as carry out some design changes to a table.

In this chapter, we will cover the following topics:

- Navigating through a datasheet.
- Adding and editing records.
- Inserting a new field using a datasheet.
- Changing field properties in a datasheet.
- Renaming a field in a datasheet.
- Deleting a field in a datasheet.
- Renaming a table in Datasheet view.

Working with Records in Datasheet View

A datasheet is one way to view and work with data in an Access table. A datasheet looks like a spreadsheet in that it has a series of rows and columns. Each row represents one record, and each column in a row represents a data item. You can scroll up, down, left, and right just as you can do for a spreadsheet.

To open a table in Datasheet view, double-click the table in the Navigation Pane. In a table's datasheet, you can work with the data as well as carry out some design changes to a table.

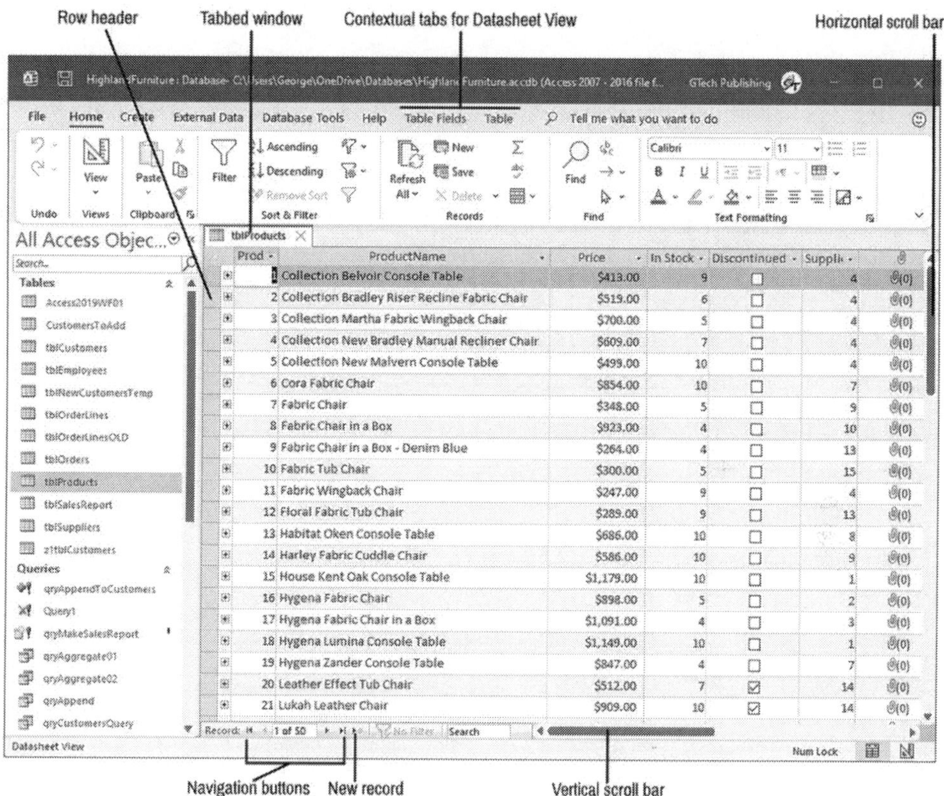

By default, Access objects are docked to the workspace as tabbed windows when opened. Personally, I've found the tabbed windows to be better at keeping the open objects organized in the workspace. But you can choose to have floating windows within the workspace.

If you wish to change this setting, follow the steps below to change the Document Window Options:

1. Navigate to **File** > **Access Options** > **Current Database**.
2. Under **Document Window Options**, select **Overlapping Windows**.
3. Click **OK** to exit Access Options.

The ideal way to enter data manually into an Access table is to use a form that allows you to enter one record at a time. You can quickly create a form bound to a particular table by using one of the form design commands on the Create tab on the Ribbon. We'll be covering Access forms in detail later in this book.

The Datasheet view is useful when performing actions where you need to view multiple records at once, for example, carrying out batch updates or deletes using commands like Find or Replace.

You can easily move in a datasheet using the mouse to click on different fields where you want to change data. Additionally, the Ribbon offers several commands that you can use to work with a datasheet like a spreadsheet.

At the bottom of the datasheet, you have navigation buttons that allow you to move between records. There are also buttons that allow you to go to the first record, last record, and create a new record.

When you're in Datasheet view, the **Home** tab on the Ribbon has several groups with commands that enable you to work with the active datasheet:

- **View:** Enables you to toggle between **Datasheet View** and **Design View**.
- **Clipboard**: The clipboard allows you to perform cut, copy, and paste commands just as you would in other Microsoft 365 applications.
- **Sort & Filter**: This group enables you to sort the rows in ascending or descending order. You can also use the filter command to limit the number of rows displayed based on the criteria set.
- **Records**: This group has commands that enable you to add, save, and delete records. You can also add a Totals row and perform spell checks.

  Under **More**, you can:
  - Adjust the row height and field width.
  - Freeze a row or field so that they stay put as you scroll.
  - Hide/unhide fields in the datasheet.

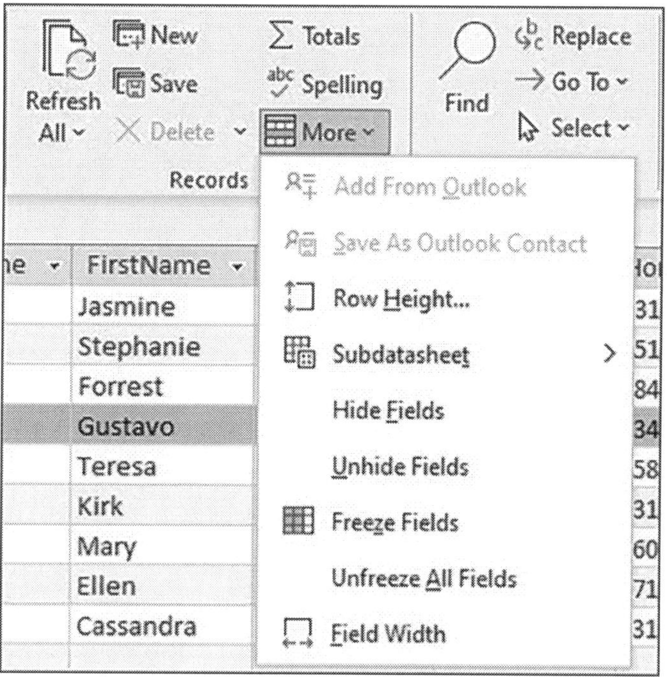

- **Find**: Commands in the Find group are identical to what you'll see in most Microsoft 365 applications. You can Find and Replace records based on a search term. You can also use commands under **Select** to select the active record or all the records in the datasheet.

- **Text Formatting**: Commands in this group allow you to change several text formatting features like fonts, alignment, and background color. You can also apply several predefined themes that will change to look and feel of the datasheet.

Adding a Record

To add a record to a table, follow the steps below:

1. Open the table in Datasheet view (double-click the table name in the Navigation Pane).

2. Click in the first empty cell at the bottom of the table. An asterisk (*) indicates the new record row.

3. If the key field is an AutoNumber, click on the second field in the row and start entering the value. As you start typing, the key field will increment automatically.

Note If the AutoNumber skips the next sequential number, it doesn't mean there's a problem. It just means a record was deleted at some point (or a data entry session was abandoned and then deleted).

---

4. To move from field to field, press **Tab**. Enter all data for the new record.

5. When you've finished entering the value for the last field, you are done. Access saves the record automatically as you are typing, so you don't need to manually save it.

6. To add a new record, simply click in the last row with the asterisk (*) and start typing.

Tip While adding a new record, if you change your mind and want to cancel the entry, press **Ctrl+Z** on your keyboard to undo the entry.

Editing a Record

To edit records in Datasheet view, follow the steps below:

1. With your table open in Datasheet view, scroll to the record you need to edit.
2. Click in the field that you want to change, and simply type in the new value over the existing value. If you have a lot of text in the field, you can press **F2** to select everything and then type in the new value. The new value will replace the old one.
3. When finished, simply press **Enter** to update the value in the field.

Deleting a Record

To delete a record in Datasheet view, follow the steps below:

1. Select the whole record by clicking the record header (this is the same as the row header).
2. Right-click anywhere in the row.
3. Select **Delete Record** from the pop-up menu.
4. Click **Yes** when Access prompts you to confirm the deletion.

Inserting a Field

1. Open the table in Datasheet view (double-click the table name in the Navigation Pane).
2. Locate the last field of the datasheet named **Click to Add**.

   If you can't see the last field, scroll all the way to the end of the datasheet to bring it into view.
3. As the name says, click the **Click to Add** header of the field. From the pop-up menu that appears, select the data type you want for the new field.

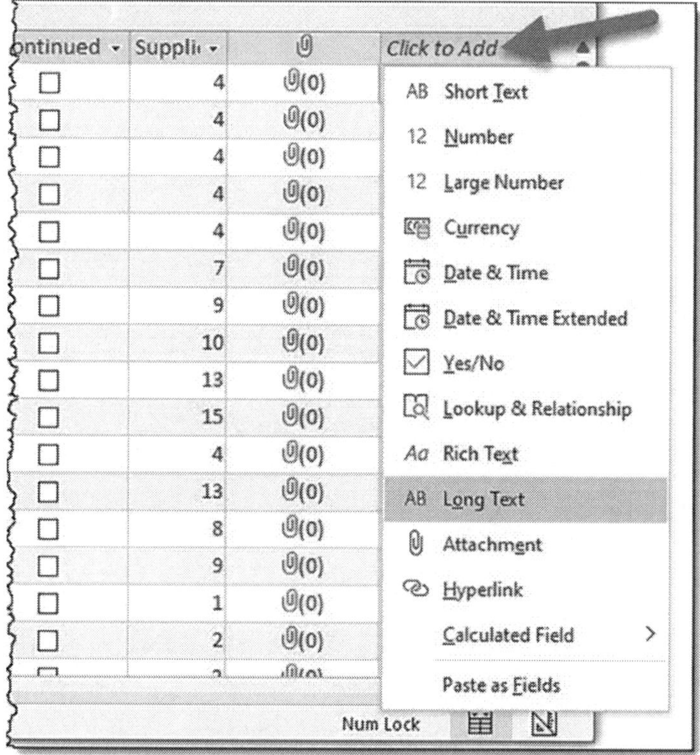

4. Access creates a new field named **Field1** (if there is no other Field1 in the table) and makes it the penultimate field. The **Click to Add** column remains at the end of the datasheet.

5. Enter the name for your new field, and press **Enter**. Access automatically highlights the new field name so that you can overwrite it with your field name.

Note If the field name is not highlighted, double-click the name to select it, type in your field name, and press **Enter**.

---

6. You can rearrange the fields so that your new field is positioned where you want it to be in the table. Click the heading of the column to select the whole column, then drag left or right to your desired location in the table.

7. Click the **Save** button in the title bar (or press **Ctrl+S**).

Making Design Changes in Datasheet View

While viewing a table in Datasheet view, you can carry out some design changes like adding fields, editing field names, changing the data type, and so on.

Note You cannot undo design changes to a table using the Undo command. When you make a change and press Enter, the table design is automatically saved. So before carrying out extensive design changes to your table, you may want to take a backup of the table.

Changing Field Properties

All fields created in Datasheet view are Short Text data types by default. If you skip the step of selecting the data type before creating a field, Access will automatically assign Short Text to the field.

Do the following to change the field type:

1. Click the first blank field under the field header.
2. Click the active field, and then on the Ribbon, click the **Table Fields** tab.
3. In the **Formatting** group, on the Table Fields tab, click the **Data Type** drop-down list and select the data type for your field.

   For some data types, you'll also need to select a format in the **Format** drop-down list.

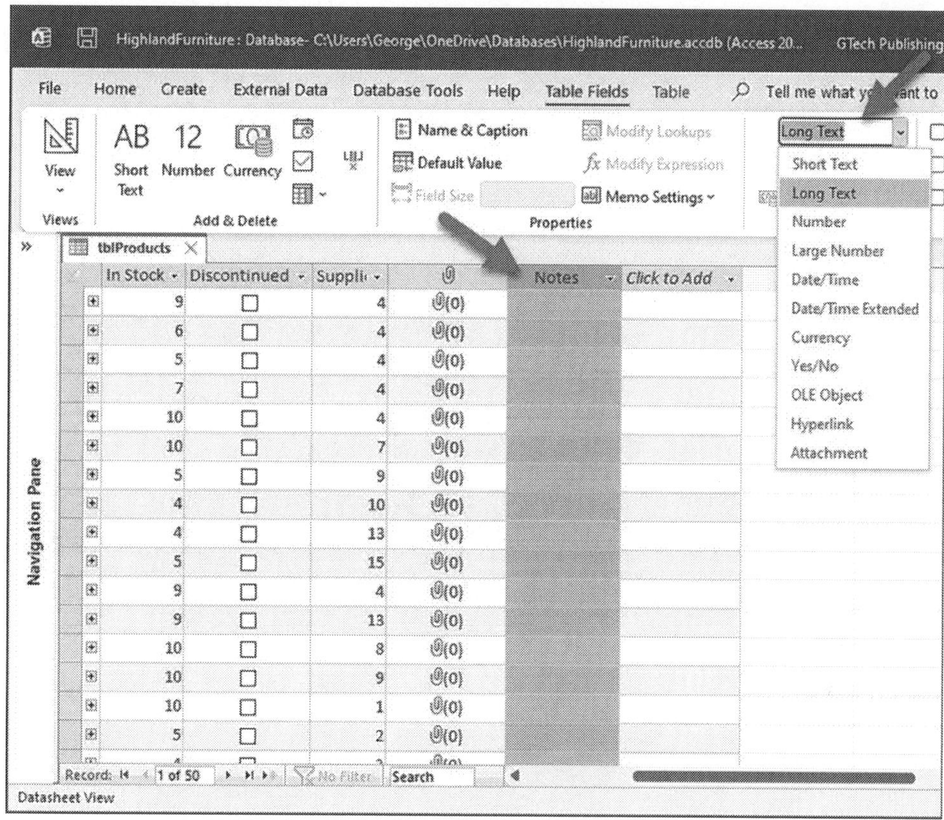

> **Note** When you change the data type of a field with existing, Access will display a warning message saying some data may be lost if you proceed. If you're happy that no existing data will be lost due to the new data type, go on and confirm the change.

4. Click the **Save** button on the title bar (or press **Ctrl+S**).

Renaming a Field

To rename a field, do the following:

1. Open the table in Datasheet view.
2. Double-click the field name. This will select the name.
3. Type in the new name over the old one.
4. Press Enter.

Deleting a Field

You cannot undo this process using the Undo command as this is a design change to the database. Hence, make sure you want to delete the field before you proceed.

To delete a field, do the following:

1. Right-click the field heading to display the shortcut menu.
2. On the shortcut menu, select **Delete Field**.
3. Access will prompt you to confirm the deletion. Click **Yes** to confirm the deletion.

Renaming a Table

To rename a table, do the following:

1. Close the table if it is open in Datasheet view or Design view.
2. Right-click the table's name in the **Navigation Pane** and select **Rename** from the shortcut menu.
3. Type in the new name and press **Enter**.

Chapter 9: Importing and Exporting Data

When working with Access, something you may often do is transfer data to and from external applications. Maybe you need to export data to Excel to create reports and charts, or you regularly import text files from a legacy system. Or perhaps you need to connect to data on an SQL Server database. Access has tools that enable you to do all that. One of the benefits of Access is its compatibility with several file formats in terms of importing and exporting data.

- In this chapter, we will be covering the following:
- How to prepare data for importing into Access.
- Importing external data from Excel, text files, and Access.
- Exporting data to Excel, Text, Access, and SQL Server.

Importing External Data

Access has two ways of accessing data from other applications:

- **Importing**: The process of importing data into Access translates the data from a foreign format into the Access database format. You can import the data into a new table (which is created during the import process), or you can append the data into an existing table.

- **Linking**: Instead of importing data into Access, you can create a link to the data from Access. This allows you to work with the records as if the data is in Access. With linked data sources, you cannot change the structure of the data in Access. When you establish a link, it will remain established until you delete the link or the data source becomes unavailable due to being moved or deleted.

You can import data from the following file sources:

File Type	File extension	Description
Excel	.XLS, .XLSX, .XLSB, .XLSM	Excel is a very common spreadsheet program used to manage and analyze data. Often, when the data becomes too complex to manage in Excel, people may want to move the data into a database application like Access. Access has seamless compatibility with Excel in terms of importing, linking to, or exporting data.
HTML	.HTM, .HTML	You can connect to tables and certain web pages and import data into Access or link to the data. For example, you can create a link to a website with live Forex data. You can refresh the link often to have current exchange rates instead of historical values.
XML	.XML	You can import XML (Extensible Markup Language) files into Access.
Text	.TXT	Text files are often used as a bridge between two incompatible systems in terms of transferring information. For example, a delimited text file may be exported from a legacy bank application, and that data can be imported into Access. The most common form of delimited text files is called Comma Separated Values - CSV. The values are separated by commas, and Access can easily read the separated data and import them into columns.

Compatible database file formats:

- **Access**: You can easily import data from other Access databases going back to Access 2000. Access versions prior to 2000 are no longer compatible.
- **ODBC**: You can use an ODBC connection (open database connectivity) to connect to server-based databases like SQL Server, Azure, and Oracle.
- **Outlook/Exchange**: You can link to your Outlook or Exchange folder from Access.
- **dBase**: You can use an ODBC connection to connect to a dBase file format.

Preparing your data for importing

To import certain file formats into Access, you need to prepare the data first to ensure the import operation goes smoothly. For database formats, you typically do not need any preparation as the data will already be organized as rows and columns in tables.

To prepare information from Excel for importing into Access, review the data using the list below:

- Double-check the data to ensure it is consistent and complete.
- The first row of the data in the spreadsheet will be the field names in Access when imported. Hence, if the first row of the data in Excel does not have column headings, you should add column headings that will represent the field names in Access.
- If you intend to append the imported data into an existing Access table, ensure the column headings in Excel are the same as the field names in Access. The order of the columns in the spreadsheet must also match the order of the fields in the Access table. Otherwise, the import will fail.
- The number of columns in the spreadsheet should not be more than 255 as Access does not support more than 255 fields in a table.
- Only include the rows and columns that you want to import. Once you start the import process, you can't skip rows. Also, if you are appending the data to an existing table, you can't skip columns.
- Ensure the data types for the cells in each column are consistent. For example, number fields should have number values, not text, and text fields should have text values. In Excel, you can change the cell format and ensure all cells in a column have a consistent format before uploading the data into Access.
- Delete all unnecessary blank rows or columns in the worksheet. If necessary, try to add any missing data before proceeding with the import operation.
- Avoid unnecessary long column headings. Keep the names as short as the kind of field names you would have in Access. The field names also need to be unique. You cannot use the same name for two fields in Access.
- If any of the cells in the worksheet has an error value, for example, **#NUM** or **#DIV**, ensure you correct them before you begin the import operation.

Importing Data from Excel

You can import Excel data into a new or existing Access table. The cells in each column in the spreadsheet must have the same format so that Access can easily assign data types to the fields. During the import process, Access will enable you to select individual worksheets or ranges in the source workbook. Hence, you can import data from individual worksheets or named ranges.

Follow the steps below to import data from Excel:

1. Open the destination Access database.
2. On the Ribbon, click the **External Data** tab. In the **Import & Link** group, click **New Data Source** > **From File** > **Excel**.

   This displays the get external data dialog box.

   Note Ensure the Excel file is closed before you select it in the next step. Otherwise, you'll get a "File in use" error message.

   ---

3. In the Get External Data dialog box, click the **Browse** button, and in the **File Open** dialog box, navigate to the Excel file, select it, and click **Open**.

   Access will enter the file path in the **File name** box.

4. In the lower part of the Get External Data dialog box, Access has import options that allow you to:
   - Import the data into a new table.
   - Append the data to a current table.
   - Create a link to the data source.

   To import the data into a new table, select the first option:

   Import the source data into a new table in the current database.

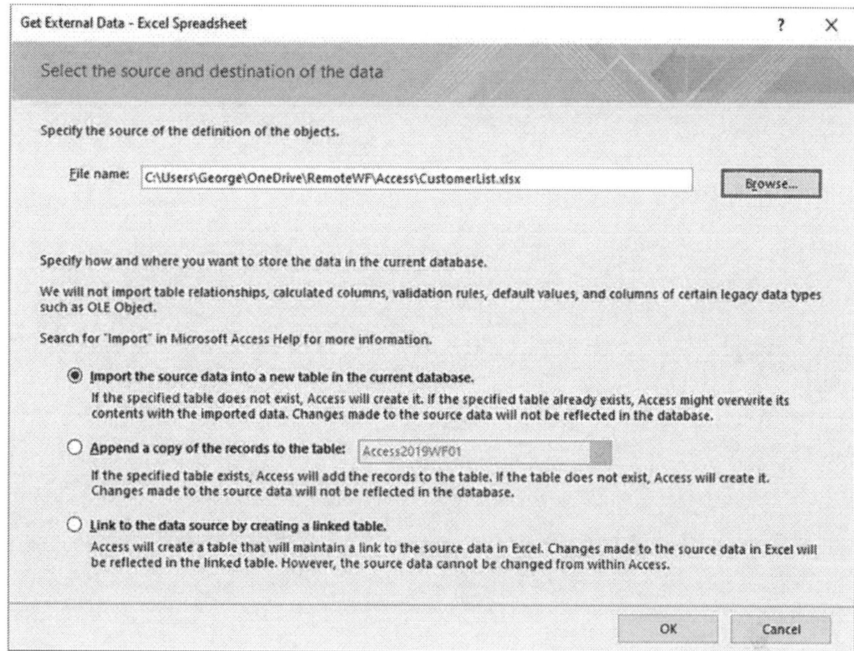

Tip When importing data into Access from a different format, always import the data into a new transient table instead of appending the data to an existing production table. Once you have the data in a new table, you can review the data and fix any issues before appending it to a production table.

This ensures you are not adding records to your production tables that may introduce errors and inconsistencies. Only choose to append the data to an existing table if you've performed this import operation before and you're familiar with the data source and data quality.

5. Click **OK** to start the Import Spreadsheet Wizard.

6. On the first screen of the **Import Spreadsheet Wizard**, select **Show Worksheets**.

Note If the data you're importing is a named range, then select **Show Named Ranges**.

7. Select the worksheet that contains the data you want to import.

   In our example, we want to import the **New Customers** worksheet.

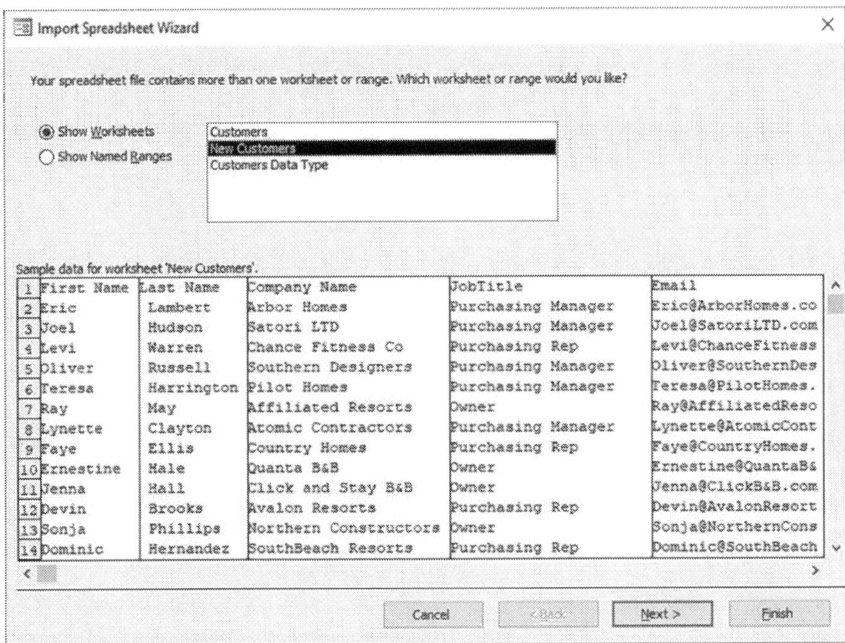

The second half of the first screen of the wizard shows you a sample of the data you have just selected. This enables you to quickly tell if you've selected the right data source.

8. Click **Next**.

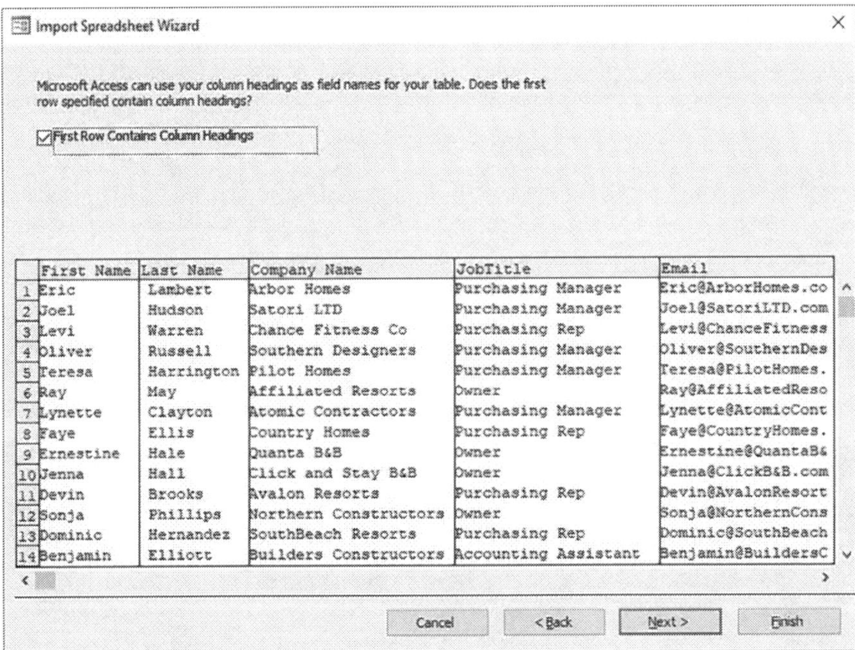

9. On the second screen of the wizard, select the check box, **First Row Contains Column Headings**. Then click **Next**.

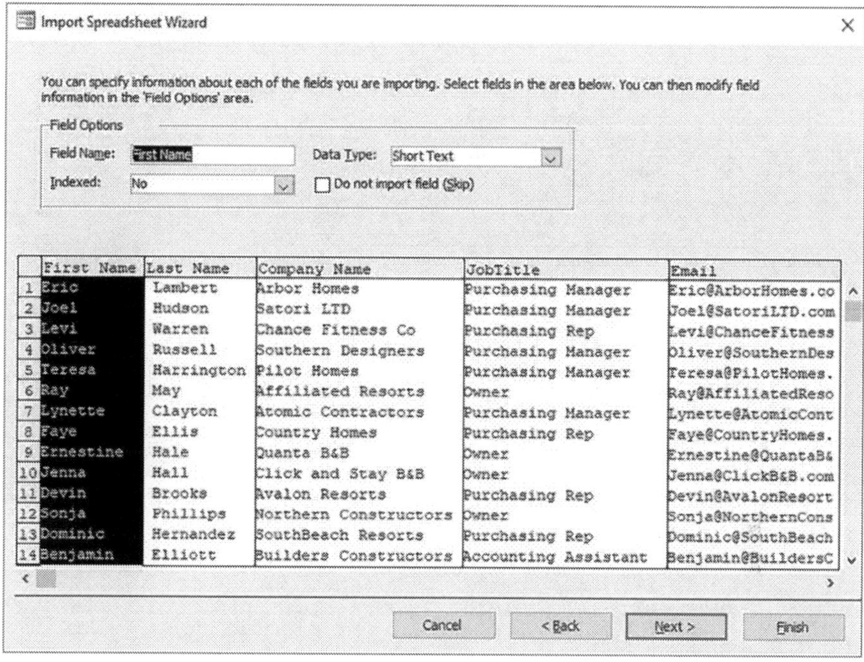

10. This screen of the wizard allows you to edit the following import settings for each field:

   - **Field Name**: If you added field names in Excel before importing the data, you don't need to enter field names here.
   - **Data Type**: Check every field in the sample to ensure Access has identified the right data type. Select the right data type for the fields you want to change.
   - **Indexed**: Ideally, you want to leave this as **No**. You can always set indexes later.
   - **Skip**: Select this checkbox if you don't want to import the field. You can only skip fields if you're importing the data into a new table.

If you need to make any changes to field names and data types, you should do it here. When you're happy with the field names and data types, click **Next**.

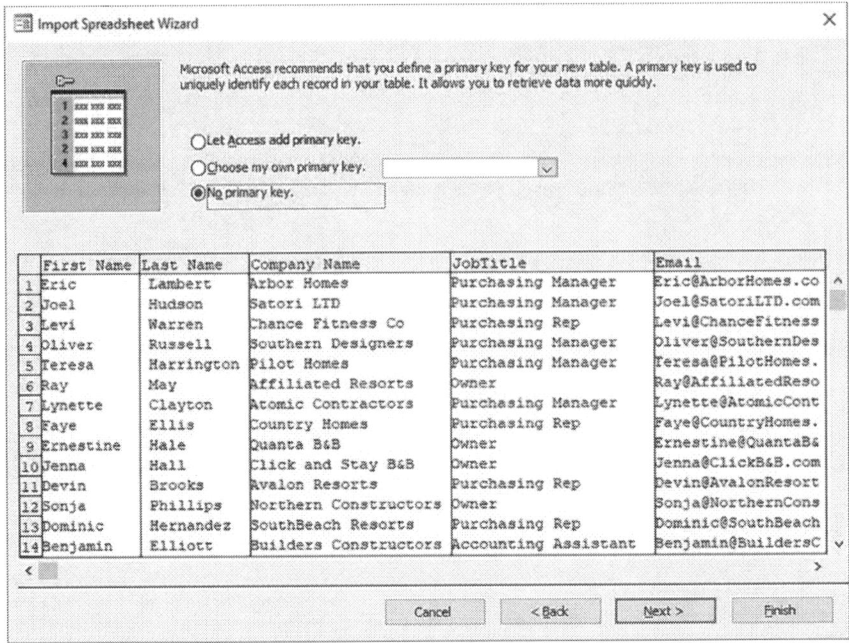

11. The next page of the wizard gives you the option to select a primary key for the table. If this is a table to temporarily hold data you intend to transfer to another table, then you do not need to assign a primary key to the table. Select **No primary key**.

Ideally, you want to avoid setting a primary key at this point because you can always specify a primary key after the table has been created and you've checked that the data is OK. However, if you must set the primary key at this point, then for an AutoNumber primary key, select **Let Access add primary key**. If you already have a field of unique values that you want to use as a primary key, then select **Choose my own primary key**, and then select the field from the drop-down list.

Click **Next**.

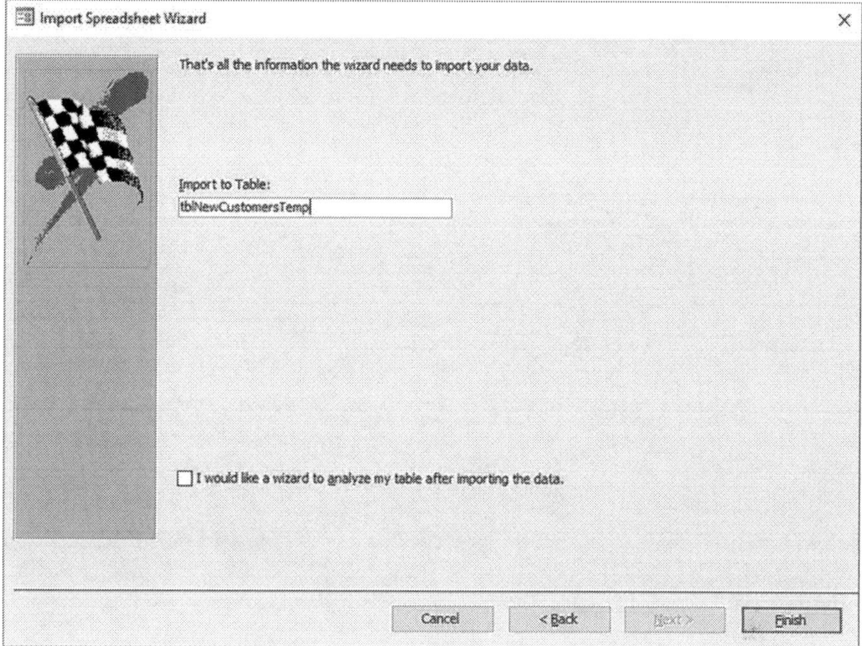

On the last screen of the wizard, enter the name of the table. Access does not allow duplicate table names, so choose a name that has not already been used on an existing table in the database.

12. Click **Finish** to close the wizard.

    Access will ask you if you want to save the import steps. If this is a one-off operation, you don't need to save the steps. However, if you intend to repeat this import process regularly, you may want to save the import steps. When you save the import steps, you can repeat the process faster next time without using the wizard.

13. Click **Close**.

    Access will create and add the table to the Navigation Pane under Tables. To view the imported data, double-click the new table in the Navigation Pane.

⚠ **Important** Whenever you import data from an external source, always review the data before use. Sometimes there could be errors, and some records may not have been imported, and you get no warning from Access. One quick check you can perform is to compare the number of records that have been imported to the number of records in the worksheet.

Importing Data from a Text File

The characters in a text file can include letters, numbers, and special characters like tabs, carriage returns, and line feeds. Access supports the importing of the following file extensions .txt, .csv, .asc, and .tab.

To import a text file, you need to structure the data in a way that allows Access to divide the data into fields and records.

Properly structured text files fall into two categories:

- **Delimited file**: Each record appears in a single line, and the fields are separated by a character called a delimiter. The delimiter can be a comma, tab, semicolon, space, and so on. This is the most common type of text file you will encounter.
- **Fixed-width file**: Each record is on a separate line, and the fields are separated by a series of blank spaces. Each column has the same width, which ensures that the values for each column start at the same point in the file. Fixed-width text files are no longer common, but legacy systems may still generate data exports in this format.

Preparing your text file for import

Before importing text files, carry out the following data preparation tasks:

- Ensure the data is organized in a consistent manner across the file. For example, you can't mix delimited records with fixed-width records in the same data source for import.
- Open the text file in Excel (or another spreadsheet application) to see if any delimiter being used is separating the fields correctly.
- Once the file is opened in Excel, you can review the data with the list above for spreadsheet data to ensure there are no issues that would prevent the data from being uploaded.
- If the delimiter is a comma, you can use Excel to save the file as a CSV file (comma-separated values).

Note The text file does not necessarily have to be a CSV file. If the delimiter used is a different character (like a semi-colon or tab), you can specify that in Access during the import process.

Importing a Delimited File

To import a text file into Access, follow the steps below:

1. Open the destination database.

2. On the Ribbon, click the **External Data** tab. In the **Import & Link** group, click **New Data Source** > **From File** > **Text File**.

   This displays the **Get External Data** dialog box.

3. In the Get External Data dialog box, click the **Browse** button. Then navigate to the text file, select it, and click **Open**.

   Access enters the file path in the **File name** box.

   For our example, we'll be importing a text file named NewCustomerList.txt.

4. On the lower part of the screen, select the first option: **Import the source data into a new table in the current database**.

   Access opens the Import Text Wizard.

Note If you're importing data from a text file for the first time, it is particularly important to create a new Access table rather than append it to an existing table. You want to make everything is OK with the data before appending it to an existing production table.

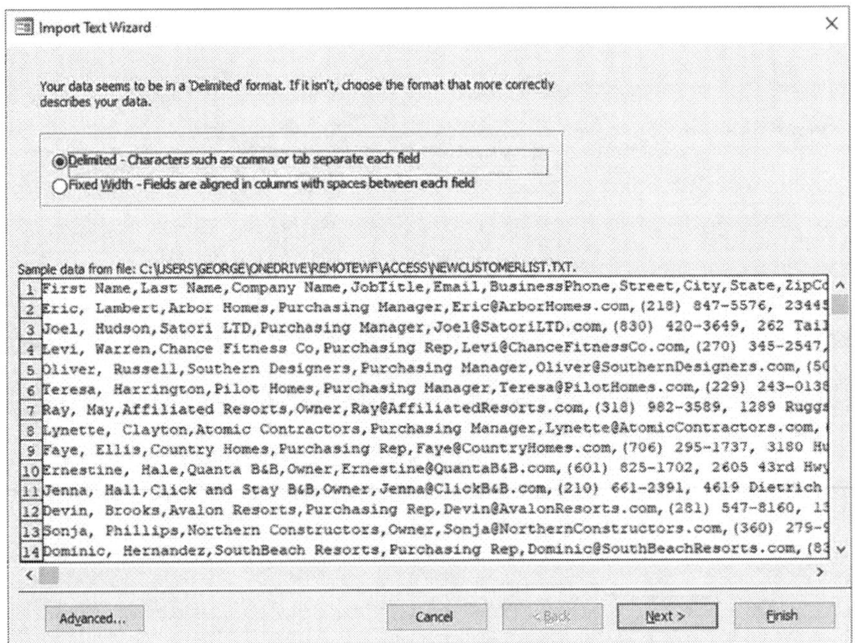

5. The first screen of the input text Wizard enables you to select which type of file you are importing. Selected **Delimited** and click **Next**.

Note If your text file is fixed width, select Fixed Width. The next page of the wizard will give you the option to define the field breaks (if different from what Access identified in the file).

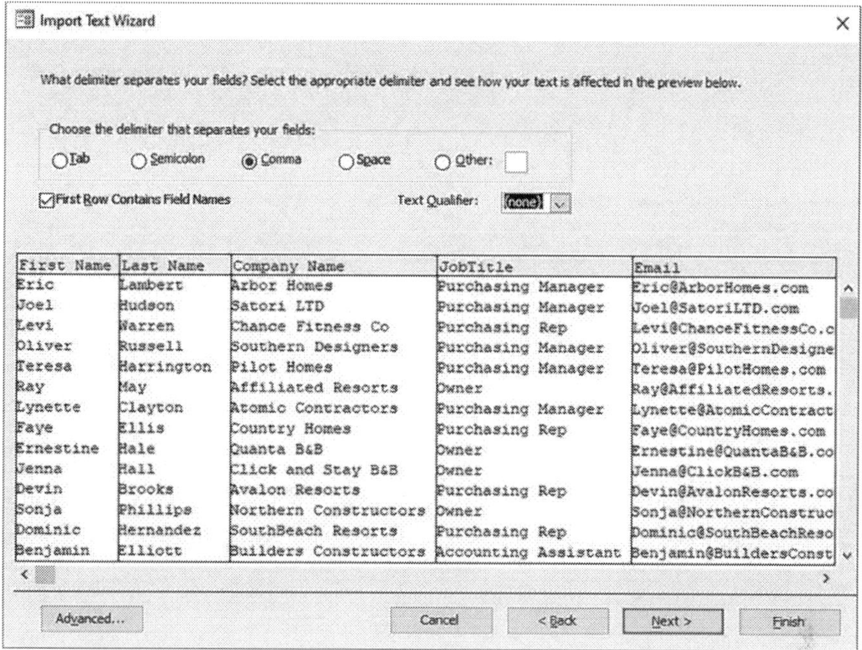

6. For a delimited text file, the second page of the wizard gives you the option of selecting the delimiter separating your fields. Access will often correctly identify the delimiter, but if your file is using a different delimiter, you can select it here.

7. If the first row of your data has field names, select the check box **First Row Contains Field Names**. Then click **Next**.

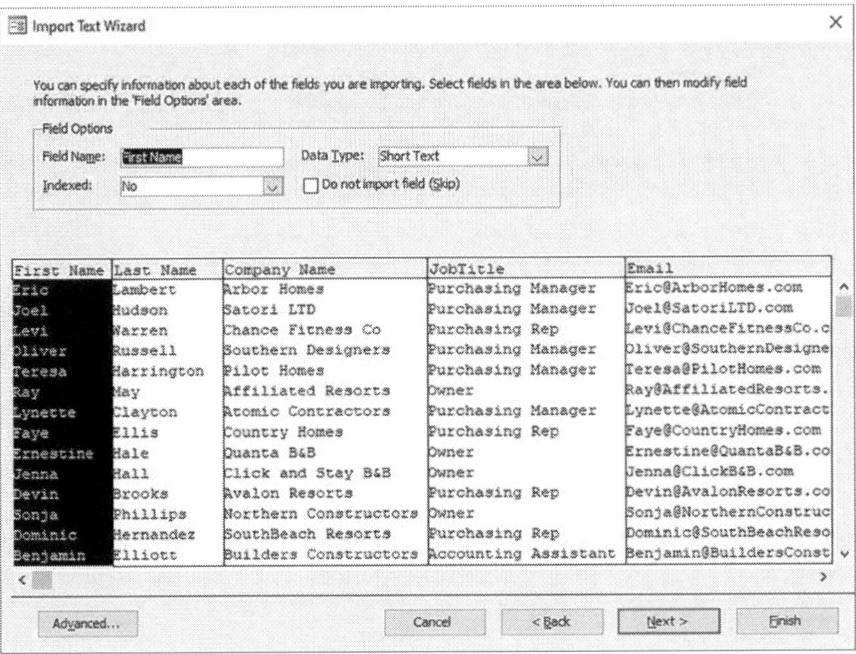

8. This screen of the wizard allows you to edit the following import settings for each field:

   - **Field Name**: If you added field names in the text file before importing the data, you don't need to enter field names here.
   - **Data Type**: Check every field in the sample to ensure Access has identified the right data type. Select the right data type for the fields you want to change.
   - **Indexed:** Ideally, you want to leave this as **No**. You can always set indexes later.
   - **Skip**: Select this checkbox if you don't want to import the field. You can only skip fields if you're importing the data into a new table.

If you need to make any changes to field names and data types, you should do it here. When you're happy with the field names and data types, click **Next**.

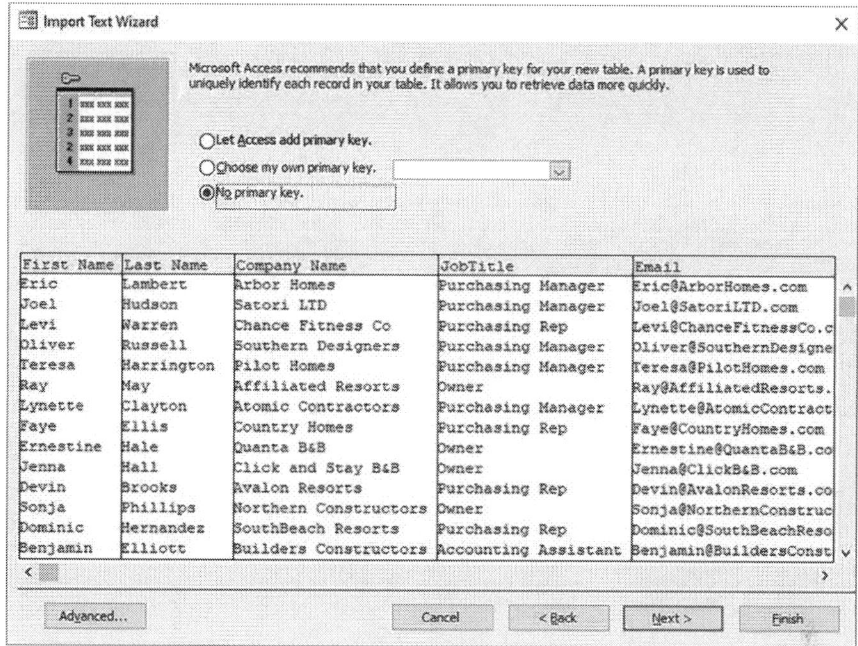

9. **Select No primary key and click Next**. You get the option to select a primary key for the table on this screen. You don't necessarily need to set a primary key now. You can always set a primary key after you have checked and fixed any import errors in the resultant table.

   If you must set a primary key here, then for an AutoNumber primary key, select **Let Access add primary key**. If you have a field in the data that you want to use as a primary key, then select **Choose my own primary key**, and then select the field from the drop-down list.

10. **Enter a unique table name and click Finish**. On the last screen of the wizard, enter a unique name for the table and click **Finish** to close the wizard.

11. **Save import changes**. At the next screen, Access will ask if you want to save the import steps. If this is a one-off import task, you don't need to save the steps. However, if this is a process you intend to repeat often, then you may want to save the import steps. When you save the import steps, you can repeat the process faster next time without going through the wizard.

    Click **Close**.

Access will import the data into a new table and add it to the Navigation Pane under Tables.

⚠ Important Whenever you import data from an external source, always review the data before deploying it in a production setting. Sometimes there could be errors, and some of the records may not be imported. Access may not necessarily inform you of this. Always check the number of records that have been imported compared to what is in the text file and if there are any blank rows.

Importing a Fixed-Width File

1. Follow steps 1 to 5 above to open your fixed-width text file in the Import Text Wizard. For this example, we will be using NewCustomers_FxedWidth.txt.

2. On the first page of the Import Text Wizard, select Fixed-Width, and click Next.

3. On the second page of the wizard, Access uses separator lines to separate the fields. You can click and move these separator lines left or right to refine the separation between the fields. Click any area in the data to add a separator line or double-click any separator line to remove it.

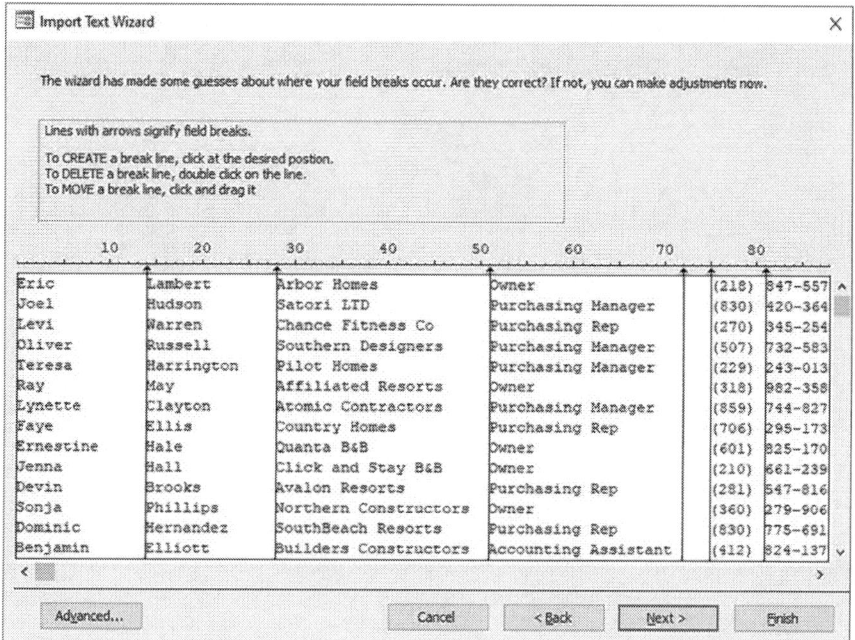

4. To set further import specifications, you can click the **Advanced** button on the Import Text Wizard to open the **Import Specification** dialog box.

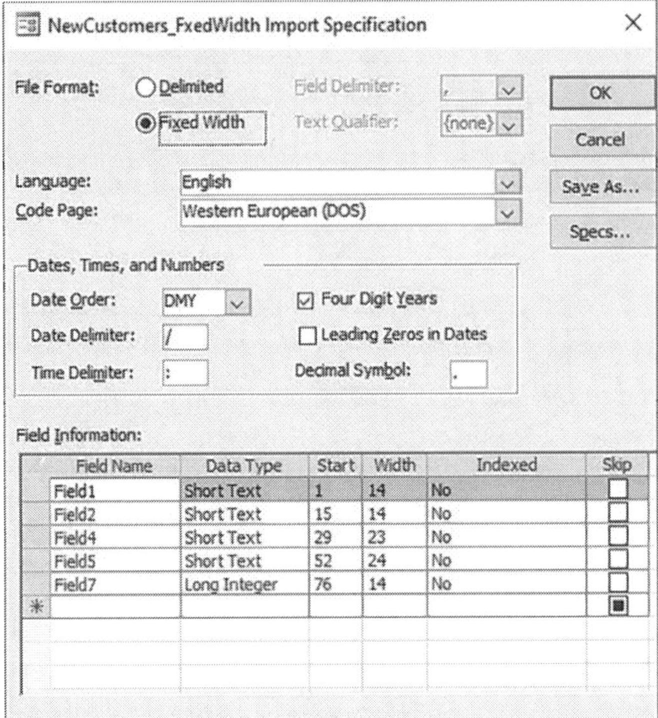

In the Import Specification dialog box, you can define import formats for date and time fields (if you have those fields in your data). You can also manually define the starting position and character length of each field and choose any field you want to skip.

Click **OK** to save your changes (if you made any) and close the Import Specification dialog box.

5. On the Import Text Wizard screen, click **Next**.

6. The next screen of the wizard allows you to edit field options like the field name, data type, and index settings. When you are done with this page, click **Next**.

7. **Select No primary key and click Next.** The wizard gives you the option to select a primary key for the table. Preferably, you want to set the primary key after the table has been created and the data has been checked.

Note If you need to set a primary key at this point, select Let Access add primary key for an AutoNumber primary. Alternatively, select Choose my own primary key if you have a field in your data that you want to use as a primary key.

8. **Enter a unique name for the table, and then click Finish**. Ensure the name is unique to avoid overwriting an existing table.

9. Select **Save import steps** if you want to save your import steps, and then click **Close.**

Importing Data from Access

Access enables you to easily import objects from another database into the current database. The steps in this section apply not just to Access tables but other types of Access objects like queries, forms, reports, macros, and modules.

Note Access 2021 can only import objects from another Access database going back to Access 2000. Access formats prior to Access 2000 are no longer supported.

To import an item into the current Access database, do the following:

1. Open the database in which you want to import the data. This is the destination database.

   For our example, the destination database will be **DataImport.accdb**.

2. On the Ribbon, select the **External Data** tab.

3. In the **Import & Link** group, click **New Data Source** > **From Database** > **Access**.

   Access displays the **Get External Data** dialog box.

   On the Get External Data dialog box, click the **Browse** button, and navigate to the source database. Select the source database and click **Open**.

   For our example, the source database is **Northwind.accdb**.

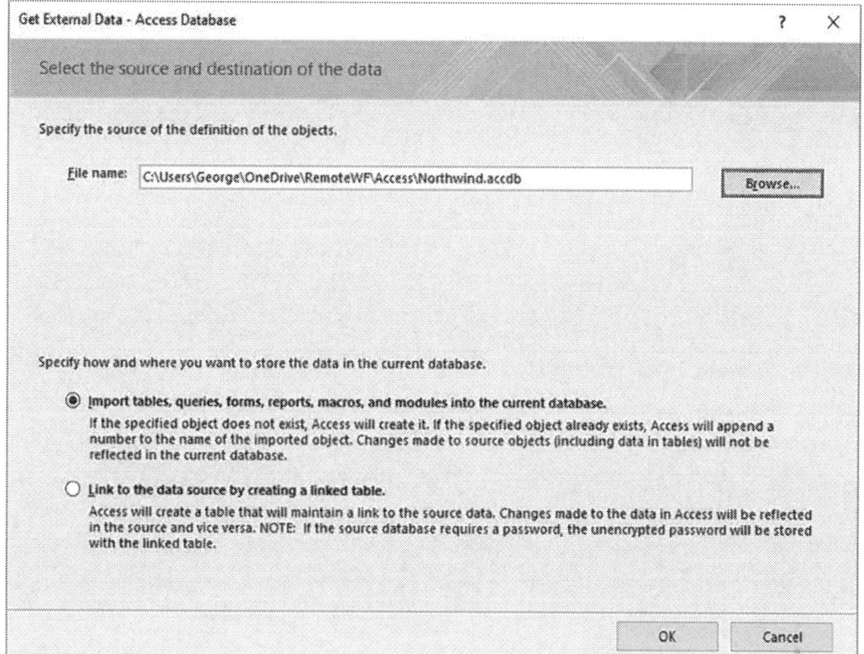

4. Choose the option to import the object and click **OK**.

In the bottom half of the Get External Data dialog box, Access provides options for importing the Access object or creating a linked table to the data source. To import the data, select the first option.

Access displays the **Import Objects** dialog box.

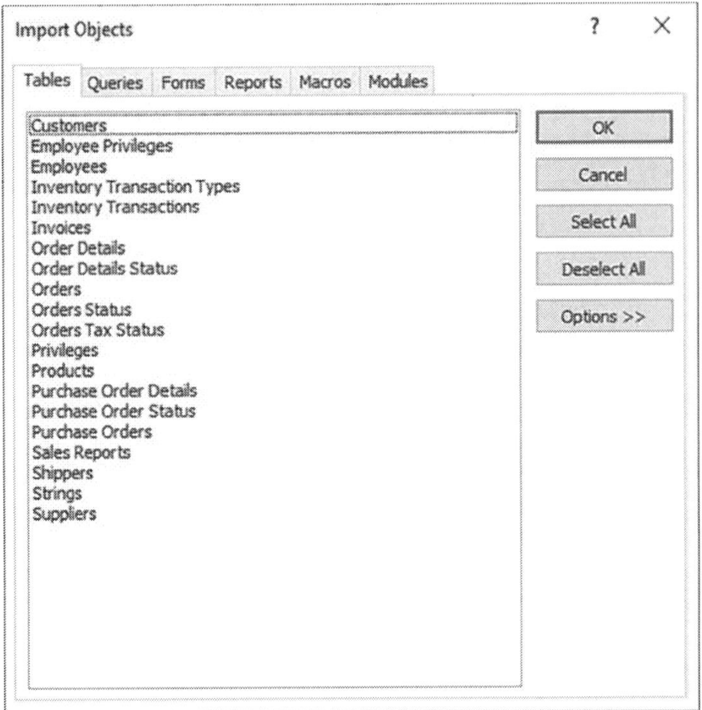

5. **Select the table you want to import and click OK**. This dialog box enables you to import tables and other Access objects from the source database.

   If an object in the destination database has the same name as an imported object, a serial number will be added to the name of the imported object to distinguish it from the existing object. Click an object on the list to select it. To deselect an item, click it again.

   This is a multi-select list. Hence you can select multiple objects by clicking additional items on the list (or on different tabs) to select them.

6. **Save the import steps (optional)**. To save the import steps, select the **Save import steps** checkbox. Enter a meaningful name and description in the boxes below.

   To run this import again later, on the Ribbon, click **External Data** > **Import & Link** > **Saved Imports**.

   Access opens the **Manage Data Tasks** dialog box where you can run saved imports.

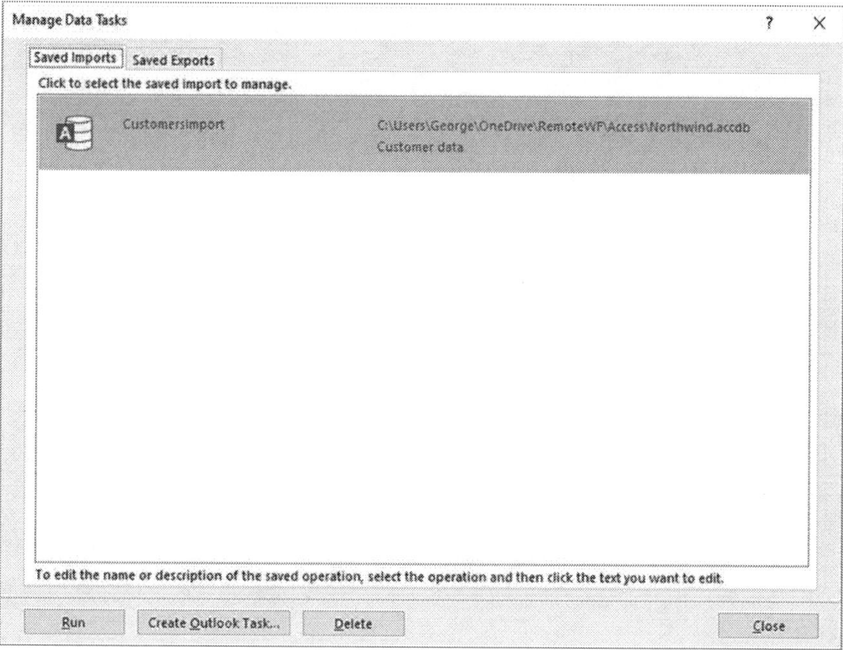

Note Each time you run a saved import, Access creates a new table (or object, if the import was for another Access object). For example, if you imported the Customers table, a table named Customers is created. If you run the same saved import again, Access will import the table again, but name it Customers1. If you run it again, Access will name it Customers2, and so on. This ensures saved imports do not overwrite existing data/objects.

Exporting Data from Access

Access provides a variety of export options, illustrating the fact that it is a great tool for uploading and transforming data that you may want to use on other platforms.

To see the export options offered by Access on the Ribbon, click the **External Data** tab. In the **Export** group, you have a variety of export formats (see image below). These formats include Excel, Text File, Access, and ODBC Database.

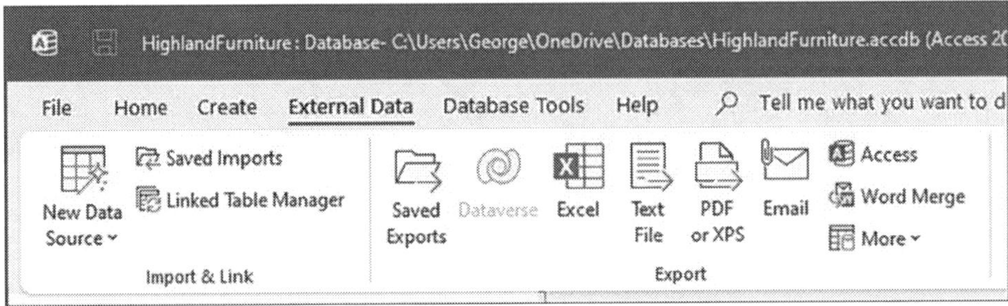

You can only export data from an Access table or query to a different file format. However, you can export all object types in Access to a different Access database.

Exporting Objects to Another Access Database

As mentioned previously, you can export every type of object in Access to another Access database. However, unlike the import process, where you can import several objects at the same time, the export process only allows you to export one object at a time.

To export an Access object to another Access database, follow the steps below:

1. Open the source database. This is the database that contains the Access object that you want to export.

2. In the Navigation Pane, select the object that you want to export.

3. On the Ribbon, click the **External Data** tab, and in the **Export** group, click the **Access** button.

4. In the **Export - Access Database** dialog box, click **Browse**, then navigate to the destination database, and select it.

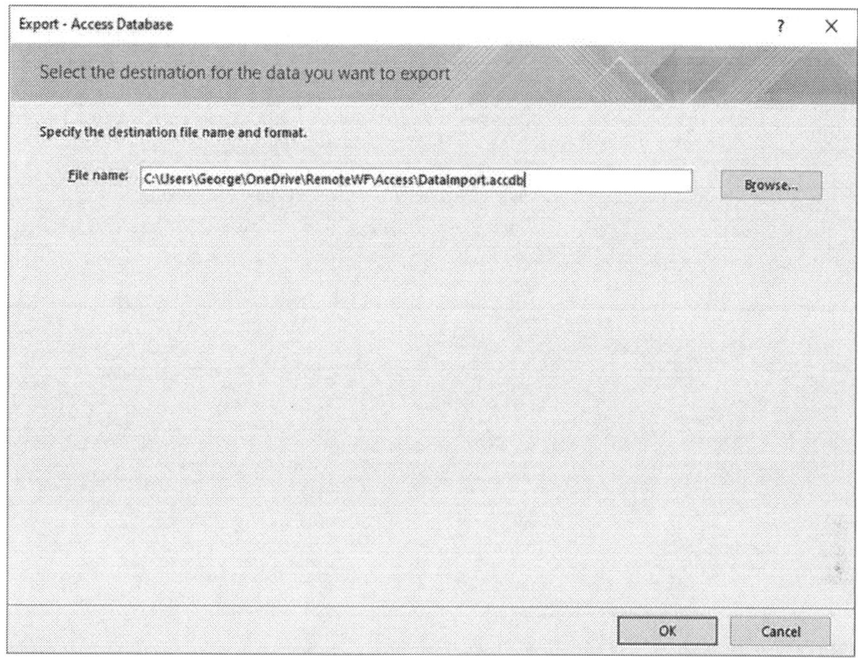

Note Make sure the destination database is not open during the export process. Otherwise, you'll encounter a lock conflict.

5. Click **OK**.

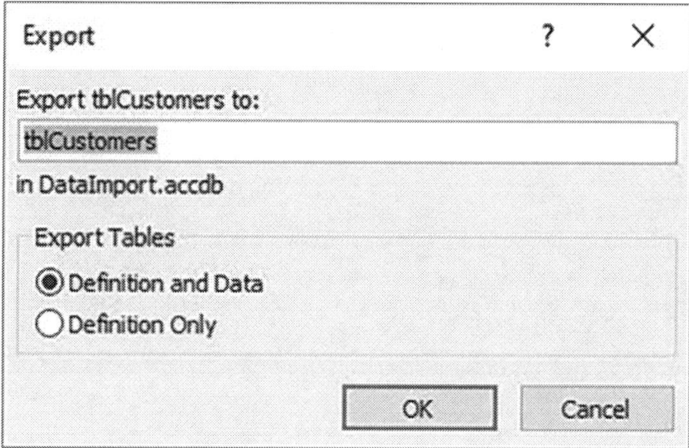

6. Click **OK** to perform the operation. In the **Export** dialog box, under **Export Tables**, you can choose to export the Definition and Data or the Definition Only.

Note When you export only the definition of a table, Access will only export the structure of the table, including any indexes, but not the records.

7. To save the export steps, select the **Save export steps** checkbox and then click **Close**.

   To view the exported object, open the destination database and locate the object in the Navigation Pane of the database.

Exporting Data to Excel

Unlike the process of importing data from Excel, exporting data from an Access table or query to Excel is quite straightforward.

To export data to Excel, do the following:

1. Open the source database.

2. In the Navigation Pane, select the table/query that you wish to export to Excel.

3. On the Ribbon, click **External Data**, and in the **Export** group, click **Excel** to launch the Export dialog box.

Tip Alternatively, you can right-click the table or query in the Navigation Pane, and from the pop-up menu, select Export > Excel.

---

4. In the **Export – Excel Spreadsheet** dialog box, click the **Browse** button and select the folder in which you want to save the file.

Important If you use the name of an existing Excel file, the export operation will overwrite the file. Access will not insert the data as a different worksheet within an existing Excel workbook. Don't use the name of an existing file if you don't want Access to overwrite it.

---

5. The default export format is an XLSX file. To change this to a different format, select a different format from the **File format** drop-down list.

6. The lower part of the dialog box has three export options:

    - **Export data with formatting and layout**: Select this checkbox if you want Access to preserve most of the formatting and layout information it can transfer to Excel.

    - **Open the destination file after the export operation is complete**: Select this checkbox if you want Access to open the Excel file after the export operation.

- **Export only the selected records**: Select this option if you're exporting a selection of records from a table/query in Datasheet view (rather than the whole object). This option is only enabled if you're exporting records from a Datasheet.

7. Click **OK**.

8. Click **Close.** You can select the **Save export steps** checkbox if you wish to save the export steps. Only do this if you intend to repeat this export operation (with the same data source) in the future.

Exporting Data to a Text File

To export data to a text file, do the following:

1. Open the source database from which you want to export data.

2. In the Navigation Pane, select the table/query that you wish to export to text.

3. On the Ribbon, click **External Data**, and in the **Export** group, click **Text File** to open the **Export - Text File** dialog box.

Tip Alternatively, you can right-click the table/query in the Navigation Pane, and from the pop-up menu, select Export > Text File.

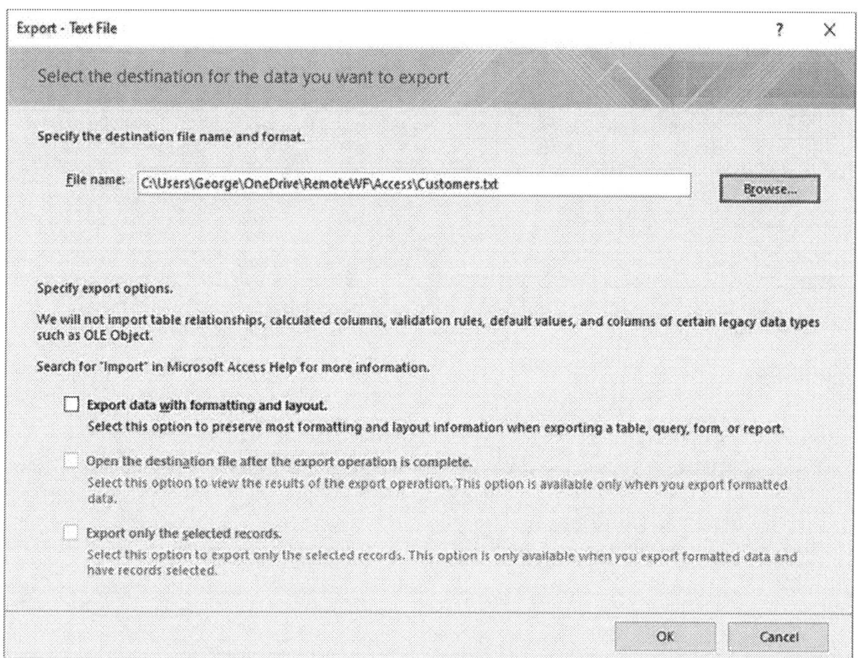

4. In the **Export - Text File** dialog box, click the **Browse** button and navigate to the folder in which you want to save the file.

Important If you use the name of an existing text file, the export operation will overwrite the file. Don't use the name of an existing file if you don't want Access to overwrite it.

---

5. In the **Export - Text File** dialog box, click the **Browse** button, select the folder in which you want to save the file, and then click **OK**.

   Access opens the Export Text Wizard box.

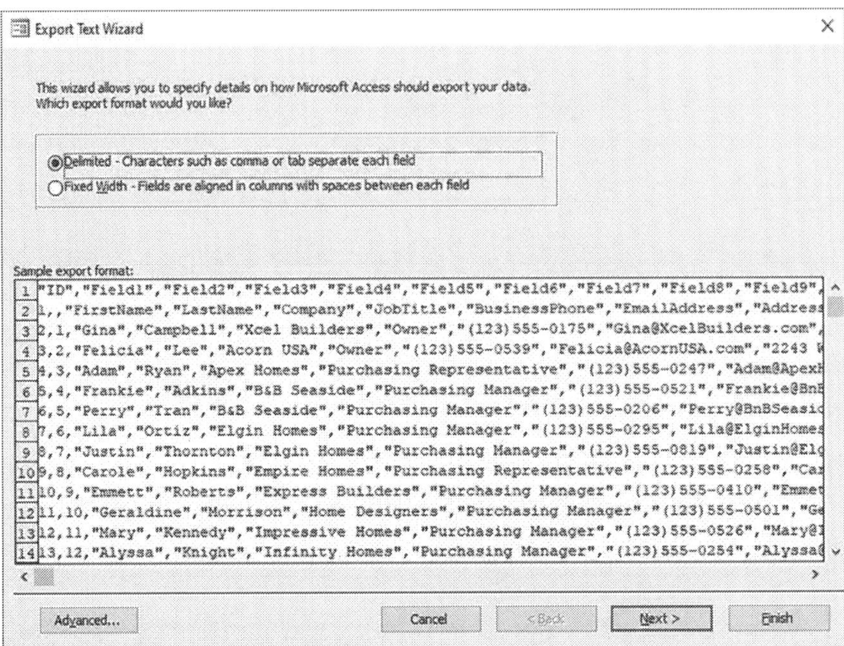

7. **Select Delimited and click Next**. On the first page of the Export Text Wizard, you have the option of exporting the data as a delimited file or a Fixed Width text file.

Note Use Fixed Width if individual data items can contain every possible character that can be used to separate the fields.

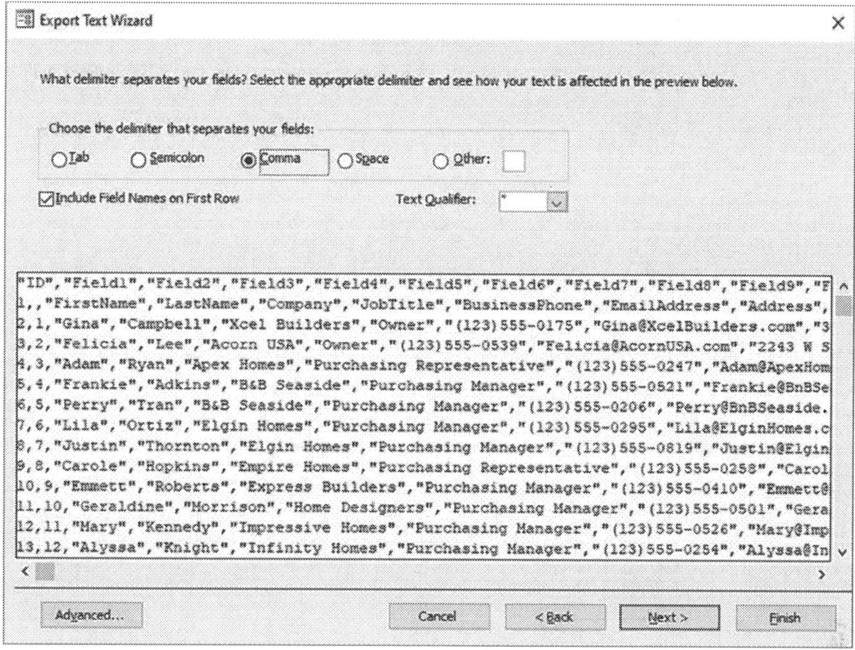

8. **Choose the delimiter that separates your fields**. On the second page of the wizard, you can choose the character you want to use for your delimiter. You can choose a tab, comma, semicolon, or space. If you can't use any of these characters, then you can choose **Other** and enter the character.

9. Select the **Include Field Names on First Row** checkbox if your data has field headings, and then click **Next**.

10. Click **Finish.** On the last page of the wizard, you have the option to rename the text file if you want. This page informs you of where the text file will be saved.

11. Click **Close.** If you wish to save the export steps, select the **Save export steps** checkbox. Only select this option if you intend to repeat this export operation (with the same data source) in the future.

Exporting Data to SQL Server

One of the pathways of moving from Access to a server-based database is to upgrade to SQL Server. You can easily export Access data to SQL Server using an ODBC (Open Database Connectivity) driver. All ODBC compliant databases are equipped with an ODBC driver that enables you to create a connection between Access and the database. Many popular databases like dBase, Oracle, MySQL, and SQL Server are ODBC compliant. In the corporate environment, SQL Server may be a good option to migrate Access data to if you're looking to move to a database server.

Note To perform the steps detailed in this section, you'll need access to an SQL Server either locally on your computer or on your network (with the required permissions).

Connecting to an SQL Server database involves two broad tasks:

1. **Create a new Data Source Name (DSN)**. The file DSN holds the information regarding the name/network path of the database server and login credentials.
2. **Use the DSN to connect to the database server**. The DSN only needs to be created once, and it can then be used multiple times to export different data sources to the database server.

The steps detailed below cover both tasks.

To export data to an SQL Server database using an ODBC driver, do the following:

1. Open the database that contains the table/query you want to export. For our example, this will be the Highland Furniture database.

2. Select the table you want to export in the Navigation Pane.

3. On the Ribbon, click **External Data**, and in the **Export** group, select **More > ODBC**.

   Access displays the Export dialog box with the name of the data source you've selected.

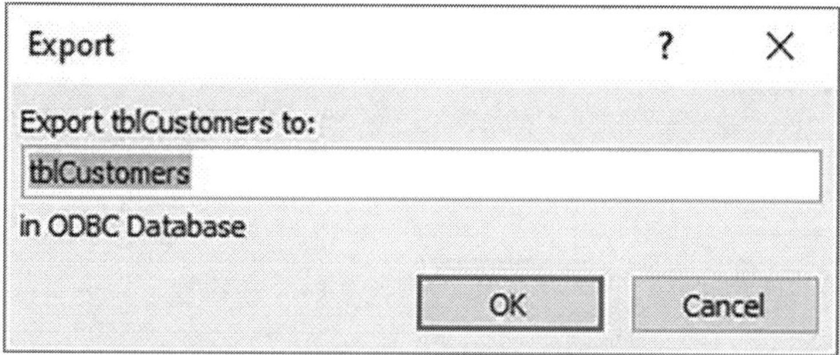

4. **Click OK.** Use the selected data source (or change the name if you want to use another data source). Access opens the **Select Data Source** dialog box.

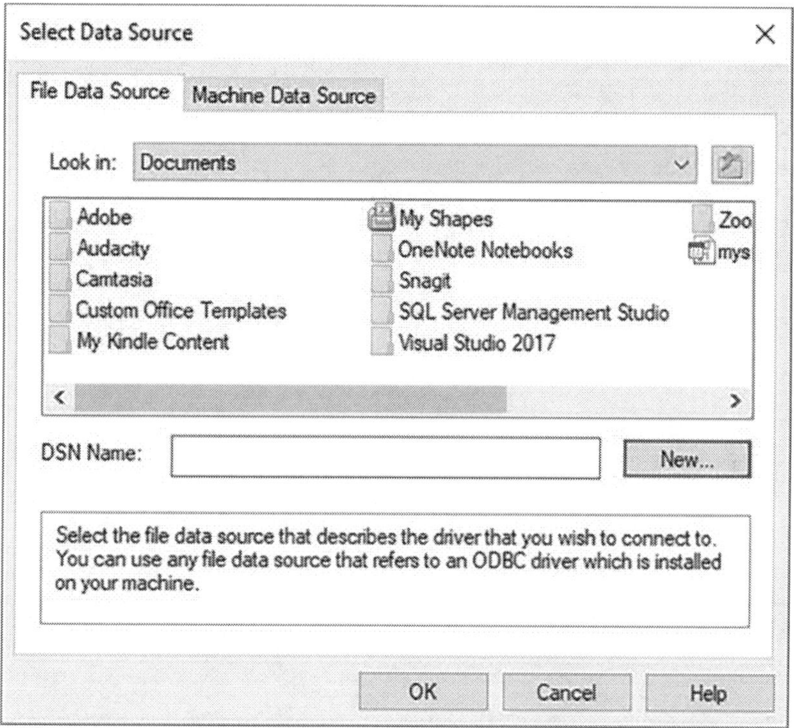

5. **Click New**. Access opens the **Create New Data Source** dialog box.

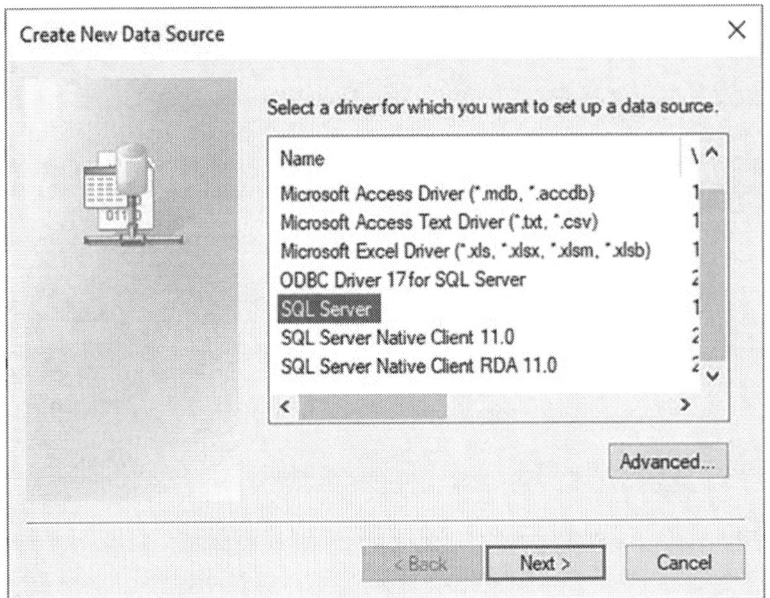

6. **Select SQL Server and click Next**. In the **Create New Data Source** dialog box, locate and select **SQL Server** from the list of drivers.

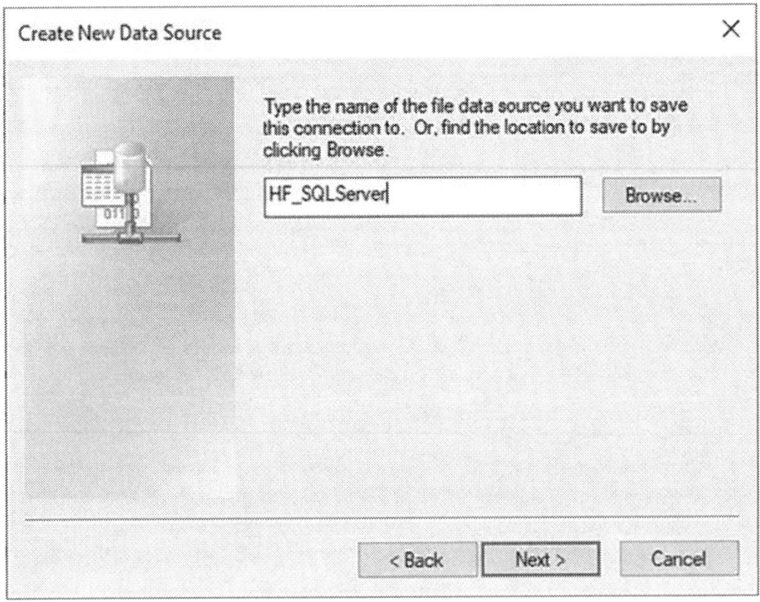

7. **Enter a name for the DSN and click Next**. Give the data source a short but meaningful name that you can remember for when you reuse the DSN. For our example, we've used the name HF_SQLServer for the Highland Furniture database on our SQL Server.

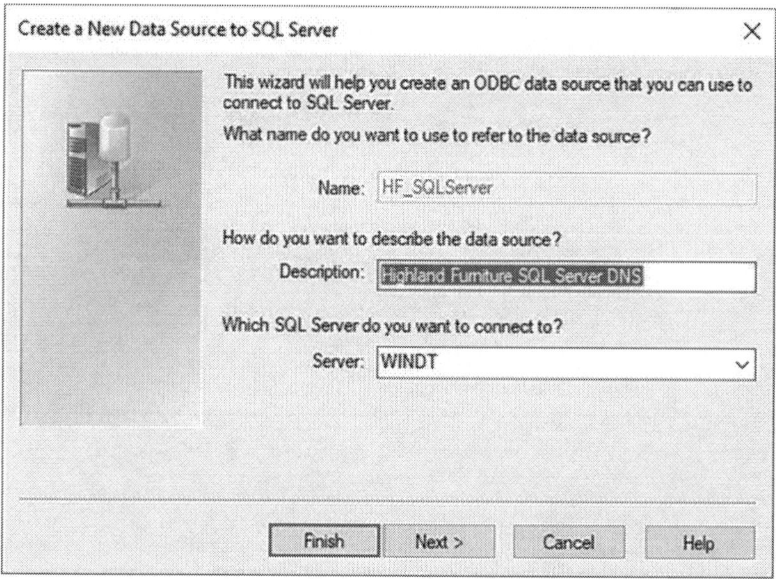

8. **Enter the description for the data source**. This helps when you've created several DSN files to the same database server.

9. **Enter the name of the SQL Server and click Next**. In the **Server** box, type in the name/network path of the SQL Server.

Note If your SQL Server is on a corporate network and administered by a database administrator, you'll need to get the database administrator to provide the network path of the SQL Server.

Tip In some situations, when you click the drop-down arrow in the **Server** drop-down list, you'll get an empty list, or your destination SQL Server may not be on the list. This is likely because the Microsoft SQL Server Browser is not running on the machine hosting that server. If the browser service is not running on the server, you can still create a DSN connection to it by directly entering the server's name (or network path) in the **Server** box.

For our example, the database server is local to the PC. Hence, we can directly enter the name of the SQL Server, which is WINDT.

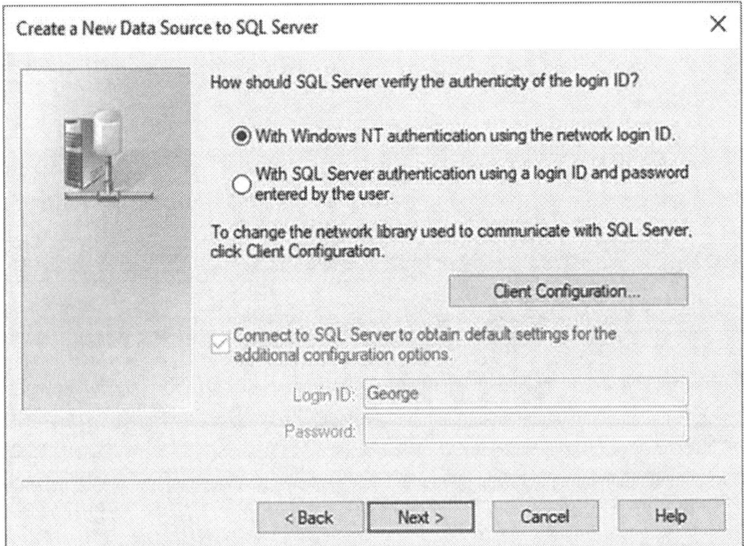

10. **Provide the SQL Server authentication information and click Next.** On the next screen, if the machine is local to the PC you're working on, use Windows NT authentication (this is the default option).

Note Use SQL Server authentication if your SQL Server is on a corporate network and you need different login credentials to access the server. Depending on how your SQL Server is managed, the login information for the database may need to be provided by your database administrator.

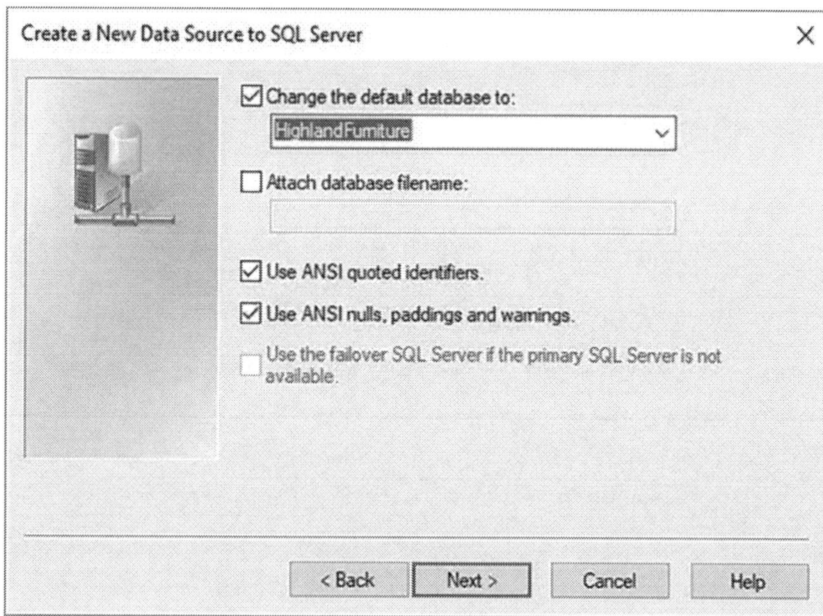

11. **Select the destination database on the server and click Next**. Select the checkbox for **Change the default database to** and select the destination database from the drop-down list.

    For our example, the destination database on the SQL Server is named **HighlandFurniture**.

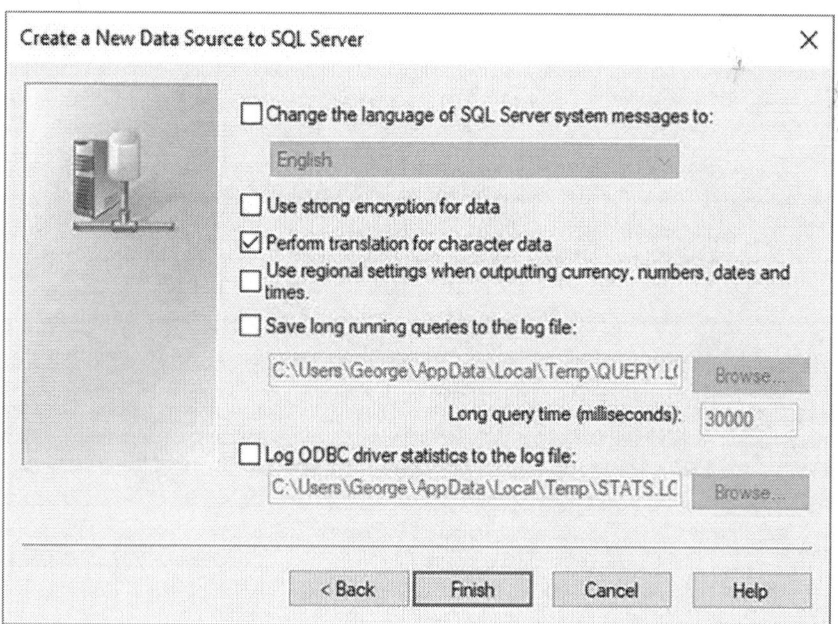

12. On the last page of the wizard, click **Finish**.

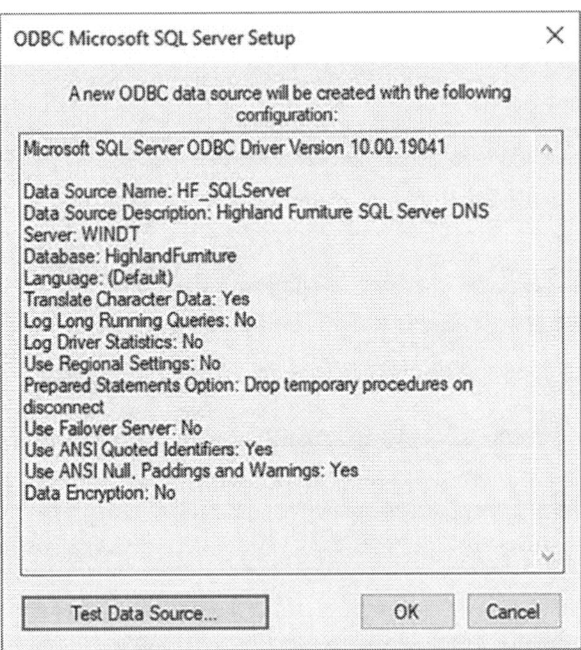

13. **Test the data source**. Access displays the **ODBC Microsoft SQL Server Setup** screen, which displays details of your ODBC driver. You can test the data source here by clicking **Test Data Source** to ensure the connection is working.

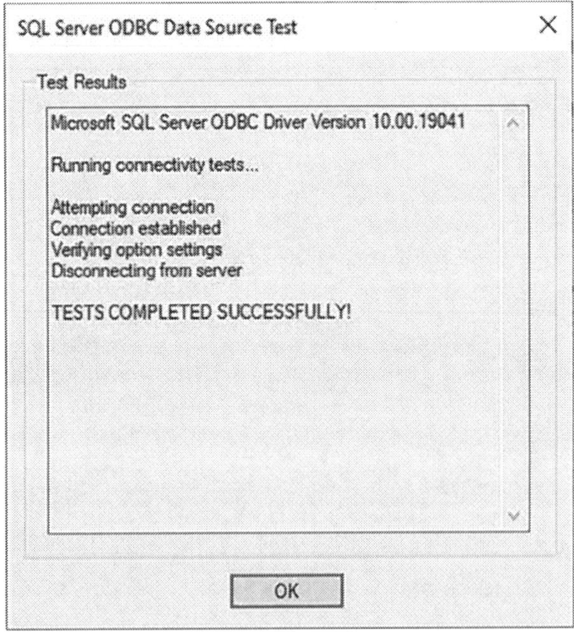

If the connection to the server is successful, Access will display the results showing that the test was completed successfully.

14. **Click OK twice to return to the Select Data Source dialog box.**

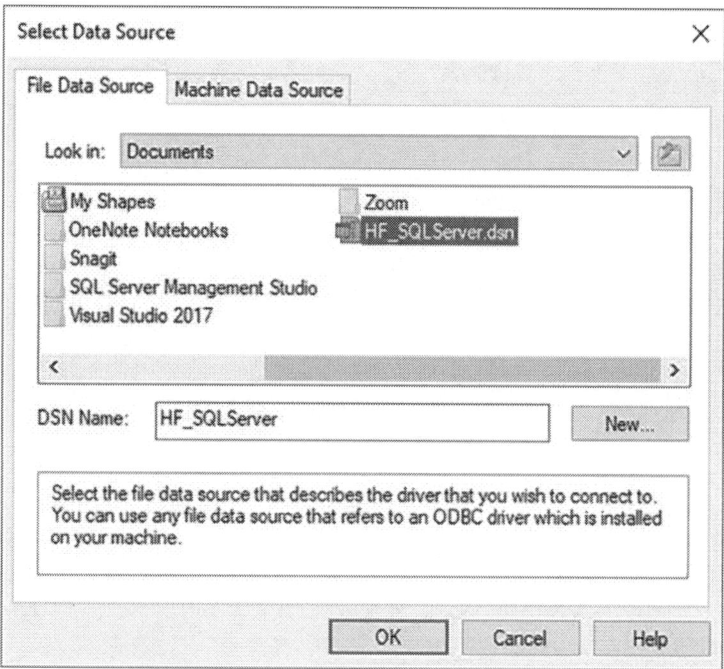

15. **Select the new DSN file and click OK.** The DSN will now be available for you to select from the **Select Data Source** dialog box. Select the file and click OK. Access exports the table to the database specified in the DSN.

You only need to create the DSN once. Once created, you can use the file whenever you want to export data from Access to that SQL Server database.

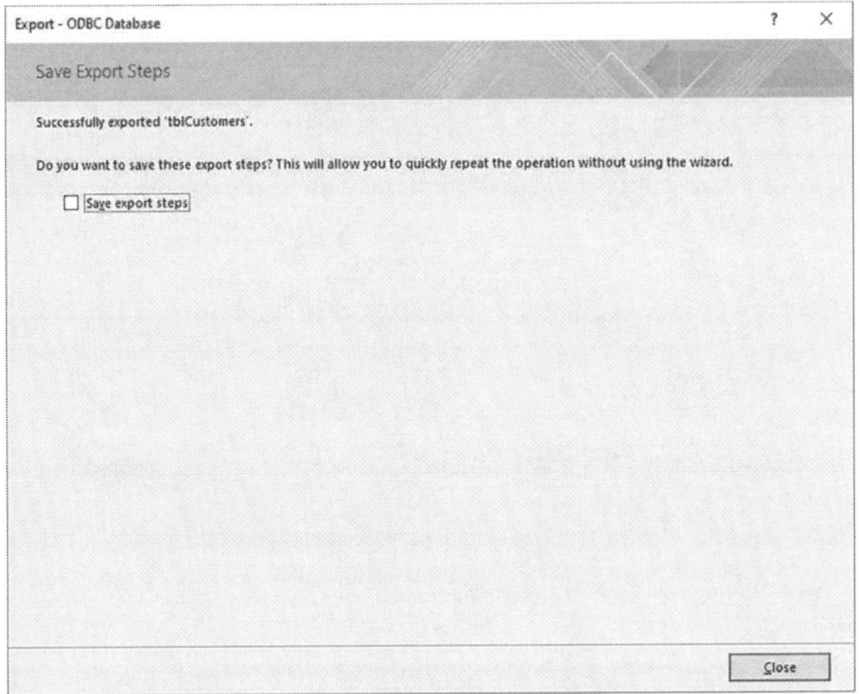

16. **Select Save export steps if you want to save the steps, and then click OK**. To view the exported data, navigate to the database with the tool you use to manage your SQL Server databases, for example, **SQL Server Management Studio**.

Expand the destination database to see the table you've just exported from Access. If you don't see the table, right-click the database name and select **Refresh** from the pop-up menu to see the latest imported objects.

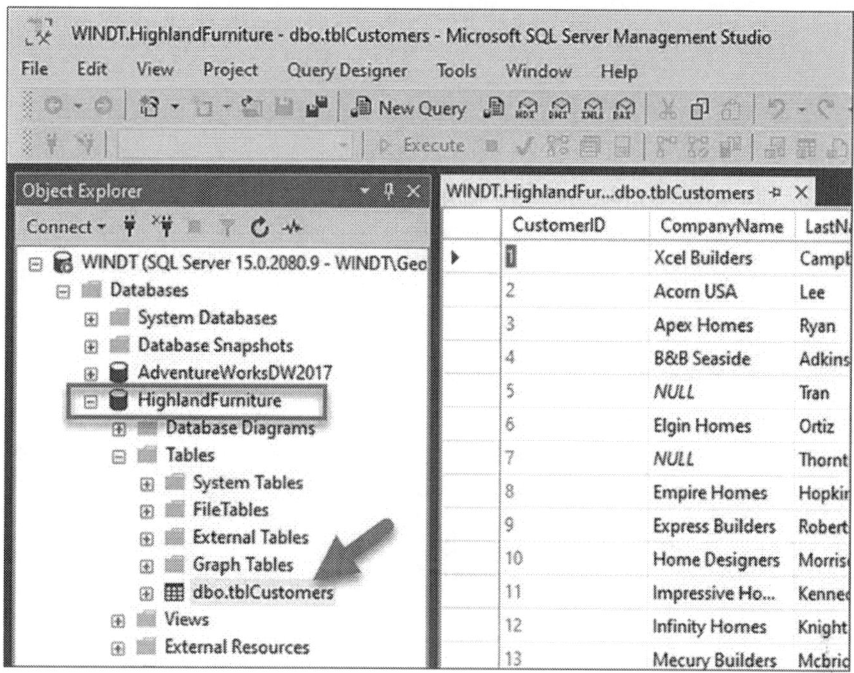

Microsoft SQL Server Management Studio

Part 4

Working with Access Forms

In Part 4

An Access form provides a user-friendly interface that lets you interact with the data in tables. Part 4 covers creating Access forms using different form generation tools, including creating complex form/subform combinations. You learn how to enhance the functionality of your forms with combo boxes, calculated fields, and command buttons. With forms, you can transform your database into an application with several user-friendly interfaces for viewing, adding, editing, and deleting data.

Contents at a Glance

Chapter 10: Creating Access Forms

An Access form provides a user-friendly interface that you can use to interact with your data. You can create a form that is bound to a particular table or query, which you can use to add, edit, delete, or just display data from that data source.

You can also create an unbound form that is not directly connected to a data source which you can use as a dialog box to open other objects like queries, forms, reports, and so on.

In this chapter, we will cover how to:

- Create a quick form with the Form Tool.
- Create a form with two types of views with the Split Form tool.
- Create a tabular form with the Multiple Items form tool.
- Create a form and subform combo using the Form Wizard.

Some Benefits of Using Forms

- **Forms are better for working with individual records.**

  Datasheets are not as user-friendly as forms when working with individual records. The constant need to scroll back and forth in a datasheet can make it more difficult to work with records. Also, the risk of inadvertently changing other records is greater with a datasheet.

- **Forms offer more flexibility in how you organize the fields.**

  Forms enable you to see the data the ideal way you want to arrange it. Forms allow you to arrange the fields in an order that's more logical to how you work. For example, you may have a comment field that requires a larger text box than what a datasheet provides. You may have a picture field to upload images, and this is best performed using a form.

- **You can update parent and child records simultaneously with forms.**

  You can interact with multiple tables on a single form. For example, you may have a main form bound to the Orders table (a parent table) and a subform bound to the OrderLines table (a child table). This enables you to update the parent and child records as a single unit. Forms essentially enable you to bring your entities back together as one object that you can update at the same time.

Overview of Form Commands

There are several commands you can use to create forms in Access. Below is a description of the main commands:

- **Form**: The Form command creates an instant form bound to a table or query with just one click. If the selected data source has a one-to-many relationship with another table defined in the Relationships pane, the Form command will create a form and a subform based on that relationship. You can modify the design of the resultant form in Layout view or Design view.

- **Form Wizard**: The Form Wizard guides you through a series of steps in creating a custom form where you choose the data source(s) and fields you want to add. The resultant form is more flexible than a form generated by the Form command in terms of making design changes.

- **Form Design** and **Blank Form**: These commands enable you to design your form from scratch. The **Form Design** command creates a blank form in *Design view,* while the **Blank Form** command creates a blank form in *Layout view.* Use these commands if the Form Wizard or any of the other form generating tools are unsuitable for the form you want to create.

- **More Forms:** The More Forms button allows you to create more forms that are automatically generated by Access, including **Multiple Items** and **Split Form**, which we'll be covering in this chapter.

In this chapter, we will focus on the Form Wizard and some of the other automatic form generation tools. With the new form tools and the Form Wizard, you rarely need to create a form from scratch these days unless you're creating an unbound form. The automatic form generation tools do the initial design work for you, and you can then focus on refining the design.

Create a Quick Form with The Form Command

You can use the Form command to create a form with just one click of the mouse. When Access generates the form, it'll place all the fields from the selected data source on the form. This enables you to start using the form immediately without any further work. However, you can make some quick design changes in Layout view before you start using the form.

To create a form with the Form command, do the following:

1. In the Navigation Pane, select the table or query for which you want to create a form. For our example, we've selected tblSuppliers (which is the Suppliers table in our database).
2. On the Ribbon, click the **Create** tab, and in the **Forms** group, click the **Form** command button.

   Access creates an instant form and displays it in Layout view.
3. On the title bar, click the **Save** button (or press **Ctrl+S**).
4. In the **Save As** dialog box, enter the name for your form and click **OK**.

If the table for which you have created the form is part of a one-to-many relationship defined in the Relationships window, Access will include the child table as a datasheet subform in the generated form.

For example, as shown in the image below, if you create a form for the Suppliers table, and you have defined a one-to-many relationship between Suppliers and Products in Relationships, Access will add the Products table as a subform under the main Suppliers form. You can delete the subform in Layout view or Design view if you don't need it as part of the design.

Note If there is more than one table in a one-to-many relationship with the data source of the main form, Access will not include any subform in the design.

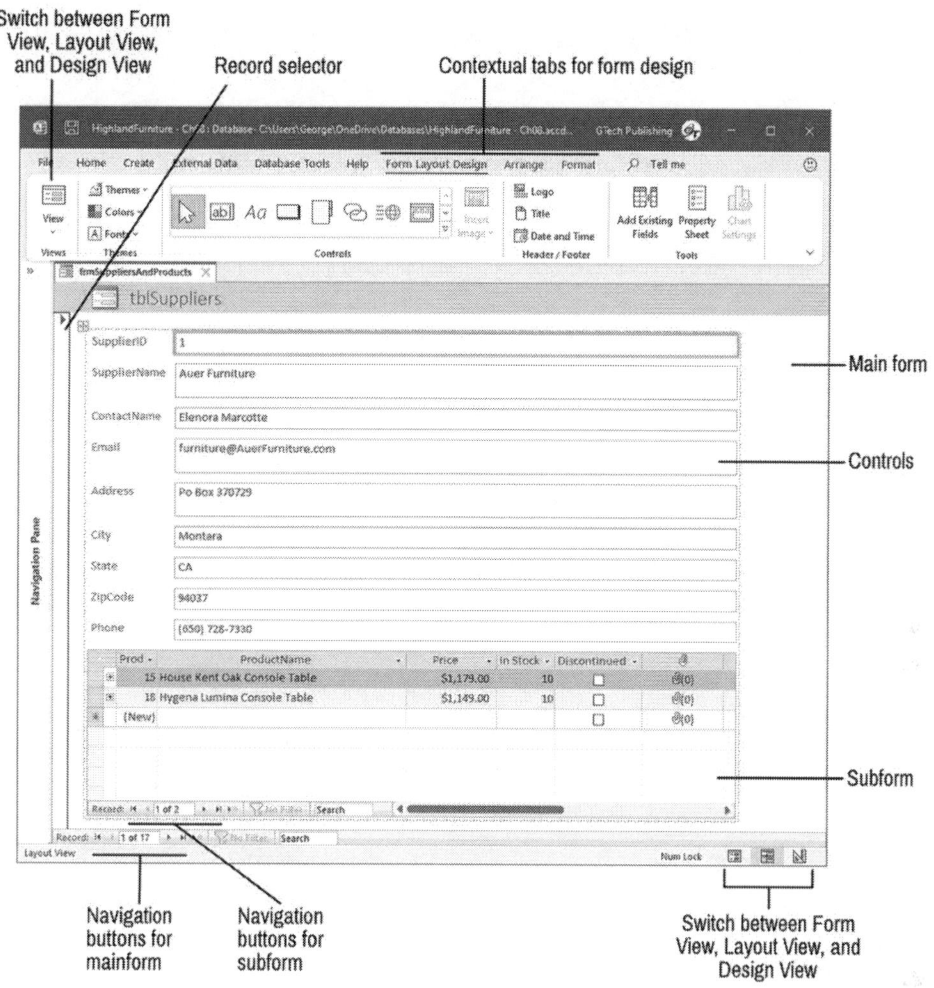

Layout view gives you the benefit of being able to design the form while viewing the data displayed on the form. This is useful because you can better resize text boxes based on the general length of the text they contain. As you can see the data, you get a better sense of how the form will look in Form view as you adjust the design.

You can adjust the size of the controls or change several properties of the labels, including font, font size, background color, and alignment. We will cover how to refine a form's design in the next chapter.

Create a Split Form with the Split Form tool

The Split Form tool enables you to create a form that displays two types of views of the table simultaneously, Form view and Datasheet view.

A Split Form is different from a form/subform combination because the two views are from the same data source rather than two different data sources. Selecting a record on one form selects the same record on the second form. You can add, edit, or delete data from the main form or subform (if the bound data source is updateable).

A Split Form gives you the combined benefits of **Form view** and **Datasheet view**. For example, you can quickly scroll up or down to locate and select a record in the datasheet and then edit the record in the form. In a form with a single view, you may have to scroll through the form, one record at a time, to find the record you want to edit.

To create a Split Form, do the following:

1. In the Navigation Pane, select the data source for the form. This can be a table or query.
2. On the **Create** tab, in the **Forms** group, click **More Forms** and select **Split Form** from the dropdown menu.

You can make changes to the form design in Layout view. For example, you can adjust the size of the text boxes depending on the length of the visible text.

Create a Form with The Multiple Items Tool

The Multiple Items command enables you to create a tabular form like a datasheet in that it displays multiple records in rows and columns. However, the Multiple Items command creates a form that is much more customizable than a datasheet. You can add graphical elements like buttons and other controls to the form. We will be covering how to refine the design of forms in the next chapter.

To create a form using the Multiple Items tool, do the following:

1. In the Navigation Pane, select the data source for the form.

2. On the **Create** tab, in the **Forms** group, click **More Forms**, and then select **Multiple Items** from the drop-down menu.

   Access creates and displays the form in Layout view. This view enables you to make changes to the form's design while viewing the data.

3. To save your form, press **Ctrl+S** (or click the **Save** button on the top-left of the Access title bar) and enter the form's name.

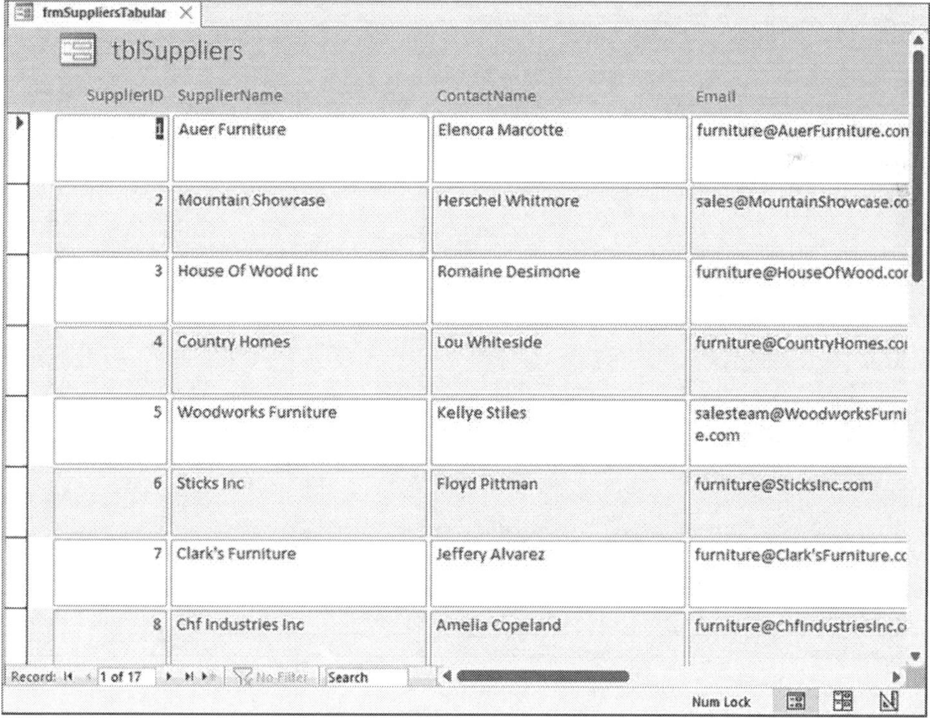

Adjusting Form Controls Independently

You may have noticed that when you create a form with one of the Form creation commands, Access puts the text boxes inside guides called layouts. When you click the layout selector on the top left of the layout, an orange grid is displayed around the controls, indicating which controls are in the layout.

When you move or resize one of the controls, Access moves or resizes all the controls within the layout. Therefore, you can't independently move or size controls in the layout. Although this grid layout can be very useful for quickly creating and modifying forms, there are times when you want to adjust controls independently. To do this, you need to first remove the control that you want to change from the layout.

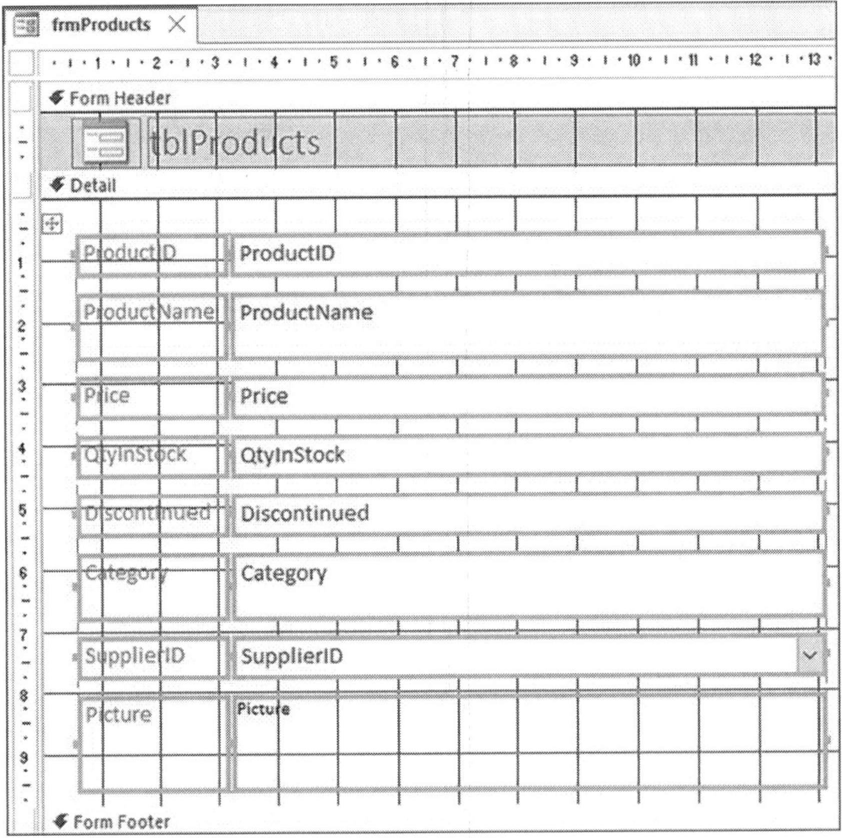

To remove one or more controls from the layout of a form created by one of the Form tools, do the following:

1. Open the form in Design view.
2. Select the control you want to remove from the layout (to select multiple controls, hold down the **Shift** key and click the required controls).
3. On the Ribbon, click the **Arrange** tab, and then click **Remove Layout**. Alternatively, right-click one of the selected controls, and on the pop-up menu, select **Layout** > **Remove Layout**.
4. Access removes the selected controls from the layout grid, enabling you to now resize or move them independently.

Note The removed controls may be positioned under the layout, making it tricky to select them. Thus, you may need to drag the layout out of the way to access the independent controls that are behind it.

Creating a Form/Subform with The Form Wizard

As mentioned earlier in this chapter, the Form Wizard gives you more flexibility in terms of what fields you want to place on the form. The Form tools simply create a form with all the fields from the chosen data source. On the other hand, the Form Wizard allows you to select specific fields that you want on the form. Once created, you'll find that the form also provides more flexibility in terms of changing the size and positions of the textboxes and the labels.

I would recommend using the Form Wizard over one of the Form tools if you want more flexibility in the size and position of your textboxes.

To create a form using the Form Wizard, do the following:

1. On the Ribbon, click the **Create** tab. In the **Forms** group, click **Form Wizard**.

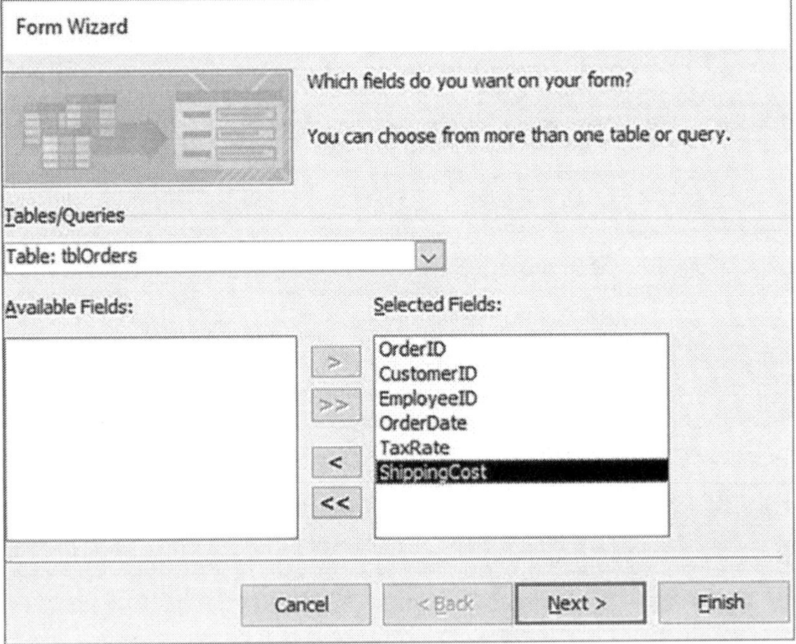

2. Select the table or query that the form will be bound to from the **Tables/Queries** dropdown list.

3. Select the field you want in the **Available Fields** list box and click the **Add** button (>) to add it to the **Selected Fields** list. Do this for all the

fields you want to add to the form. To add all the fields, click the Add All button (>>).

4. If you're creating a form/subform combination, after selecting the fields for the first table, you need to repeat the process for the second table. Select the second table in the **Table/Queries** drop-down list, and then add the fields you want for the subform to the **Selected Fields** list. Then click **Next**.

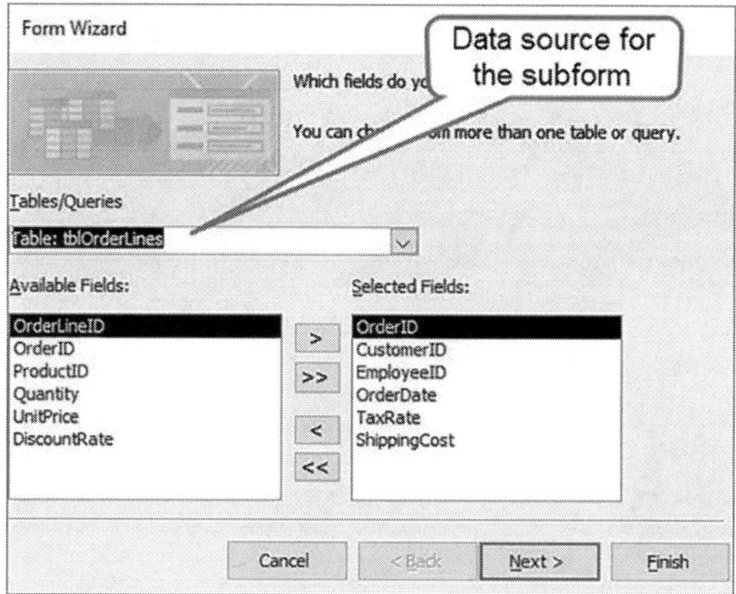

5. On the next page, select how you want to view the form and subform. In a one-to-many relationship, the subform will be bound to the child table. Ensure **Form with subform(s)** is selected, then click **Next**.

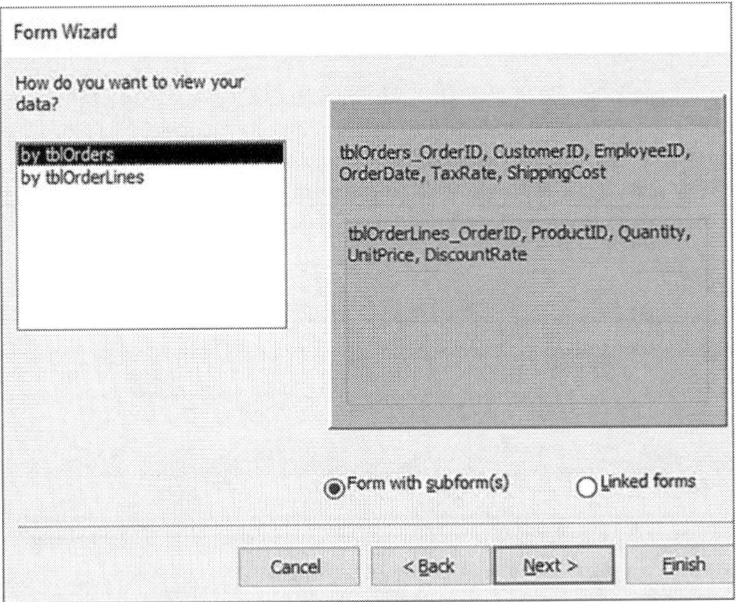

6. Choose to display the subform as a **Datasheet** on the next page, then click **Next**.

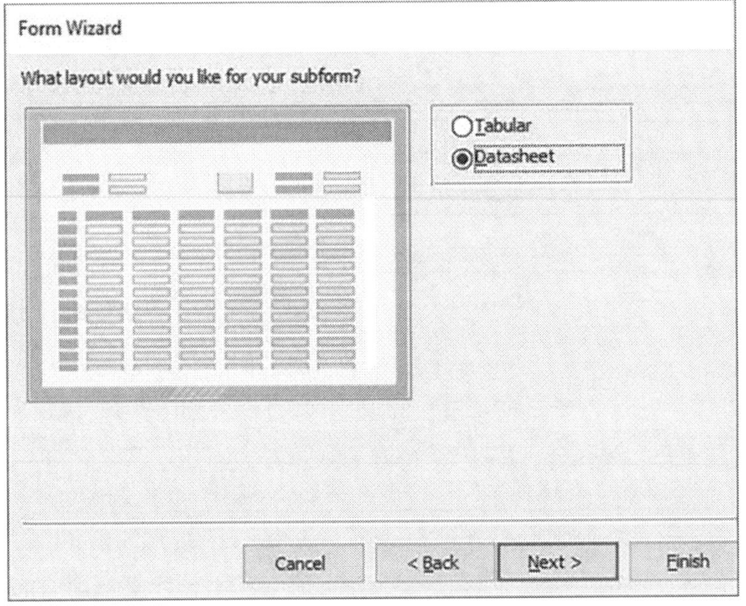

Note If you're creating a single form (with no subform), you'll get the option to choose between Columnar, Tabular, Datasheet, and Justified layouts. If you want the fields next to their labels going down the form in a column, then select Columnar.

7. On the next page, enter meaningful names for the form and subform so that they're easily identifiable in the Navigation Pane. You can choose to open the form in Form view so that you can determine what changes are required to finalize the form. On most occasions, you'll need to do some design fine-tuning after creating a form with the Form Wizard.

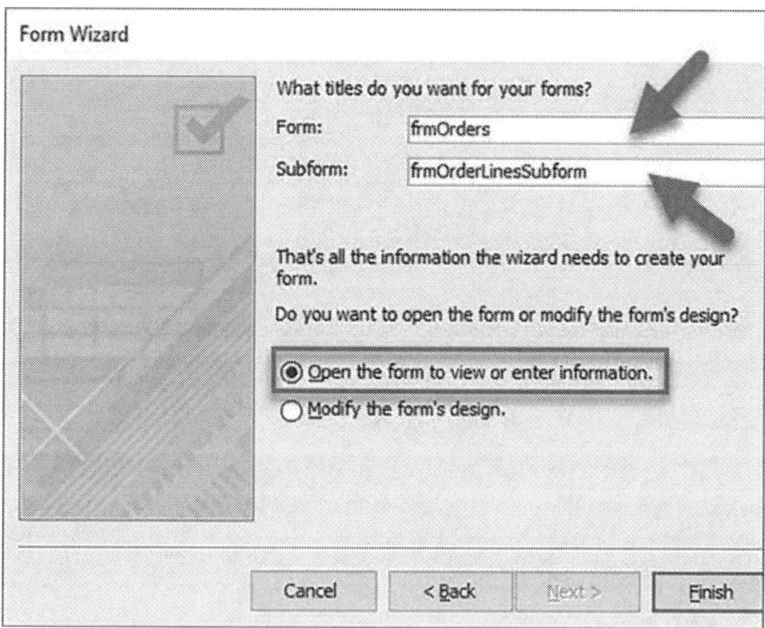

8. Click **Finish** when done.

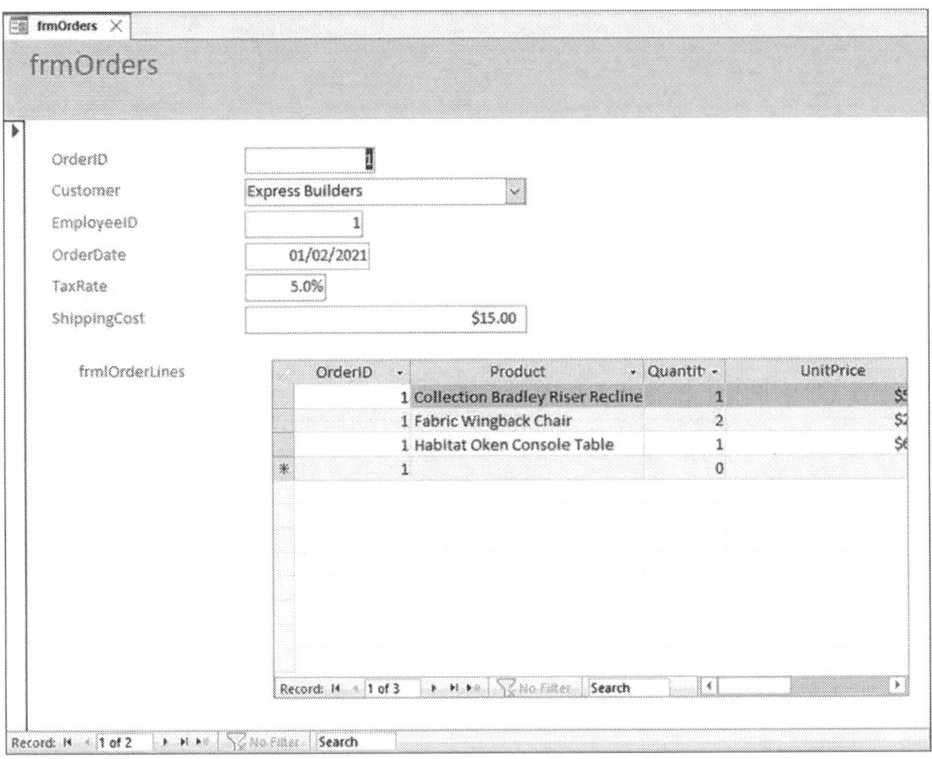

Access will display the form in Form view. As you can see, we need to make a few design changes to make the form more user-friendly.

Chapter 11: Fine-tune Your Form's Design

If you are new to Access, you should start with one of the form tools or the Form Wizard described in the previous chapter to create your forms. The automated form tools have been improved over the years, making it unnecessary to create a bound form by starting with a blank form. The form tools do most of the initial work, leaving you to focus on fine-tuning the design. Form tools like the Form Wizard are not perfect, and the forms they create usually require some design refinements to finalize them.

In this chapter, we'll cover how to use calculated fields, drop-down lists, and buttons to enhance the functionality of your forms. We will refine the design of the Orders form we created in the previous chapter by resizing some of the text boxes, adjusting the text and alignment of the labels, and finally, adding a button to close the form.

This chapter will cover:

- An overview of the different form views.
- Working with form controls.
- Using the Property Sheet to modify control properties.
- Formatting controls and control captions.
- Working with a subform.
- Creating form headers and footers.
- How to add combo boxes to your form.
- How to add calculated fields to your form.

The Three Form Views

There are three views you'll be switching between as you design and view your form, and these are Form view, Layout view, and Design view.

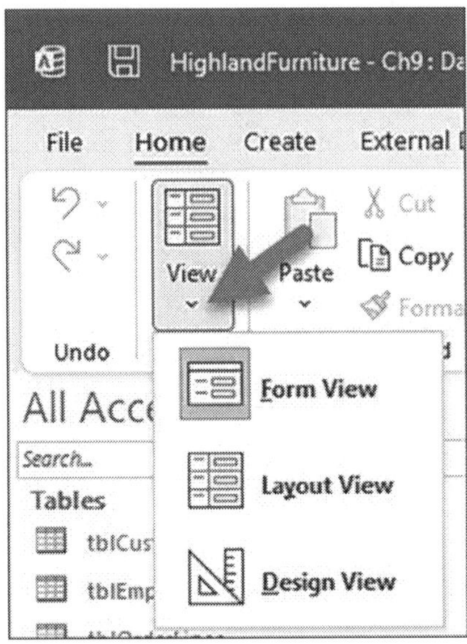

- **Form view:** This view displays the form with data. You can enter, edit, and use the navigation buttons to scroll through the records. You cannot make any design changes in Form view.

- **Layout view:** This view displays forms with the data in the controls visible. The visible data makes it easier to resize data-bound controls like text boxes and combo boxes based on the length of the data they contain. You can change the design of the form in Layout view, but you can't carry out record operations. Use Layout view to see the underlying data as you resize, format, or reposition controls.

- **Design view:** One of the benefits of Design view is that the form design surface has horizontal and vertical rulers as well as gridlines. This makes it easier to move, reposition, and organize the controls on the form. Use Design view when you need to reposition and arrange controls on the form more precisely.

Tip You can quickly switch between Form view, Layout view, and Design view by clicking the view buttons on the status bar of the Access window (bottom right).

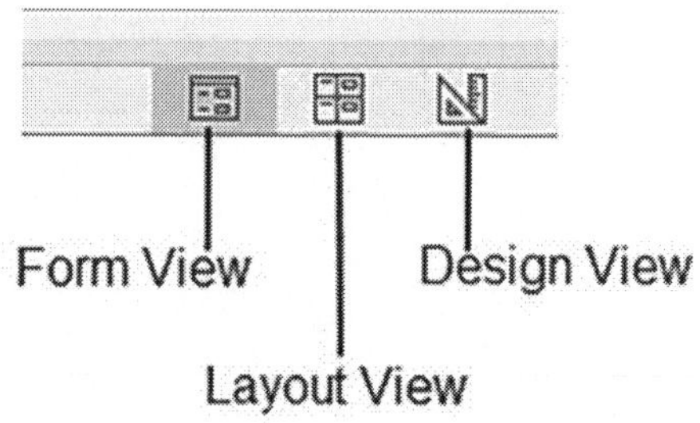

Introducing the Property Sheet

One way to change the properties of an Access object is to use the object's Property Sheet. An Access form and most controls have properties that you can change with the Property Sheet. Elements of a form like the header and footer also have their own set of properties you can change with the Property Sheet.

Displaying the Property Sheet

To display the Property Sheet, do the following:

1. Open the form in Design view or Layout view.

2. On the Ribbon, click the **Form Design** tab, and in the **Tools** group, click **Property Sheet**.

Tip With the form in Design view or Layout view, you can press **F4** to display the Property Sheet.

Access displays the **Property Sheet** and docks it to the right side of the workspace by default.

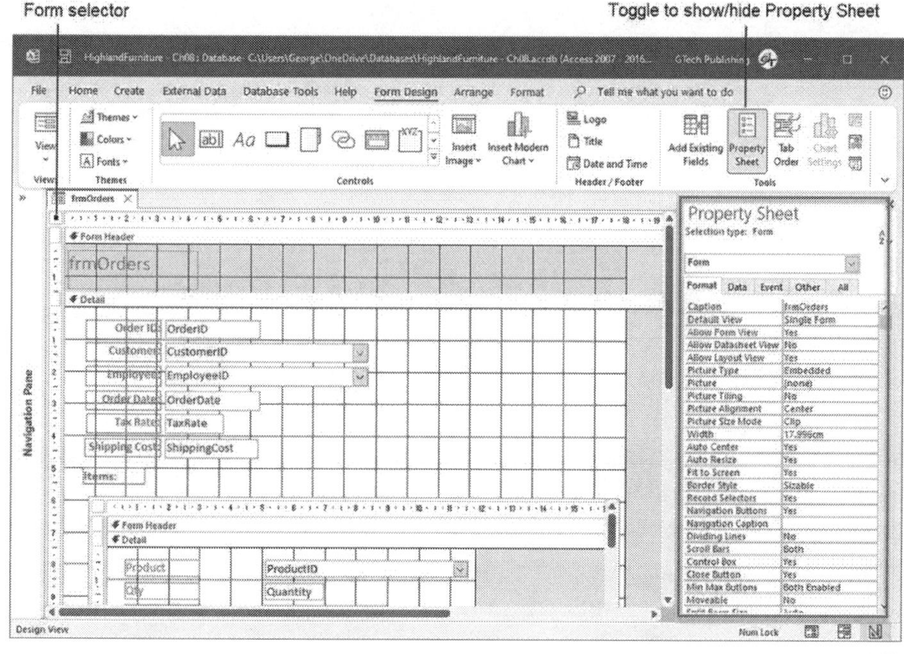

How to Reposition the Property Sheet

The Property Sheet is docked to the right side of the Access workspace by default. However, you can move it to the left or make it a floating window if you want.

You can reposition the Property Sheet in the following ways:

- **Floating**: To undock the Property Sheet, move your mouse over the top area of the Property Sheet panel until it changes to a four-directional arrow. Click and drag it away from the edge of the workspace. The Property Sheet becomes a floating window.
- **Dock to the previous location**: To dock the Property Sheet to its last location, move the mouse pointer over the top area of the Property Sheet until it changes to a four-directional arrow, then double-click. Access will automatically dock it to its previous location.
- **Dock left**: To dock the Property sheet on the left of your workspace, undock it from the right and gradually drag it left, over the left edge of the Access window. Once the dialog box is about halfway over the left edge of the Access window, it automatically docks to that side of the workspace.
- **Dock right**: If the Property Sheet is docked to the left of your workspace and you want to move it to the right, undock it from the left side and

gradually drag it right. Once the dialog box is about halfway over the right edge of the Access window, it automatically docks to that side of the workspace.

Resizing the Property Sheet

To increase the size of the Property Sheet or its columns, do the following:

- To increase the width of the Property Sheet, move your mouse pointer over its left edge until it turns into a two-headed arrow, then click and drag left.

- To increase the size of the columns showing the property names and corresponding values, move your mouse over the dividing line (the line that separates the property name and the value) until the mouse changes to a sizing cursor. Then drag right to increase the size of the property column or left to increase the size of the value column.

Getting Acquainted with the Property Sheet

The Property Sheet has several tabs used to categorize the properties:

- **Format**: Contains formatting properties.
- **Data**: Contains properties for controls that handle data like text boxes, combo boxes, and list boxes.
- **Event**: Any macros or event procedures (VBA code) attached to the object are set here.
- **Other**: Miscellaneous properties that do not fit into any other category.
- **All**: All the properties for the object are listed here.

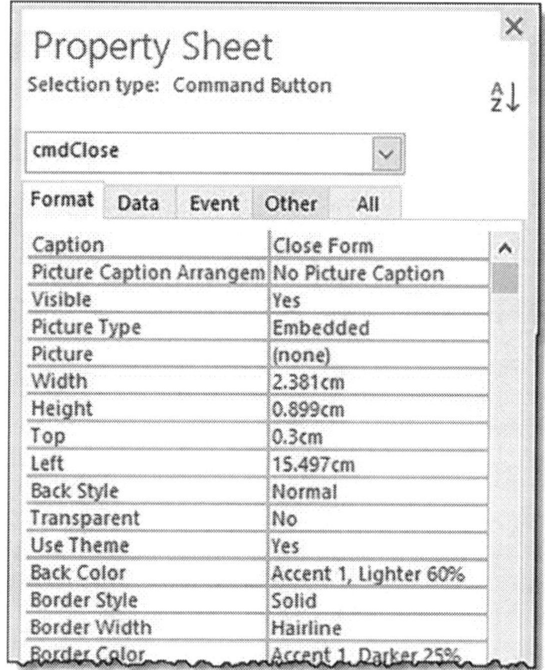

The number of properties displayed in the Property Sheet depends on the control selected. Some controls have more properties than others. The property names are pretty self-explanatory. For example, if you add a new text box control to your form, you can change the border style to transparent with the **Border Style** property on the **Format** tab. You'll choose **Transparent** from the list of options provided for the Border Style.

You can use the property sheet to change most of the properties you can change using commands on the Ribbon. You can also alter many properties using the

Property Sheet for which there are no commands on the Ribbon. Many properties provide a drop-down list of values from which you can choose.

How to Display Form and Control Properties

You can use one of the following methods to display the properties of a form or control:

- With the Properties Sheet open, click on any control or form section to display its properties in the Property Sheet. To display the properties of the form itself, click the form selector (this is the top left area of the form, between the horizontal ruler and vertical ruler).
- In the Property Sheet pane, select the name of the control or form section from the **Selection type** drop-down list to display its properties.
- Right-click the control (or form section) and select **Properties** from the pop-up menu. To display the properties of the form, right-click the form selector and select **Properties** from the pop-up menu.

Working with Form Controls

A form control is a design element you can place on a form like a text box, combo box, label, line control, or button.

Controls fall primarily into two categories:

- Those used to display data on the form.
- Those used to design and organize the interface of the form.

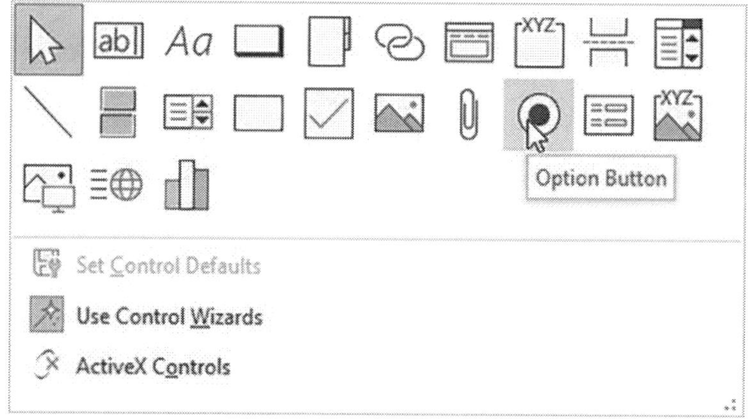

Move your mouse pointer over a control to see its name

Below are the most popular form controls used in Access:

- **Text box**: As the name implies, a text box is used for entering or displaying text. A text box can be bound to an underline data source (like a table or query), or it could be unbound and based on an expression that performs a calculation using values from other fields.

- **Label**: A label is often used to describe a field on the form, like a text box or combo box.

- **Combo box**: A combo box is like a text box, but it has an attached list of value choices you can select instead of entering the value manually.

- **List box**: The list box has a list of options you can select. However, unlike a combo box, multiple items are visible simultaneously. A list box also displays a scroll bar when the items in the list exceed the control's height.

- **Checkbox**: This is a box attached to a Boolean field that stores true/false, on/off, or yes/no values. You can use the drop-down list or a checkbox for a yes/no field.

- **Line**: You can use a line control to denote a separation on the form. For example, to add clarity to a continuous form, you may want a separation line after each record.

- **Button**: A button is used to run a macro or an event procedure that can be used to carry out different types of actions in the application. We'll be covering buttons later in this chapter.

- **Subform**: Enables you to insert a form within another form. The subform is usually bound to the child table of a one-to-many relationship, where the main form is bound to the parent table. Subforms are used to display child records in a one-to-many relationship.

Resizing a Control

To change the size of a text box control, do the following:

1. Open the form in Layout view or Design view.
2. Click the text box to select it. The edges of the text box will be highlighted.
3. If the form is in Layout view, move your mouse over one of the highlighted edges until the pointer changes to a double-headed arrow.

Note If the form is open in Design view, move your mouse pointer over one of the 'sizing handles' in the upper, lower, and right edges of the control (see the image below) until the pointer changes to a double-headed arrow.

---

4. Click and drag to increase or decrease the length or height.

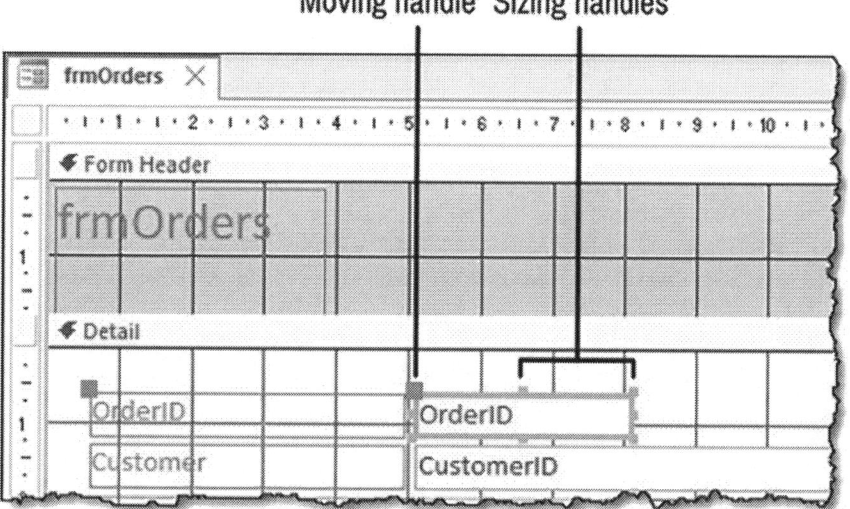

Moving a Control

You can use one of the following methods to reposition a control on the form:

- Click the control once to select it. Move your mouse over any of the highlighted edges until the mouse pointer changes to a four-directional arrow. Click and drag the control to any position on the form.

- Click the control and hold down the mouse button. You'll notice that the cursor has changed to a four-directional arrow. Drag the mouse to move the control to a new position on the form.

- Click the control once to select it. Use the arrow keys on the keyboard to move the control left, right, up, or down. Each keypress moves the control by 1 pixel. Use this method if you only want to move the control slightly.

Tip To select more than one control, click the first control to select it, and then hold down the **Shift** key as you click on the additional controls. You can resize or move controls that have been selected together.

Changing the Captions of Labels

One design change you should make as you refine the design of your form is to edit the labels attached to bound controls with more meaningful names (rather than the table field names). You may also want to make some formatting changes like bolding the captions and changing their alignment.

To overwrite the caption of a label, do the following:

1. Double-click the label, and Access will select the whole caption.
2. Type over the current caption and press Enter.

To edit the caption of a label without overwriting it, do the following:

1. Click the label to select it.
2. Click once again in the label to get the insertion point blinking in the text.
3. Use the left or right keys to move the insertion point to the part of the text you want to edit and type in the label.

Changing the Format of a Label Control

To change the format of the caption on a label, click on the **Format** contextual tab on the Ribbon. You can use commands in the **Font** group to change the font, size, and alignment of the caption on labels. You can also use commands in the **Control Formatting** group to change the style of the control, like the fill color and outline.

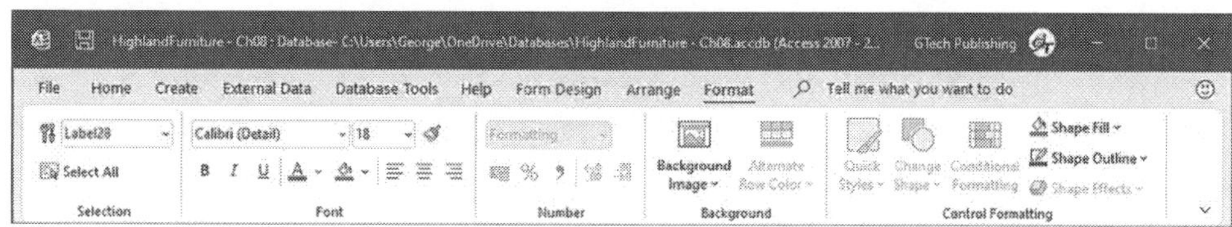

Aligning Controls and Captions

To select multiple controls so that you can change them together, click the first control to select it, and then hold down the **Shift** (or **Ctrl**) key and click the other label controls to select them.

To right-align controls on the form, do the following:

1. With the form open in Design view, click the **Arrange** tab.
2. Select all the controls you want to align right.
3. In the **Sizing & Ordering** group, click the **Align** button and select **Right** from the drop-down menu.

This right-aligns the selected controls.

To right-align text/captions on controls, do the following:

1. With the form in Design view, click the **Format** tab.
2. Select all the labels with captions that you want to right-align.
3. In the **Font** group, click on the **Align Right** button.

This should right-align the captions on the labels.

Moving and Resizing a Subform Control

A subform is a control just like any of the other form controls. The Form Wizard will automatically add a subform control to a form if the data source has a one-to-many relationship. If you're designing your form from scratch in Design view, you can manually add a subform control to the design.

After creating your form/subform with the Form Wizard, you'll often need to reposition and resize the subform as well as adjust the size of its columns to fit the data.

The subform has labels just like the main form. When you change the caption of the labels, this will be reflected on the column headings of the datasheet (if your subform is a datasheet) in Layout view and Form view.

To resize or change the position of the subform, do the following:

1. Display the main form in Layout view.

2. Click anywhere in the subform. Access will highlight the edges of the subform, indicating it is selected.

3. On the top left corner of the subform control, you'll see the layout selector. Move the mouse over the layout selector until it changes to a four-directional arrow. Then click and drag the subform to where you want it on the form.

4. You can resize the subform by moving the mouse pointer over the highlighted edges until it changes to a double-headed arrow, and then drag until it is the size that you want.

5. When done, click **Save** on the title bar (or press **Ctrl+S**).

To resize a column on a datasheet subform, do the following:

1. Position the mouse pointer over the right edge of the column you want to resize until it changes to a double-headed arrow.

2. Click and drag left/right to decrease/increase the width of the column.

3. Click **Save** on the title bar (or press **Ctrl+S**).

To resize a row in a datasheet subform, do the following:

Place the mouse pointer between any two record selectors in the datasheet and drag until the rows are the size that you want. Save your change by clicking the **Save** button on the title bar (or press **Ctrl+S**).

Note You cannot resize rows individually. When you resize one row, all the rows are resized.

After carrying out several formatting changes, our Orders form looks like the image below:

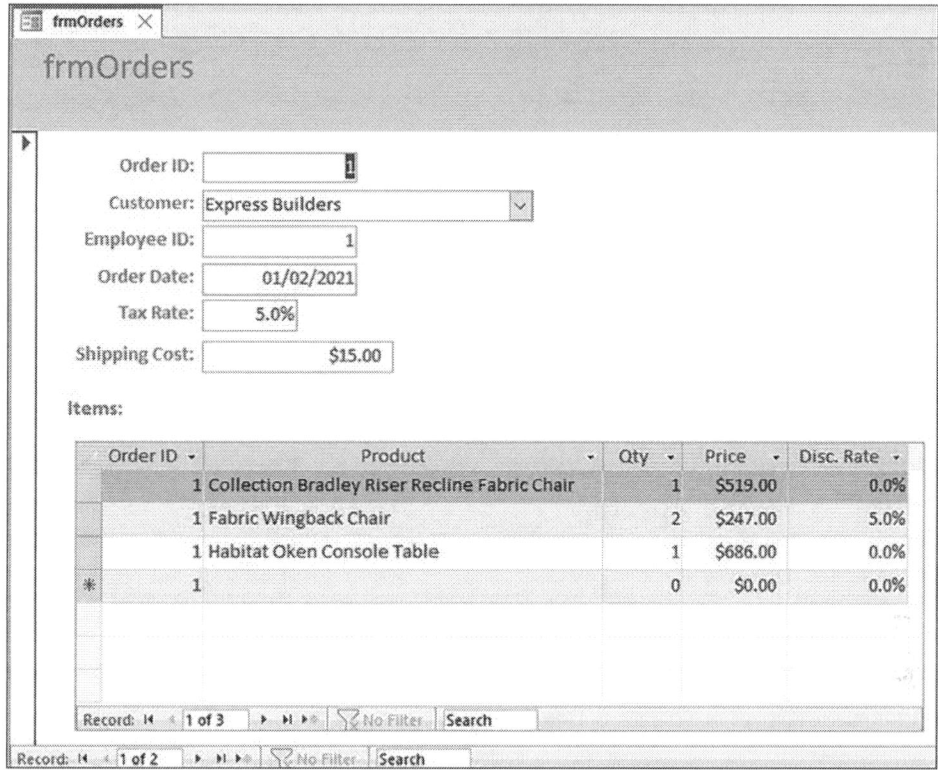

There are still some design changes required. For example, the form needs:

- The header needs a meaningful title and a logo (applicable if your company has a logo).
- A footer with a button to close the form.
- A few unbound text box fields to show the calculated values we would like to display on the form. For example, tax amount, order line total, and order total can all be calculated using expressions. This gives the data more meaning.

We will be making these changes in the coming sections.

Form Headers and Footers

A form has three sections separated by horizontal bars called section selectors.

- Form Header
- Detail
- Form Footer

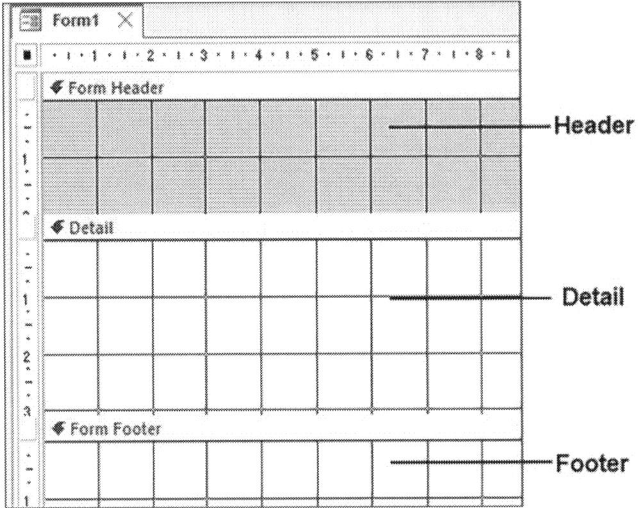

The form Detail section usually contains most of the controls that display data. The other sections are used for controls you always want to be visible on the form. Depending on the size of the form, the Detail section can scroll up or down. However, the form header and footer always remain on the screen.

The header is usually used for a company logo and the title of the form. The form footer is useful for any button controls that you always want to be visible, for example, a button to close the form or a button to launch another process that is part of your workflow.

To further refine the design of our Orders form created by the Form Wizard in chapter 10, we'll make a couple of changes to the form's header and footer.

Header and footer changes required for the Orders form:

- Add a company logo to the form header.
- Change the form title to something more meaningful.
- Add a form footer and a button used to close the form.

Designing the Form Header

The image below shows the Orders form in Design view immediately after being created by the Form Wizard. Notice that the Design view has horizontal rulers, vertical rulers, and gridlines on the form design surface. Also, notice the section selectors that separate the various sections of the form.

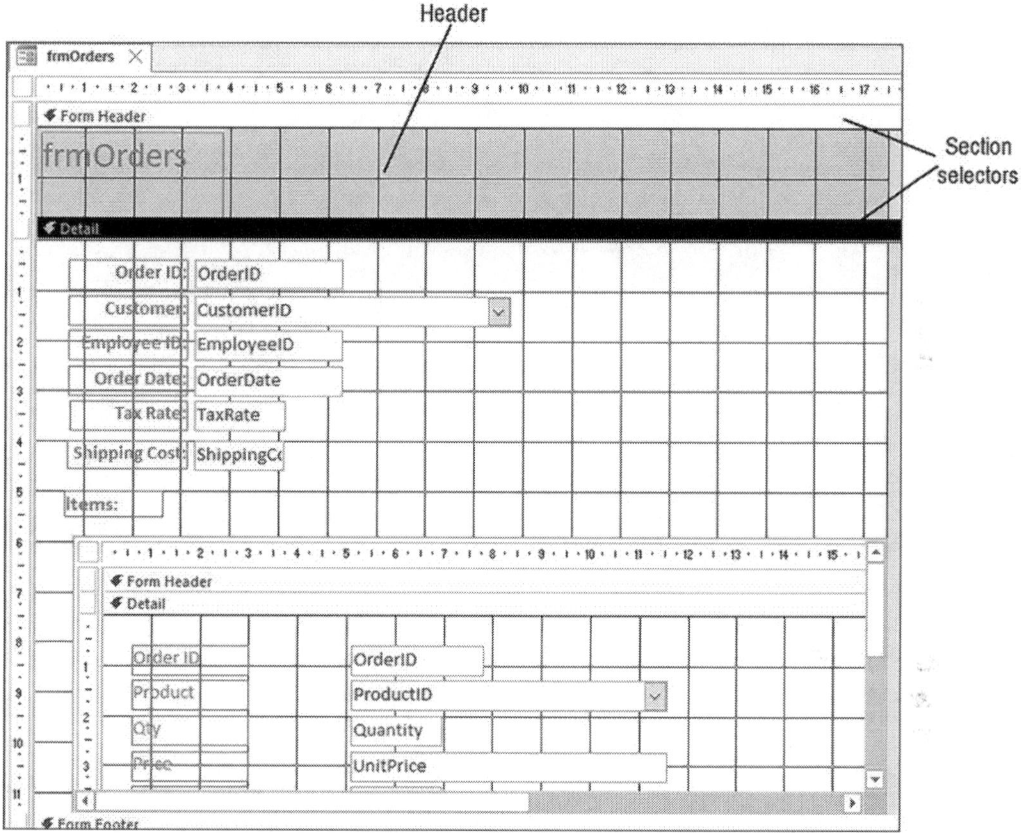

When you create a form with the Form Wizard, the form header is displayed, but the footer is not visible. The header will contain a label with the name of the form.

To increase or decrease the size of the Form Header:

1. Open the form in Design view (if it is not open already).
2. Move your mouse pointer over the top of the **Detail** section selector (the horizontal bar between the header and the body) until the mouse pointer changes to a sizing cursor.
3. Drag down (or up) to resize the header to the size you want.

Adding an Image to the Header

To add a company logo to the form header, do the following:

1. Click the form header (or click the **Form Header** section selector) to make it active.
2. On the Ribbon, click the **Form Design** tab. In the **Controls** group, click **Insert Image** > **Browse** to open the **Insert Picture** dialog box.
3. Select the logo or image you want to add to the form header and click **Open**.

   Access will insert the image in the form header.
4. Use your mouse to reposition the image where you want it in the header. For example, you may want to align it left.

Note You can also use the **Logo** command, in the **Header / Footer** group, on the **Form Design** tab to insert a logo in the form header. However, the **Image** control is more flexible in terms of positioning the logo.

Editing the Title Label in the Header

To edit and reposition the form title, do the following:

1. With the form in Design view, select the label in the form header, and then click inside the label to edit the text. You should see the insertion point in the text.
2. You can select the whole text and overwrite it or edit the text.

   For instance, for the Orders form, the title is *frmOrders*, and we just need to change this to *Orders*.
3. Click on the **Format** tab. On this tab, you can use various commands in the **Font** group to change the font, font size, font color, background color, and alignment.
4. Use the sizing handles on the label control to adjust its height and width to fit the text.
5. When you're happy with the format of the title, you can reposition the label in the header using the horizontal ruler and gridlines as your guide. Drag the label to where you want it on the header with your mouse.

The edited header should now look like this:

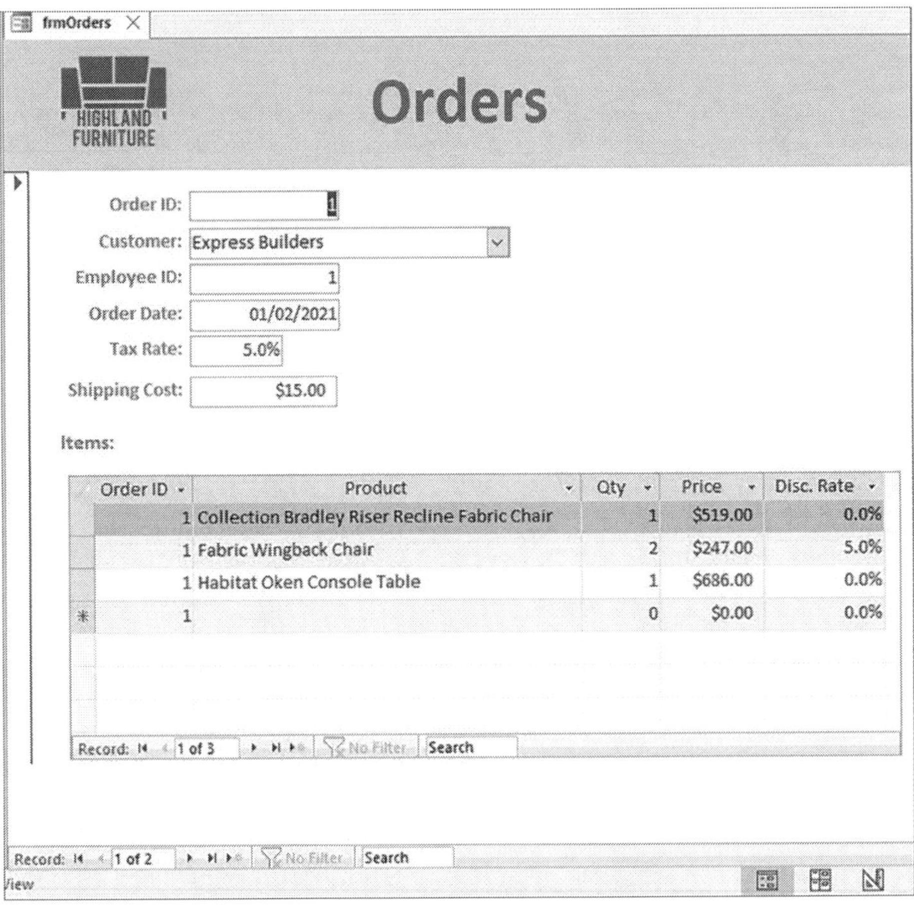

Adding a Footer

To display the form footer (if it isn't visible), do the following:

1. Open the form in Design view.
2. Click the **Form Footer** section selector (the horizontal bar at the bottom of the Detail section).
3. Move your mouse pointer over the bottom of the Form Footer section selector until the mouse pointer changes to a sizing cursor.
4. Drag down to increase the size of the form footer.

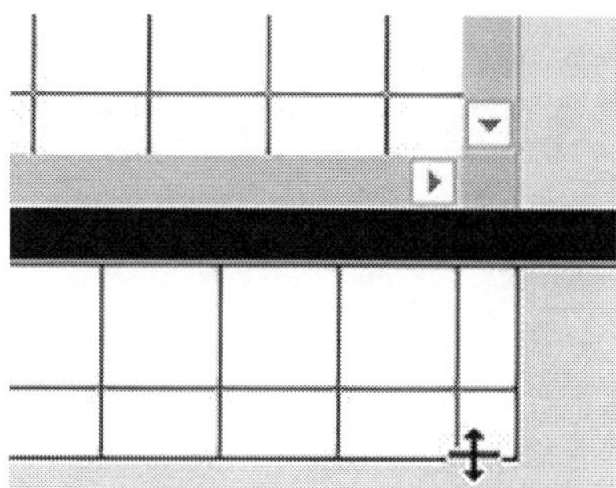

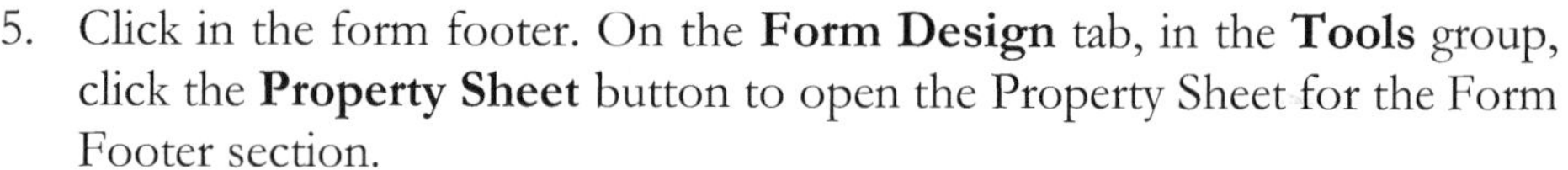

5. Click in the form footer. On the **Form Design** tab, in the **Tools** group, click the **Property Sheet** button to open the Property Sheet for the Form Footer section.

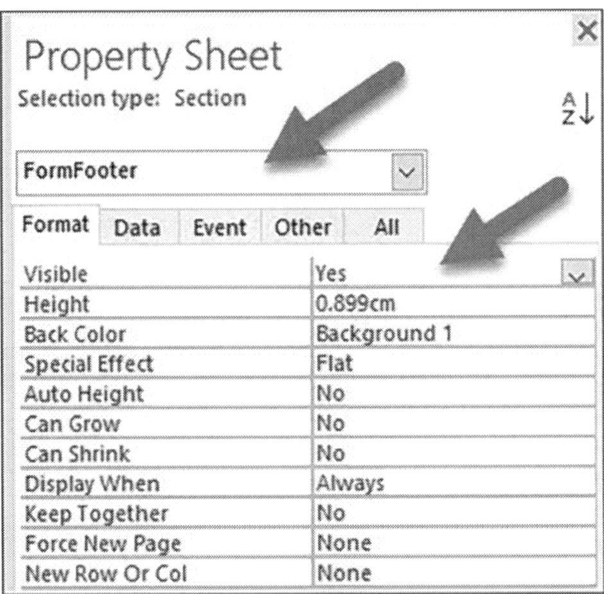

6. On the **Format** tab of the Property Sheet, ensure the **Visible** property is set to **Yes** (this is the default).

Changing the Fill Color of any section of the form

You can change the background color (back/fill color) of any section of the form to match the style of your application. For example, you may want the header and footer to have a different fill color from the details section.

To change the back/fill color of a section of the form, do the following:

1. Right-click anywhere in the section.
2. On the pop-up menu, select **Fill/Back Color**
3. Select the fill color of your choice from the color palette.

Note You can also change back/fill color with the **Background color** button in the **Font** group on the **Format** tab (when the form is in Design view).

Adding a Button to the Footer

You can add buttons to your form using the Command Button Wizard for various actions, including:

- Record navigation, like going to the previous or next record.
- Record operations, like adding and deleting records.
- Form operations, like closing the form or opening another form.
- Quitting the database.
- Running a query or running a macro.

You can put a button anywhere on the form, but one benefit of putting it in the footer is that the footer is always visible even if you have to scroll up or down to see some controls in the Detail section.

To add a Close button to a form, do the following:

1. Open the form in Design view.

2. On the **Form Design** tab, in the **Controls** group, click the **Button** control.

3. Ensure **Use Controls Wizards** is selected (this is selected by default).

4. Click in the Form Footer and use your mouse to draw the button. Access will add a button on the form and launch the Command Button Wizard.

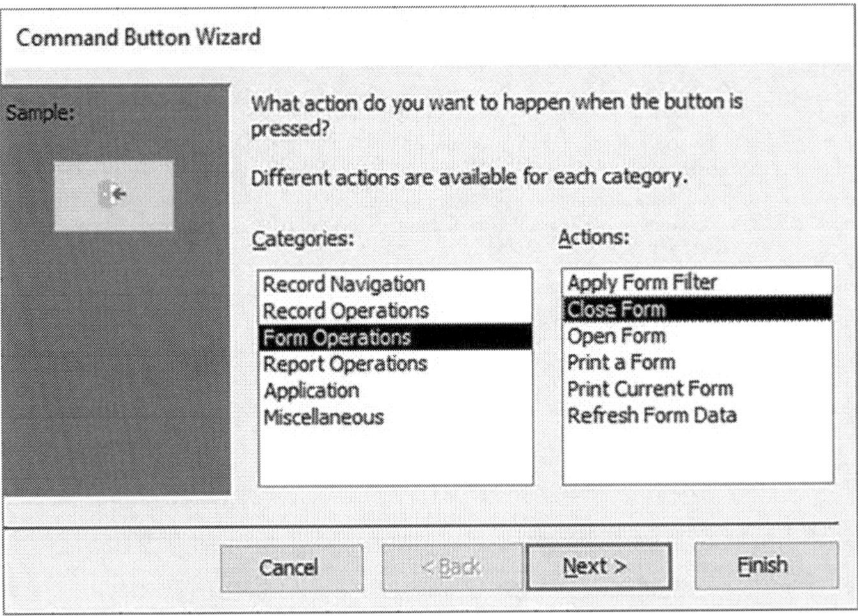

5. In the **Categories** list, select **Form Operations**, and in the **Actions** list, select **Close Form**, then click **Next**.

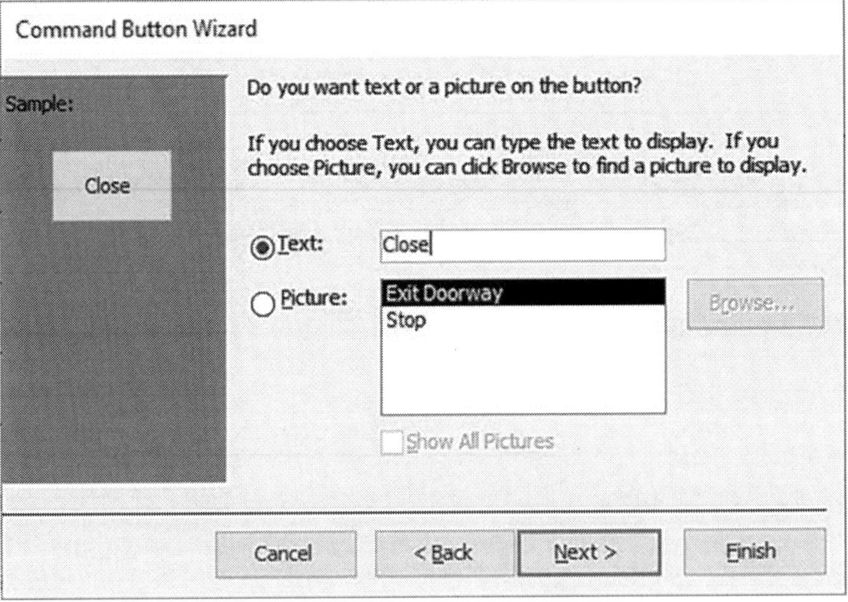

6. On the next page, select **Text** and enter the text that will be the caption on the button, then click **Next**.

Note You can also select **Picture** and use the default **Exit Doorway** icon (or click the **Browse** button and insert your own image/icon if you have a custom icon you want to use for the button).

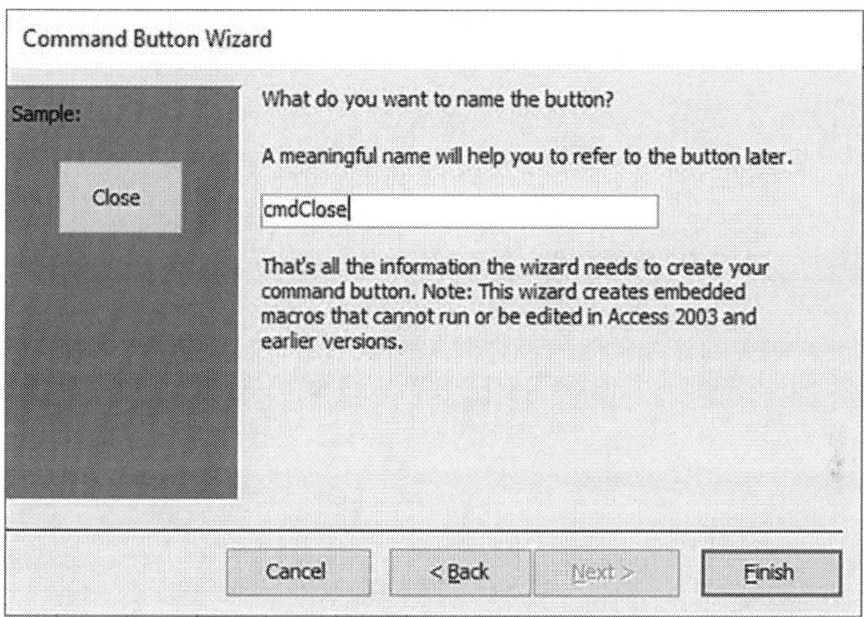

7. On the final page, enter the name of the button and click **Finish**.

Note You can change several properties of the button control using commands on the **Format** tab like the font and size of the button's caption, background color, Shape Fill, Shape Outline, and Shape Effects.

8. When done, click the **Save** button in the title bar (or press Ctrl+S).

9. To test the button, switch to Form view and then click the new button to close the form.

Tip Although Access creates an embedded macro for the button, it is important to use a meaningful name like "cmdClose" when naming the button ("cmd" is a prefix for command buttons using the Leszynski naming convention for Access databases). The name makes it easier to identify the button in code modules if you decide to create an event procedure for the button in the future.

After applying the changes discussed above to the Orders form for the Highland Furniture database, the form looks like the image below:

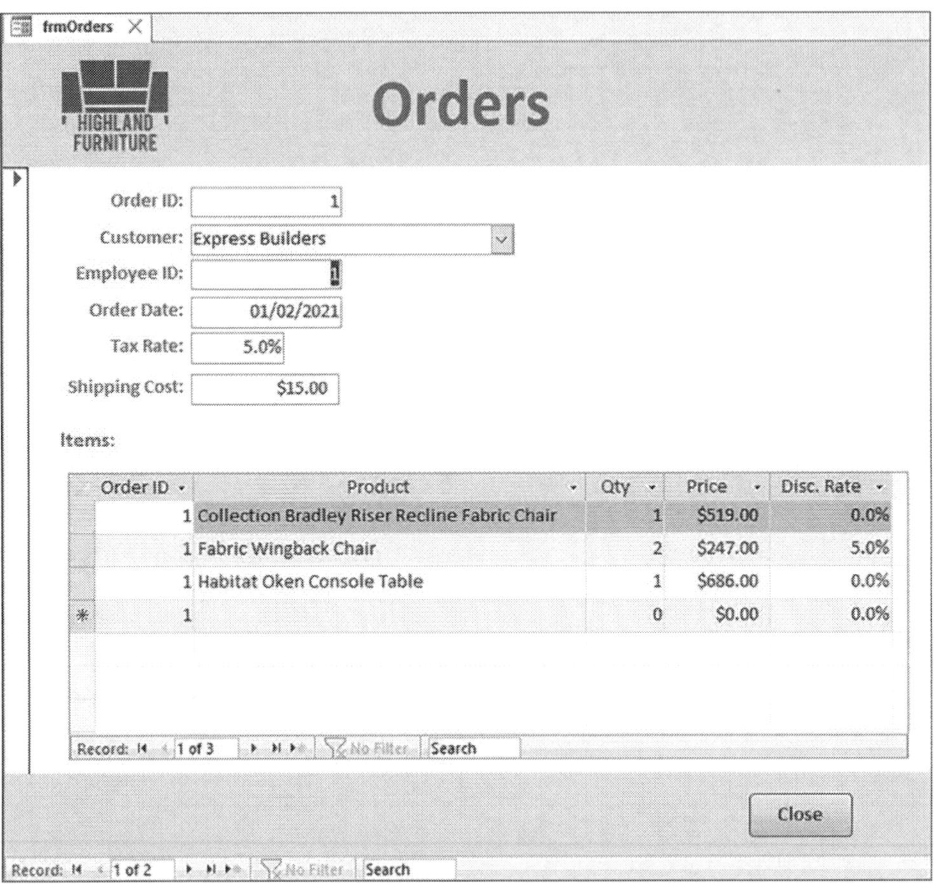

Adding a Combo Box to a Form

The combo box is a control that enables you to easily create drop-down lists that pull data from different data source types. This can make data entry easier and less error-prone for users as a combo box provides the user with a list of valid values for the field. A combo box can have a set list of values or be bound to a dynamic list from a table or query.

To illustrate the use of a combo box control, we will use the Orders form for the Highland Furniture database we created in the previous chapter. The Orders form (bound to tblOrders) has a field named EmployeeID, which is used to link each order to the employee in tblEmployees who processed it.

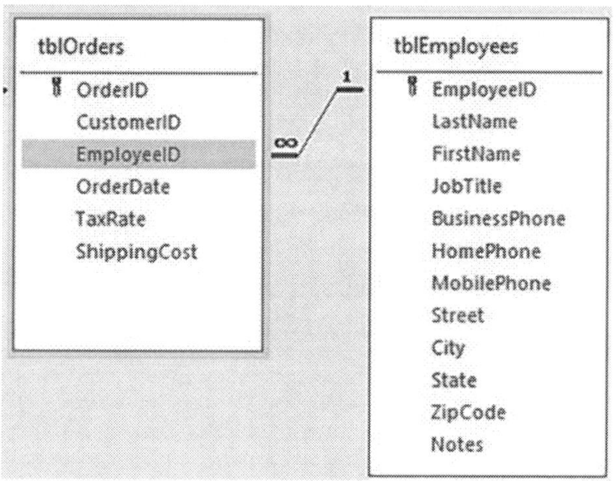

Each order has one employee, and each employee can process multiple orders.

Instead of manually looking up the EmployeeID from the Employees table, we can create a drop-down list with the names of the employees in tblEmployees. The user can then select the related employee from the drop-down list using their proper name rather than an ID. When a name is selected, even though the name is displayed on the form, Access stores the EmployeeID in tblOrders. Thus, users can enter employee details when creating or editing records without needing to know their ID.

Tip To make the process of form design even easier, you should create a Lookup field in your table for each field that you expect will need a combo box on a form. The lookup list then becomes automatically available as a combo box on every form you create that is bound to that table.

Converting a Bound Text Box to a Combo Box

When you create a form bound to a table, Access creates a text box for each number field, including foreign key fields. You can convert a text box to a combo box for any foreign key field that does not have a combo box.

For example, in our Orders form (see below), the Employee ID field is populated with an ID number. Using the Employee ID, in this case, is not user-friendly because a person viewing or editing the record can't easily tell whom that ID belongs to. Ideally, we want the name of the employee displayed on the form rather than their ID. Thus, we should change the textbox to a combo box showing the employee's name.

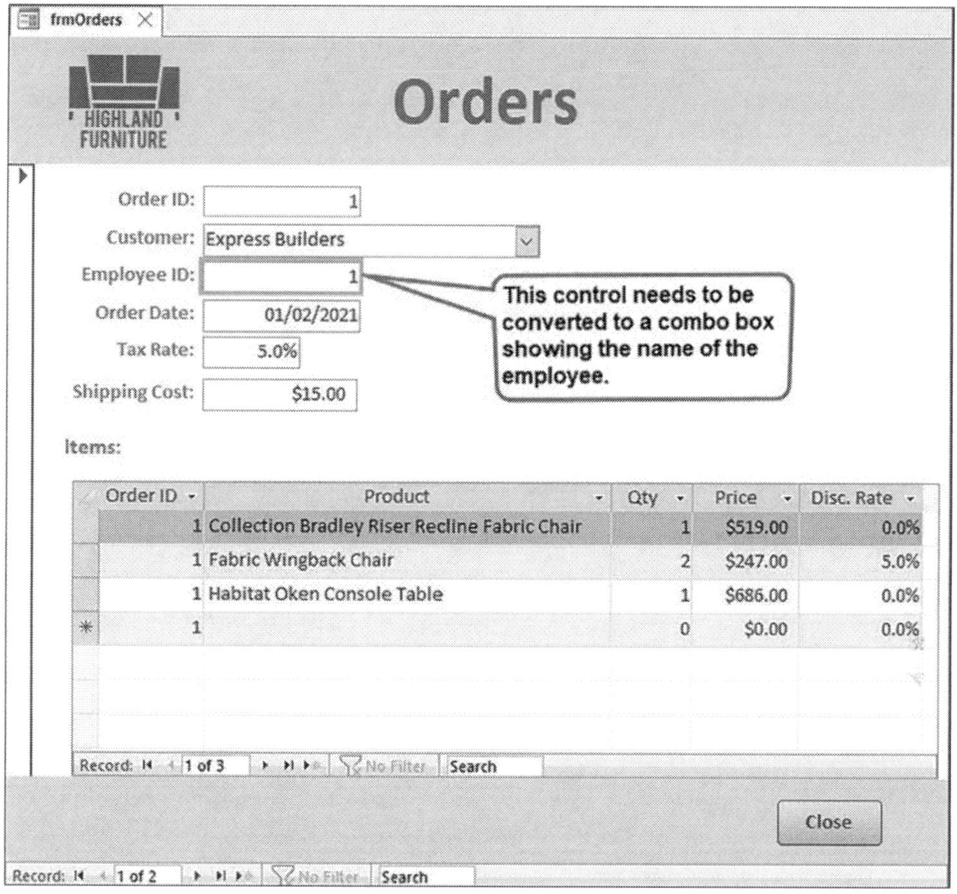

To convert a text box on a bound form to a combo box, do the following:

1. Open the form in Design view.

2. Right-click the text box, and from the pop-up menu, select **Change To** > **Combo Box**.

3. Right-click the new combo box, and from the pop-up menu, select **Properties**.

   This displays the Property Sheet for the combo box (if the Property Sheet is not already open).

4. On the **Data** tab of the Property Sheet, ensure **Row Source Type** is set to **Table/Query**.

5. In the **Row Source** property box, click the **Builder button** (with the ellipsis).

This opens a Query Builder window.

6. To add a field to the query design grid, double-click the field in the table in the top pane. Access will add the field in the next available column in the query design grid. Alternatively, select a field in the table in the top pane and then drag and drop it on a column in the query design grid.

7. Add the ID field you want to store in the table and the field you want to display on the form.

   In our example, we want to store the Employee's ID and display the employee's name. Thus, we add **EmployeeID** to the first column in the query design grid. For the second column, we want to display the employee's full name (i.e., first name and last name*)*, so we need to use the following expression:

   Employee: [FirstName] & " " & [Lastname]

   This expression tells Access to concatenate the FirstName and LastName fields to form a full name and then name the column **Employee**.

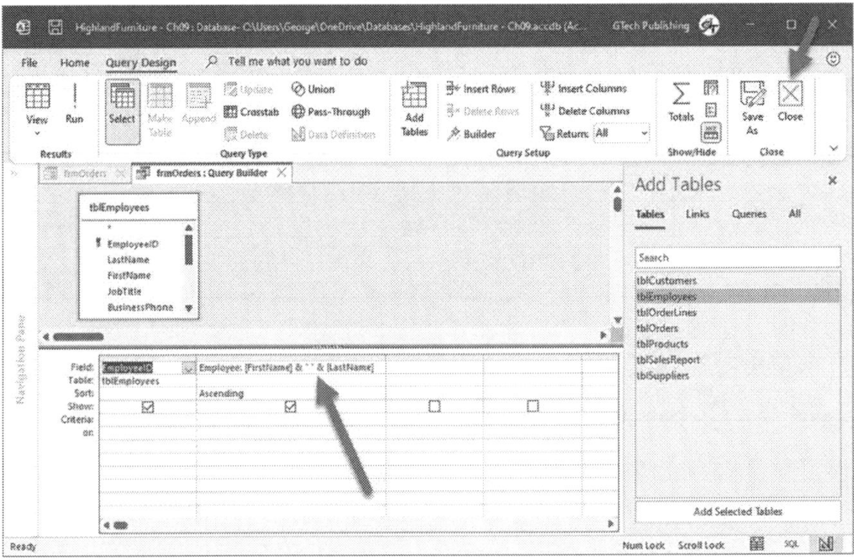

8. (Optional) You can view the results of the query by clicking the **Datasheet View** button in the **Results** group of the **Query Design** tab. To return to the Query Builder, click the **Design View** button.

9. On the **Query Design** tab, in the **Close** group, click the **Close** button.

Access will ask if you want to save the changes made to the SQL statement in the **Row Source** property of the control.

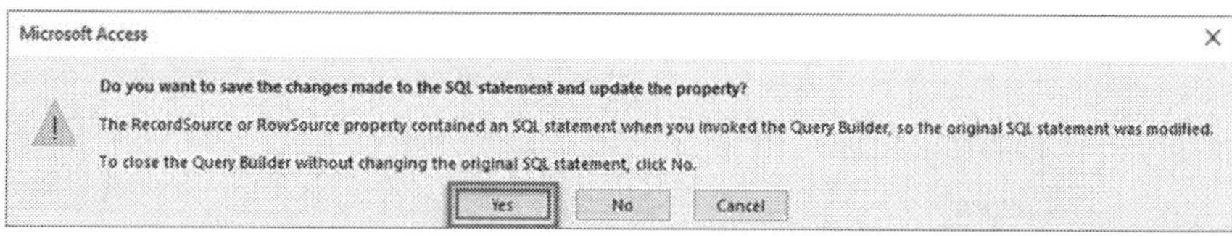

10. Click **Yes**.

    Access will then insert the SELECT statement in the **Row Source** property.

11. Next, ensure the **Bound Column** is set to 1 (this means the first column of the table is the column bound to the underlying field).

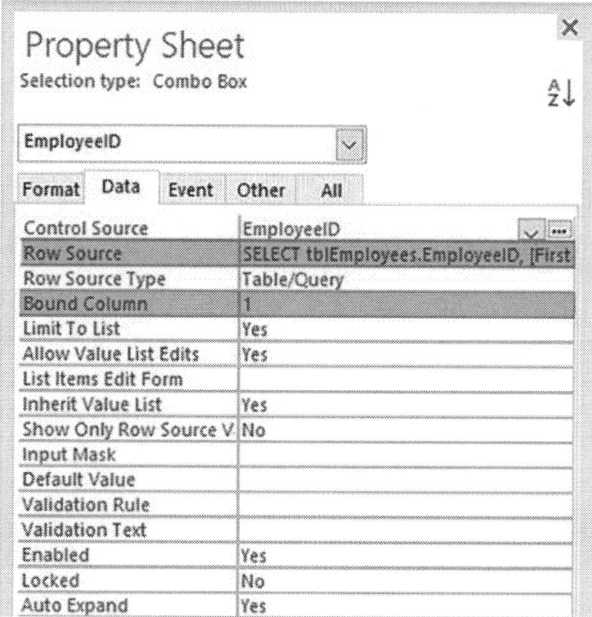

12. On the **Format** tab of the Property Sheet:

    - Set the **Column Count** to 2.
    - Set the **Column Widths** to 0cm;6cm (or to the width of your combo box, which you can find in the **Width** property further down the Property Sheet).
    - Set the **List Rows** to 8.

      This limits the visible rows in the combo box to 8. The scroll bar can be used to access the other values.

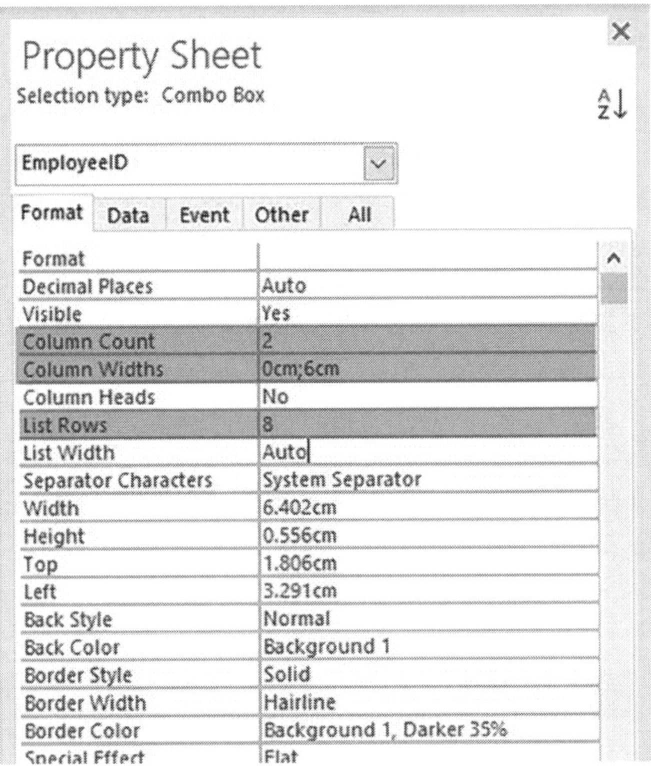

These settings tell Access to make two columns available to the combo box but to hide the first column (which is the ID field). This is because we want to display the value in the second column on the form and store the value of the first column in the table.

13. When done, click **Save** in the title bar (or press **Ctrl+S**).

Display the form in Form view to test the combo box.

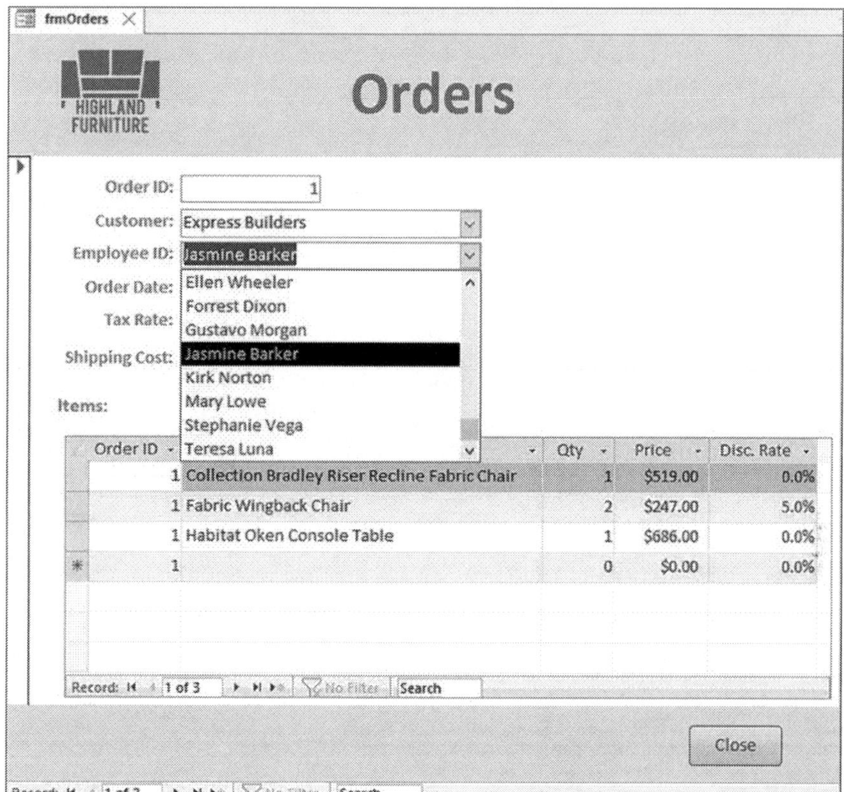

The finished combo box should look like the image above. Note that when entering or editing an order, the user enters the employee's name using the combo box, but Access stores the employee's ID with the order.

Adding a Combo Box with the Combo Box Wizard

You can also insert a combo box control on a form from the **Controls** group on the **Form Design** tab.

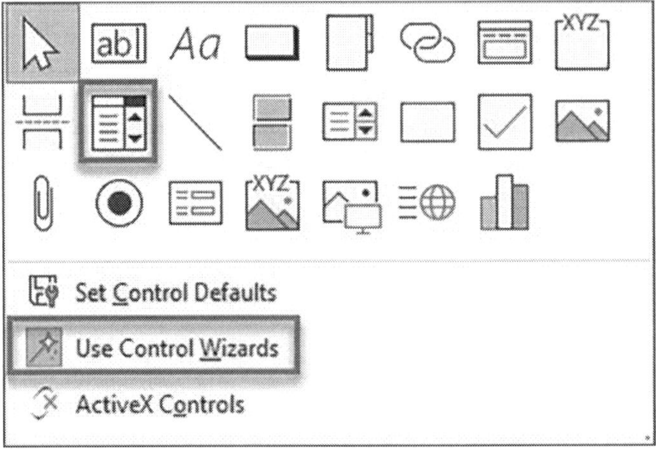

Ensure **Use Control Wizards** is selected when inserting a combo box on a form so that Access initiates the Combo Box Wizard. The wizard will guide you through the steps of selecting and setting the values you want to display in the list, how you want the list displayed, and which bound field you want to update with the data. The wizard can apply all the settings we covered in the steps above for manually creating a combo box.

Adding Calculated Fields

When we created our database tables, we made sure we didn't include any data items that were calculated fields, which are against the rules of normalization. However, we need to view calculated fields on forms, reports, and queries to give the data more meaning.

The Orders form of the Highland Furniture database will need three calculated fields:

- **Line total:** Calculates the quantity, price, and discount rate (if any is applied).
- **Total amount:** Sums all the items on the order plus the shipping cost (if any) and the tax rate.
- **Tax value:** Calculates the tax value from the Total amount. This value may be required by the customer for accounting purposes.

These values will be displayed in unbound text boxes on the form and subform using expressions. The calculated values will not be stored in the database and are for reporting purposes only. In a well-designed database, we don't need to store calculated values as we can always generate them from the data entered in the bound controls.

Adding a calculated field to the subform

Follow the steps below to add a calculated field to the subform:

1. Open the subform in Design view.

2. Insert a text box control at the bottom of the form, under the bound controls.

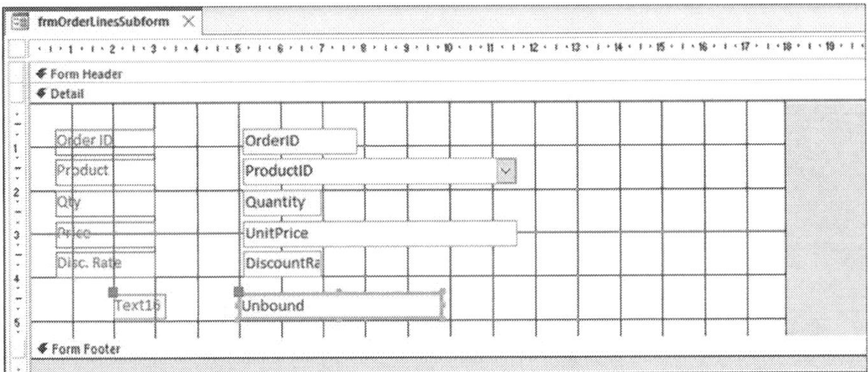

3. Double-click the label control associated with the text box and enter the caption *Line Total*. This will be the caption of the new column we are creating in the subform. You can also change the caption in the Property Sheet of the label.

4. Right-click the text box and select **Properties** from the pop-up menu to display the **Property Sheet** (if it's not already open).

5. In the Property Sheet for the new text box, click the **Data** tab.

6. In the **Control Source** property box of the **Data** tab, click the **Builder button** (with the ellipsis) to open the **Expression Builder**.

   The Expression Builder is a tool that helps you to build your expression by providing all the elements you'll need to formulate the expression in one place. The Expression Elements include the names of fields on the form, built-in functions, operators, constants, and other elements you can use to build your expression.

7. The expression used to calculate the line total for our example is as follows:

   =IIf([DiscountRate]>0,([Quantity]*[UnitPrice])-([Quantity]*[UnitPrice]*[DiscountRate]),[Quantity]*[UnitPrice])

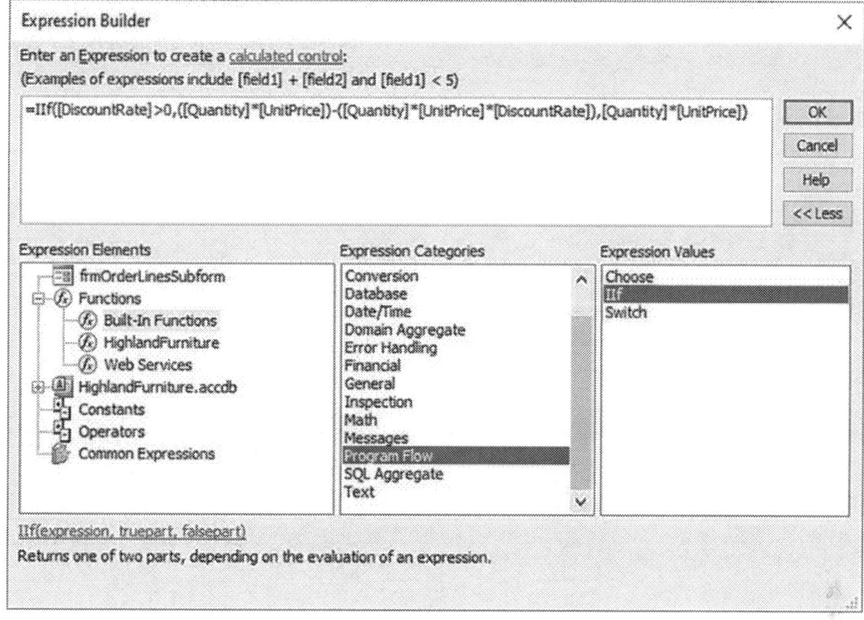

This expression says:

If the discount rate is greater than zero, then multiply the quantity by the unit price and then subtract the discount amount. If the discount rate is zero, then only multiply the quantity by the unit price.

8. Once you're happy with your expression, click **OK** to close the expression builder and insert the expression in the **Control Source** field of the Property Sheet.

9. Next, click on the **Format** tab of the Property Sheet and set the **Format** property to **Currency** (or the data type for your data).

10. Click the **Save** button on the title bar (or press **Ctrl**+**S**).

11. Test your form by clicking the **View** button in the **Views** group on the **Form Design** tab.

The finished subform with the new column should look like this:

Order ID	Product	Qty	Price	Disc. Rate	Line Total
1	Collection Bradley Riser Recline Fabric Chair	1	$519.00	0.0%	$519.00
1	Fabric Wingback Chair	2	$247.00	5.0%	$469.30
1	Habitat Oken Console Table	5	$686.00	5.0%	$3,258.50
0		0	$0.00	0.0%	$0.00

Calculating the Sum on the Subform

Next, we need to add two calculated controls on the parent form:

- Order Total
- Tax Value

To retrieve the order total value from the subform, we need to add a text box control on the footer of the subform that sums up the line total. This control will not be visible when the subform is in datasheet view because the datasheet doesn't have a footer. However, we can access the value in the control from the parent form.

To add a totals control to the footer of the subform, do the following:

1. Open the subform in Design view (for our example, this will be frmOrderLinesSubform).

2. Add a text box control to the footer of frmOrderLinesSubform and name it LineTotalSum using the Property Sheet (the **Name** property of a text box is on the **Other** tab of its Property Sheet).

3. Copy the **IIf** expression from the Control Source property of the Line Total control and paste it in Notepad or any other text application.

4. In Notepad, enclose the expression with the **Sum** function like this:

   =Sum(IIf([DiscountRate]>0,([Quantity]*[UnitPrice])-([Quantity]*[UnitPrice]*[DiscountRate]),[Quantity]*[UnitPrice]))

5. Now, copy and paste this expression in the **Control Source** property of the LineTotalSum text box in the footer of frmOrderLinesSubform.

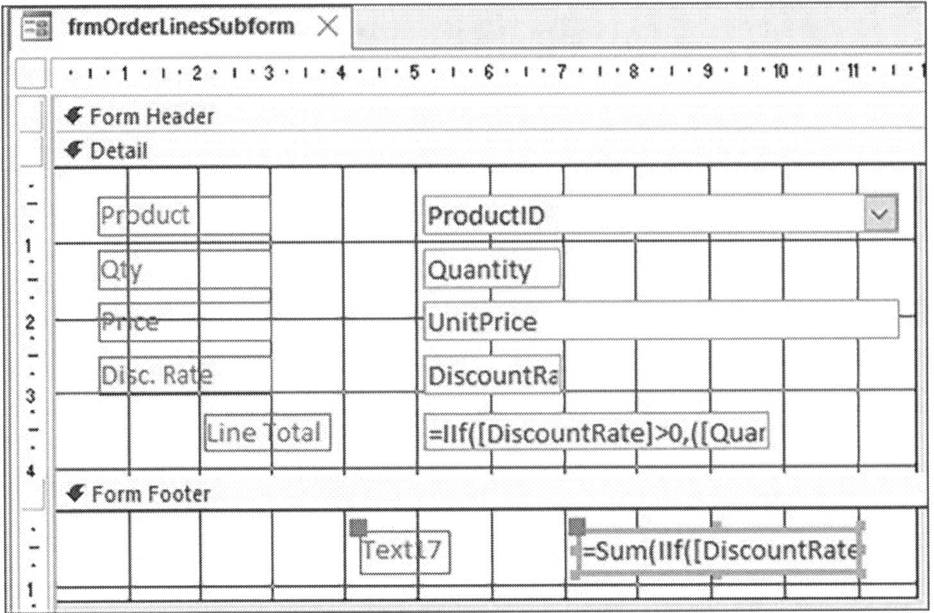

6. Click the **Save** button on the title bar (or press **Ctrl+S**).

The LineTotalSum text box now provides a sum for all the line items in the subform, but we will only be using this value on the parent form.

Adding Calculated Controls to the Parent Form

To create a control on the parent form for the Order Total, do the following:

1. Open the parent form in Design view (for our example, this will be frmOrders).

2. Add a new text box to the bottom right of the form, just under the subform, and name it **OrderTotal**.

3. In the label control of the new text box, enter *Order Total* as the caption.

4. In the **Control Source** property of the text box, enter the following expression:

   ```
   =[frmOrderLinesSubform].[Form]![LineTotalSum]+
   [ShippingCost]
   ```

   This expression accesses the value in the LineTotalSum control in the subform and adds the shipping cost from the parent form to the total.

5. On the **Data** tab of the Property Sheet of the OrderTotal control, set the **Enabled** property to **No.**

   This setting disables the text box, making it read-only. It is also slightly greyed out so that users can see that it's read-only.

6. On the **Format** tab of the Property Sheet, said the **Format** property to **Currency** (or the data type for of your control).

7. Next, we want to display the Tax Value for the order. To derive the Tax Value, we need to multiply the expression we used for the order total with the TaxRate bound control.

8. Follow the steps already described above to place a new text box control on the parent form, just under the Order Total text box, and name it TaxValue.

9. Copy the expression from the Control Source property of the Order Total text box and paste it in the Control Source property of the TaxValue text box. Then multiply the expression by the Tax Rate, like this.

   ```
   =([frmOrderLinesSubform].[Form]![LineTotalSum]+
   ```

```
[ShippingCost])*[TaxRate]
```

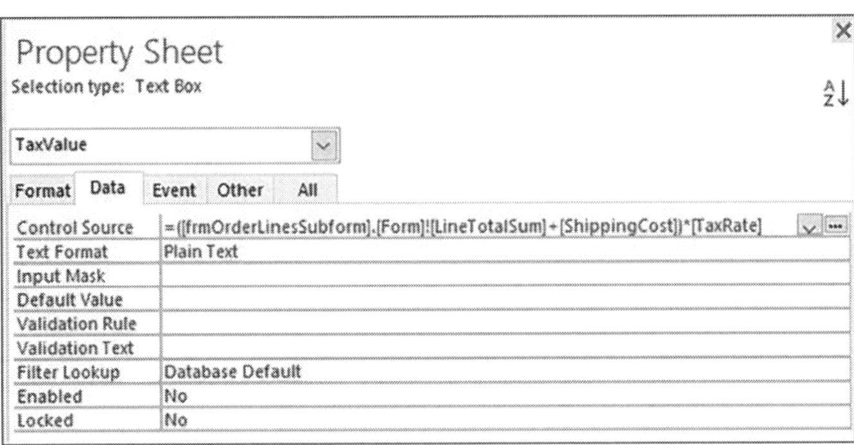

10. On the **Format** tab of the Property Sheet, said the **Format** property to Currency.

11. Click the **Save** button on the title bar (or press **Ctrl+S**).

12. Test your form by clicking the **Form View** button in the **Views** group on the **Form Design** tab.

With the calculated controls added to the form and subform, the finished form should now look like this (image below):

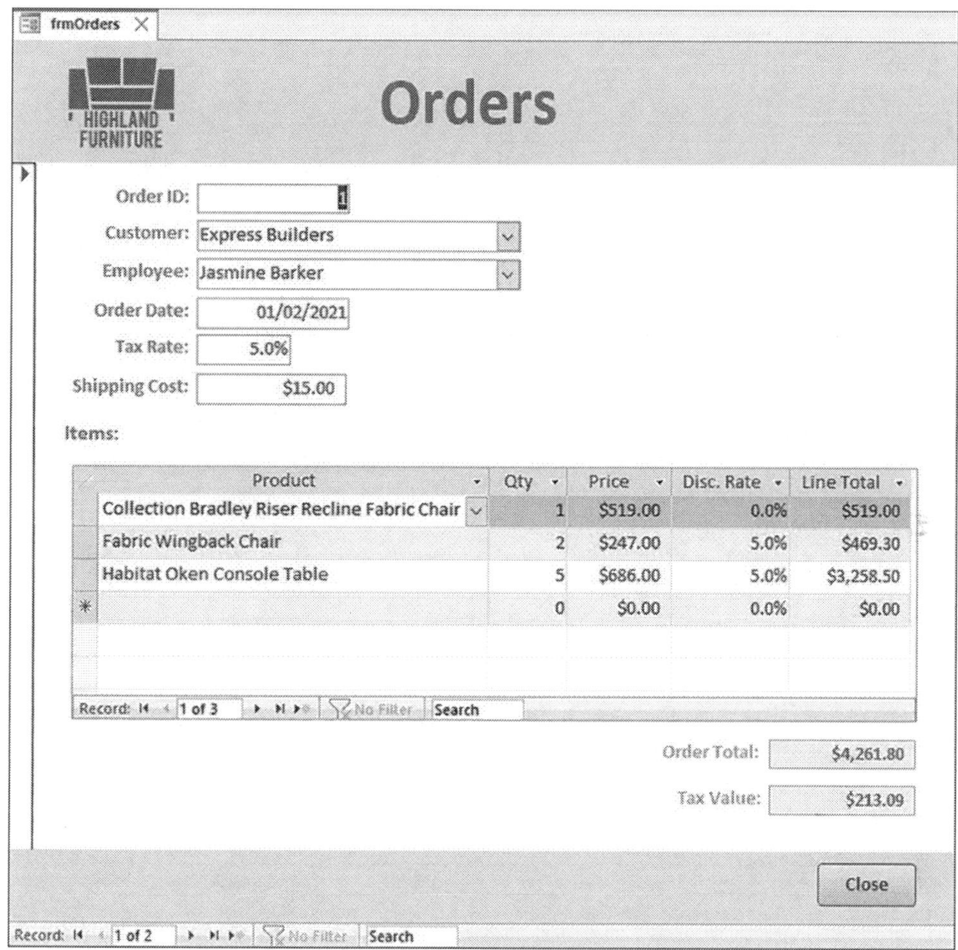

Chapter 12: Working with Data on Access Forms

Now that we've finished designing our forms, it is time to use them. In this chapter, we will cover how to navigate through records, create new records, delete records, and more.

In this chapter, we will cover the following:

- How to navigate the records on a form.
- How to enter, edit, and find records on a form.
- How to save, clear, and delete records on a form.

Navigating, Creating, and Finding Records

Use the buttons on the lower left of the form for navigation and creating a new record:

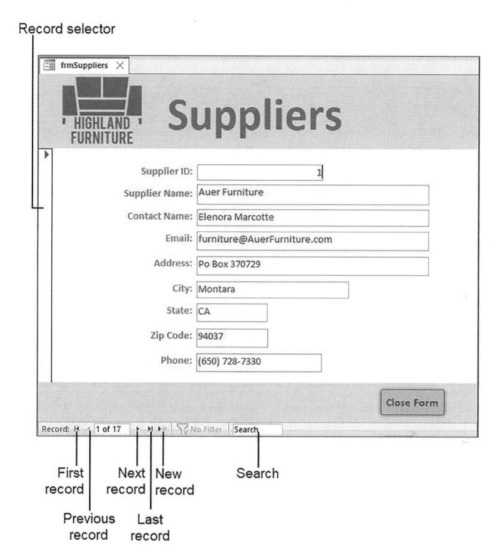

- To move forward, click the **Next record** button (>).
- To move back, click the **Previous record** button (<).
- To move to the first record, click the **First record** button (<|).
- To move to the last record, click the **Last record** button (>|).
- To initiate a new record, click the **New record** button (>*).

- To search for data, enter a search term in the **Search** box, and Access will go to the first record that contains your search term. For example, if you enter "Dunn" in the Search box, Access will automatically go to the first record that contains Dunn.

Saving, Clearing, and Deleting Records

Saving records in Access is different from other applications as you don't need to manually save your data after entry. When you enter a record in Access, as soon as you move to a new record, Access automatically saves the data. Thus, you won't easily lose data in Access.

If you want to be extra careful, you can manually save a record before moving away from it by clicking the **Save** button, in the Records group, on the Home tab. Alternatively, you can press Ctrl+S on your keyboard).

To delete the contents of a field, do the following:

1. In Form view, press the tab key on your keyboard to go to the field containing the data you want to delete.
2. Access will select the contents of the field.
3. Press the **Delete** key on your keyboard to delete the contents of the field.

Note If you mistakenly deleted data in a field, you could use the **Undo** button in the **Undo** group on the **Home** tab to undo the change.

To delete an entire record, follow the steps below:

1. While in Form view, navigate to the record that you want to delete.
2. Click the Record Selector button (located on the left edge of the form).
3. On the **Home** tab, in the **Records** group, click the **Delete** button.
4. Access displays a message box asking you to confirm the deletion. Click **Yes** on the message box to delete the record.

Note Access cannot undo deleted records. Thus, you want to make sure you're viewing the correct record before you delete it. Also, back up your database file often in case you need to restore a deleted record.

What if Access is unable to delete the record?

Occasionally you may encounter a situation where you're unable to delete a record because it has related records in another table. If the record you're trying to delete has related records in a child table and the relationship has **Enforce Referential Integrity** enabled (but not **Cascade Delete Related Records**), Access will display a message telling you that the record cannot be deleted.

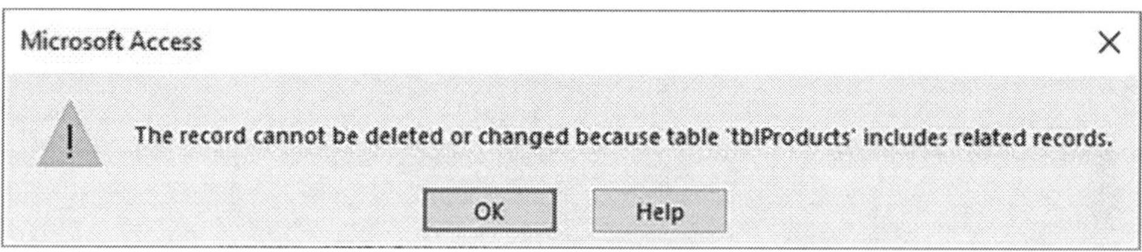

You'll need to edit the relationship in the Relationships window and disable **Enforce Referential Integrity** before you can delete the record. If you want to also delete all related records, then you need to enable both **Enforce Referential Integrity** and **Cascade Delete Related Records**.

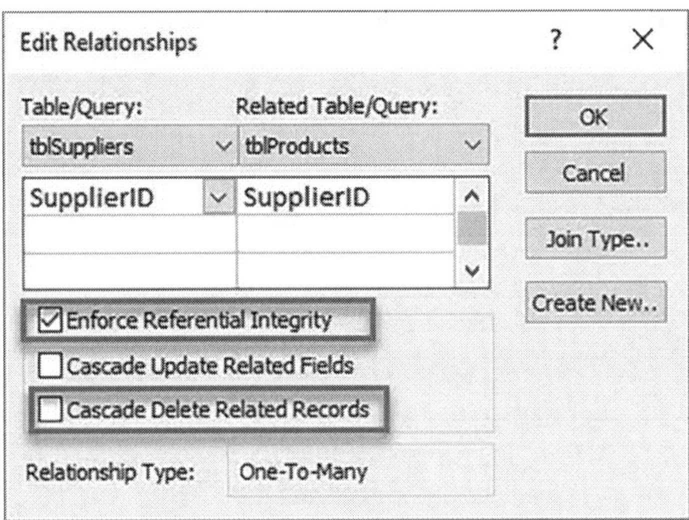

Note Select **Cascade Delete Related Records** with caution. Depending on your business rules, when one record is deleted, you may not always want Access to automatically delete related records.

Part 5

Creating Access Queries

In Part 5

Access queries are like questions that you ask your database to find and return information. You can also use queries to perform actions that transform the data in tables like bulk updates or deletes. Access provides a powerful Query by Example interface that allows you to create queries graphically. For that reason, Access is often used as a data transformation tool for data imported from other applications like Excel and SQL Server.

Contents at a Glance

Chapter 13: Selecting Data with Queries

A query is a database object, just like the other objects in the Access Navigation Pane. Once you create the query and save it to the database, it becomes available for reuse. You can run the query multiple times or edit its design. A query does not store data in the database. Rather, it retrieves and displays data from tables or performs data transformation actions against tables.

You can select data from one or more tables using queries. In one scenario, you may just want to list the telephone numbers of contacts, which would require querying one table. In another scenario, you may want to find all the items ordered by a particular customer, which would involve a query with multiple tables.

This chapter covers the following:

- An overview of the types of queries you can create in Access.
- Creating and running Select queries.
- Grouping and aggregating data in Select queries.
- Using the Query Wizard for other types of Select queries.
- Using operators and expressions in Access queries.
- Creating and running parameter queries.

Types of Queries in Access

You can use queries for different types of tasks in Access, so there are different types of queries you can create. However, the queries in Access fall into two main categories, select queries, and action queries.

Select Queries

Select queries enable you to view information from one or more data sources. You can filter the data with criteria and specify what fields to display. For instance, you can create a select query that returns only the product name and quantity for orders where the City is "NY."

With a parameter query, you can create a more flexible query that prompts for the criteria each time it is run. These are useful for situations where you run a similar kind of query using different criteria. Thus, for the query example mentioned above, instead of making "NY" part of the query design, you would insert a parameter under the City field. Access would then prompt the user for the name of the city each time the query is run to display results for that city.

Select queries do not transform the data in the database. They simply select and display data based on the criteria provided.

Action Queries

Action queries perform data transformation actions on your database. They change your data, so you should be more careful when creating and running action queries.

There are four types of action queries in Access:

- **Make Table query**: You can create a new table using fields and data from another table in your database.
- **Append queries**: You can create a query that retrieves data from one or more tables and adds (appends) it to another table.
- **Update query**: You can use an update query to edit and change data in a table. You can enter criteria to specify which rows should be updated. An update query enables you to review the planned changes before you execute the query. For example, you may have imported some data, and you want to change all the fields with the value "New York" to "NY." You

can create an update query that searches for all records with "New York" and updates the values to "NY."

- **Delete query**: Access enables you to create a query that will delete records, usually based on criteria specified. For example, our business rules may specify that we can only keep records in our database going back ten years. So, we can create a delete query that filters the results to records that are over ten years old and then deletes them.

With VBA coding, you can run multiple queries in transactions. For example, you could create queries that copy data to an archive table successfully before deleting them from the main table.

Creating Select Queries

A select query selects records from your database and displays the results based on the criteria you've set. You can use a select query if you want to view data from only certain fields in a table, from multiple tables simultaneously, or view data based on certain criteria.

For example, let's say for the Highland Furniture database, we want to view all products that are $1,000 or above.

The steps below show how to create a select query that returns products that are $1,000 or more in the Products table of the Highland Furniture database:

1. Open the database, and on the **Create** tab, in the **Queries** group, click **Query Design**.

   This opens the query design window.

2. In the **Add Tables** pane (see image below), double-click **tblProducts**. This adds the table to the table/query pane (top).

Note You can display the Add Table pane by clicking the **Add Tables** button in the **Query Setup** group on the **Query Design** tab.

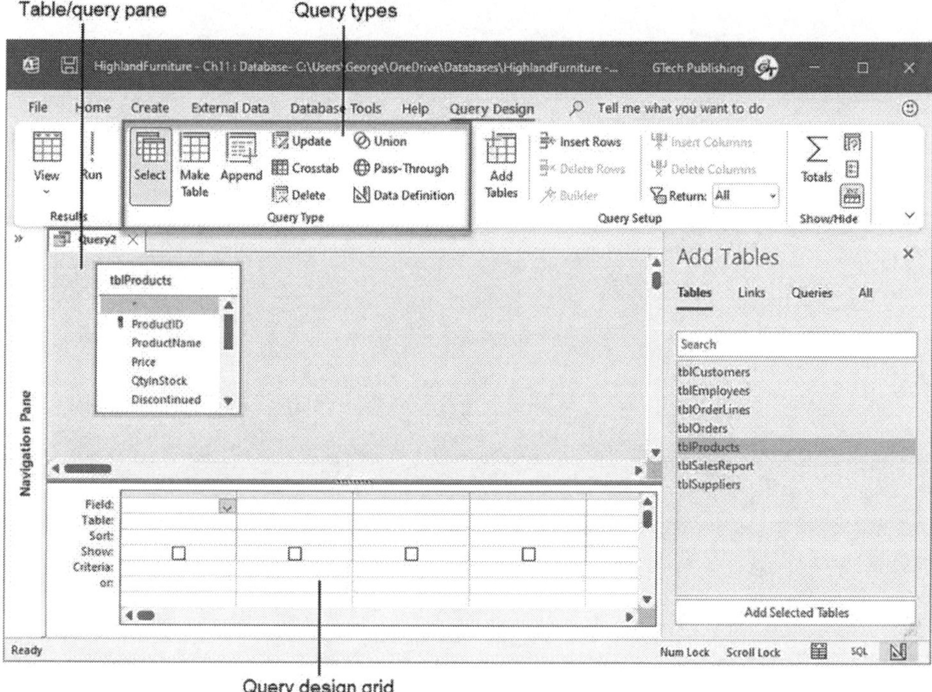

3. In tblProducts, let's say we want to see the **ProductName** and **Price** fields. Double-click ProductName and Price to add them to the query design grid.

Note You can also drag fields from the table/query pane and drop them in specific columns in the query design grid. To change the position of a column in the query design grid, select the column and drag left or right. To select a column, move your mouse pointer over the top part of the column until you see a down-pointing arrow, and then click. To remove a column, select the column and press **Delete** on your keyboard.

---

4. To add criteria to the query, under the Price column, in the **Criteria** row of the query design grid, enter this expression: **>= 1000**. This tells Access to only return records where the price is $1,000 or above.

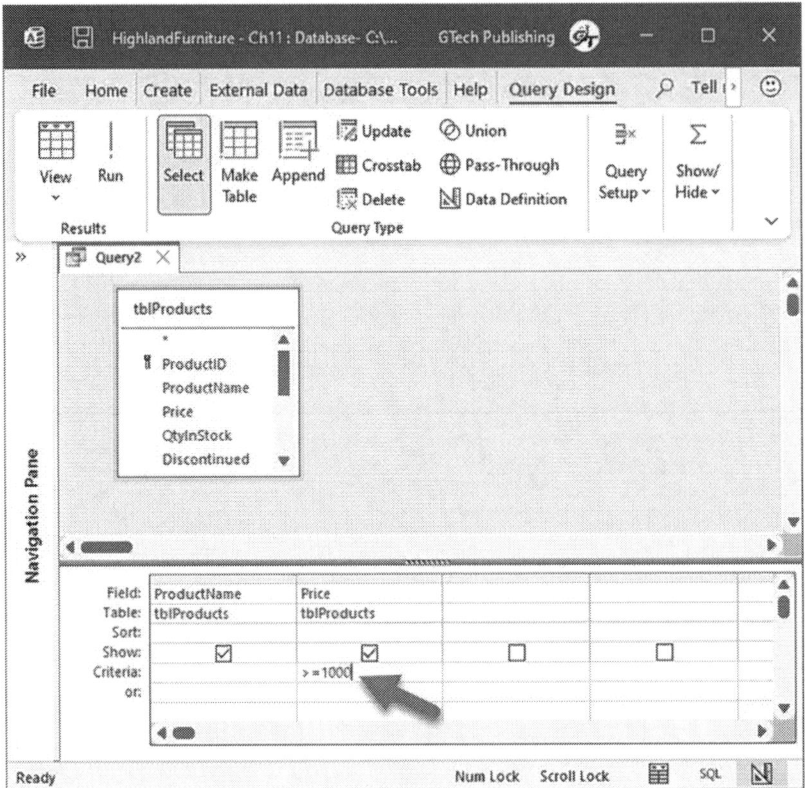

5. On the **Query Design** tab, in the **Results** group, click the **Datasheet View** button. This gives you a preview of the results.

   Access displays the results in a datasheet.

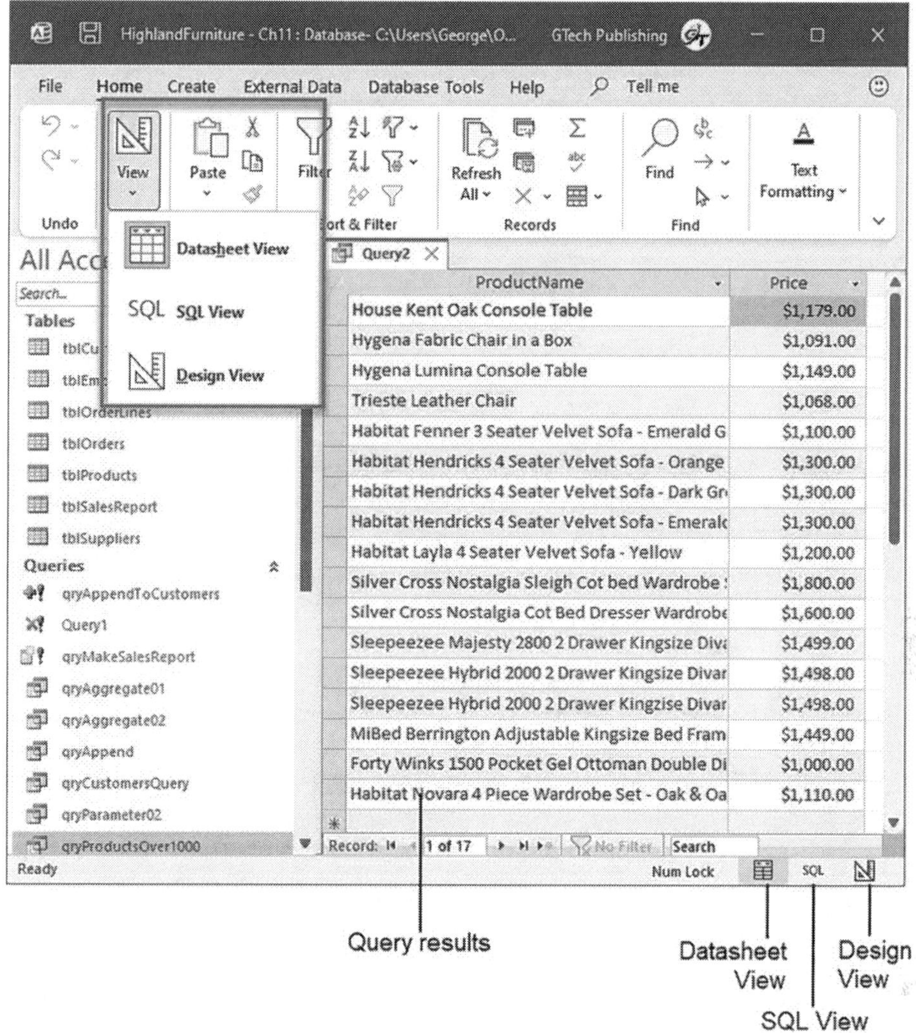

6. To go back to the query design window, click the **Design View** button (on the **Home** tab or the status bar).

7. To save the query, click on the **Save** button on the title bar. In the **Save As** dialog box, enter a meaningful name to give you an indication of what the query is about, for example, "qryProductsOver1000". Then click OK.

   Access saves the query as a query object in the database, making it available in the Navigation Pane under **Queries**.

Tip You can also use the **Run** command button to execute a select query, but the Datasheet View button is sufficient to view the results of select queries. Ideally, you want to make a habit of using the Datasheet View button to view the result of your queries before executing them. Reserve the Run button for executing action queries that you've already reviewed in Datasheet view (to ensure the query is affecting the correct records before being run).

Tip The drop-down arrow on the Views button allows you to switch between Datasheet view, SQL view, and Design view. You can also use the buttons on the right of the status bar (bottom-right of the window) to switch between views.

Using Multiple Criteria

For example, let's say we want a query that returns customers whose state is "NY," "CA," or "WA."

We can use the **Or** operator to create an expression in the Criteria row for the State column like this:

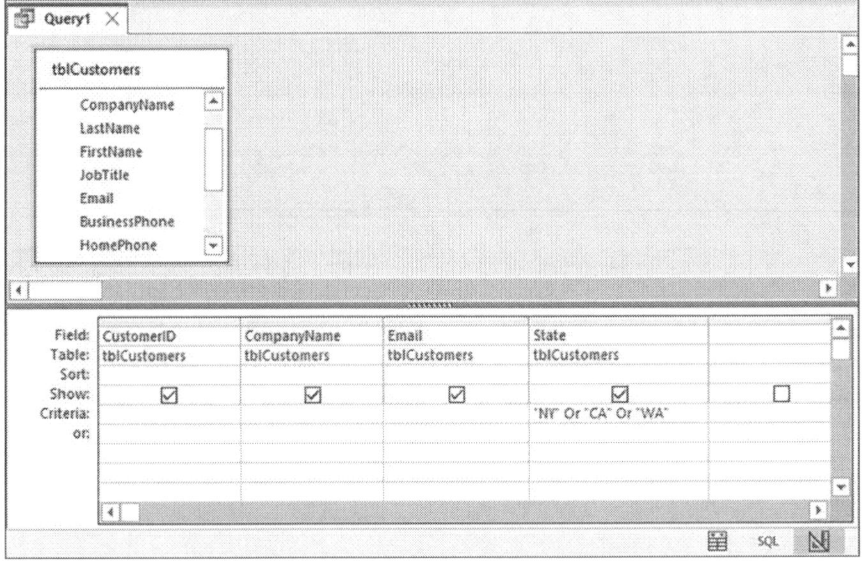

You can also use the **or** row in the query design grid to specify additional criteria like this:

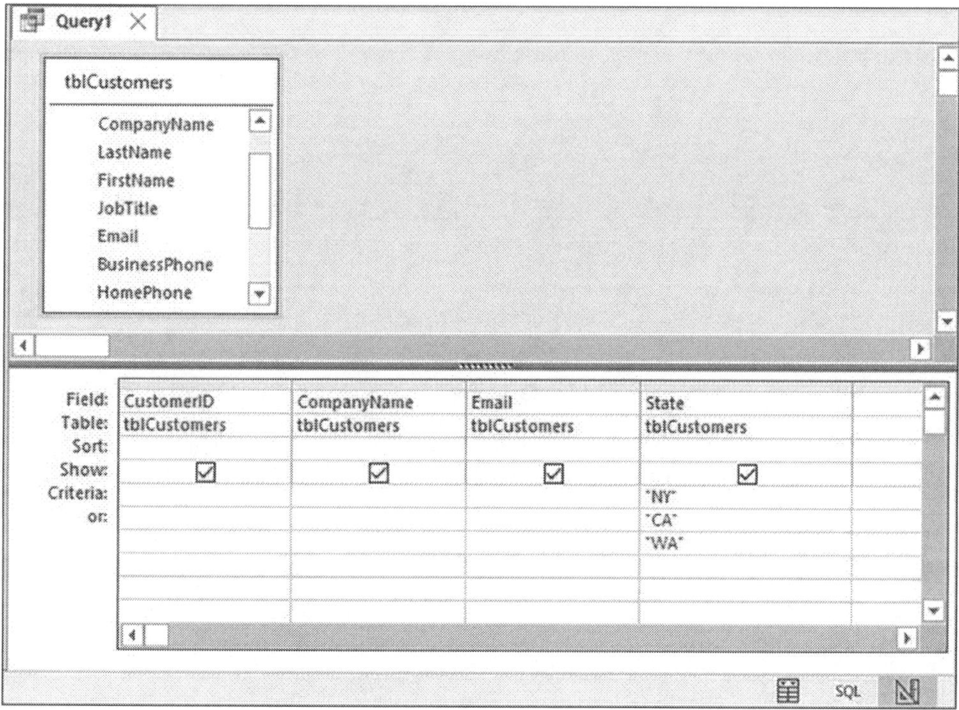

Both methods return the same results:

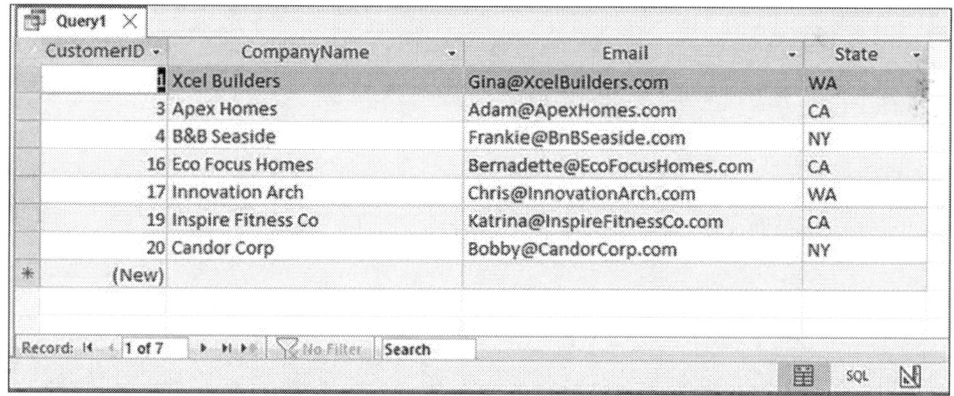

CustomerID	CompanyName	Email	State
1	Xcel Builders	Gina@XcelBuilders.com	WA
3	Apex Homes	Adam@ApexHomes.com	CA
4	B&B Seaside	Frankie@BnBSeaside.com	NY
16	Eco Focus Homes	Bernadette@EcoFocusHomes.com	CA
17	Innovation Arch	Chris@InnovationArch.com	WA
19	Inspire Fitness Co	Katrina@InspireFitnessCo.com	CA
20	Candor Corp	Bobby@CandorCorp.com	NY
(New)			

Record: 1 of 7 No Filter Search

We can also use multiple columns to filter the data. For example, let's say we want to view customers from NY, IL, or NV whose job title is "Purchasing Manager." We'll create a query like this:

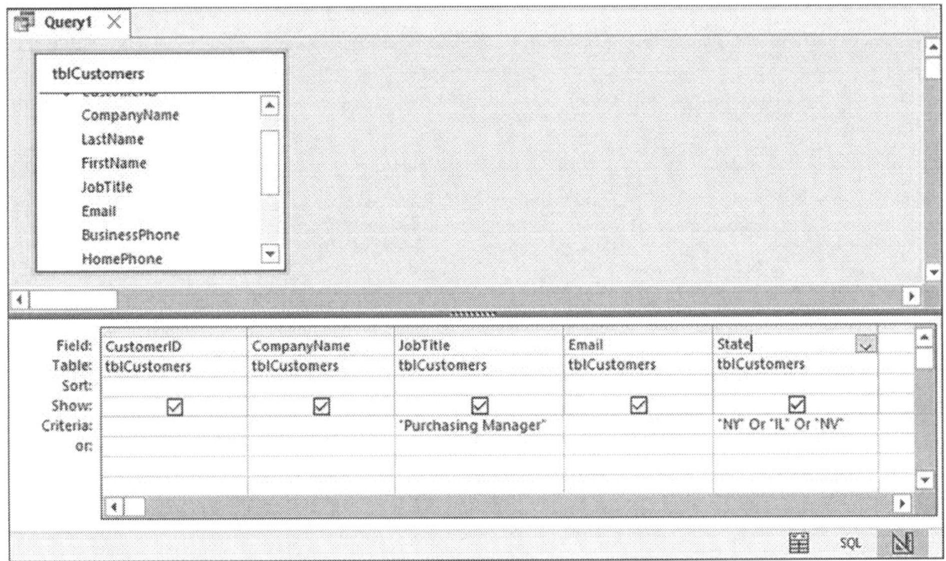

The query will produce these results:

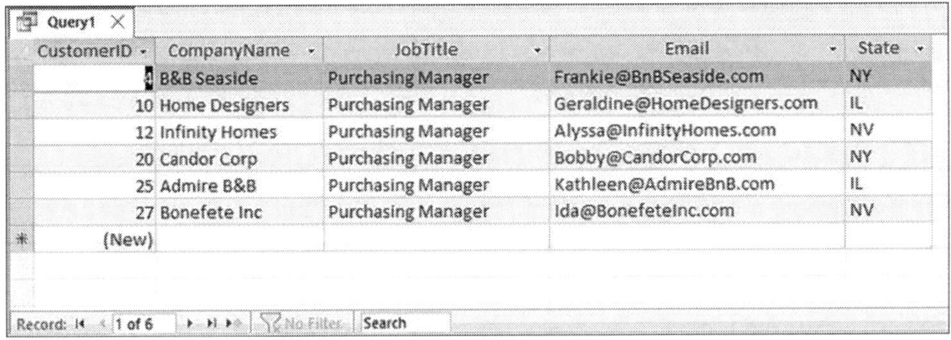

CustomerID	CompanyName	JobTitle	Email	State
4	B&B Seaside	Purchasing Manager	Frankie@BnBSeaside.com	NY
10	Home Designers	Purchasing Manager	Geraldine@HomeDesigners.com	IL
12	Infinity Homes	Purchasing Manager	Alyssa@InfinityHomes.com	NV
20	Candor Corp	Purchasing Manager	Bobby@CandorCorp.com	NY
25	Admire B&B	Purchasing Manager	Kathleen@AdmireBnB.com	IL
27	Bonefete Inc	Purchasing Manager	Ida@BonefeteInc.com	NV
(New)				

Record: 1 of 6 No Filter Search

Select Queries with Multiple Tables

If your database is well structured with entities split into individual tables, then you'll often need to combine different tables to create queries that answer your questions. For example, let's say we want to see a list of employees and the orders they created by date. We would add the Employees and Orders table to the query.

Tip When creating a query involving two or more related tables, Access will use the relationships defined in the Relationships window to establish joins between the tables in the query. Thus, if you have permanent links between tables like primary key/foreign key relationships, always establish them in the Relationships window before creating queries involving those tables.

See the chapter on relationships to learn how to create relationships between tables. If you want to create a temporary relationship just for a query, you can do this in the query design window, and that relationship will apply only to that query object.

Join Types

If the tables being used for a query do not have a defined relationship, you can create joins between the tables in the query design window. Joins are only associated with the query in which they've been created. If you're often creating the same joins in your queries between two tables, then those tables probably need a permanent relationship defined in Relationships. Joins are particularly useful when your query's data sources are other queries.

- **Inner Joins**: An inner join returns records from one table only when it finds matching records in the other table. To create a join, you need two tables that have at least one field with the same datatype and similar values. For example, if we want to see a list of employees and the dates of orders they processed, with an inner join, we'll only see a list of employees that have a matching order. Most joins you'll create will be inner joins. However, there are occasions when you need outer joins to answer your questions.

- **Outer Joins:** In contrast to inner joins, outer joins return all the data from one data source and some of the data from another data source. For instance, if you want to see which products are not selling, you create a query that shows all the products from the product table and any records with matching Product IDs in the Order Lines table. Products that have no orders will have no values in fields from the Order Lines table.

In summary, inner joins let you know when something has happened, while outer joins let you know when something hasn't happened.

Creating a Select Query with Two Or More Tables

To create a query with multiple tables, do the following:

1. Open the database. On the **Create** tab, in the **Queries** group, click **Query Design**.

2. Add the tables/queries you need as data sources to the table/query pane.

   The data sources could be tables or saved queries. For example, if you've already created a query to find all the orders for a given month, you can use that query and the Employees table to show all the orders employees created for that month.

3. Create joins between related data sources. To add a join between data sources where a relationship hasn't been defined, click the field in one table or query and drag it to a corresponding field in the other table or query. Access will create an inner join by default.

   To view the join properties, right-click the line between the tables and select **Join Properties** from the pop-up menu.

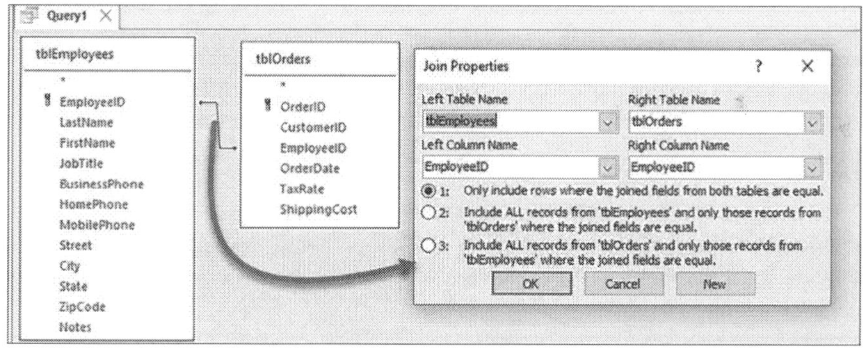

Note If you already have an existing relationship between the data sources added to the query design window, that relationship will be applied to the query. Thus, you won't need to create a join in the query.

---

4. Add the fields you want to display to the query design grid.

5. Run the query.

The results will show data items from the two tables.

Query1

FirstName	LastName	OrderDate
Jasmine	Barker	01/02/2021
Jasmine	Barker	01/07/2021
Jasmine	Barker	01/07/2021
Jasmine	Barker	05/07/2021
Jasmine	Barker	06/07/2021
Jasmine	Barker	15/07/2021
Stephanie	Vega	01/07/2021
Stephanie	Vega	01/07/2021
Stephanie	Vega	03/07/2021
Stephanie	Vega	15/07/2021
Forrest	Dixon	30/04/2021
Forrest	Dixon	03/07/2021
Forrest	Dixon	01/07/2021
Forrest	Dixon	05/07/2021
Gustavo	Morgan	01/07/2021
Gustavo	Morgan	30/06/2021
Gustavo	Morgan	02/07/2021
Gustavo	Morgan	31/07/2021
Gustavo	Morgan	21/07/2021
Ellen	Wheeler	06/07/2021

Record: 1 of 20 No Filter Search

Aggregate Queries

Often, when we run queries, we want to summarize or group the data using one of the fields to get an aggregate value.

For example, how many orders were placed per month in the last year? What are the top 10 selling products? Which salesperson made the most sales last year?

In this section, we'll discuss the **Total** row in the query design grid, which allows you to summarize data in an Access query. The Total row enables you to group data as well as calculate aggregates using different aggregate functions.

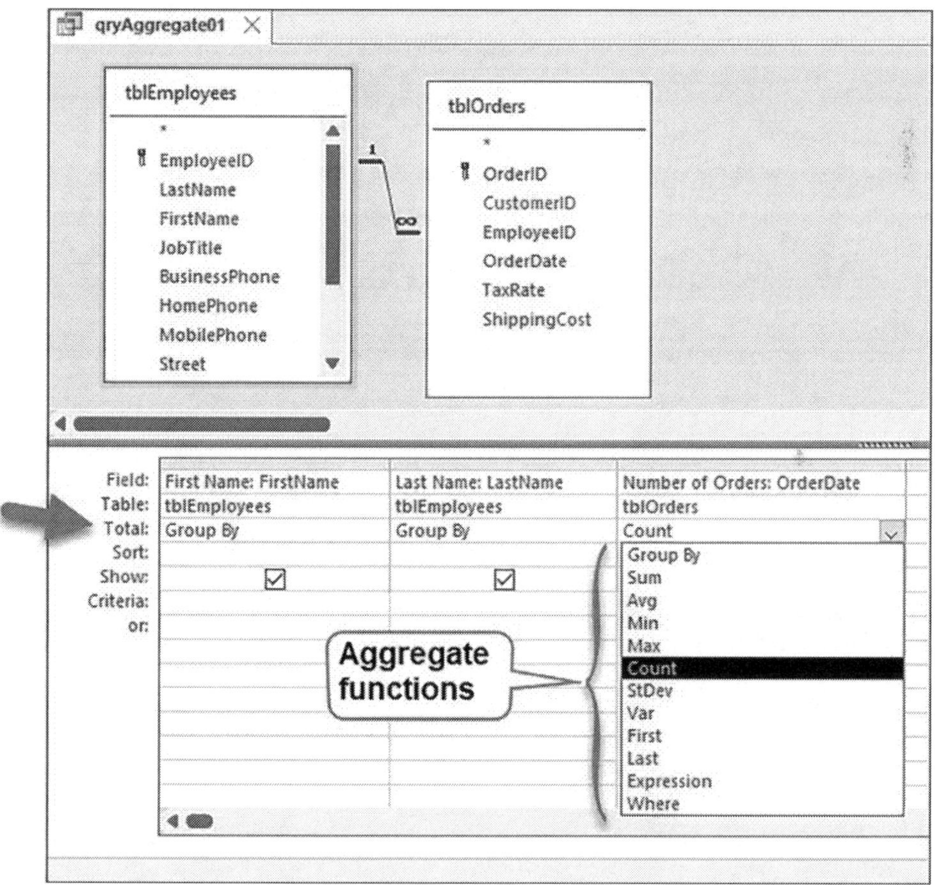

Aggregate Functions

The table below describes the aggregate functions available in the Totals row:

Function	Description
Group By	Groups the records by the values in the field.
Sum	Sums the values of a field or group if the data is grouped.
Avg	Calculates the average of a field or a group if the data is grouped using another field.
Min	Identifies the lowest value in a field or group.
Max	Identifies the highest value in a field or group.
Count	Returns the count of the values in a field or group.
StDev	Calculates the standard deviation of the values in a field or group.
Var	Calculates the variance of the values in a field or group.
First	Displays the first record in the field (or each group if the data is grouped by another field).
Last	Displays the last record in a field or each group (if the data is grouped by another field).
Expression	Used for calculated fields. This tells Access the field name is a custom name.
Where	The Where clause is used to specify criteria for the query to filter the records. The field used for this clause is not displayed as part of the query results.

To use these functions with multiple fields in the query design grid, you must first group your records using the **Group By** function. The **Group By** function groups repeating values into one. For example, if we have a query of employees and orders, we can group the records by employee name and count the number of orders processed by each employee.

Normally, you would use **Group By** in text or ID fields and use the other aggregate functions on numeric fields. The items you'll use the most in the Total row are Group By, Sum, and Count.

In the example below, we group the query with employees and orders to count the number of orders for each employee.

To group the data in a query, do the following:

1. Open an existing query (or create a new query) that contains the data you want to summarize in Design view. In our example, we'll be using the query created in the previous example showing employees and the dates of orders they've created.

2. To display the **Total** row in the query design grid, click the **Totals** button in the **Show/Hide** group on the **Query Design** tab.

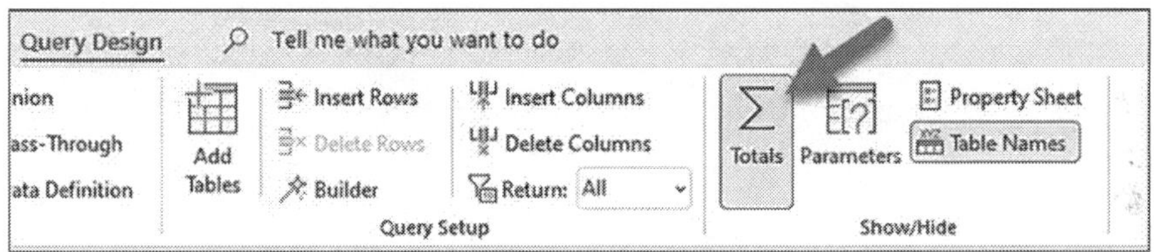

3. Access automatically fills the Total row for every field in the query design grid by default with Group By. Leave this default for the fields you want to group. In our example, it would be FirstName and LastName.

4. In the Total row for the field that you want to calculate, select the function you want to use. This field would usually have non-repeating values. In our example, we want to display the number of orders per employee. Hence, we can use the OrderDate field and the **Count** function.

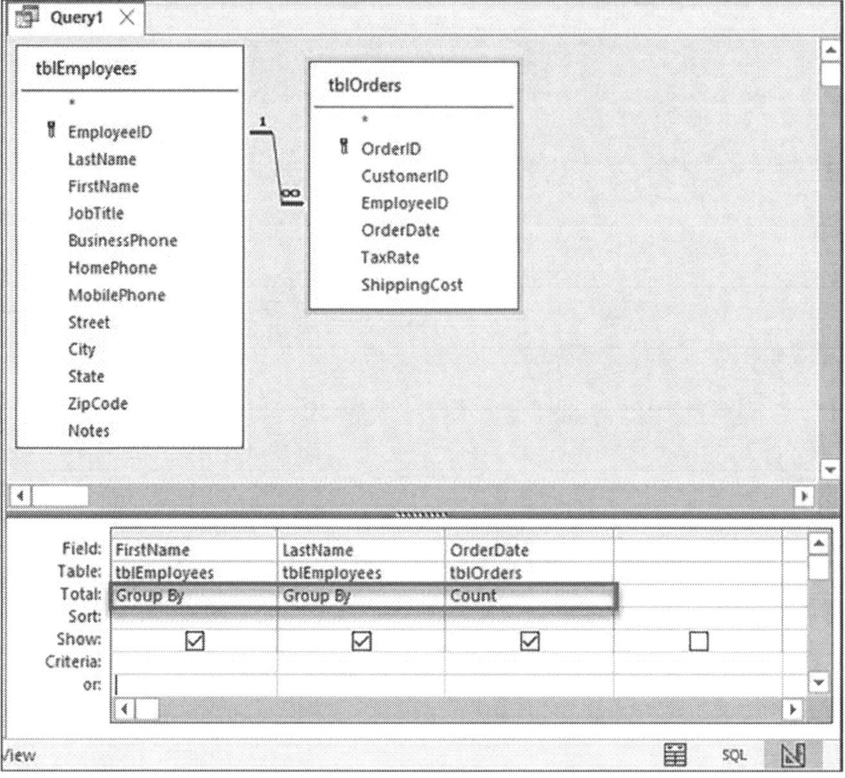

5. Run the query.

   You'll get a result with summarized data like this:

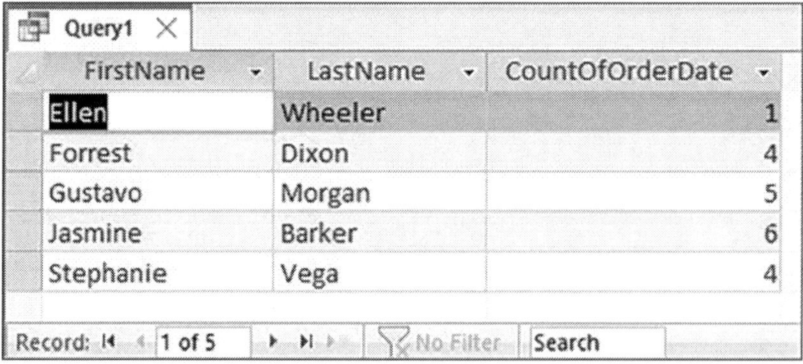

Query1

FirstName	LastName	CountOfOrderDate
Ellen	Wheeler	1
Forrest	Dixon	4
Gustavo	Morgan	5
Jasmine	Barker	6
Stephanie	Vega	4

Record: 1 of 5 No Filter Search

Notice that the names are now grouped, and the OrderDate field (captioned CountOfOrderDate) now displays the count of order dates. This query gives us a quick snapshot of the number of orders each employee has created.

Sorting Fields

You can sort columns in the results in ascending or descending order by using the **Sort** row in the query design grid. For example, to sort the CountOfOrderDate in our result in ascending order, we would select **Ascending** in the **Sort** row under OrderDate.

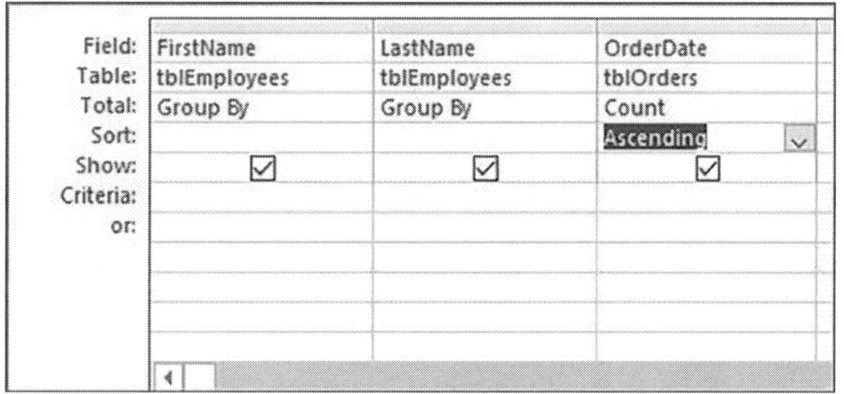

When you run the results, you'll get the records sorted in ascending order. Thus, in our results, we can quickly see that Ellen has created the least number of orders, and Jasmine has the most.

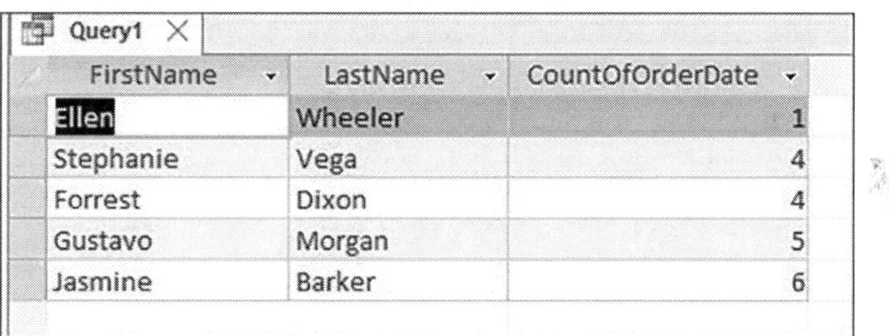

Query1

FirstName	LastName	CountOfOrderDate
Ellen	Wheeler	1
Stephanie	Vega	4
Forrest	Dixon	4
Gustavo	Morgan	5
Jasmine	Barker	6

Using Aliases for Column Names

When you use one of the aggregate functions like Count or Sum, Access automatically changes the caption of the field when you view the data in Datasheet view to something like CountOfOrderDate. In this case, Access is informing you that the values in that column are a count. In some cases, this renaming may be confusing, especially if you want to export the data and distribute these results to other people. Hence, you may want to give the field a more meaningful name. You can give the field an alternate name that is easier to understand in the query results. This is called an alias.

To create an alias, preface the field name with the text you want to see as the field name followed by a colon.

For our example, we will change the **OrderDate** field to **Number of Orders: OrderDate**.

This tells Access that we want the OrderDate field to show as **Number of Orders** (instead of CountOfOrderDate) when our data is grouped and aggregated.

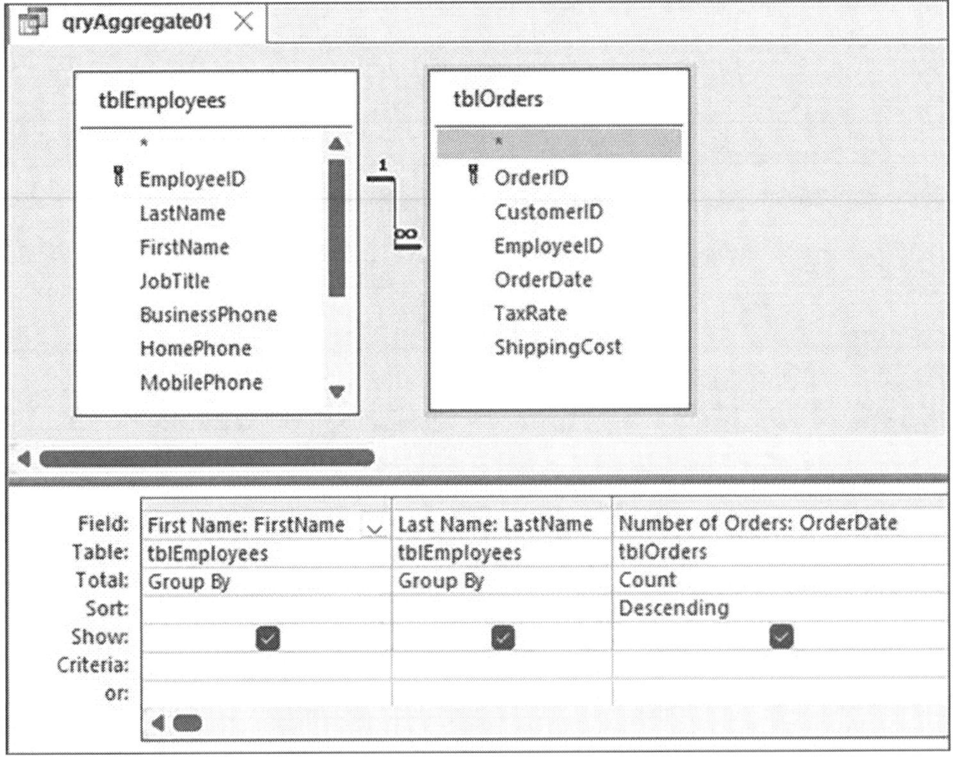

When we run the query, the results will look like this:

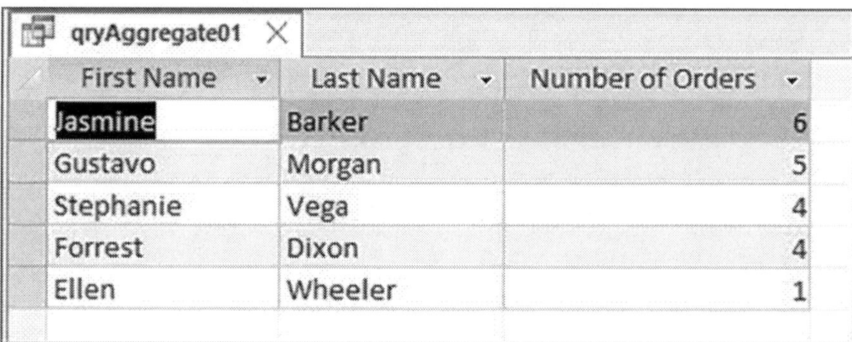

qryAggregate01

First Name	Last Name	Number of Orders
Jasmine	Barker	6
Gustavo	Morgan	5
Stephanie	Vega	4
Forrest	Dixon	4
Ellen	Wheeler	1

Using multiple aggregate functions

You can use multiple aggregate functions in the same query. For instance, we can count the number of products an employee sold as well as the total value of those products.

We can edit the query above and insert the necessary fields. We would need three tables from the Highland Furniture database – tblEmployees, tblOrders, and tblOrderLines. tblOrderLines enables us to add the ProductID and UnitPrice fields to our query.

Note To add additional tables to a query, you can drag the tables from the Navigation Pane unto the query design window or add the tables from the **Add Tables** pane.

Our query with the new fields added from tblOrderLines will look like this:

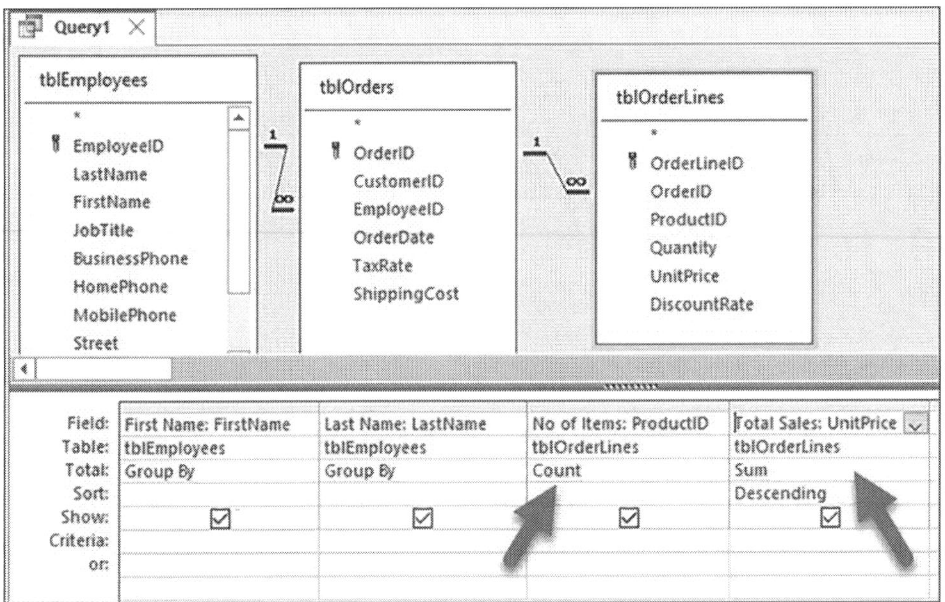

Note the **Count** and **Sum** functions used to aggregate the values for the ProductID and UnitPrice fields, respectively.

Also, notice that you can use a meaningful caption for the column heading by entering the caption you want to see with a colon before the field name.

When we run the query, we get the following results:

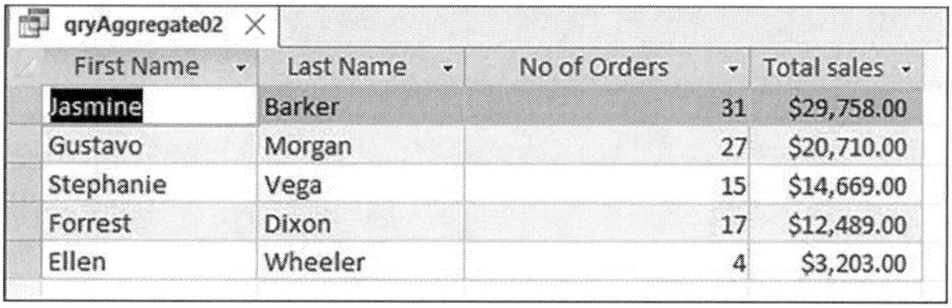

qryAggregate02

First Name	Last Name	No of Orders	Total sales
Jasmine	Barker	31	$29,758.00
Gustavo	Morgan	27	$20,710.00
Stephanie	Vega	15	$14,669.00
Forrest	Dixon	17	$12,489.00
Ellen	Wheeler	4	$3,203.00

We can see from the query that Jasmine has the highest number of sales and Ellen has the lowest.

Using The Query Wizard

The Query Wizard in Access is not recommended for general select queries. However, it is most useful when creating specialized queries like a Crosstab query, Find Duplicates query, and an Unmatched query. These queries are more complex than standard select queries, so it can be useful to have the wizard guide you through the steps of creating these query types.

You can launch the Query Wizard by clicking the **Query Wizard** button, which can be found in the **Queries** group, on the **Create** tab of the Access Ribbon.

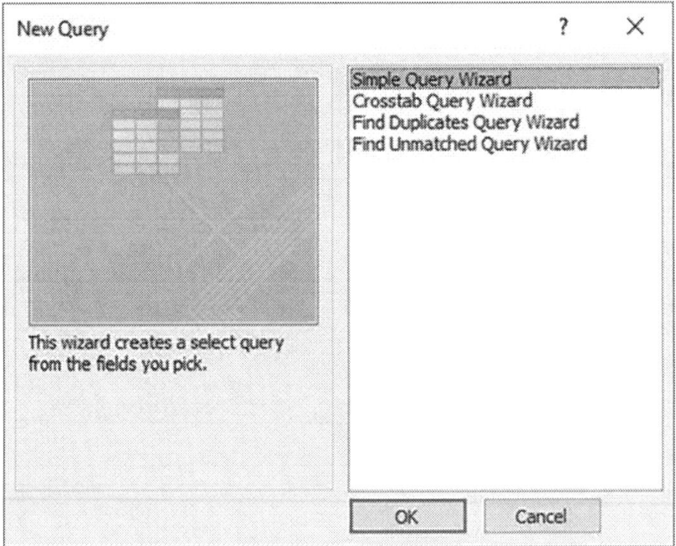

The Query Wizard offers the following options:

- **Simple Query Wizard**: This option helps you create a simple Select query based on the table and fields you've selected. The wizard also enables you to add summary calculations like Sum, Avg, Min, and Max to the query. To add criteria to your query, you'll need to edit the query in the query design window after the wizard has created it. Unless you're creating the most basic Select query, you should use the Query Design command to create your Select queries from scratch. The query design window gives you more flexibility in specifying criteria.

- **Crosstab Query Wizard**: A crosstab query summarizes large data sets for analysis, similar to spreadsheet pivot tables. If you're not familiar with creating crosstab queries in Access, then the wizard will guide you through the steps in creating one.

- **Find Duplicates Query Wizard**: As the name suggests, this query type will help you identify duplicate records in a table. Find Duplicates is a type of select query, so no change action is performed against the database. After the query finds the duplicates, you can determine if they are genuinely redundant and need to be removed.

- **Find Unmatched Query Wizard**: Occasionally, you may want to compare two tables and identify records in one of the tables without corresponding records in the other table. The easiest way to do this is to use the Find Unmatched Query Wizard. After the wizard creates the query, you can edit the query's design to add or remove fields or edit the joins between the two tables to specify the fields you want to match.

  One application for this type of query is tidying records in related tables. For example, if you don't enable Referential Integrity in a relationship between two tables, it's possible to insert records in the child table without matching records in the parent table. The Find Unmatched Query Wizard can enable you to find and remove such records from the database when required.

Operators and Expressions

A calculated field in a query combines values from other fields in the data source to perform calculations. It is often a good idea to create any calculated field in the query used to power a report rather than on the report itself. The calculations you will create in Access will often involve using standard operators and built-in functions in Access. In this section, we'll cover the most common operators used in expressions in Access queries.

Operators in Access

You can create expressions with simple arithmetic operators like addition and multiplication or built-in functions like IIf, Mid, and Datediff. You'll find an Access equivalent for most functions you can use in Excel.

Arithmetic Operators

Use arithmetic operators to calculate a value from two or more numbers or to change the sign of a number from positive to negative or vice versa.

Operator	Purpose	Example
+ (plus sign)	Addition	[UnitPrice]+[DiscountRate]
– (minus sign)	Subtraction	[UnitPrice] – ([UnitPrice] * [DiscountRate])
* (asterisk)	Multiplication	[Quantity] * [UnitPrice]
/ (forward slash)	Division	[Total]/[ItemCount]
\ (back slash)	Integer division	102 \ 7 = 14
^ (caret)	Exponentiation	Number ^ Exponent
Mod	Modulo	10 Mod 4 = 2

Comparison Operators

Comparison operators allow you to compare two values and produce a logical result that is either True, False, or Null.

Operator	Purpose
=	Equal to
>	Greater than
<	Less than
>=	Greater than or equal to
<=	Less than or equal to
<>	Not equal to

Note If either the first or second value is null, then the result will be null. The result of any comparison with a null value is unknown because null represents an unknown value.

Logical Operators

Logical operators, also known as Boolean operators, combine two Boolean values and return True, False, or Null. Logical operators are usually used with Program Flow functions like the IIf function.

Operator	Purpose	Example
And	Returns TRUE if both expressions are true. Otherwise, it returns FALSE.	[Price] > $100 And [Quantity] > 3
Or	Returns TRUE if any part is true. Otherwise, it returns FALSE.	[Price] > $100 Or [Quantity] > 3
Not	Performs a logical negation on an expression. That is, it reverses true and false. For example, 'Not A=B' returns TRUE if A=B is false and returns FALSE if A=B is true.	Not [Quantity] = 0

Note There are other logical operators in Access, but these three are the ones you're most likely to ever use.

Concatenation Operators

Use concatenation operators to combine two text values (or strings) into one.

Operator	Purpose	Example
&	Combines two strings into one.	[LastName] & ", " & [FirstName]
+	Combines two strings into one. However, unlike the ampersand, if one of the operands is null, then the entire expression evaluates to null.	[FirstName] + " " + [LastName]

Tip Always use the & (ampersand) operator for string concatenations. The & operator will always return a string when you concatenate two values. Conversely, the + (plus) operator might cause unexpected results in some situations (for instance, where one of the operands is null).

Special Operators

The following operators are like Boolean operators as they return True or False depending on the result of the evaluation.

Operator	Purpose	Example
Is Null or Is Not Null	Used to determine if a value is Null or Not Null.	Field1 Is Not Null
Like	Used to match string values when used with wildcard operators (?) and (*).	Field1 Like "Habitat*"
Between val1 And val2	Used to determine whether a numeric value is found within the given range.	Field1 Between 1 And 100 Or Field1 Between #01-01-22# And #12-31-22#
In(val1,val2...)	Used to determine whether a value is found within the given set of values.	Field1 In ("apple","pear","peach") Or Field1 In (6,25,46,51)

Built-in Functions in Access

The expressions you build may occasionally require text, date, SQL aggregate, or program flow functions to achieve the desired outcome. You can find the full list of built-in functions and descriptions of their arguments in the Expression Builder in Access.

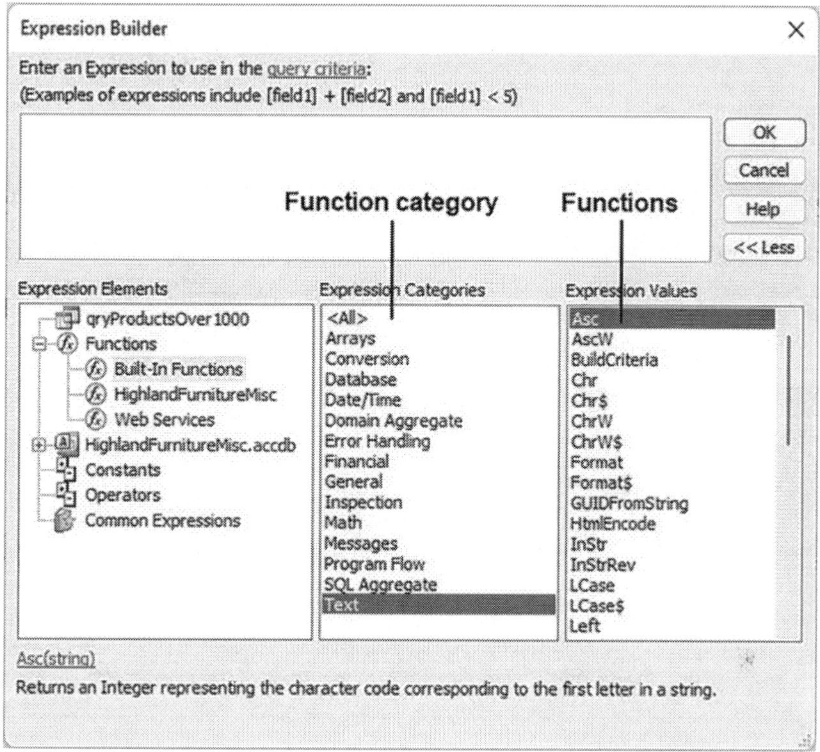

Using Expressions in a Query

Let's say we want to display a list of products purchased in the Highland Furniture database. We want to show the line total for each line item (this will take account of the quantity sold, price, and any discount applied).

To build this query, we would need to add three tables to the query:

- tblOrders
- tblOrderLines
- tblProducts

From the three tables above, we'll add the fields we want to display in our query in the query design grid as described in previous sections.

Where things get interesting is in creating the custom field that calculates the line total. Here we'll use the Expression Builder to create the expression that performs the calculation.

Tip The Expression Builder is a tool in Access you can use to build expressions in tables, queries, forms, and reports. It provides all the elements and references to database objects you need to build your expression in one place, including syntax suggestions and tips. The Expression Elements include the names of fields on the form, built-in functions, operators, constants, and other elements you can use to build your expression. Use the Expression Builder if you need help with the syntax of a function.

Using the Expression Builder

1. To open the **Expression Builder**, right-click the field name where you want to create the expression and select **Build** from the pop-up menu.

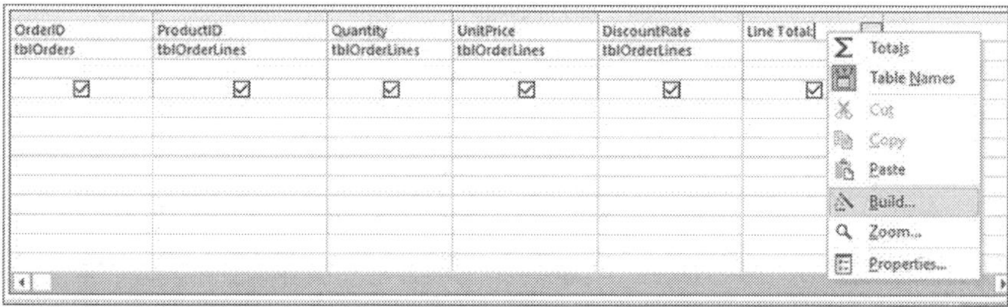

Note Another way to open the Expression Builder is to click the **Builder** command button, which is in the **Query Setup** group, on the **Query Design** tab.

---

2. In the Expression Builder dialog box, navigate to **Built-In Functions** > **Program Flow** > **IIf.**

3. Double-click the IIf function to enter the syntax in the text box for the expression. The Expression Builder provides help for the syntax of the function. Also, at the bottom of the window, there is a link to the Access help page for the selected function.

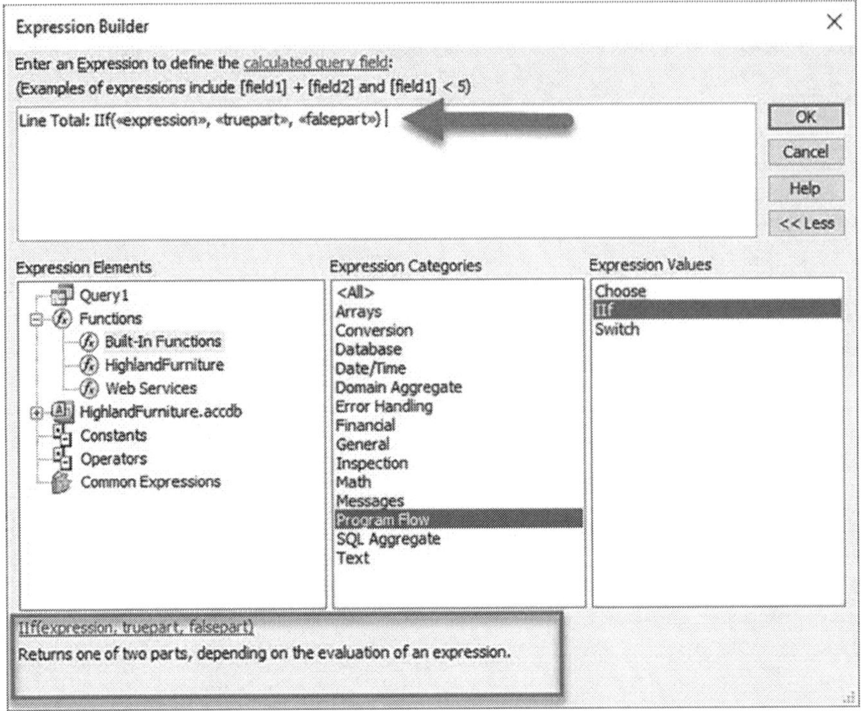

4. We will be using the following conditional expression to calculate the Line Total:

   IIf([DiscountRate]>0,([Quantity]*[UnitPrice])-([Quantity]*[UnitPrice]*[DiscountRate]),[Quantity]*[UnitPrice])

   This expression says:

   If the discount rate is greater than zero, then multiply the quantity by the unit price and then subtract the discount amount. If the discount rate is zero, then only multiply the quantity by the unit price.

   Once entered, the expression should look like this:

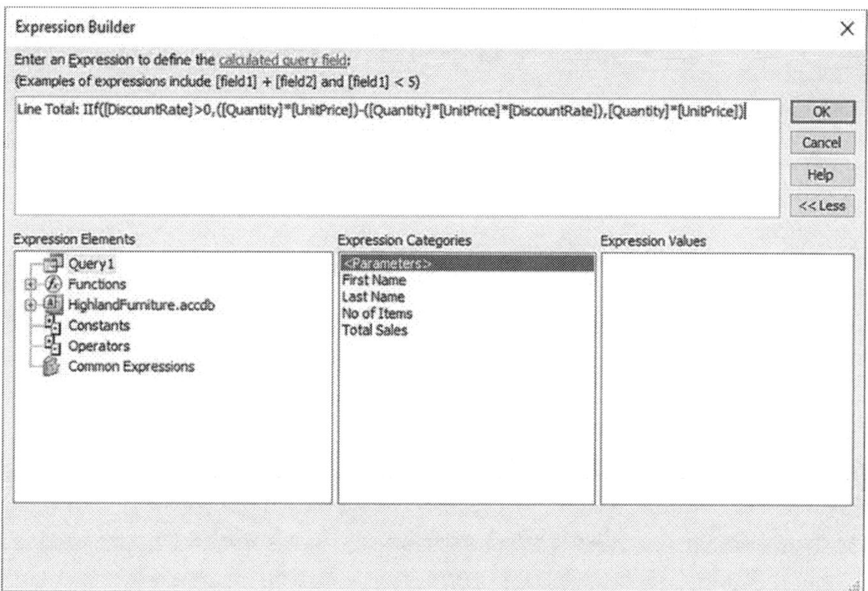

5. Click OK to save the expression in your query and close the Expression Builder.

6. Run the query to view the results. The Line Total field should now display the total for each line item.

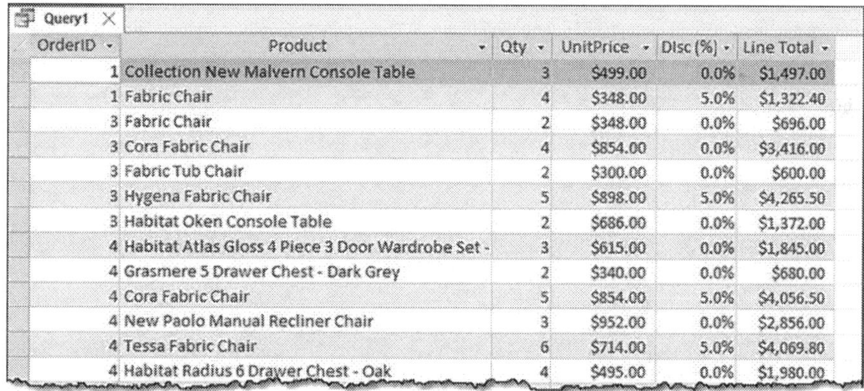

Query1

OrderID	Product	Qty	UnitPrice	Disc (%)	Line Total
1	Collection New Malvern Console Table	3	$499.00	0.0%	$1,497.00
1	Fabric Chair	4	$348.00	5.0%	$1,322.40
3	Fabric Chair	2	$348.00	0.0%	$696.00
3	Cora Fabric Chair	4	$854.00	0.0%	$3,416.00
3	Fabric Tub Chair	2	$300.00	0.0%	$600.00
3	Hygena Fabric Chair	5	$898.00	5.0%	$4,265.50
3	Habitat Oken Console Table	2	$686.00	0.0%	$1,372.00
4	Habitat Atlas Gloss 4 Piece 3 Door Wardrobe Set -	3	$615.00	0.0%	$1,845.00
4	Grasmere 5 Drawer Chest - Dark Grey	2	$340.00	0.0%	$680.00
4	Cora Fabric Chair	5	$854.00	5.0%	$4,056.50
4	New Paolo Manual Recliner Chair	3	$952.00	0.0%	$2,856.00
4	Tessa Fabric Chair	6	$714.00	5.0%	$4,069.80
4	Habitat Radius 6 Drawer Chest - Oak	4	$495.00	0.0%	$1,980.00

Creating a Parameter Query

A parameter query allows you to supply a filter at run-time because the criteria value is not specified as part of the query design. Rather, a parameter query has a placeholder (called a parameter) for the criteria. When you run the query, Access prompts you to enter the criteria. If you frequently run variations of a similar query, instead of creating multiple versions of the query, you can create just one query and use a different filter each time you run it.

Continuing from the previous example where we had a list of order lines, let's say we wanted to view the sales figures filtered by employee name.

To build the new query, we would need to add the Employees table to the existing tables in the table/query pane:

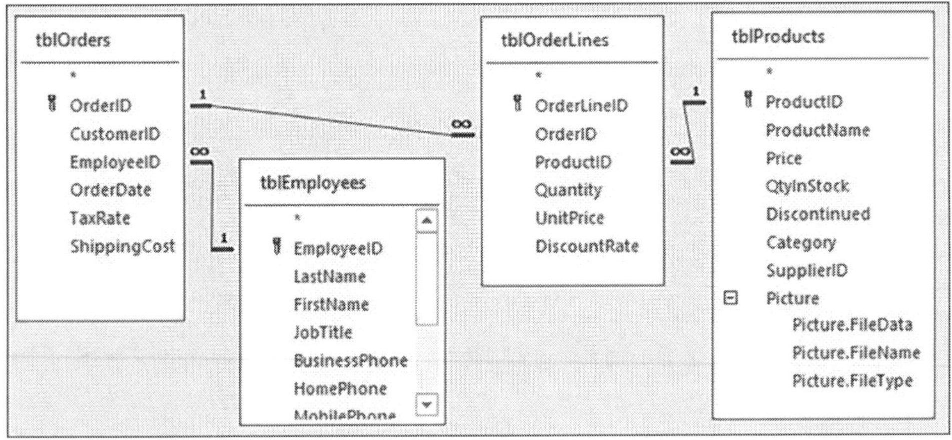

1. To create a single column for the employee's name (FirstName and LastName), we can use an expression to concatenate both fields into one like this:

   Employee: [FirstName] & " " & [LastName]

   Note See previous sections in this chapter for how to create expressions and field aliases.

2. To create the parameter, we enter the parameter expression in the **Criteria** row of our newly created Employee field in the query design grid. For example:

```
Like "*" & [Please enter the employee's name] & "*"
```

The **Like** keyword used here with the ampersand (&) and wildcard (*) means the user does not necessarily need to enter the exact name being used for the filter. The parameter allows the user to type in either the first name, surname or just some characters to return a variety of results.

For instance, if the user enters "Dixon," the query returns all names that include Dixon.

If the user enters (*), the query returns all the records.

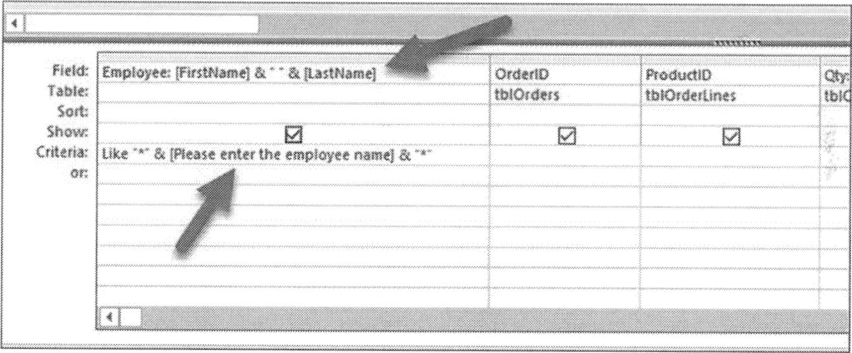

The string *[Please enter the employee's name]* is the parameter prompt. The square brackets tell Access that you want the query to ask for input, and the text enclosed in the brackets is the message the user sees.

3. Run the query and enter the parameter value at the prompt. Then click **OK** (or press ENTER on your keyboard).

Enter Parameter Value ? ×
Please enter the employee name
Forrest
OK Cancel

For our example, when we enter "Forrest" and click OK.

Access displays all records that include Forrest in the Employee field, as shown in the table below.

Query1

OrderID	Product	Qty	UnitPrice	Disc (%)	Line Total
1	Collection New Malvern Console Table	3	$499.00	0.0%	$1,497.00
1	Fabric Chair	4	$348.00	5.0%	$1,322.40
3	Fabric Chair	2	$348.00	0.0%	$696.00
3	Cora Fabric Chair	4	$854.00	0.0%	$3,416.00
3	Fabric Tub Chair	2	$300.00	0.0%	$600.00
3	Hygena Fabric Chair	5	$898.00	5.0%	$4,265.50
3	Habitat Oken Console Table	2	$686.00	0.0%	$1,372.00
4	Habitat Atlas Gloss 4 Piece 3 Door Wardrobe Set -	3	$615.00	0.0%	$1,845.00
4	Grasmere 5 Drawer Chest - Dark Grey	2	$340.00	0.0%	$680.00
4	Cora Fabric Chair	5	$854.00	5.0%	$4,056.50
4	New Paolo Manual Recliner Chair	3	$952.00	0.0%	$2,856.00
4	Tessa Fabric Chair	6	$714.00	5.0%	$4,069.80
4	Habitat Radius 6 Drawer Chest - Oak	4	$495.00	0.0%	$1,980.00

Getting the Criteria from a Form

For a more user-friendly experience, we can go a step further and use a combo box on a form to supply the criteria for a parameter query. In place of the parameter in the previous example, we would enter a reference to the combo box on the form.

The image below shows a simple form that has one combo box called Employee.

The **Employee** combo box has a record source that combines the FirstName and LastName fields from the Employees table (tblEmployees) into one value. We'll use this as the criteria for the Employee field in the query from the previous example.

The View Data button on the form has a macro in its **On Click** property that runs the parameter query (qryParameter02), which takes its criteria from the combo box on the form.

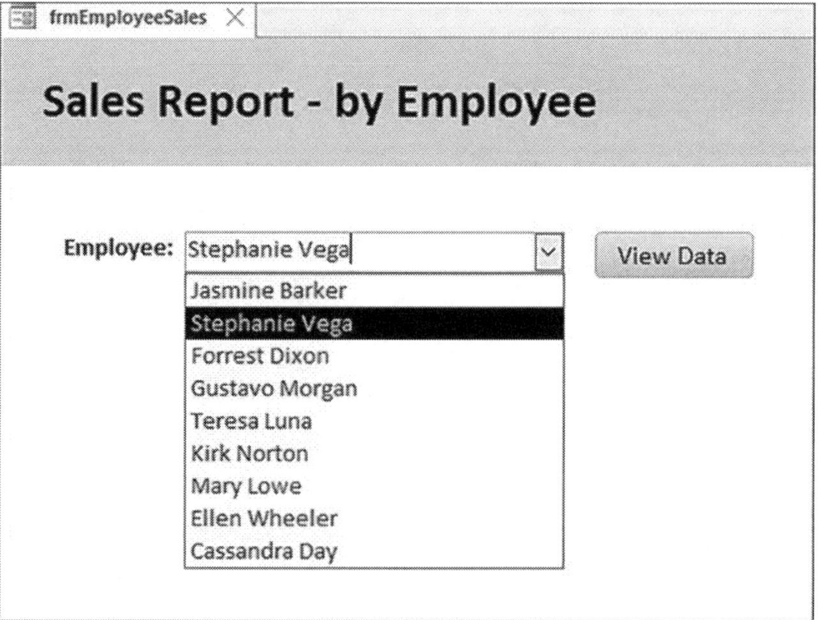

Note

For how to create a combo box on a form, please see **Adding a Combo Box to a Form** in chapter 11.

With the form created, follow the steps below to enter a reference to the combo box on the form as the query's parameter:

1. Open the query in Design view and ensure the form you'll be referencing in the query is open in any view.

2. Click in the **Criteria** row under the Employee field and delete the previous parameter expression.

3. On the **Query Design** tab, in the **Query Setup** group, click the **Builder** command button to open the **Expression Builder**.

4. In the Expression Builder, in the **Expression Elements** list, navigate to the form.

   In our example, this would be:

   HighlandFurniture.accdb > Forms > Loaded Forms > frmEmployeeSales.

5. In the **Expression Categories** list, double-click the name of the combo box to enter its full reference in the Expression Builder box.

   For our example, the following reference is entered in the Expression Builder box:

   [Forms]![frmEmployeeSales]![cboEmployee]

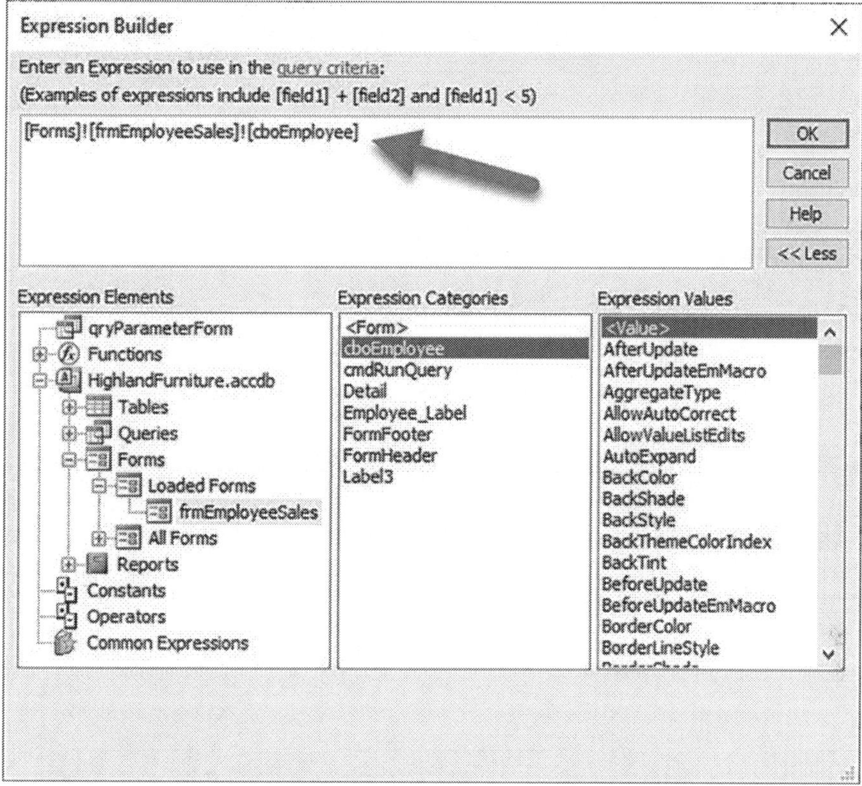

6. Click **OK** to enter the value in the Criteria row of the Employee field.

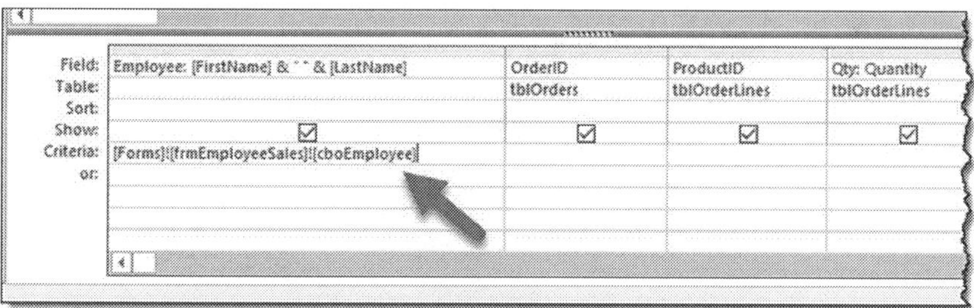

7. Click the **Save** button on the title bar (or press Ctrl+S) to save the query.

8. Close the query.

9. Switch to the form (in Form view) and test your query by selecting a value from the combo box and clicking the View Data button.

This opens the query, showing the records related to the selected employee.

frmEmployeeSales | qryParameter02

Employee	OrderID	Product	Qty	UnitPrice	Disc (%)	Line Total
Stephanie Vega	9	Grasmere 5 Drawer Chest - Dark Grey	1	$340.00	0.0%	$340.00
Stephanie Vega	9	Grasmere 5 Drawer Chest - Dark Grey	3	$340.00	0.0%	$1,020.00
Stephanie Vega	9	Fabric Chair	6	$348.00	5.0%	$1,983.60
Stephanie Vega	9	Habitat Oken Console Table	1	$686.00	0.0%	$686.00
Stephanie Vega	9	Hygena Zander Console Table	1	$847.00	0.0%	$847.00
Stephanie Vega	10	Sleepeezee Majesty 2800 2 Drawer Ki	5	$1,499.00	5.0%	$7,120.25
Stephanie Vega	10	Sleepeezee Hybrid 2000 2 Drawer Kin	5	$1,498.00	5.0%	$7,115.50
Stephanie Vega	12	Sleepeezee Majesty 2800 2 Drawer Ki	5	$1,499.00	5.0%	$7,120.25
Stephanie Vega	12	Sleepeezee Hybrid 2000 2 Drawer Kin	5	$1,498.00	5.0%	$7,115.50
Stephanie Vega	12	New Paolo Manual Recliner Chair	10	$952.00	10.0%	$8,568.00
Stephanie Vega	16	Hygena Lumina Console Table	2	$1,149.00	0.0%	$2,298.00
Stephanie Vega	16	New Paolo Manual Recliner Chair	1	$952.00	0.0%	$952.00
Stephanie Vega	16	Verona 1 Shelf Telephone Table	1	$883.00	0.0%	$883.00
Stephanie Vega	16	Trieste Leather Chair	1	$1,068.00	0.0%	$1,068.00
Stephanie Vega	16	Habitat Novara 4 Piece Wardrobe Set	1	$1,110.00	0.0%	$1,110.00
*	(New)					

Chapter 14: Action Queries

As mentioned earlier, in addition to queries that display data, Access provides action queries that transform the data in your tables when run.

Many people tend to export data to Excel for data transformation tasks, but you can perform any data transformation task you can carry out in Excel even better in Access using queries. Access is also better at handling larger datasets. You've probably seen, through the Expression Builder, the array of operators and functions available in Access for building expressions. Pretty much any function you can use in Excel for data transformation is also available in Access.

Think of an action query like a select query where the query returns a set of records based on the fields you've selected, and any criteria set. However, the action query performs some action on those results. The action the query performs will depend on the query type. Action queries cannot be used as data sources for forms and reports as they do not return a dataset.

Important

Action queries will change data in your database permanently, meaning you can't undo the changes with the Undo command on the Ribbon. Therefore, it's always a good idea to back up a production database before running any action queries. If anything goes wrong, you can always restore the data from the backup.

In this chapter, we will cover the following:

- Updating records in a table with an Update query.
- Appending records to a table with an Append query.
- Deleting records from a table with a Delete query.
- Creating a new table based on an existing data source with a Make Table query.

Update Query

An update query does not add any new rows or columns to your table. Rather, it edits/changes data items that are already present. You can review the data to be updated before running the query.

For an update query example, let's say in the Highland Furniture database, we have a supplier that has gone out of business. We want to mark all the products supplied by this supplier as discontinued until we can find another supplier for them (or alternative products). When we deplete the items currently in stock for these products, we will not seek to replenish them because our database will inform us that they are currently discontinued.

To create an update query, do the following:

1. Open the database in which you want to create the query and click the **Create** tab on the **Ribbon**.

2. In the **Queries** group, click the **Query Design** button.

   The query design window opens with the **Add Tables** pane on the right of the window.

3. Click and drag the table you want to update from the **Navigation Pane** onto the table/query pane. Alternatively, you can double-click the table in the **Add Tables** pane to add it to the table/query pane.

4. In the table/query pane, double-click the fields you want to add to the query design grid. These will be the fields you want to update and any fields you'll be using to apply criteria. For our example, this will be the *Discontinued* and *SupplierID* fields.

5. Click the **Query Design** tab on the Ribbon, and in the **Query Type** group, select **Update**.

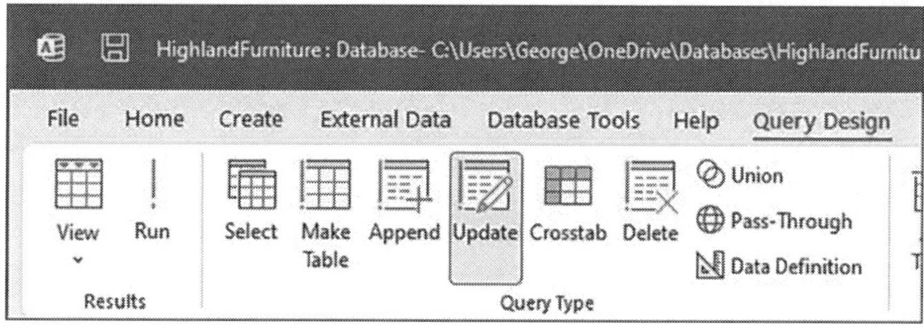

Making it an Update query adds the **Update To** row on the query design grid.

6. In the **Update To** row of the field, you want to update, enter the new value (or expression) to update the field.

7. If you're providing criteria, in the **Criteria** row, enter the criteria value (or expression) under the column you're using to filter the data.

   For our example (see image below), we're updating the **Discontinued** field to **Yes**, and only for records where the **SupplierID** is **14**.

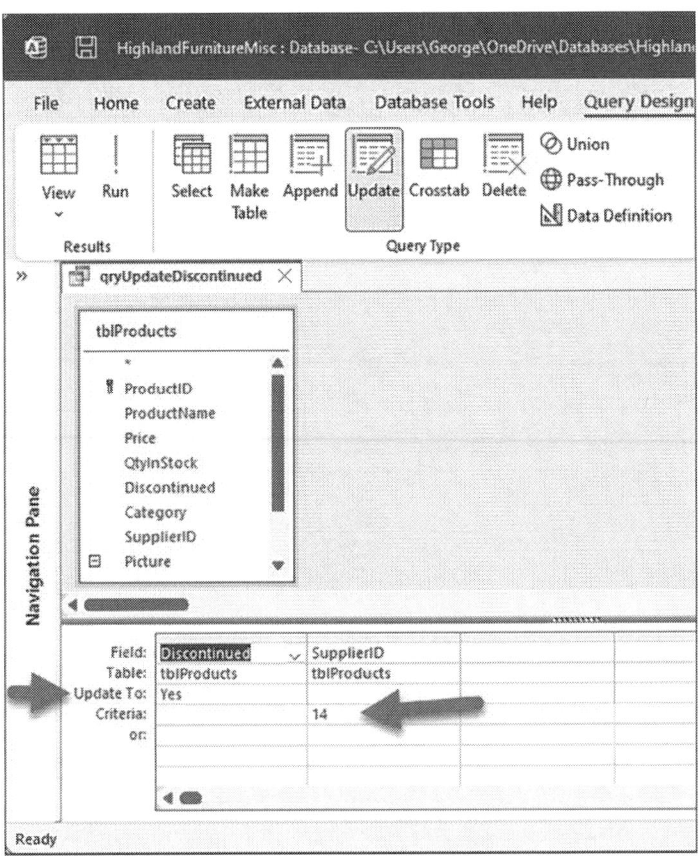

8. **Review the rows that will be affected**. On the Query Design tab, in the Results group, click **View**. In Design view, the View button displays the query in Datasheet view.

   If everything looks good regarding the number of rows being affected, you can then proceed with running the query.

9. **Run the query**. On the Query Design tab, in the Results group, click **Run**.

   Access prompts you to confirm the update. Note the message telling you that you can't Undo the command or reverse the changes once done.

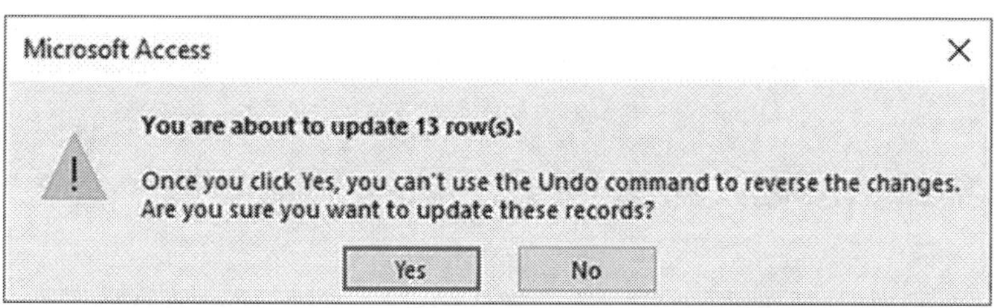

10. Click **Yes** if you're happy to go ahead with the update.

As mentioned earlier, an Update query can't be undone using the Undo command so ensure you back up your data before you run Update queries.

Append Query

You can use an append query to copy records from one data source to another table based on the fields and criteria you've defined in the query. The append query adds the results of your query as new rows to the end of a table. An append query is useful when you want to copy large sets of data from one data source into a table.

For example, if you imported data from Excel or a CSV file that you want to add to a table, you can first import the data into a temporary table and use an append query to transfer the data into the destination table.

An append query is useful for archiving data. When archiving data, you often need to use an append query to copy the data from a production table to the archive table before running a delete query to remove the data from the production table.

Important points to consider regarding append queries:

- An append query may not always append all the records you wanted to append because Access found issues with the data. Hence, when you run an append query, always pay attention to the messages Access displays regarding how many rows are being appended.
- The source and destination fields must be of the same data type. For instance, you cannot append values from a text field to a number field.
- If your destination table uses an AutoNumber field as the primary key, ensure the source data has no primary key field. The primary key values will be automatically generated when the records are added to the destination.

To illustrate an Append query, let's say we have a list of customers in an Excel spreadsheet that we want to add to our Customers table in Access. We'll first import the list into Access as a temporary Access table and then append the values from that table into the Customers table.

To create an Append query, do the following:

1. Open the database with the source and destination tables and click the **Create** tab on the **Ribbon**.

2. In the **Queries** group, click the **Query Design** button.

   The query design window opens with the **Add Tables** pane on the right of the window.

3. Double-click the source table in the **Add Tables** pane to add it to the table/query pane. Alternatively, click and drag the table you want from the **Navigation Pane** onto the table/query pane.

   For our example, the source table is CustomersToAdd.

4. Double-click the field names in the table that you want to add to the destination table. To add all the fields from the source table, double-click the table name in the table/query pane. This selects all the fields in the table. You can then drag and drop them on the query design grid.

5. Click the **Query Design** tab on the Ribbon, and in the **Query Type** group, select **Append**.

   Access displays the **Append** dialog box.

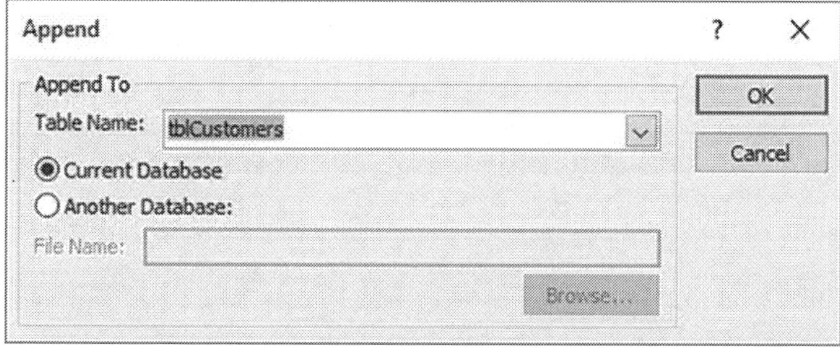

6. Select the destination table from the **Table Name** drop-down list.

7. Ensure **Current Database** is selected (this is the default), and then click **OK** to close the dialog box.

   Access adds the **Append To** row in the query design grid just above the Criteria row.

In the Append To row, Access will pre-populate any field in the destination table that matches a field in the source table.

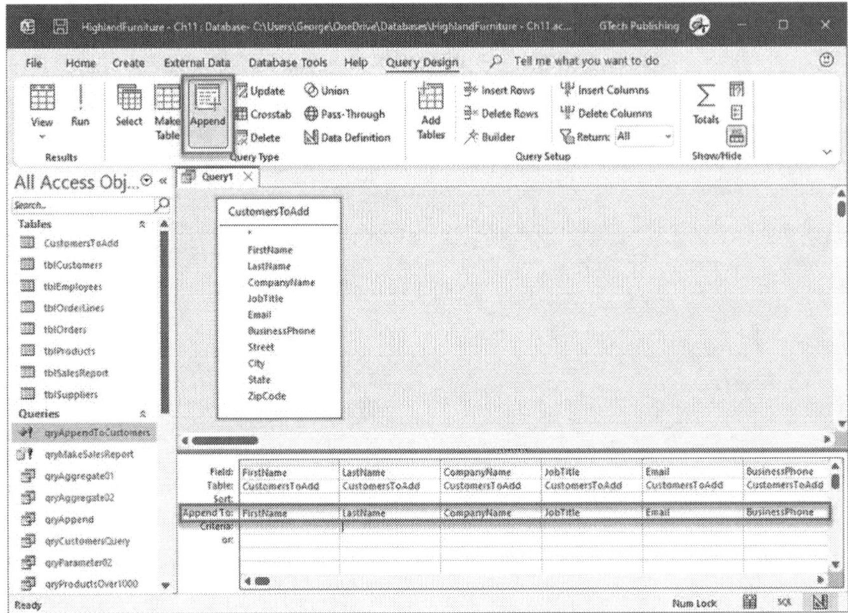

Note For the fields in the source table that have different names from their destination-table counterparts, you need to select the fields manually. You can do this by clicking the **Append To** row in a column with a missing field name and selecting the field name of the destination from the drop-down list.

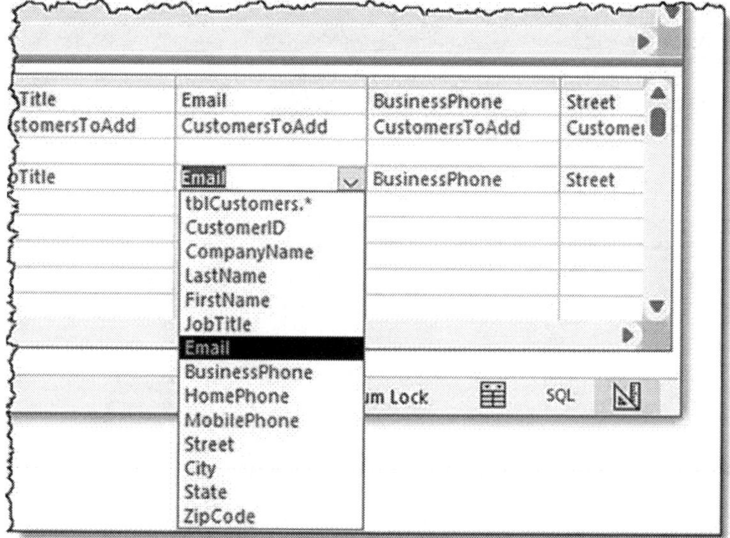

8. You can add criteria to the **Criteria** row in the query design grid if necessary. For example, you may only want to append records from the source that meets some criteria to the destination.

9. In the **Results** group, on the **Query Design** tab, click the **Run** button to run the query.

   Access prompts you to confirm the append action. The message box tells you how many records will be added.

   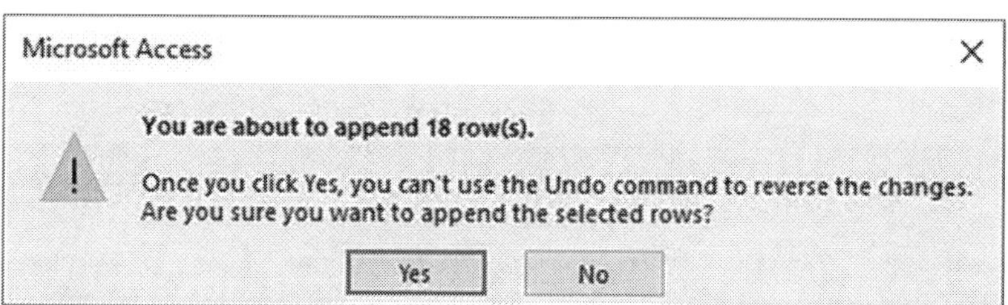

   As the message box points out, you cannot undo the results. Hence you want to ensure you back up your database file (or make a backup copy of the table) before you run an append query.

10. Click **Yes** in the message box to confirm the request and to run the query.

11. To save your append query, click the **Save** button on the title bar (or press **Ctrl+S**). In the **Save As** dialog box, enter the name for the query and click **OK**.

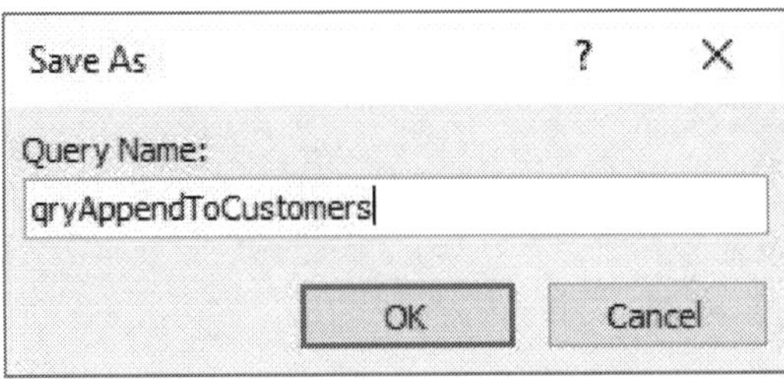

Manually Undoing Appends

If you run an append query by mistake or the data introduced errors, you can remove the unwanted data by doing the following:

- You can delete the appended records manually from the destination table using a delete query that selects the newly added records.
- Revert to a backup table (if you have made one), then fix the problem with the append query and rerun it.

Delete Query

A delete query deletes records from a table based on the criteria you set. Although you can delete records by hand manually, there are occasions it is more efficient to use a delete query. For example, when you have a lot of records to delete, or you need to apply complex criteria to select the records to be deleted, it is best to use a delete query.

Of all the action queries in Access, the delete query is the most dangerous because it can delete all the data in a table in an instant with no Undo option. Thus, you need to take particular care when running delete queries.

Delete queries are often used on tables with transient data. For example, let's say every quarter we need to run a sales report. It may be more efficient to generate that report using queries and store the data in a table which can then be sent to the sales team so they can run their reports and analysis. At the end of each quarter, the data is deleted, and the table is repopulated with new data.

To avoid losing data due to accidental deletions, get in the habit of taking one or more of the following actions:

- Always use the Datasheet View button to review the records you're about to delete before using the Run button to run the query.
- Make a copy of the table before running the query. See **Organizing Access Objects** in **chapter 3** for how to make a copy of an Access table.
- Make a backup of the database before running a delete query.

To illustrate a delete query, let's say we generated a sales report and stored the data in a transient table which was passed to the sales team. However, they've come back saying they wanted a sales report of only the high-end products that are $800 and above. We can either regenerate the data or simply delete all the records in our transient table that are less than $800. Deleting the unwanted records would be the most efficient move here.

To create a delete query, do the following:

1. Open the database with the table for which you want to delete data and click the **Create** tab on the Ribbon.

2. In the **Queries** group, click the **Query Design** button.

   The query design window opens with the **Add Tables** pane on the right of the window.

3. In the **Add Tables** pane, double-click the table you want to run the delete query on.

   For our example, the table is **tblSalesReport**.

4. From the field list of the table, double-click the asterisk (*) to add it to the query design grid. This represents all the fields in the table. You should also add any field(s) you'll be using for your criteria as separate fields.

5. Click the **Query Design** tab on the Ribbon, and in the **Query Type** group, select **Delete**.

   Access adds the **Delete** row to the query design grid just above the Criteria row. Access adds **From** to the Delete row under the field with the asterisk. The **Where** keyword is added under any other added field being used for the criteria.

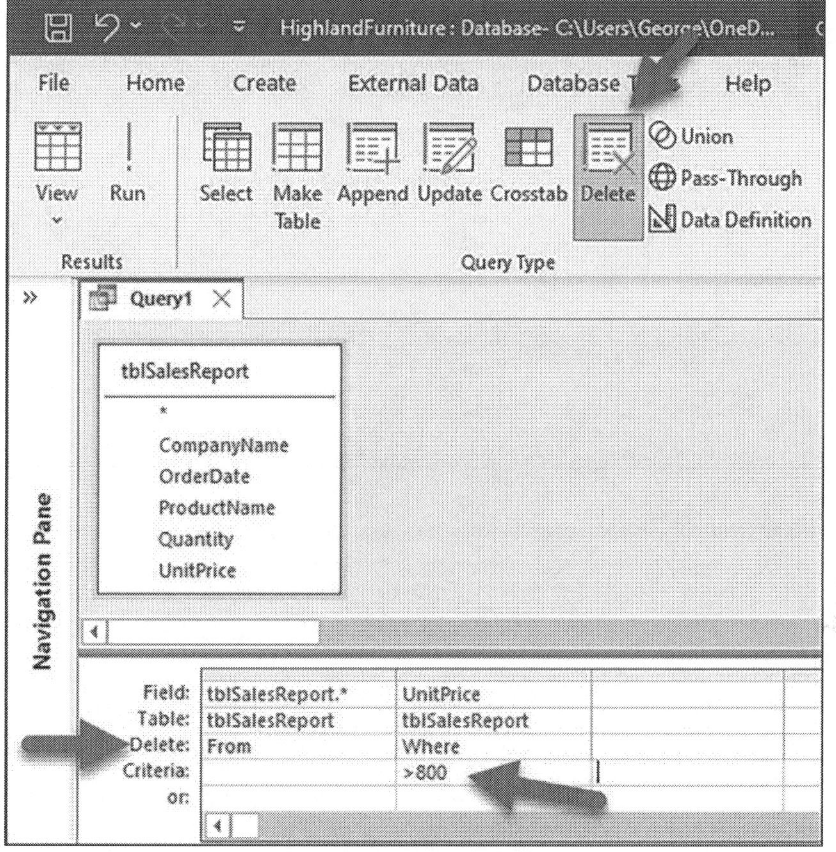

6. **Do one of the following to review the query before running it:**

   - View the rows set to be deleted from the table by clicking the **View** button, in the Results group, on the Query Design tab. The View button displays the query in Datasheet view without executing it.

   - Alternatively, you can change the query back to a select query by clicking **Select** in the Query Type group on the Query Design tab. Then run the query to see which records will be deleted. If everything looks OK, change the query back to a delete query.

7. Click the **Run** button (in the **Results** group, on the **Query Design** tab) to run the query.

   Access will display a message box telling you how many records will be deleted. If you're unsure at this point, you can still cancel the action by clicking **No** in the message box.

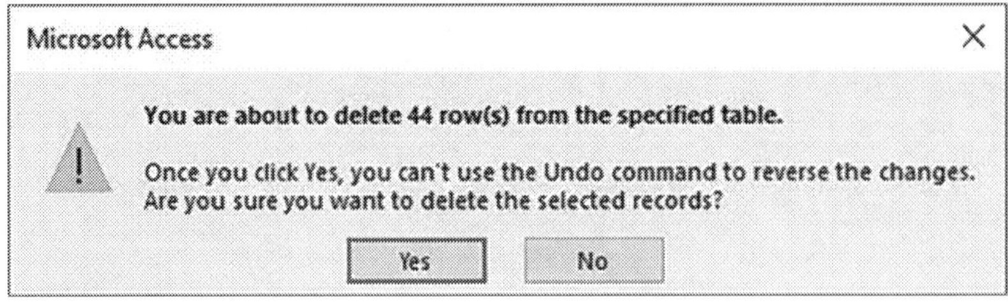

Important As mentioned previously, a Delete query will delete records permanently from the selected table, and there is no way to undo the action with an Undo command. Thus, it is important to make a copy of the table or backup your database file before running a delete query on a production database.

8. Click **Yes** to run the query and delete the records.

9. To save your delete query, click the **Save** button on the title bar (or press **Ctrl+S**). In the **Save As** dialog box, enter the name for the query and click **OK**.

Make Table Query

A make table query creates a new table based on data from existing tables, and it enables you to capture the results of your query in a new table. Make table queries come in handy for data transformation tasks. For example, when you import data from different external sources, you may need to use make table queries in the process of organizing the data.

Make table queries are also used for tables with transient data. For example, let's say every month, the sales team needs historical sales data for analysis and reports. It may be more efficient to generate the data using queries and storing the records in a separate table which can then be sent to the sales team. This means that we don't need to give the sales team direct access to the live data. After creating the table, we could periodically populate this table with new data or refresh the data.

Important

If you specify the name of an existing table for your new table in a make table query, when you run the query, Access will inform you that you're about to overwrite an existing table. If you select **Yes**, Access will delete the existing table and create the new one in its place. Always read the messages from Access carefully before running action queries.

If you unintentionally overwrite an existing table with a make table query, you will not be able to undo the action and recover the old table. Hence, always choose the names for your make table queries carefully, ensuring they do not match any existing tables you don't want to overwrite.

Let's say you've been asked to provide the sales department with a list of customer orders, including the order date line-item details. You can use a make table query to make this information available to the sales team.

To create a make table query, do the following:

1. Create a query with all the tables you need and add the fields to the query design grid.

   The query for our example would need tblCustomers, tblOrders, tblOrderLines, and tblProducts.

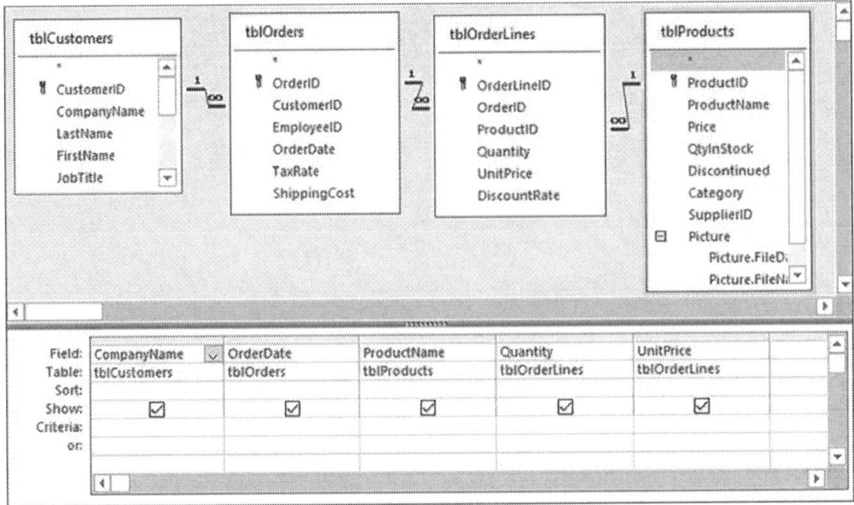

2. Click the **Query Design** tab on the Ribbon, and in the **Query Type** group, click the **Make Table** button.

   Access displays the **Make Table** dialog.

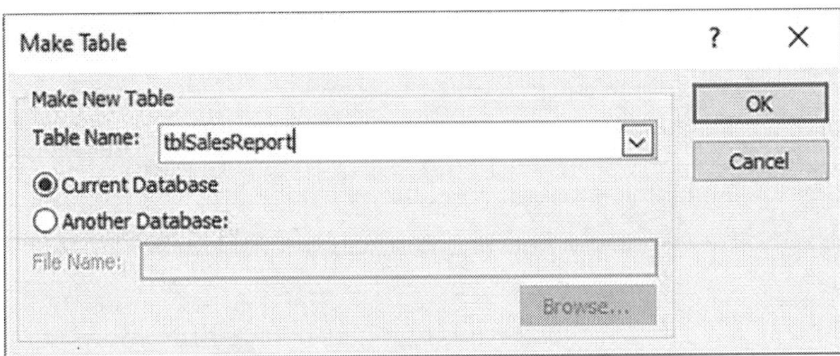

3. In the Table Name field, enter the name of the new table and click **OK** to close the dialog box.

4. Click the **Run** command to run your query.

   If there is an existing table with the same name as the new table, Access will ask you if you want to overwrite it. Pay close attention to the messages at this point to avoid unintentionally overwriting an existing table.

   If you entered a unique name, Access displays a message with the number of rows to be copied into the new table. Pay attention to this message. For example, if the number of rows appears to be wrong, you can cancel the action and revise the query before running it again.

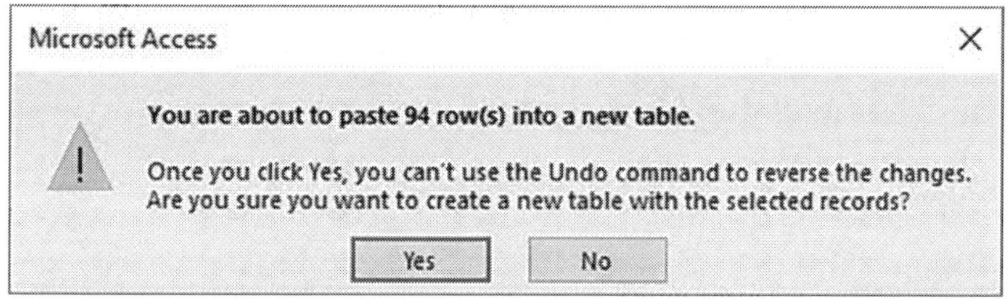

5. Click **Yes** to confirm the action and create your new table.

You'll find the new table in the Tables group in the Navigation Pane.

Chapter 15: Data Transformation in Access

When working with lots of data from different data sources, you may often receive data that needs to be cleaned up before it can be used in a production environment. Data transformation tasks could include removing duplicates, removing blanks, removing unwanted spaces, cleaning up text, standardizing data types, and restructuring the data.

Before you can add imported data to production tables or use them for any kind of meaningful analysis, it is important to review and clean up the data if necessary. This chapter will cover some of the data transformation tasks you are most likely to encounter when working with data in Access.

In this chapter, we will be covering the following:

- How to find duplicate records using a query.
- How to remove duplicate data once found.
- Finding and filling in blank fields.
- Splitting one field into two or more fields.
- Concatenating text items.
- Changing the case of text values.
- Removing leading and trailing spaces from text.
- Finding and replacing text.

Finding duplicate records

One of the common data clean-up tasks is finding and removing duplicate records. Duplicate records will introduce discrepancies in any analysis performed with the data. Access has a simple wizard that enables you to quickly identify duplicate records in a dataset.

To identify duplicate records in a table, follow the steps below:

1. Open the database that contains the table in which you want to identify duplicate records and select the table in the Navigation Pane.

2. On the Ribbon, click the **Create** tab, and then in the **Queries** group, click the **Query Wizard** button.

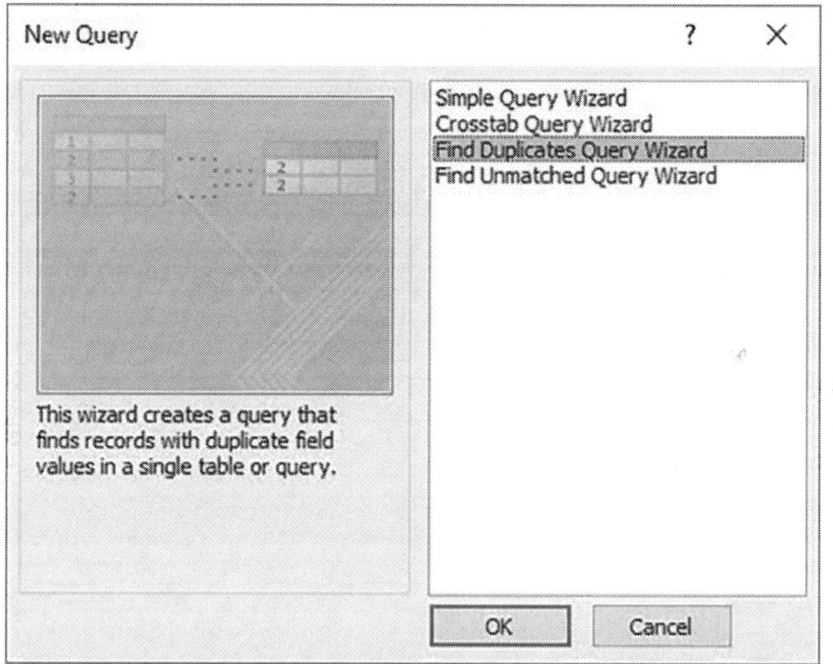

3. In the New Query dialog box, select **Find Duplicates Query Wizard** and then click **OK**.

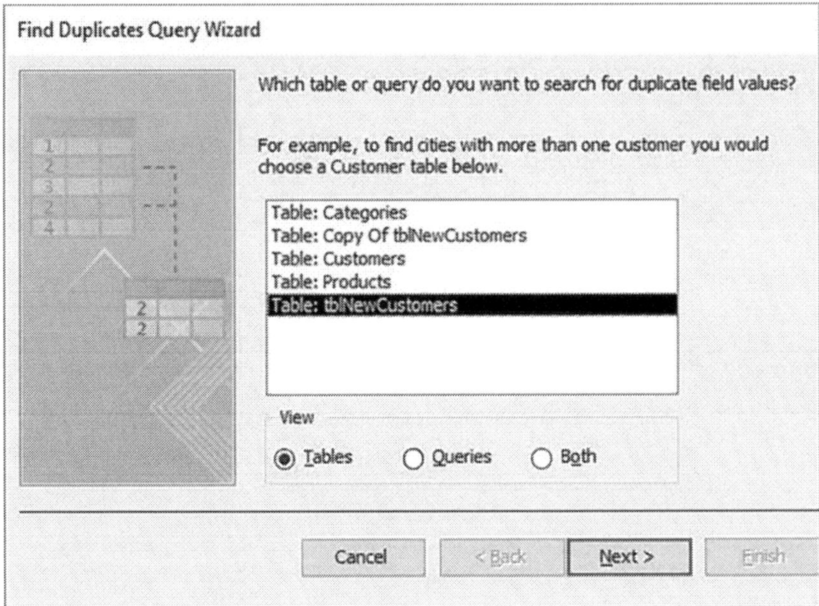

4. In the **Find Duplicates Query Wizard** dialog box, select the data source, and then click **Next**.

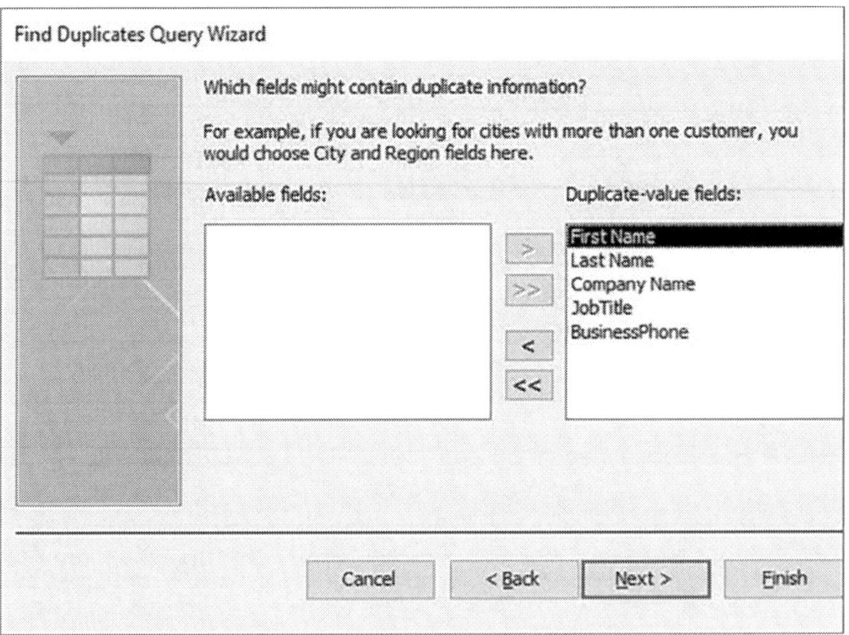

5. Select the fields that best define a unique record in your dataset and add them to the **Duplicate-value fields** box.

Note You may not necessarily need all the fields. For example, in a table with products that are supposed to have unique product numbers, you may only need the product number field to identify any duplicate records.

6. On the last page of the wizard, name your query, and then click **Finish**.

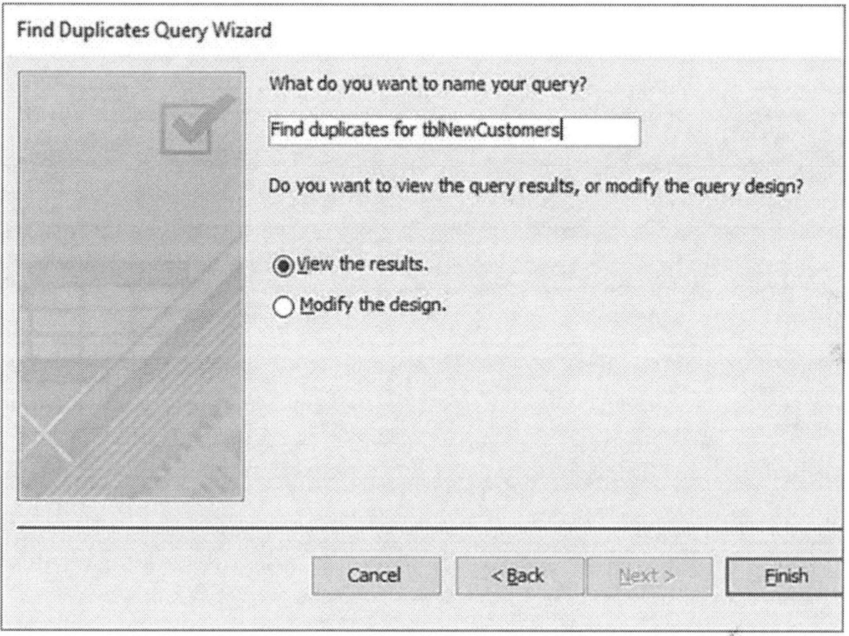

Your Find Duplicates query will open, allowing you to view any duplicate records that have been found.

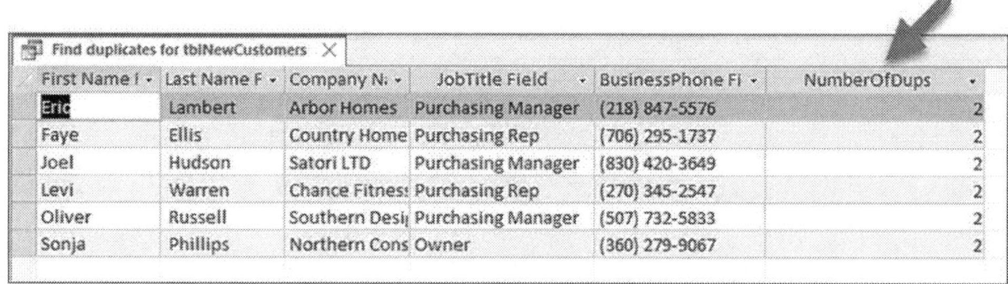
Find duplicates for tblNewCustomers

First Name I	Last Name F	Company N:	JobTitle Field	BusinessPhone Fi	NumberOfDups
Eric	Lambert	Arbor Homes	Purchasing Manager	(218) 847-5576	2
Faye	Ellis	Country Home	Purchasing Rep	(706) 295-1737	2
Joel	Hudson	Satori LTD	Purchasing Manager	(830) 420-3649	2
Levi	Warren	Chance Fitnes:	Purchasing Rep	(270) 345-2547	2
Oliver	Russell	Southern Desi	Purchasing Manager	(507) 732-5833	2
Sonja	Phillips	Northern Cons	Owner	(360) 279-9067	2

Access displays the list of records with duplicates. The last field, named **NumberOfDups**, provides a count of how many instances of a particular record are in the dataset. For example, if NumberOfDups is 2, it means there are two instances of that record in the dataset.

Removing duplicates

Once you've identified duplicates in a dataset, one quick trick to remove the duplicates is to run a Make Table query with unique records.

To remove duplicates from a data set, do the following:

1. Open the database that contains the dataset with the duplicate records.
2. On the Ribbon, select the **Create** tab, and in the **Queries** group, click on **Query Design**.
3. Add the source data to the table/query pane of the query design window.

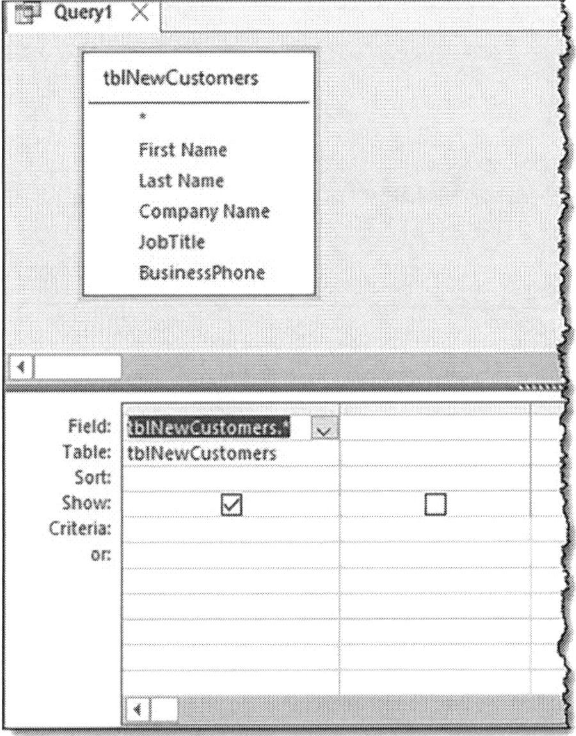

4. Double-click the asterisk in the field list to add it to the query design grid (this adds all the fields to the query).
5. Display the Property Sheet for the query by clicking the **Property Sheet** button in the **Show/Hide** group on the **Query Design** tab.

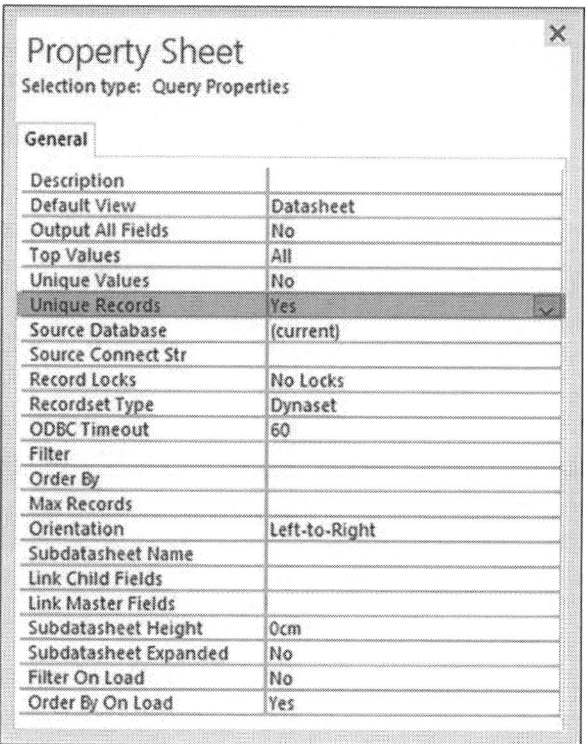

6. In the Property Sheet for the query, change the **Unique Records** property to **Yes**.

7. On the **Query Design** tab, in the **Results** group, click the **View** button to review the results of the query. Access displays the records in a Datasheet view. You will notice that all the duplicates have been removed from the dataset.

8. Click the **View** button again to return to the query design window.

9. On the Query Design tab, in the Query Type group, click the **Make Table** button.

10. In the Make Table dialog box, enter a unique name for the table and click **OK**.

11. On the Query Design tab, in the Results group, click **Run**.

    Access will display a message telling you the number of records it is about to insert into your new table.

12. Click **Yes** to proceed.

A new table with the unique records will be created, and you can access it from the Navigation Pane.

Filling in Blank Fields

Often, you may encounter a dataset with fields that contain empty values, which are known as null values. Nulls are not necessarily bad if they are part of your data design, as you can use null fields to find and filter records. However, you may have situations with an imported dataset where you need to replace null values with an empty string or zero (0).

To fill null fields in your dataset with zeros, do the following:

1. Create an update query and add the field you want to update in the query design grid.

For details on how to create an update query, see chapter 14.

2. Enter the keyword **Is Null** in the Criteria row and enter **0** in the Update To row.

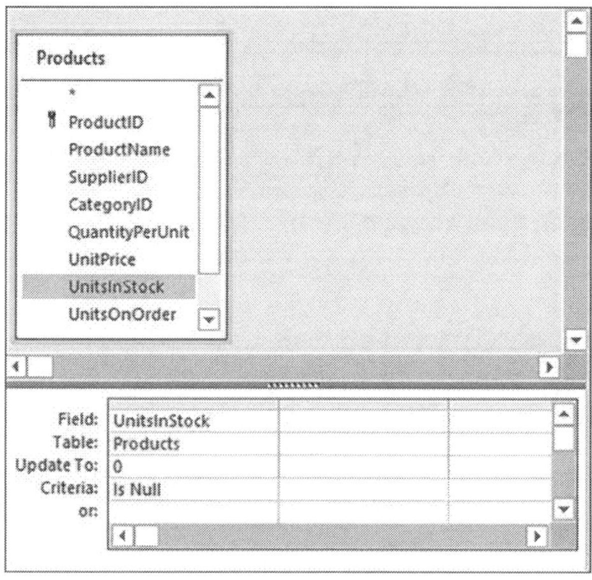

In the example above, we want to find all null values in the **UnitsInStock** field and update them to zero (0).

3. Review your query before you run it.

Splitting Fields

The need to split a value into two or more parts is one of the tasks you will often encounter when transforming data in Access. A common example is splitting a full name field into first name and surname fields. Just like Excel, there are several functions in Access you can use to manipulate and restructure strings.

Tip To see the full list of the functions you can use to manipulate strings in Access queries, open the **Expression Builder** and navigate to **Built-In Functions** > **Text**.

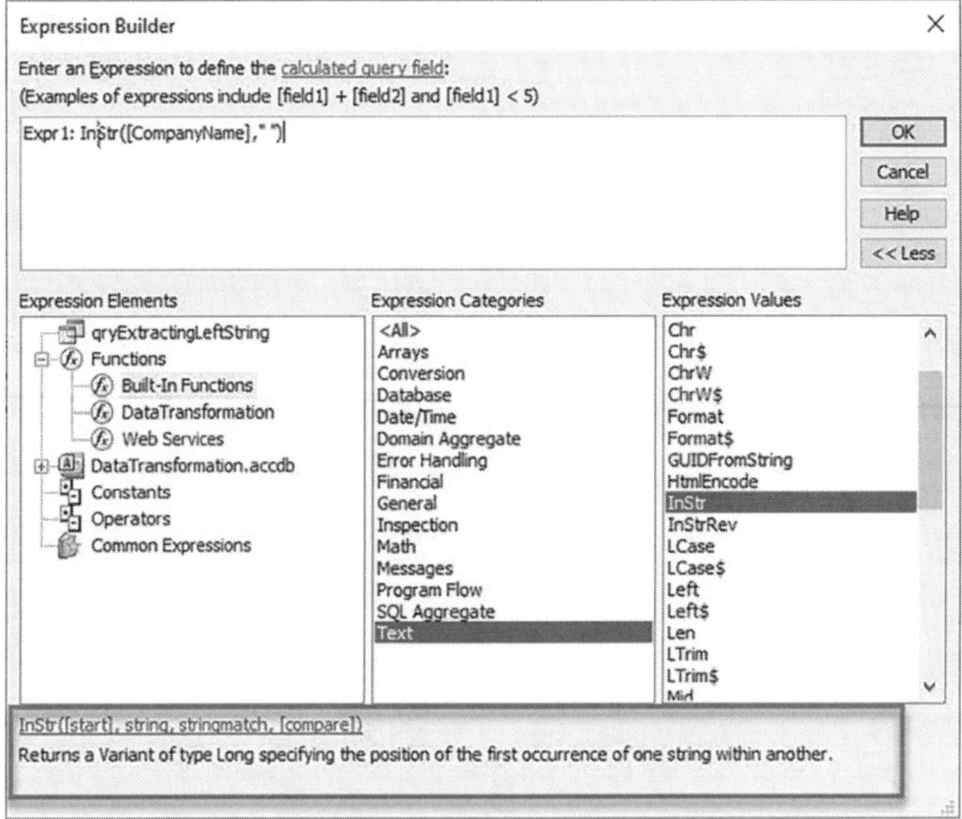

For more on the Expression Builder, see **Using the Expression Builder** in chapter 13.

In the example below, we're splitting a Full Name field into FirstName and LastName. We'll use a combination of the Access functions described below to split the string in the field.

Overview of the text functions used in the required expressions:

Function	**Left**
Syntax	Left (string, length)
Description	Returns a string containing a specified number of characters from the left side of a string based on the *length* provided.

Function	**Right**
Syntax	Right (string, length)
Description	Returns a string containing a specified number of characters from the right side of a string based on the *length* provided.

Function	**InStr**
Syntax	InStr([start], string1, string2, [compare])
Description	Enables you to search for a character (or string) within a string. InStr returns the position (a number) of the first instance of one string within another. The *start* and *compare* arguments are optional.

Function	**Len**
Syntax	Len(string)
Description	Returns the length of a string as a number.

Let's say we've imported some data containing the names of clients, and we want to split the Full Name field into two fields, First Name, and Last Name. The image below shows the data in its original form.

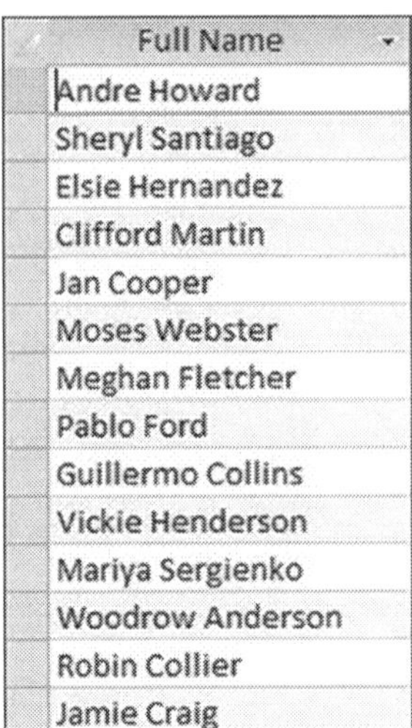

Full Name
Andre Howard
Sheryl Santiago
Elsie Hernandez
Clifford Martin
Jan Cooper
Moses Webster
Meghan Fletcher
Pablo Ford
Guillermo Collins
Vickie Henderson
Mariya Sergienko
Woodrow Anderson
Robin Collier
Jamie Craig

Follow the steps below to split the Full Name field into first name and last name fields:

1. Create a select query and add the table with the field you want to split.

2. To extract the first name, create a field that uses a combination of the Left and InStr functions to extract the string to the left of the space between the names.

```
FirstName: Left([Full Name],InStr([Full Name]," ")-1)
```

3. To extract the last name, create a field that uses a combination of the Right, Len, and InStr functions to extract the string to the right of the space between the names.

```
LastName: Right([Full Name],Len([Full Name])-InStr([Full
Name]," "))
```

Here is the result of the extracted names compared to the full names.

Full Name	FirstName	LastName
Andre Howard	Andre	Howard
Sheryl Santiago	Sheryl	Santiago
Elsie Hernandez	Elsie	Hernandez
Clifford Martin	Clifford	Martin
Jan Cooper	Jan	Cooper
Moses Webster	Moses	Webster
Meghan Fletcher	Meghan	Fletcher
Pablo Ford	Pablo	Ford
Guillermo Collins	Guillermo	Collins
Vickie Henderson	Vickie	Henderson
Mariya Sergienko	Mariya	Sergienko
Woodrow Anderson	Woodrow	Anderson
Robin Collier	Robin	Collier

Concatenating Text

Instead of splitting the name, what if we wanted to rearrange the name to look like *LastName, FirstName?*

We can use the concatenation operator for this. The concatenation operator combines strings from two or more fields into one string.

To create the solution from the query we used in the previous example, we can use the following expression as an additional field in the query to create the new name field.

```
Surname First: [LastName] & ", " & [FirstName]
```

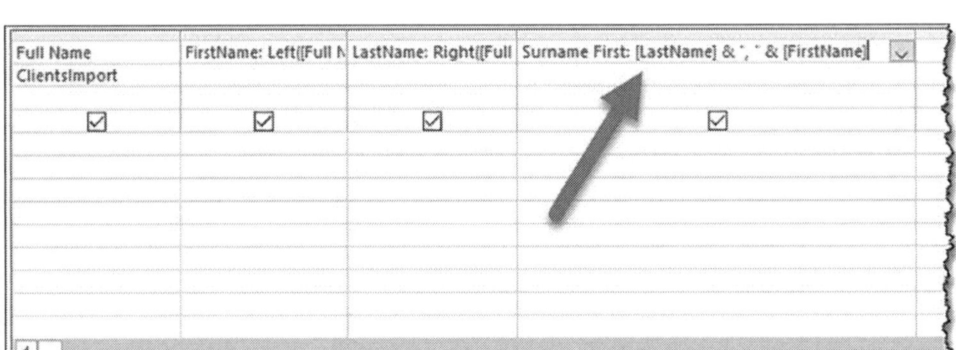

Notice that this expression uses the alias names of the two previous expressions that extracted the first name and last name.

The result, compared to the other fields, will look like this:

Full Name	FirstName	LastName	Surname First
Andre Howard	Andre	Howard	Howard, Andre
Sheryl Santiago	Sheryl	Santiago	Santiago, Sheryl
Elsie Hernandez	Elsie	Hernandez	Hernandez, Elsie
Clifford Martin	Clifford	Martin	Martin, Clifford
Jan Cooper	Jan	Cooper	Cooper, Jan
Moses Webster	Moses	Webster	Webster, Moses
Meghan Fletcher	Meghan	Fletcher	Fletcher, Meghan
Pablo Ford	Pablo	Ford	Ford, Pablo
Guillermo Collins	Guillermo	Collins	Collins, Guillermo
Vickie Henderson	Vickie	Henderson	Henderson, Vickie
Mariya Sergienko	Mariya	Sergienko	Sergienko, Mariya
Woodrow Anderson	Woodrow	Anderson	Anderson, Woodrow
Robin Collier	Robin	Collier	Collier, Robin

For more on the concatenation operator, see **Concatenation Operators** in chapter 13.

Changing Case

When working with imported data, one of the tasks you may need to perform is to change the case of text values in a field. For example, you could get records from a mainframe database that are all in uppercase or lowercase. The StrConv function in Access allows you to convert text to a different case.

StrConv Function

Syntax: StrConv(string, conversion [, LCID])

Description of arguments:

Argument	Description
string	Required. This is the string to be converted.
conversion	Required. This is a numeric constant specifying the type of conversion you want. See the list of constants below.
LCID	Optional. Only required if the LocaleID is different from the system LocaleID. The system LocaleID is the default.

Values for the conversion argument:

Value	Description
1	Converts the specified string to uppercase.
2	Converts the specified string to lowercase.
3	Converts the specified string to proper case. That is, the first letter of every word in the string is converted to uppercase.

In the example below, we have received a list of customers in lower case. We want to convert the Cust ID field to uppercase and the other fields to proper case.

Cust ID	Company Name	Contact Name
alfki	alfreds test	maria anders
anatr	ana trujillo emparedados y helados	ana trujillo
anton	antonio moreno taquería	antonio moreno
arout	around the horn	thomas hardy
cactu	cactus comidas para llevar	patricio simpson
centc	centro comercial moctezuma	francisco chang
chops	chop-suey chinese	yang wang
commi	comércio mineiro	pedro afonso
consh	consolidated holdings	elizabeth brown
dracd	drachenblut delikatessen	sven ottlieb
dumon	du monde entier	janine labrune
eastc	eastern connection	ann devon
ernsh	ernst handel	roland mendel
famia	familia arquibaldo	aria cruz
fissa	fissa fabrica inter. salchichas s.a.	diego roel
folig	folies gourmandes	martine rancé
folko	folk och fä hb	maria larsson

To perform the conversions for the table above, do the following:

1. Create a make table query with the table containing the lowercase values as the data source.

2. Add the following expressions for the fields of the query (use the Expression Builder if necessary):

```
CUSTID: StrConv([Cust ID],1)
```

```
CompanyName: StrConv([Company Name],3)
```

```
ContactName: StrConv([Contact Name],3)
```

3. Run the query to make a new table with the converted text.

The data in the new table will now look like this:

CUSTID	CompanyName	ContactName
ALFKI	Alfreds Test	Maria Anders
ANATR	Ana Trujillo Emparedados Y Helados	Ana Trujillo
ANTON	Antonio Moreno Taquería	Antonio Moreno
AROUT	Around The Horn	Thomas Hardy
CACTU	Cactus Comidas Para Llevar	Patricio Simpson
CENTC	Centro Comercial Moctezuma	Francisco Chang
CHOPS	Chop-suey Chinese	Yang Wang
COMMI	Comércio Mineiro	Pedro Afonso
CONSH	Consolidated Holdings	Elizabeth Brown
DRACD	Drachenblut Delikatessen	Sven Ottlieb
DUMON	Du Monde Entier	Janine Labrune
EASTC	Eastern Connection	Ann Devon
ERNSH	Ernst Handel	Roland Mendel
FAMIA	Familia Arquibaldo	Aria Cruz
FISSA	Fissa Fabrica Inter. Salchichas S.a.	Diego Roel
FOLIG	Folies Gourmandes	Martine Rancé

Removing Leading and Trailing Spaces

Leading and trailing spaces in values is something you may encounter when working with data imported from other systems. These extra spaces can lead to inconsistent results when analyzing the data. The **Trim** function in Access can be used to remove all leading and trailing spaces from text.

Syntax: Trim(text)

The single argument is the text you want to trim.

Example:

In the example below, our table has four distinct US states in 14 records. However, if we group this data, we get eight records instead of four. This error occurs because some of the values have leading and trailing spaces that make them appear distinct to Access.

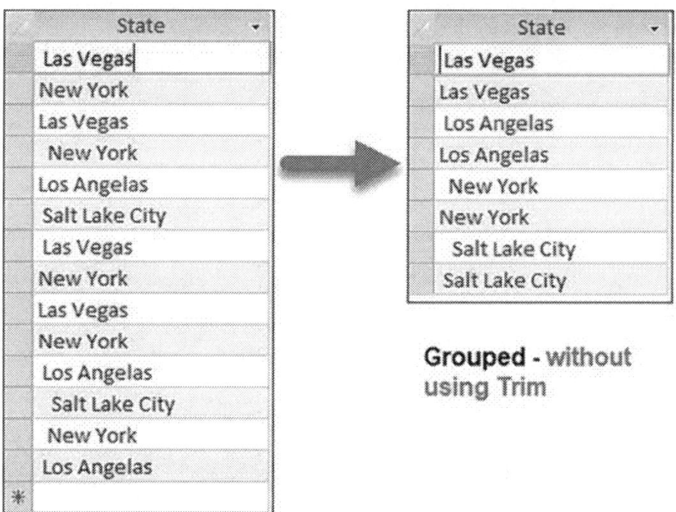

To resolve this issue, we apply the Trim function to the State field in our Update or Make Table query. Enter the following expression in a field in the query design grid:

```
StateTrimmed: Trim([State])
```

This will produce the following outcome:

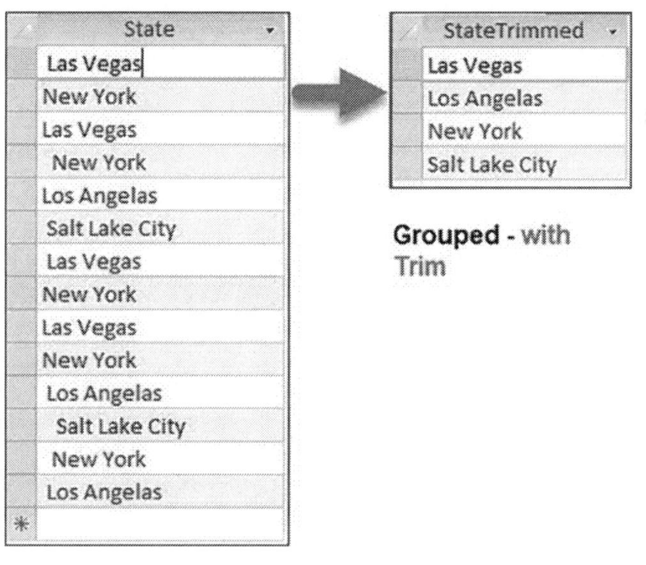

Finding and Replacing Text

Let's say you wanted to find all instances of "Limited" in your database and replace them with "LTD" to ensure that term is used in a consistent way in your database.

Now, you could use the Find and Replace dialog box (available in Access and other Microsoft 365 applications) to find and replace small amounts of data. However, the Find and Replace tool would be inefficient for the task if the number of records you need to change run into hundreds of thousands. When you have hundreds of thousands of records, the **Replace** function is more suitable for the task.

The Replace function finds a string within another string and replaces it with a replacement string that you've specified.

Syntax:

Replace(expression, find, replace [, start] [, count] [, compare])

Description of Arguments

Argument	Description
expression	Required. This is the full string that contains the substring you want to replace. In a query, this would be the target field.
find	Required. This is the substring you want to find and replace.
replace	Required. This is the replacement substring.
start	Optional. The position you want to start the search within the full string. If omitted, the default is 1.
count	Optional. This represents the number of found instances of the substring you want to replace within the full string. If omitted, the default value is -1, which means replace all instances.
compare	Optional. The kind of comparison you want to use. The options are binary, textual, or the default setting. The default setting is used if omitted. For more details on this argument, see Access Help.

Examples:

- Replace("Satori Limited", "Limited", "LTD") would return *Satori LTD*.
- Replace("200 pounds", "pounds", "lbs") would return *200 lbs*.
- Replace("7832 Landing Drive", "Drive", "Dri") would return "*7832 Landing Dri*".

The following query finds all instances of "Limited" in the CompanyName field and replaces them with "LTD".

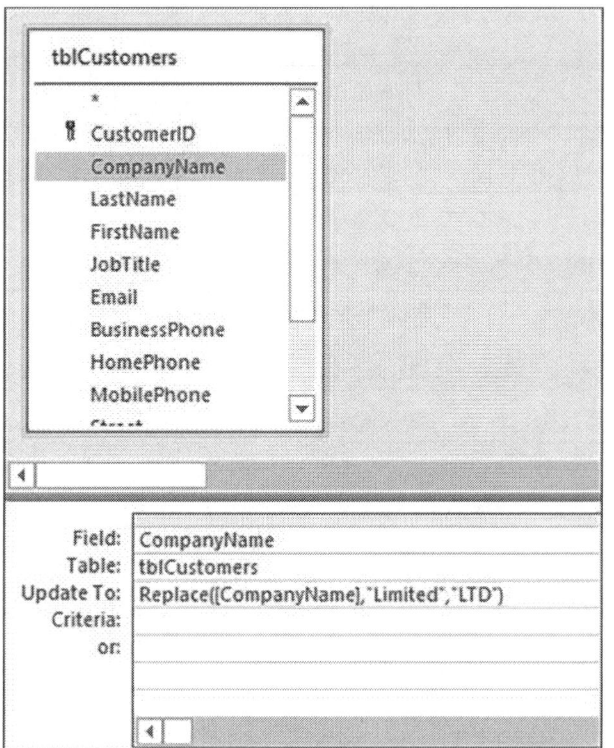

Note For more details on how to create and run Update queries, see chapter 14.

Part 6

Presenting Data with Access Reports

In Part 6

Access reports allow you to present information in a more understandable way than can be done with a query. Access provides easy-to-use reporting tools that enable you to format and summarize data into meaningful information for analysis. In Part 6, you learn how to quickly create different report types and how to refine and enhance reports with controls, properties, grouping, sorting, and totals. You also learn how to configure a report's page setup for printing a hard copy.

Contents at a Glance

Chapter 16: Creating Access Reports

Access provides powerful reporting tools that enable you to format and summarize data into meaningful information for analysis. Reports allow you to present data in a more user-friendly way than can be achieved with a query alone. You can add different grouping levels, totals, statistical comparisons, and graphics to Access reports. The main difference between forms and reports is that forms are meant for data input and edits while reports are for presenting data.

On some occasions, users prefer exporting data from Access to a spreadsheet program like Excel to produce reports like pivot tables and other types of summaries. This is okay for historical data, but if you want a dynamic report that reflects any source data changes in real-time, you should use an Access report. Any exported information needs to be refreshed constantly if the source data is often changing.

In this chapter, we will cover the following topics:

- An overview of the tools you can use to create reports in Access.
- The types of reports you can create in Access.
- How to use a query to power your report.
- Creating a report with a Report Wizard.

Report Creation Tools

On the Create tab of the Access Ribbon, there are several ways you can create a report:

- **Report tool**: This tool enables you to quickly create a simple tabular report based on a table or query. The report generated by this option is quite basic and looks like a table or query in Datasheet view. If you need something more sophisticated, you're better off either creating the report with the Report Wizard or from scratch with a blank report, as it would be faster than enhancing a report created by the Report tool.

- **Report Wizard**: The Report Wizard takes you through several pages, enabling you to select options to create your report. You can create something more complex than what you can create with the Report tool. The report wizard enables you to choose what fields you want on the report, what fields to group or sort, and what type of report to create. On most occasions, you'll still need to spend some time refining the design of a report created by the Wizard to make it operational.

- **Report Design** and **Blank Report** tools: You can create a report from scratch with either the Report Design or Blank Report tools. The Report tool opens a blank report in Layout view, while Report Design opens a blank report in Design view.

  When designing a report from scratch, I recommend working in Design view, especially when you have grouped data. You'll be able to view and work with the different groups (and sections) better. Design view also has horizontal and vertical rulers as well as gridlines, making it easier to position controls on the report.

In this chapter, we will be coving the Report Wizard as it is the best starting point if you're new to Access reports.

Report Types

There are three basic report types used in Access:

- Tabular
- Columnar
- Mailing labels

Tabular reports

Tabular reports display the data in rows and columns, similar to a spreadsheet or datasheet. Unlike a datasheet, however, a tabular report can have grouped data with subtotals or any other aggregate data for each group. You could also have page totals and grand totals in the report.

An example of a tabular report:

HIGHLAND FURNITURE

Suppliers and Products

Supplier Name	City	Product Name	Price
Auer Furniture	Montara, CA		
		House Kent Oak Console Table	$1,179.00
		Hygena Lumina Console Table	$1,149.00
Central Plains Millwork Inc	Laughlin, NV		
		Habitat Atlas Gloss 4 Piece 3 Door Wardrobe Set - Grey	$615.00
		Silver Cross Nostalgia Cot Bed Dresser Wardrobe Set- White	$1,600.00
		Silver Cross Nostalgia Sleigh Cot bed Wardrobe Set- White	$1,800.00
Chf Industries Inc	Mcallen, TX		
		Grasmere 5 Drawer Chest - Dark Grey	$340.00
		Habitat Oken Console Table	$686.00

Columnar reports

A columnar report displays the records in a single column, usually with just one or a few records per page (in a continuous report). This is similar to a data entry form that displays one record at a time. Columnar reports are ideal for displaying the full details of a record, especially when one or more of the fields needs a lot of space to be fully displayed, for example, a comment or an image field. Columnar reports are also ideal for displaying parent and child records from two tables together. A typical example of this is an invoice. An invoice has a main record with related line items that you want to display together.

An example of a columnar report:

Labels

Labels are a special type of report that you can create using the Label Wizard in Access. The Label Wizard enables you to select fields from a data source (usually address fields) and then create a report that can be printed as address labels. With most communication now carried out electronically by email, this feature is no longer as popular as it used to be. But it is available whenever you want to generate labeling for letters or other physical items.

An example of a Labels report:

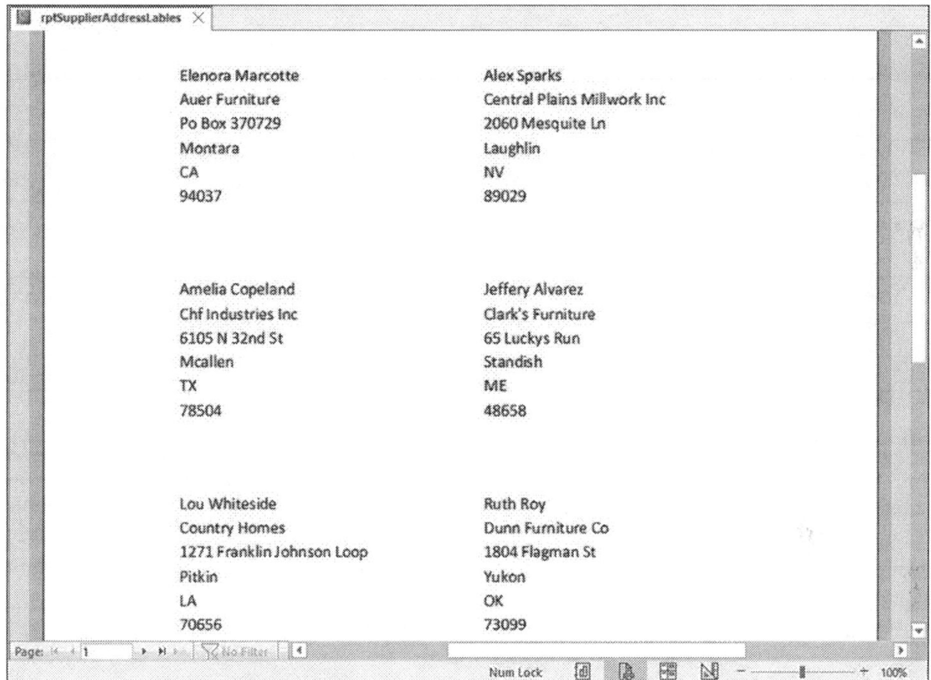

Using a Query as the Data Source

The ideal type of data source for a report is a query. There are some benefits in using a query as the data source of your report rather than a table:

- A query enables you to include only the fields required for the report. In some cases, this could make the report run faster, especially if the query is only selecting a subset of the data from a very large table.
- A query allows you to include fields from multiple related tables. For example, if the main table for the report has a foreign key field like Customer ID, but you want to display the customer's name on the report. You can include the name field from the Customers table in the query that you use to power the report.
- A query enables you to include calculated fields.
- If you decide you want one or more additional fields after creating the report, you can edit the query and include the required fields.

In the following example, we will create a report that lists orders in the Highland Furniture database, including the items per order. We also want to display the subtotal for each order and sort the data using the order date.

The tables from which we need to pull the required fields for this report are:

- tblOrders
- tblOrderLines
- tblCustomers
- tblProducts

Thus, we can proceed to create a query that includes these four tables, and the query would look like the query in the image below:

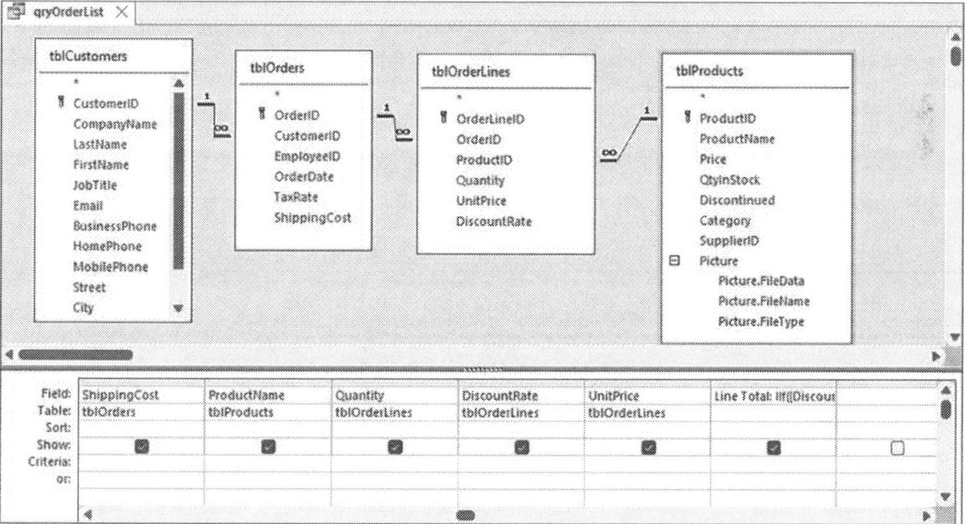

Notice that the CompanyName and ProductName have been pulled from tblCustomers and tblProducts instead of using the ID fields in the main tables containing the order details.

The **Line Total** field in the query is a calculated field that multiplies the price, quantity, and discount rate (if one applies).

To only apply the discount when it's greater than 0%, the IIf function has been used to create a conditional expression that calculates this value:

=IIf([DiscountRate]>0,([Quantity]*[UnitPrice])-([Quantity]*[UnitPrice]*[DiscountRate]),[Quantity]*[UnitPrice])

This expression says:

If the discount rate is greater than zero, then multiply the quantity by the unit price and then subtract the discount amount. If the discount rate is zero, then only multiply the quantity by the unit price.

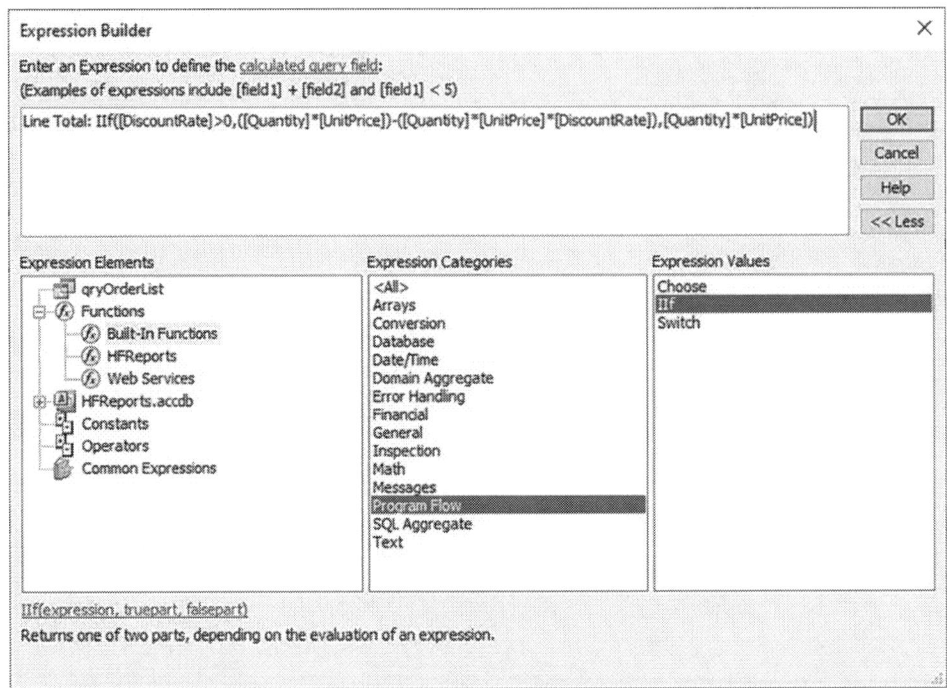

Note For more on creating queries and calculated fields with the Expression Builder, see chapter 13.

With the data source for our report now created, we can now create the report.

Creating A Report with the Report Wizard

If you are new to Access reports or your knowledge is basic, then the Report Wizard is a good place to start when creating reports. The Report Wizard strikes a fine balance between using the Report tool (which is only ideal for very simple reports) and the Report Design tool (which requires you to create all fields, sections, and groupings manually).

Some benefits of using the Report Wizard over a blank report:

- You can generate a report very quickly using the wizard. Thus, you can use an iterative process of generating the report multiple times, each time with different options and settings, until you get your desired outcome.
- If you're new to Access reports, you may find creating sections for grouping data confusing. The wizard enables you to select any fields you want to group by, and it creates the necessary sections to handle the grouping.
- The Report Wizard can automatically detect one-to-many relationships in your source data and group the data on the report accordingly.
- Even if you're proficient with Access reports, you can still use the Report Wizard to quickly generate a base report on which you build. The wizard does the basic things like adding the fields to the report and creating any required sections, leaving you to focus on formatting and other fine-tuning activities.

To create a report with the Report Wizard, do the following:

1. In the Navigation Pane, select the query that you want to use for the report. In our example, this will be the query we just created called **qryOrderList**.

2. On the Ribbon, click on **Create**, and then in the **Reports** group, click **Report Wizard**.

   Access opens the Report Wizard.

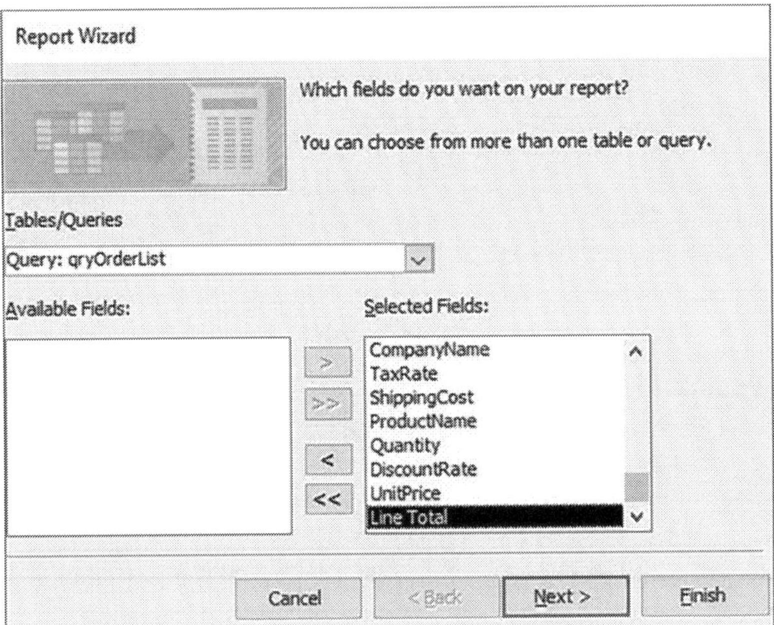

3. **Choose the fields you want for your report and click Next.**

   Select the data source from the **Tables/Queries** drop-down list (if the default one selected is not the query you want to use for the report).

   The **Available Fields** box lists all the fields in your query. Click the **Add All** button (**>>**) to move all the fields to the **Selected Fields** box or use the **Add** (>) button to select one field at a time (if you don't want to use all the fields).

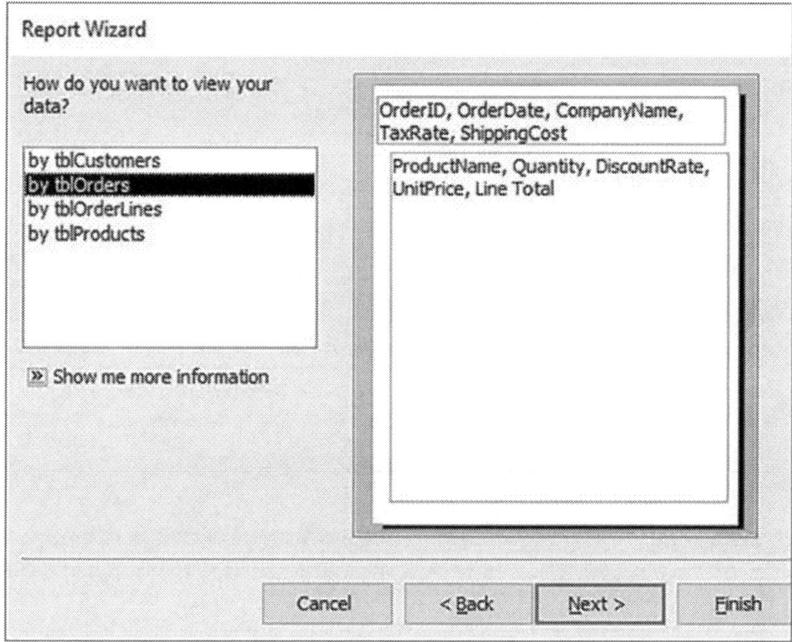

4. **Specify how you want to view the data and click Next**.

Access will ask you how you want to view your data. If your query is made up of several related tables, in the left box, select the parent table in the one-to-many relationship.

For our example, this will be the Orders table (**tblOrders**), as we want to display each order with its associated order lines.

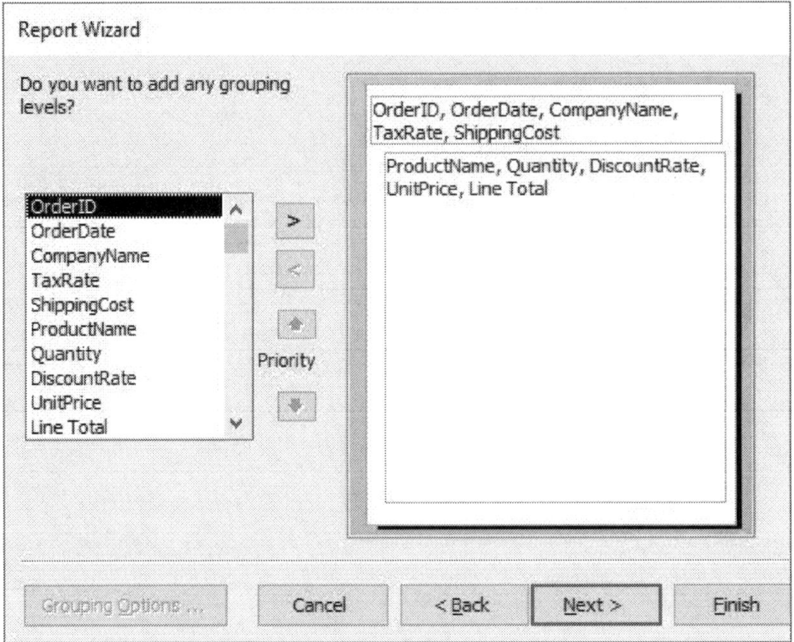

5. **Select the field you want to group by and click Next**.

   On this page (image above), Access asks you if you want to add any grouping levels. The data for our example comes from two main tables in a one-to-many relationship. In the previous step, Access recognized the structure of the data and already arranged our fields in a one-to-many grouping. Hence, we don't need to add any further grouping levels here. However, if your data is not already grouped, you can add grouping levels on this page by selecting the field you want to group by on the fields list and clicking **Add**.

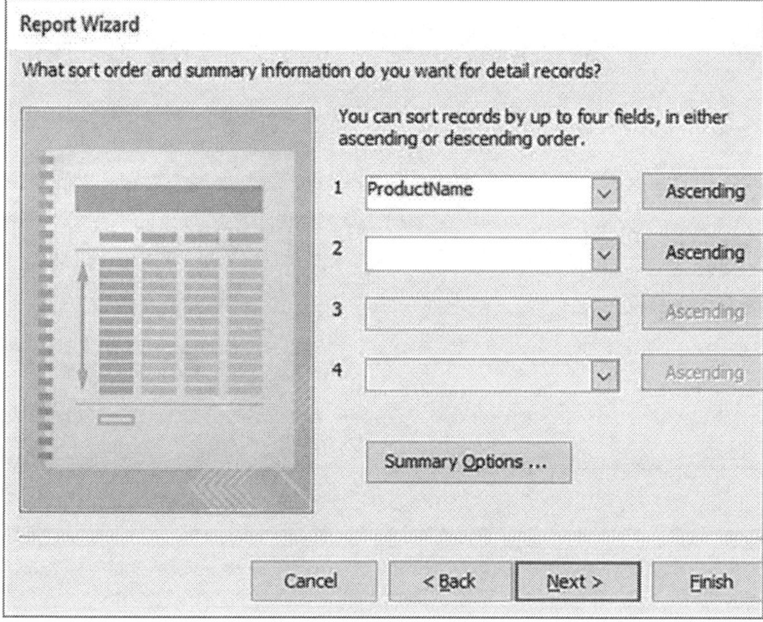

6. **Select a sort field and click Next**.

This page of the wizard (image above) enables you to sort your data in either ascending or descending order using several fields.

For our example, we will sort the list items by ProductName, but this is not a necessity. Depending on your data, you may want to leave this unsorted so that the items are displayed in the order they were entered.

Note The **Summary Options** button on this page allows you to create aggregate summaries, including Sum, Avg, Min, and Max, for each record in the detail section. We don't need these summaries for our example.

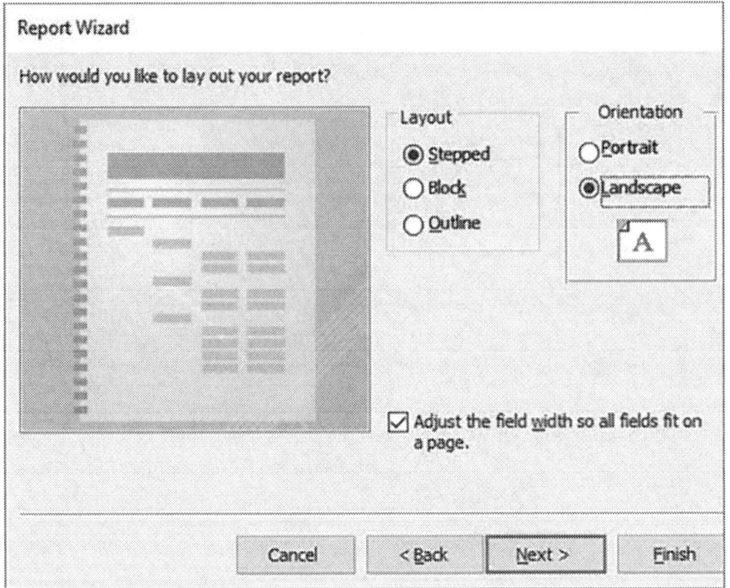

7. **Select your Layout and Orientation.**

On this page of the wizard (image above), you get options for choosing the **Layout** and **Orientation** of the page.

- **Under Layout, choose Stepped**. The layout determines how the fields are organized on the report. As you select an option, the image on the left displays a graphic of the layout. The **Stepped** option indents each group, making it easier to read the report.

- **Under Orientation, choose Landscape**. If you have five or more fields in your report, and you want all the fields (columns) to fit into the width of one page, I recommend choosing Landscape. This ensures the data is more evenly spread to make the report more legible. Note that you can always change the orientation of the report later if your option here turns out to be unsuitable.

- Select **Adjust the field width so all fields fit on a page** (this is the default). When selected, this option attempts to arrange all the fields on one page. It doesn't always do a perfect job if the report has a lot of fields. Hence, you may need to adjust the fields manually when editing the report's design.

Click **Next**.

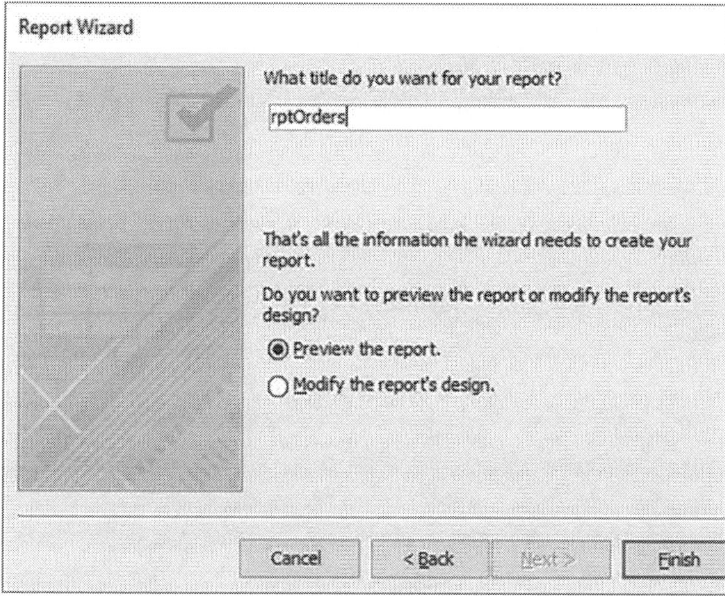

8. On the last page of the wizard, enter a meaningful name for your report and click **Finish**.

9. Access displays the report in Print Preview mode.

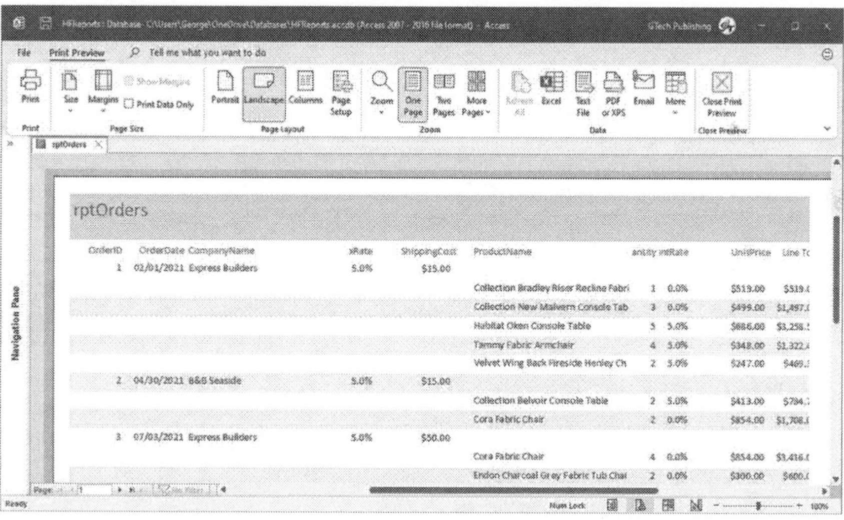

As you can see from the image above, the report generated by the wizard is not exactly perfect, but it is a good starting point. We will be covering how to refine the report's design in the next chapter.

Chapter 17: Refining a Report's Design

After creating a report with the Report Wizard, the report will be displayed in print preview mode. You can review the report and identify what revisions are needed to polish up the report. This chapter will focus on the design changes you can make to handle more complex data arrangements.

In this chapter, we will cover the following topics:

- Refining reports created by the Report Wizard.
- Changing report properties using the Property Sheet.
- How to add, move, and resize controls on a report.
- Formatting report controls.
- Adding report sections and creating group headers and footers.
- Adding calculated fields to aggregate data in group footers.

Required Changes for the Orders Report

The Orders report created with the Report Wizard in chapter 16 requires some design changes to refine the report.

The list below is an overview of the refinements required:

- **Resize and reposition some fields on the report so that they fit into the width of one page.** Even though we selected the option in the wizard to fit the fields on one page, it doesn't always get it right. Depending on the number of fields you have, they may spill into a second page.

- **Edit and format the field labels in the page header.** We need to give the field labels more appropriate names instead of the field names from our tables. We also want to bold the field labels and use a line control to create a separation between field labels and field controls.

- **Add a section footer for each order.** We can add any summary information for each group in the group footer. The wizard can automatically create a group header for any of your fields, but you have to create the group footer manually.

- **Add a calculated field to the group footer for each order.** This will involve using an expression in an unbound textbox control. The data is grouped by order ID, and under each group, we want to calculate the total for that order.

- **Format the report title.** Give the report a more appropriate title and formatting style in place of the default title created by the wizard.

- **Add the company logo to the report title.** It is often a good idea to add your company branding or logo to your report header.

The following sections in this chapter will go through how we would generally perform each of these design changes on the report.

The Four Report Views

To change the view of the report, use the view buttons on the lower-right of the status bar of the screen (see image below).

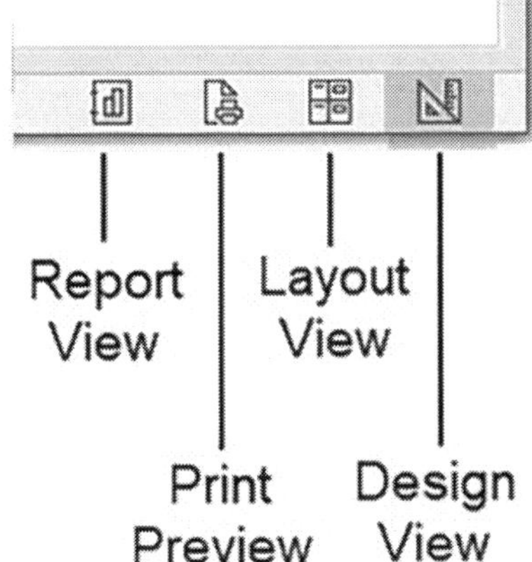

- **Report View**: Displays a screen version of the report.
- **Print Preview**: Displays a preview of the print version of the report.
- **Layout View**: Enables you to perform design changes on what is closer to a preview of the report.
- **Design View**: Enables you to perform design changes using the report design window.

You can also change the view of the report by right-clicking the report selector button (upper-left corner of the report, between the rulers). From the pop-up menu, you can select Report View, Layout View, Design View, or Print Preview.

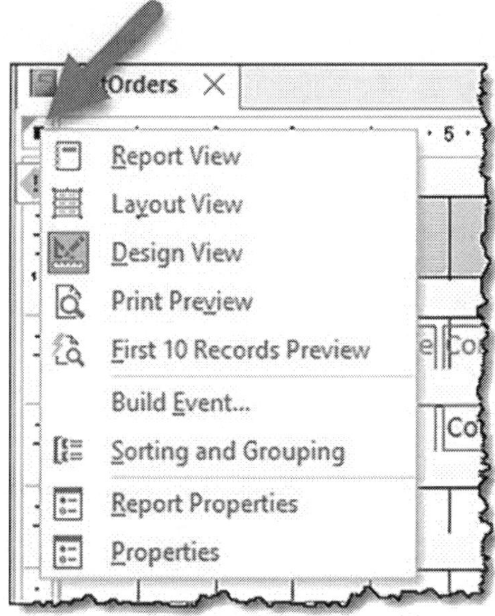

Views for Editing a Report

You can change the design of a report using Design view or Layout view. Each view has its advantages regarding what design changes you want to make.

- **Design view**

  This view is good for adding new controls and elements to a report, for example, text boxes, labels, and lines. This view is also good for positioning controls on the report as it has grid lines, including horizontal and vertical rulers. If you're adding elements to different sections of the report, it's better to work in Design view as it is easier to differentiate the sections in this view.

- **Layout view**

  This view displays the report with the data as it would look in Report view. Resizing controls while the data is visible helps with sizing accuracy. When changing control styles and text formats, you'll see the changes as they would look in Report view, which helps with formatting accuracy. Layout view also shows you the page boundaries, which makes it easier to place your controls within the page layout.

Using the Property Sheet

An Access report and most of the controls on the report, including the different report sections, have properties that you can adjust using the Property Sheet.

Note For more details on how to use the Property Sheet, see **Introducing the Property Sheet** in chapter 11.

Displaying the Property Sheet

To display the Property Sheet, do the following:

1. Open the report in Design view or Layout view.
2. Click the item you want to modify. For example, it can be a text box, a label, or a report section.
3. On the Ribbon, click the **Report Design** tab, and in the **Tools** group, click **Property Sheet**. Another way to display the properties for a report element is to right-click the item and select **Properties** from the pop-up menu to display its Property Sheet.

   If the Property Sheet is already open, clicking the item will display the properties for that control.

   Tip With the report in Design view or Layout view, you can press **F4** to display or hide the Property Sheet.

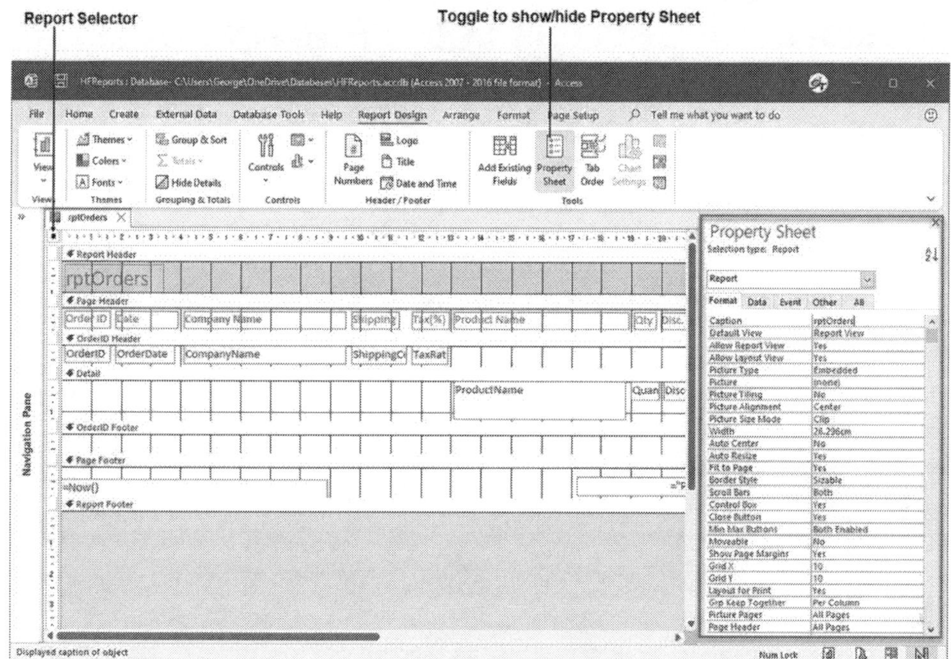
Report Selector
Toggle to show/hide Property Sheet

Selecting Controls in the Property Sheet

At the top of the Property Sheet, the *Selection type* shows the type of control or report element currently being displayed. The drop-down list displays the name of the control or report element. For example, if the item selected is a text box, the *Selection type* will be *Text Box*, and the drop-down list will have the name of the text box.

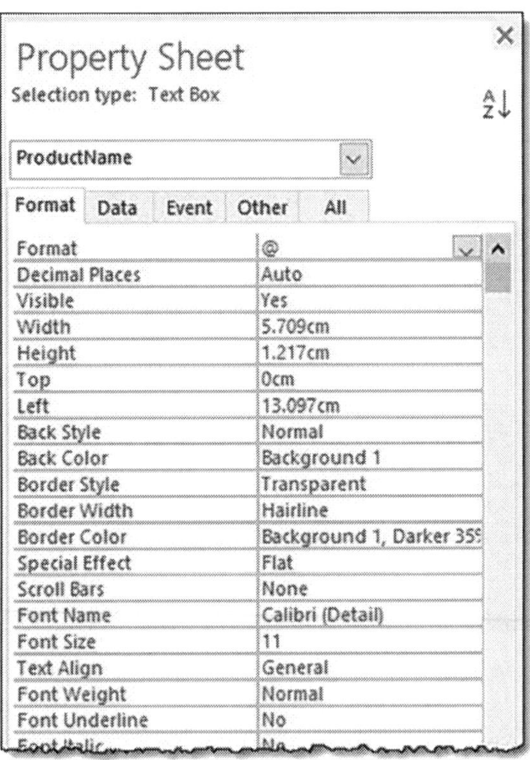

You can use the drop-down list to change the element of the report you want to display in the Property Sheet. For example, if you want to display properties for the Detail section, you'll click the drop-down arrow on the drop-down list and select Detail from the list.

Selecting Report Properties

While designing a report, you may occasionally need to display the properties of the report itself rather than its sections. This could be confusing at first because clicking any section of the report displays properties for that section in the Property Sheet.

You can display the report properties in one of the following ways:

- Right-click the report selector (the square box located between the horizontal and vertical rulers) and select Properties from the pop-up menu.

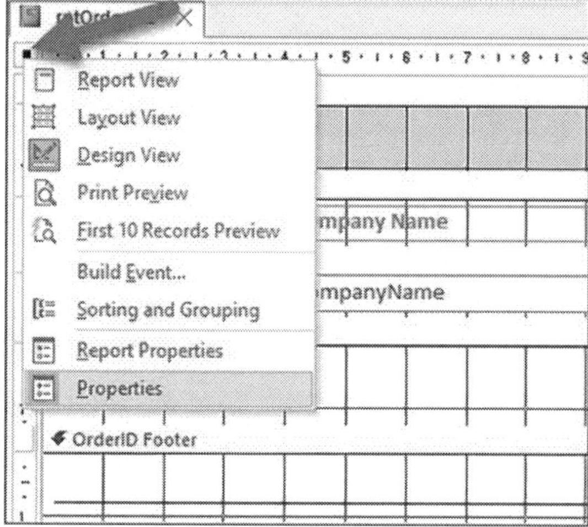

- Right-click anywhere on the report and select Report Properties from the pop-up menu.

- If the Property Sheet is already open, then click the report selector to display its properties.

- Double-click the report selector to display its Property Sheet.

You can use the Property Sheet of a report to change its Record Source (on the Data tab) and various formatting properties that are self-explanatory on the **Format** tab.

Working with Report Controls

A report control is a design element you can place on a report like a text box, label, image, or line.

Controls fall mostly into two categories:

- Controls that are used to display data on the report.
- Controls that are used to design and organize the interface of the report.

Move your mouse pointer over a control to see its name.

Below are the most common report controls used in Access:

- **Text box**: As the name implies, a text box is used for displaying text. A text box can be bound to a field in the report's data source, or it could be unbound and used to perform a calculation using values from other fields.

- **Label**: Labels are used for report titles, field titles, and any other piece of static text you want to add to the report.

- **Line**: Use a line control to create a separation where you need one on the report. For example, you may want a separation line after every group to better define the groups on the report.

- **Image**: The image control enables you to add an image to any section of the report.

Resizing and Repositioning Controls

To resize a text box control on the report, do the following:

1. Open the report in Design view.
2. Click the text box to select it. The edges of the text box will be highlighted.
3. Move your mouse over one of the 'sizing handles' in the upper, lower, and right edges of the control (see image below) until the pointer changes to a double-headed arrow.

Note
If the report is in Layout view, move your mouse over one of the highlighted edges until the pointer changes to a double-headed arrow.

4. Click and drag to increase or decrease the length or height.

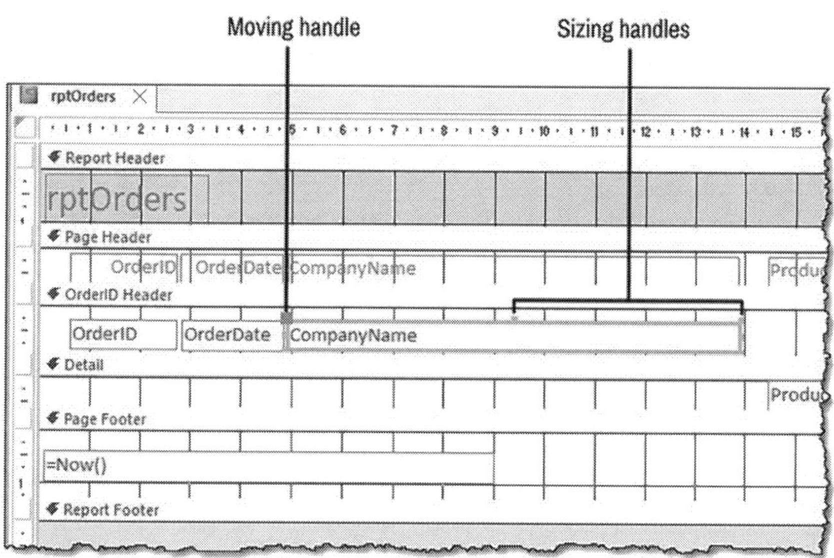

To reposition a control, use one of the following methods:

- Click the control once to select it. Then move your mouse over any of the highlighted edges until the mouse pointer changes to a four-directional arrow. Click and drag the control to any position on the report.

- Click the control and hold down the mouse button. You'll notice that the cursor has changed to a four-directional arrow. Drag the mouse to move the control to a new position on the report.

- Click the control once to select it. Use the arrow keys on the keyboard to move the control left, right, up, or down. Each key press moves the control by only 1 pixel at a time. Hence, this method is useful if you want more precision in positioning a control on the report.

Tip To select more than one control, click the first control to select it, and then hold down the **Shift** key whilst clicking additional controls. You can resize or move controls that have been selected together.

To check the page layout, view the report in Layout view to see the page margins.

Note If the page margin lines are not visible when you're in Layout view, in the **Page Size** group, on the **Page Setup** tab, select **Show Margins**.

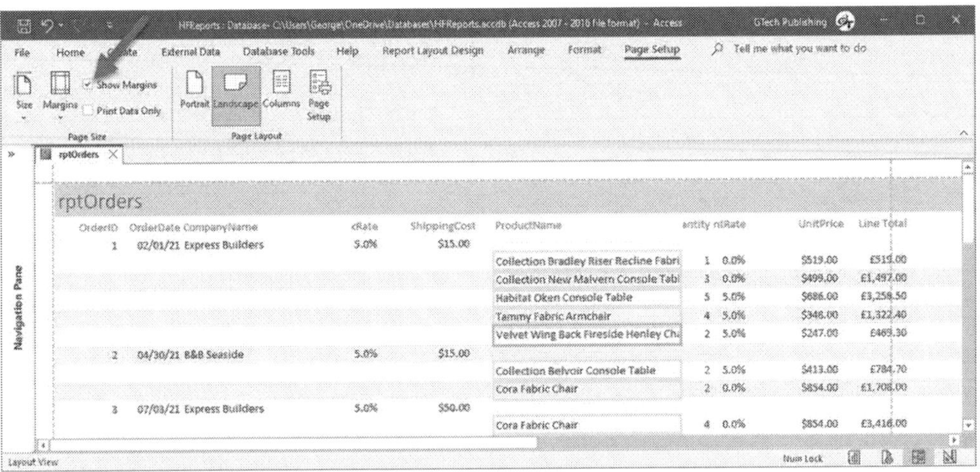

After resizing and repositioning the controls on our report, it should look like this:

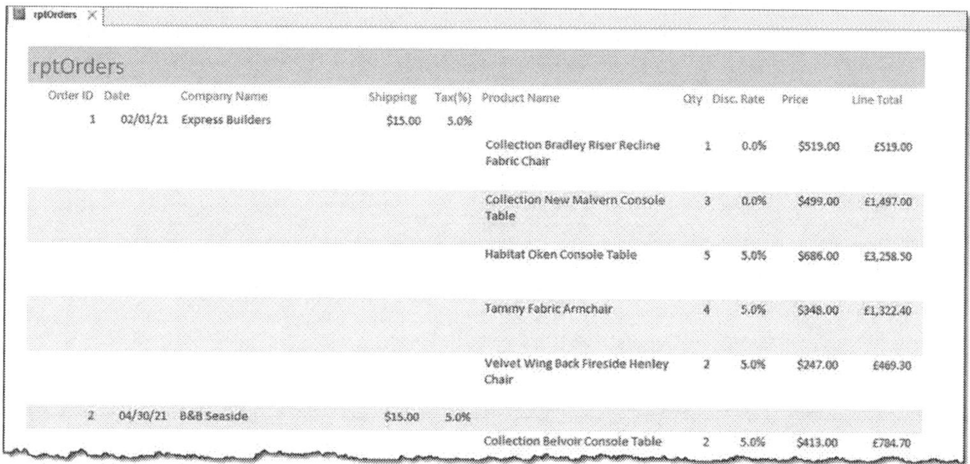

Editing Label Captions and Formats

One design change you'll often have to make after creating your report with the Report Wizard is to edit the field labels so that they are more user-friendly (instead of the table field names). You may also want to make some formatting changes like bolding the text and changing their alignment.

On the Format tab of a label's Property Sheet, you can change its caption as well as adjust many format properties. For example, if you wanted to bold the text in a label, you would select **Bold** in the **Font Weight** property.

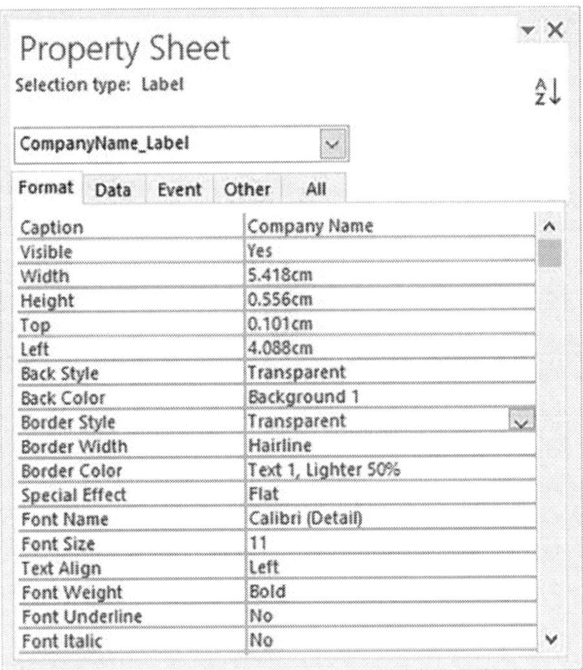

You can also manually overwrite the text in a label by double-clicking the label. Access will select the whole text, enabling you to enter a new caption. To edit the text of a label (if you don't want to completely overwrite it), select the label and then click once in the label. You'll see the insertion point blinking in the text. You can then edit the text by moving the insertion point left or right and typing in the label.

Editing Text Box Formats

You can change the formatting of a text box using the text box Property Sheet. On the Data tab, you can change the Control Source. You can set it to one of the fields bound to the report or enter an expression (for an unbound control).

You can change several formatting properties on the Format tab of the Property Sheet. For example, Border Style, Back Color, Font Name, Font Size, Font Weight, Text Align, and so on.

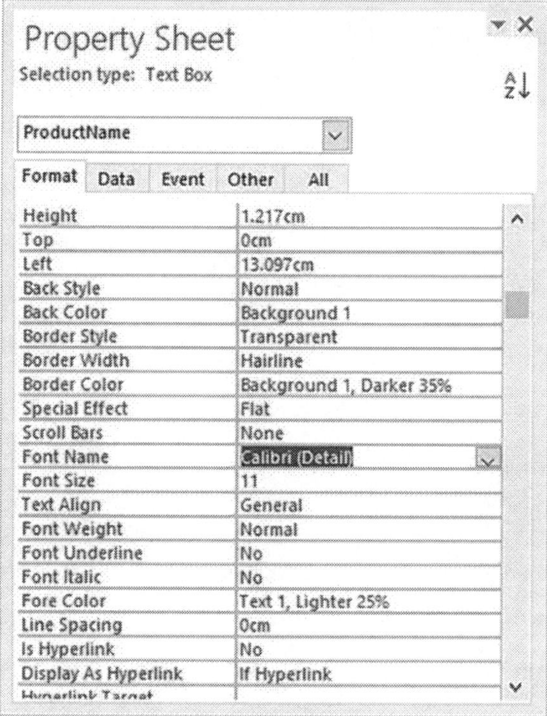

You can also change some formatting properties on the Access Ribbon.

To change the formatting of the text box using commands on the Ribbon, do the following:

1. Open the report in Design view.
2. Select the Text Box control.
3. Click the **Format** tab on the Ribbon.

   The commands in the **Font** and **Control Formatting** groups are similar to commands you'll see in other Microsoft 365 applications.

4. You can use commands in the **Font** group to change the font, size, and text alignment of the text in labels and text boxes.
5. You can also use commands in the **Control Formatting** group to change the style of the control, like the fill color and outline.

Aligning Controls and Captions

To select multiple controls so that you can change them together, click the first control to select it, and then hold down the Shift (or Ctrl) key and click the other controls to select them.

To right-align the labels on a report, do the following:

1. With the report open in Design view, click the **Arrange** tab.
2. Select all the labels you want to right-align.
3. In the **Sizing & Ordering** group, click the **Align** button and select **Right** from the drop-down menu.

This right-aligns the selected label controls.

To right-align the label captions (text), do the following:

1. With the report in Design view, click the **Format** tab.
2. Select all the labels with captions that you want to right-align.
3. In the **Font** group, click on the **Align Right** button.

This right-aligns the captions on the labels.

Adding A Line Control

You will often need to add lines to your report to separate different sections. For example, you could add a line in the report header, under the field headings, to separate them from the values. You may also add a line to a group footer to delineate the end of a group and the start of another.

To add a straight line across any section of the report, do the following:

1. Open the report in Design view.
2. On the **Ribbon**, in the **Controls** group, select the **Line** control.

   The mouse pointer will change to an image indicating the line control is selected.
3. Hold down the **Shift** key, then click in the report section where you want to add the line and drag from left to right.

Tip Holding down the **Shift** key while drawing a line ensures you draw a straight line.

---

4. To increase or reduce the size of a line, click the line to select it, then hold down the **Shift** key and drag the sizing handle (on the right or left) of the line to resize it.

Working with Report Sections

Access reports are divided into several sections. The information that is displayed in each section depends on what groups you have and your chosen layout. It is important to understand Access report sections if you want to change a report with groups created by the wizard or if you want to add/remove groups manually.

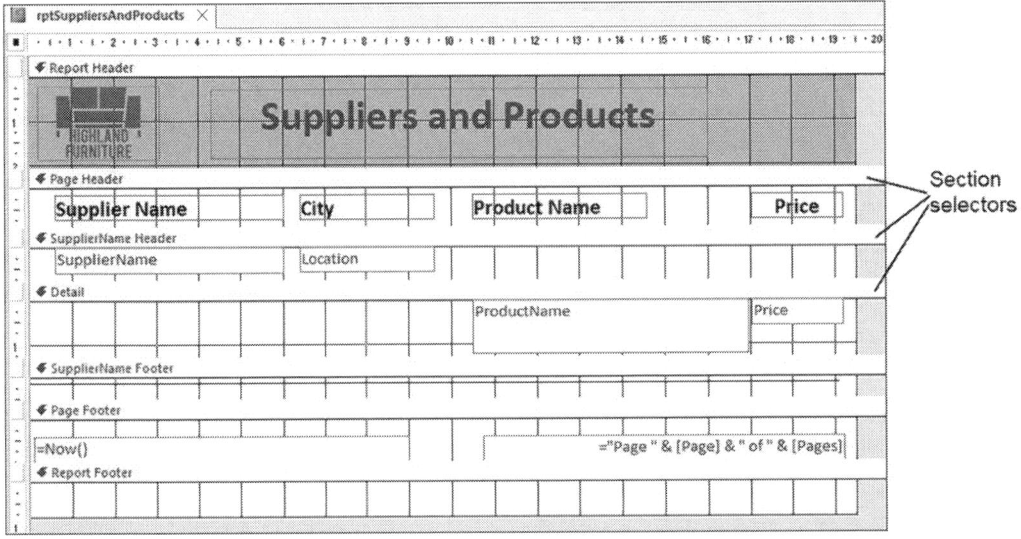

The different groups you'll find in a report are as follows:

- **Report header and footer**: These sections appear only once in the report, that is, at the start and end of the report. The report header can be used to provide general information about the report, for example, the title of the report, the date, and the version. You can use the report footer for information like a copyright notice, author name, email address, phone number, and other contact details.

- **Page header and page footer**: These sections appear just once at the top and bottom of every page. Any information in the page header section will be displayed on the header of all printed pages, and any information in the page footer section will be displayed on the footer of every printed page. Thus, these sections are useful for any information you want to be repeated at the top and bottom of each page.

  Typical pieces of information that can go in the page header and footer are your company logo and the date the report was printed. What appears on the page header also depends on the layout of the report. If the report is a tabular layout (columns and rows), the field names will be in the report header so that they appear on each page. The page footer is normally used to hold the page number and the report date.

- **Group headers and footers**: Group headers and footers are used to group data in a parent-child relationship (one-to-many relationship). The fields in the group header are from the parent table and are only displayed once per group. That is, instead of the data repeating for every related record, it is displayed once in the group header. For example, if you're listing suppliers with multiple products, the supplier's name and ID fields will be in the group header while the product fields will be in the Detail section. The group footer is normally used for aggregate information like a count, sum, average, or subtotal.

- **Detail**: The detail section is good for displaying any repeating data. If your data has a parent-child relationship, then the detail section will contain the child records.

Resizing a Section

To resize a section in your report, with the report in Design view, move the mouse pointer over the bottom edge of the section until the pointer changes to a sizing cursor (see image below), then click and drag up or down.

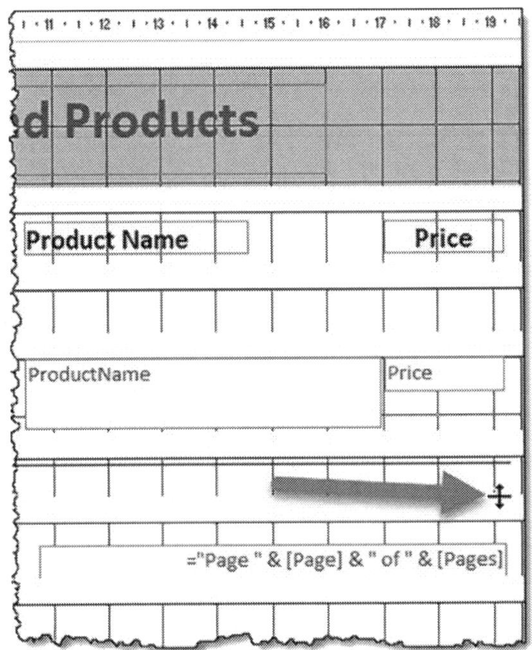

Formatting a Section

To display the Property Sheet for a section of the report, right-click the section and select **Properties** from the pop-up menu. For example, if you wanted to display the Property Sheet for the report header, you would right-click the report header and select Properties.

If the Property Sheet is already open and you want to display the properties for a section, simply click the section to display its properties.

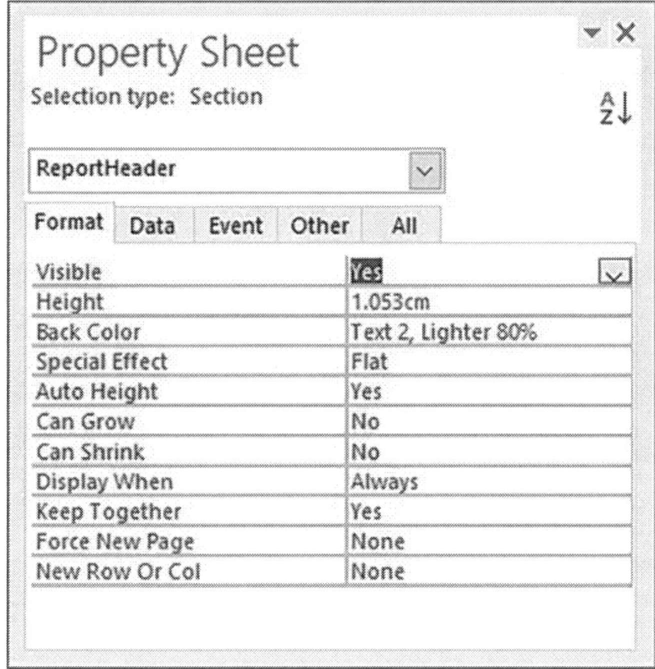

The Property Sheet provides several properties that you can use to customize a section.

- **Visible**: This allows you to set the visible property of a section to **Yes** or **No**. When set to No, the section is not rendered when the report is printed.

- **Height**: You can adjust the height of a section with this property, but it's often easier to resize a section manually with your mouse.

- **Back Color**: To change the background color of a section, click the small button with the eclipses in the Back Color drop-down list. This will open a color palette from which you select your desired background color.

- **Special Effect**: You can choose between Flat, Raised, and Sunken for this property. The default value is Flat.

- **Force New Page**: On some occasions, you may want to force a new page before a section, after a section, or both. For example, if your data is grouped and you want each group to be printed on a different page, you would select **After Section** for this property.

All the other properties are usually best left at their default values.

How to Group and Sort Records

When you create a report with the Report Wizard, and you tell the wizard to group one or more fields, the wizard will create the necessary group sections in the report for you. However, when refining the report, you may want to add more groups, change the grouped fields, or add fields to the group header. You may also want to create a section footer to add summarized information for that group. To make these changes, you need to understand how to add report sections and groupings.

Note Before making any major changes to your report's design, you can create a copy of the report as a backup. To create a copy of a report, right-click the report in the Navigation Pane and select **Copy** from the pop-up menu. Then, right-click a blank area in the Navigation Pane and select **Paste** on the pop-up menu.

To manually create a group in your report, you need to use the **Group & Sort** command in the **Grouping & Totals** group in the menu.

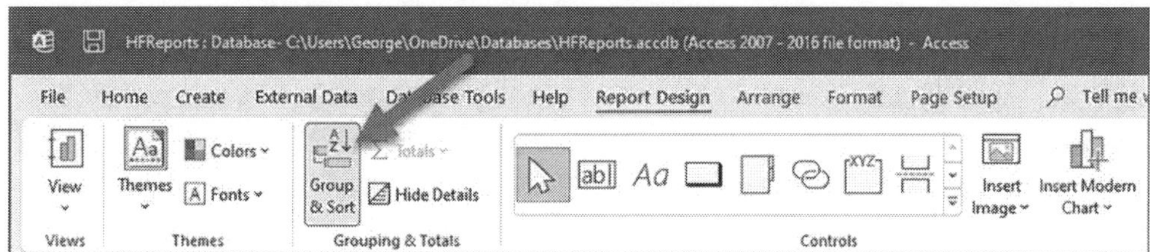

To display the Group, Sort, and Total panel, do the following:

1. Open your report in Design view.
2. Click the **Report Design** tab.
3. In the **Grouping & Totals** group, click the **Group & Sort** button (this is a toggle button that you can use to display or hide the Group, Sort, and Total panel).

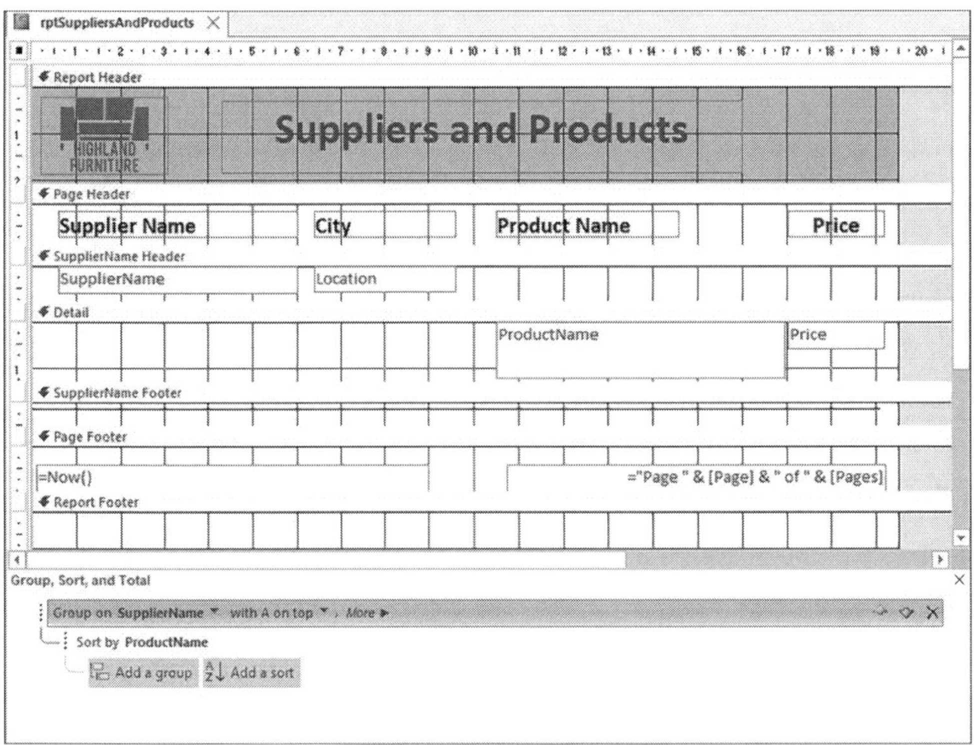

The **Group, Sort, and Total** panel enables you to group and sort the records in your report. You can use this panel to add section headers, section footers, and any fields you want to sort by. On this panel, you can also remove groups and sorting settings.

To create a new group using the Group, Sort, and Total panel, do the following:

1. Open your report in Design view.

2. On the Ribbon, click the **Report Design** tab, and in the **Grouping & Totals** group, click the **Group & Sort** button.

   The Group, Sort, and Total panel will be displayed at the bottom of the report.

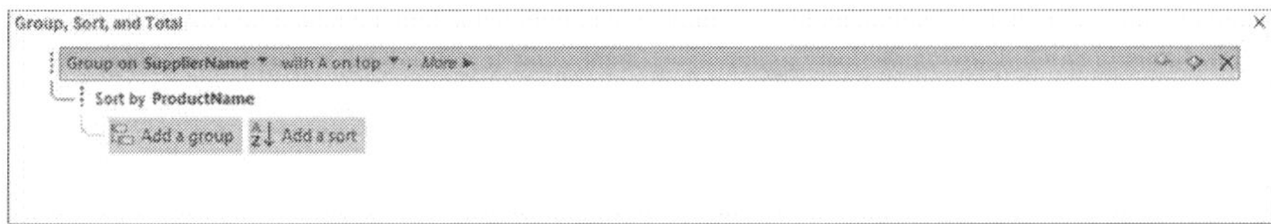

   You will see any existing groups or sorting in this panel. The hierarchical order of the grouping and sorting information in the report is displayed here. A group starts with **Group on**, followed by the name of the field used for the grouping. Any sorting will start with **Sort by**, followed by the name of the field used for the sorting.

3. Click **Add a group** to add a new group to your report. On the pop-up menu, select the field you want to use for the grouping.

   Access displays a list of available fields you can use to group the data.

4. To add a footer to the group, click the **More** button to expand the 'Group on' bar. The expanded bar displays additional settings for the group.

   If the group doesn't have a footer, **without a footer section** will be one of the settings on the bar. Click the drop-down arrow next to this setting and select **with a footer section** from the drop-down list.

   To remove an existing footer, do the reverse. To collapse the bar, click the **Less** button.

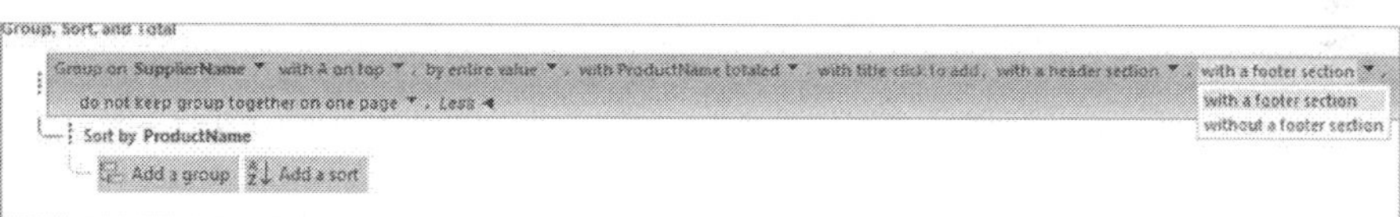

Note This panel also allows you to add aggregate information like count, sum, and average to your section footer. We'll be covering how to add aggregate information later in this chapter.

---

5. Click **Add a sort** to add a sorting field. Then select the fields you want to sort by from the pop-up menu.

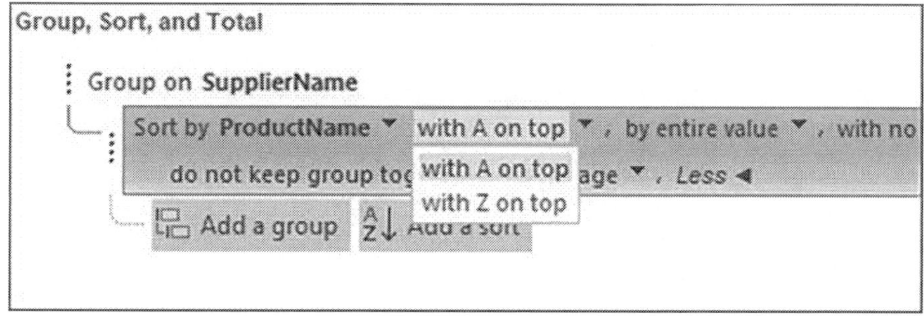

Access displays a list of available fields you can use to sort the data.

To change the sort order, expand the **Sort by** panel and click **with A on top**. Here you get options to sort the data using that field in ascending or descending order.

6. To close the Group, Sort, and Total panel, click the close button (x) on the upper-right corner of the panel. Alternatively, on the Ribbon, click the **Group & Sort** button in the **Grouping & Totals** group. This button is a toggle button that toggles the Group, Sort, and Total panel on or off.

The Group, Sort, and Total panel makes it easy to organize groups and other sections on your report.

Adding Fields to the Group Header

After you create a group using the Group, Sort, and Total panel, you need to manually move any fields currently on your report into the new section header.

For example, let's say we created a report to display suppliers and products, with each supplier having multiple products. If we add a section for the SupplierName field to our report, we need to move the SupplierName field into the SupplierName section header and leave the fields for the product in the Detail section.

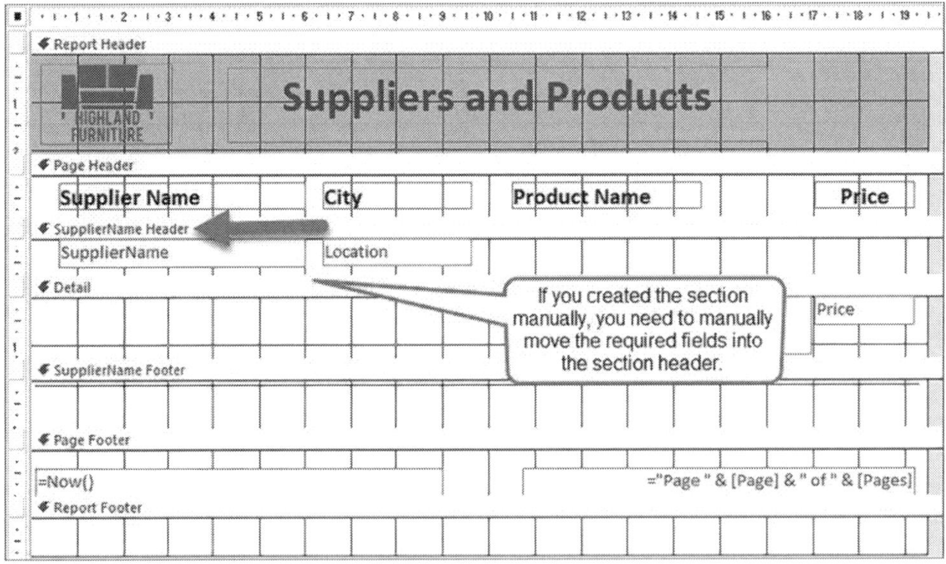

Add Calculated Fields to the Group Footer

To illustrate how to add a calculated field to the footer of a group, we need to revisit the **Orders report** we created in chapter 16.

The report is grouped by OrderID, and each order can have one or more items. To add the total value for each order to the footer of each group, we need to add a field that sums the Line Total field (see image below).

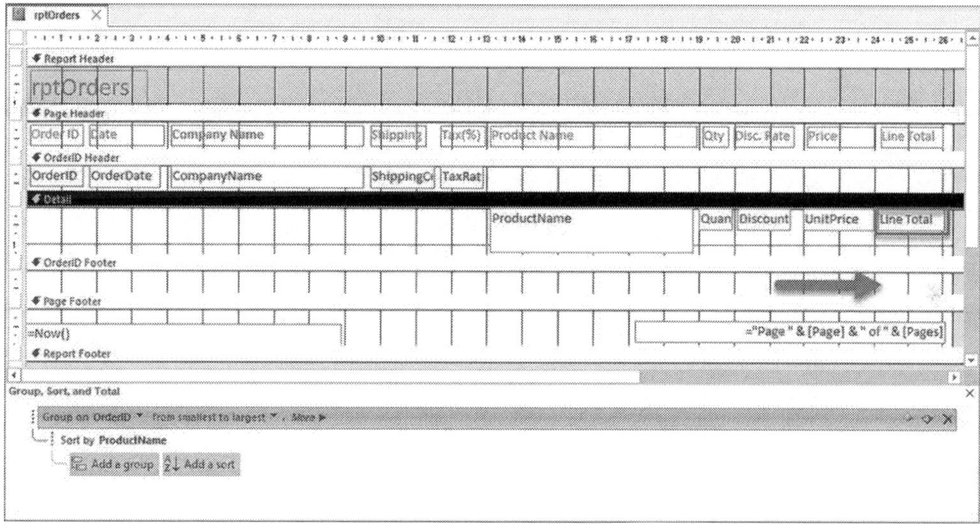

There are two ways you can add aggregate information to a group footer:

- You can use the **Group, Sort, and Total** panel to add totals to the report.
- You can manually insert an unbound text box control and use an expression to calculate the total.

To add aggregate information to your group footer using the Group, Sort, and Total panel, do the following:

1. With your report open in Design view, display the **Group, Sort, and Total** panel.

2. Click the **Group on** panel for the field that you want to summarize in the footer.

3. Click **More** to expand the bar.

4. Click the drop-down arrow next to **with no totals**. If you have not set any totals for the group prior, you'll see this option.

   Access displays the **Totals** pop-up menu.

5. In the **Total On** dropdown list, select the field you want to summarize. For example, if we want to sum the Line Total, we will select the Line Total field.

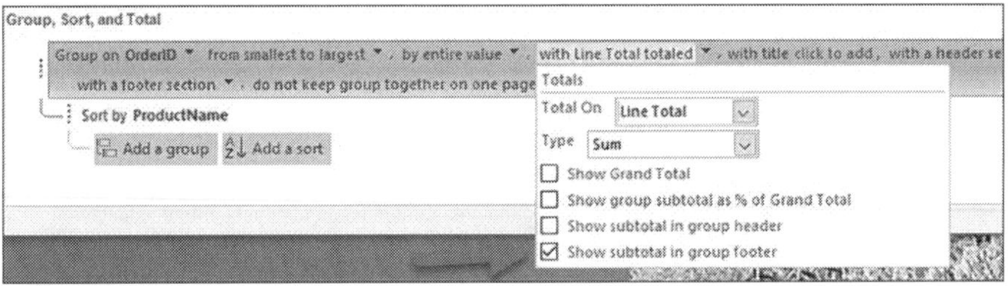

6. In the **Type** drop-down list, select the aggregate function you want to use.

   If the field you selected in Total On is a text field, you'll get the options of **Count Records** and **Count Values** in Type.

   If the field you selected in Total On is a number field, you'll get options in the Type drop-down list to aggregate the data using Sum, Average, Count Records, Count Values, Maximum, Minimum, Standard Deviation, or Variance.

7. Select **Show subtotal in group footer**.

   Access inserts a textbox in the group's footer with an expression to perform the calculation. For our example, Access inserts a text box with the following expression:

=Sum([Line Total])

8. When we view the report now in Print View, we'll have the total for each order after every group.

Manually Add a Calculated Field to Your Report

You can use the Group, Sort, and Total panel to insert simple aggregate values for fields in the group. However, you may have a more complex calculation to perform, and in such cases, it is often easier to manually insert a text box control and expression for the calculation.

Follow the steps below to manually add a calculated field to the footer of your report:

1. Open the report in Design view.

2. On the **Report Design** tab, in the **Controls** group, select the icon for the Text Box control.

3. Click in the group footer (or the section of your report where you want to place the text box). The text box and its label are added to the report.

4. Right-click the label for the text box and select **Properties** from the pop-up menu to display the **Property Sheet**.

   On the **Format** tab of the Property Sheet:

   - Change the **Caption** of the label to a name that best describes your text box, for example, Order Total.
   - Change the **Font Weight** property to **Bold**.
   - Set the **Text Align** property to **Right**.

5. Click the text box to display its properties in the Property Sheet.

   - On the **Format** tab, change the **Border Style** to **Transparent**.
   - On the **Data** tab, in the **Control Source** property, click the **Builder button** (with the ellipsis) to open the **Expression Builder**.

     For our example, we want to calculate the order total. Hence this would include the line total as well as the shipping cost and tax rate.

The following expression will do the job:

```
=(Sum([Line     Total])+[ShippingCost])+((Sum([Line
Total])+[ShippingCost])*[TaxRate])
```

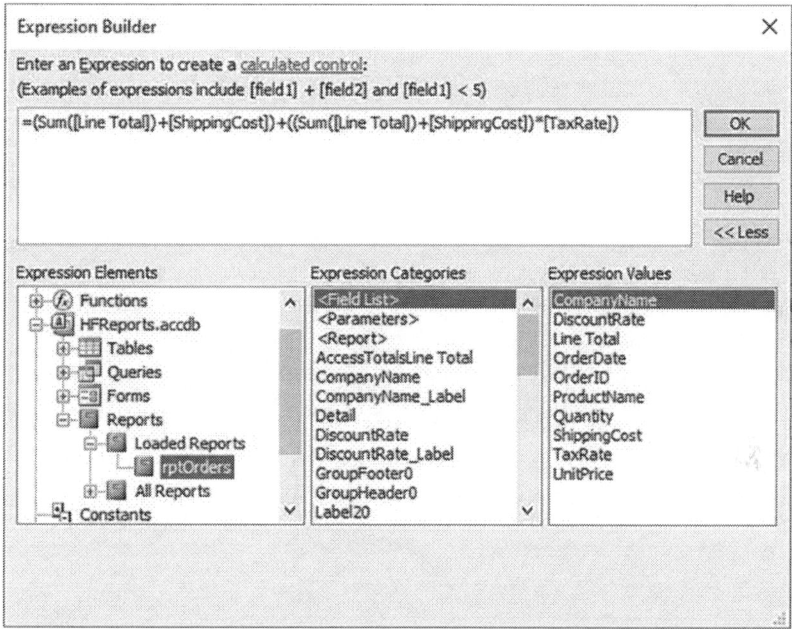

The expression above adds the line total and the shipping cost. It then calculates the tax rate and adds it to the total.

Tip The Expression Builder makes it easier to build complex expressions by having all the elements you need to construct your syntax in one place. However, you don't necessarily need to use the Expression Builder if your expression is simple. You can just enter the expression directly in the **Control Source** property. For example: *=Sum([Line Total]).*

---

6. When done, click **OK** to close the Expression Builder.

7. Save your report, and switch to Print Preview (or Report View) to view the new summary information you've added to the group footer.

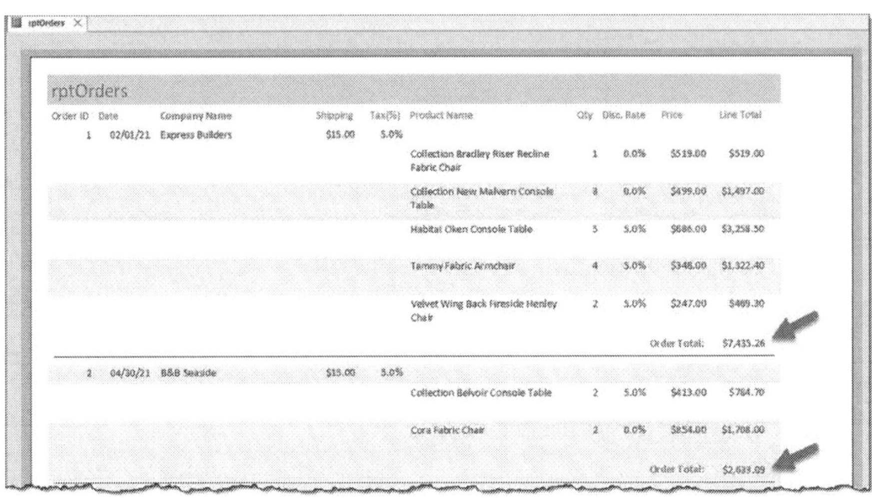

Note For more on creating expressions with the Expression Builder, see **Using the Expression Builder** in chapter 13.

Removing a Group

To remove a group in the **Group, Sort, and Total** panel, click the delete button on the right end of the 'Group on' panel for that field. Access will inform you that any controls in the group header or footer will be deleted.

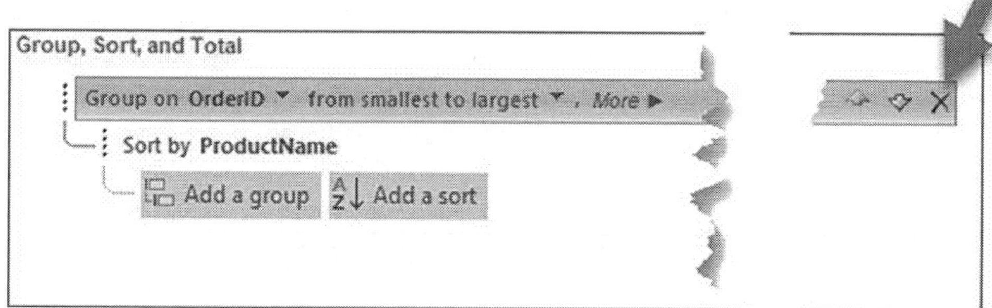

Note When you delete a group, all fields in the group's header and footer are also removed. Therefore, if you want to keep those fields in the report, ensure you move them into the Detail section before deleting the group.

Chapter 18: Mailing Labels and Printing

Another type of Access report you can create is a Labels report. The Labels command in Access is mainly used for mailing labels, but you can create different types of labels. You can use a Labels report to generate labels for one or multiple addresses in your database. For example, you may want to generate mailing labels for all suppliers in your database in a bulk mailing campaign or generate a mailing label for one customer.

Users mostly create labels with the intention of printing hard copies to be attached to letters or physical items requiring labeling. Thus, we will also cover printing Access reports in this chapter and the various print options and settings available.

This chapter covers how to:

- Create mailing labels using the Label Wizard.
- Print a hard copy of your report.
- Configure page setup and print options.

Creating a Mailing Label

Using Access to generate your labels can be easier to manage than using an application like Microsoft Word. With your data in Access, you could have names and addresses in tables you can easily convert to mailing labels. Having the data in a database instead of a flat-file also makes it easier to manage. Access gives you better tools to organize and manage data than a word processor or spreadsheet application. This is one reason you may want to use an Access database to generate mailing labels rather than Word or Excel.

Tip You can use an Access Labels report for different types of labels and not just for mailing labels. For example, you can print labels for products, cabinets, shelves, crates, and other items that you want to label. The advantage Access provides is that you can organize this information in database tables as opposed to a flat-file. You then have the tools to automatically generate labels from the database.

Before starting the Label Wizard, decide what table or query you will use as the data source for your labels. You can use a single table that contains names and addresses, like customers, for example, or you can use a query with a selection of fields from one or more tables.

You can also use a parameter query if you want to have the option of printing just one address.

Note For more on how to create queries, including parameter queries, see chapter 13.

To generate a Label report, do the following:

1. In the Navigation Pane, select the table/query for which you want to generate labels.

2. On the Ribbon, click **Create**, and in the **Reports** group, click **Labels**.

   Access opens the **Label Wizard**.

3. **Select the specifications for the label, and then click Next**. If you have a specific manufacturer for the stationery you use for your labels, click the **Filter by manufacturer** drop-down list. This list has the specifications for hundreds of labels from popular label manufacturers. If you can find yours in the list, select it, and the wizard will set up the report dimensions in the list above.

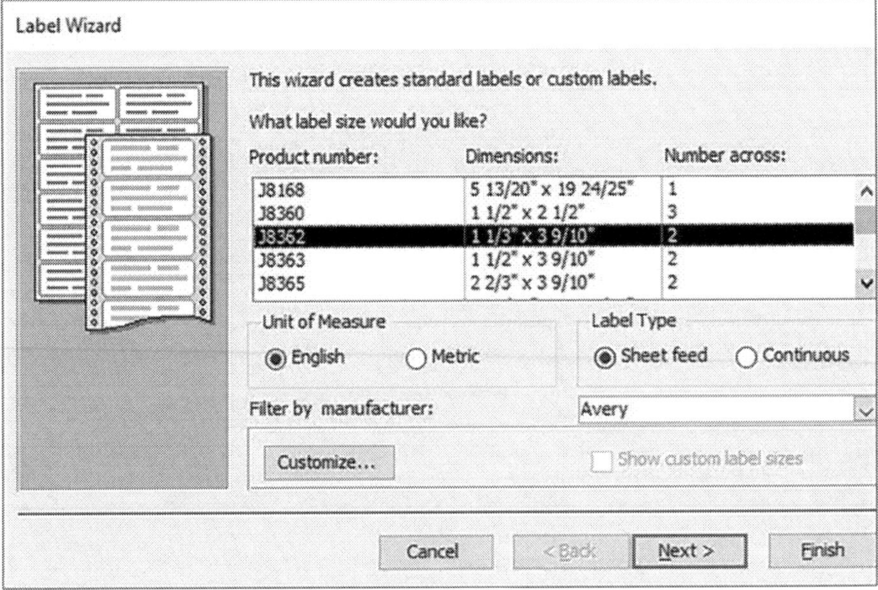

   If you don't know the manufacture of your label, then leave the default value, which is Avery.

   At the top of this page, a list shows several label specifications. You can select an option from the list that best suits your requirements. You can choose between 2 across, 3 across, or 1 across.

4. **Configure the text appearance and click Next**. On this page, you can select the font, font size, and font weight. You can also choose to italicize

or underline the text. On the left of the page, Access shows you a sample of the text appearance.

Tip As the wizard generates the labels automatically, you can always generate the report multiple times until it meets your requirements. So don't get too caught up in figuring out the right choices here. You can experiment with different options and run the wizard multiple times until the generated label is what you want.

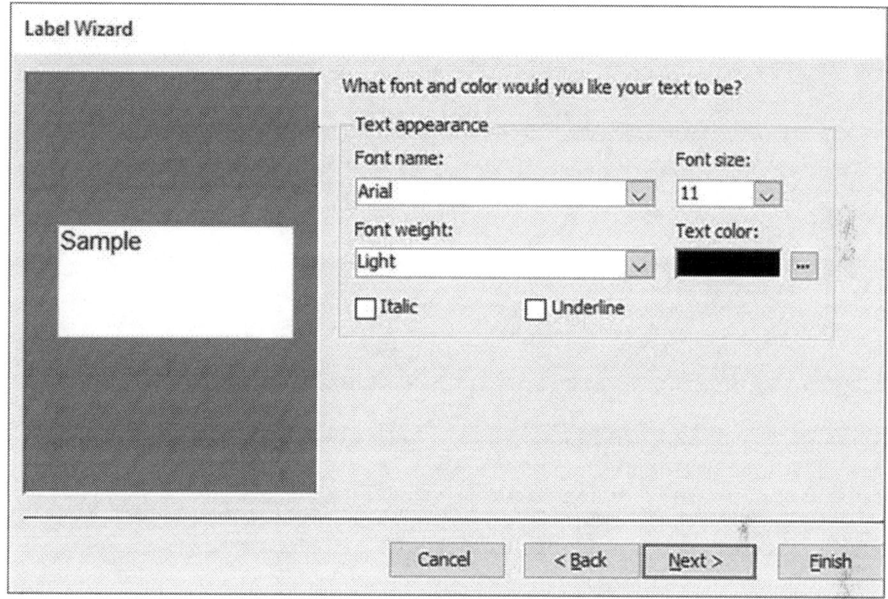

Click **Next**.

5. **Select the fields you want in the label and click Next**. Select a field name in the **Available fields** list, then click the add button (>) to add it to the **Prototype label** list.

   If you want the next field to be on a new line, press the **Enter** key in the Prototype label field to move the cursor to the next line. Repeat this process for the other fields you want to add to the label. The Prototype label field gives you a preview of how the fields are arranged on each label. You can also add characters to the label like commas here.

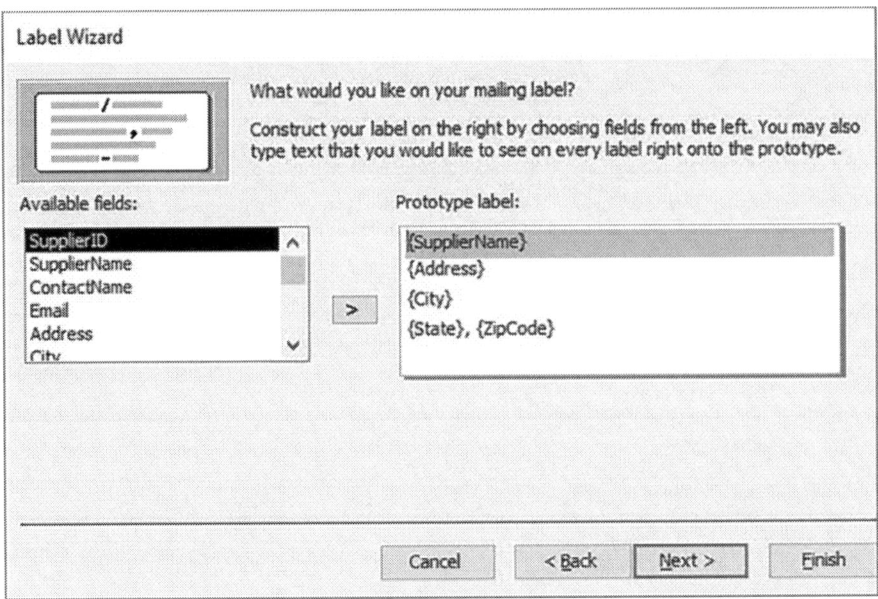

Click **Next**.

6. On the next page, select the fields that you want to sort the labels by. For example, you may want to sort the labels by supplier name or city.

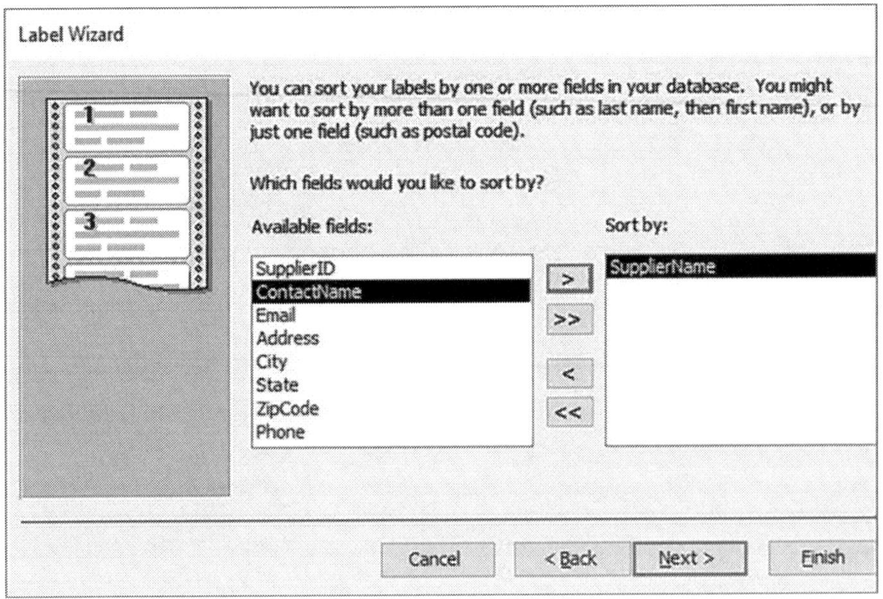

Click **Next**.

7. Enter an appropriate name for the report so that it is identifiable in the Navigation Pane. Choose the option to see the labels as they will look when printed and click **Finish**.

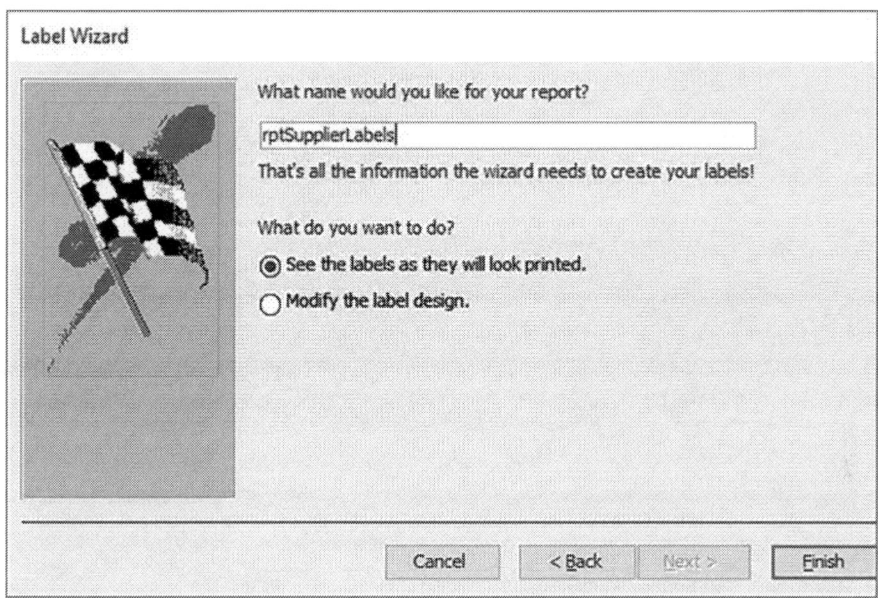

8. Access displays a print preview of the labels. To print your labels, insert the paper for the labels in your printer, and then click the **Print** command on the **Print Preview** tab.

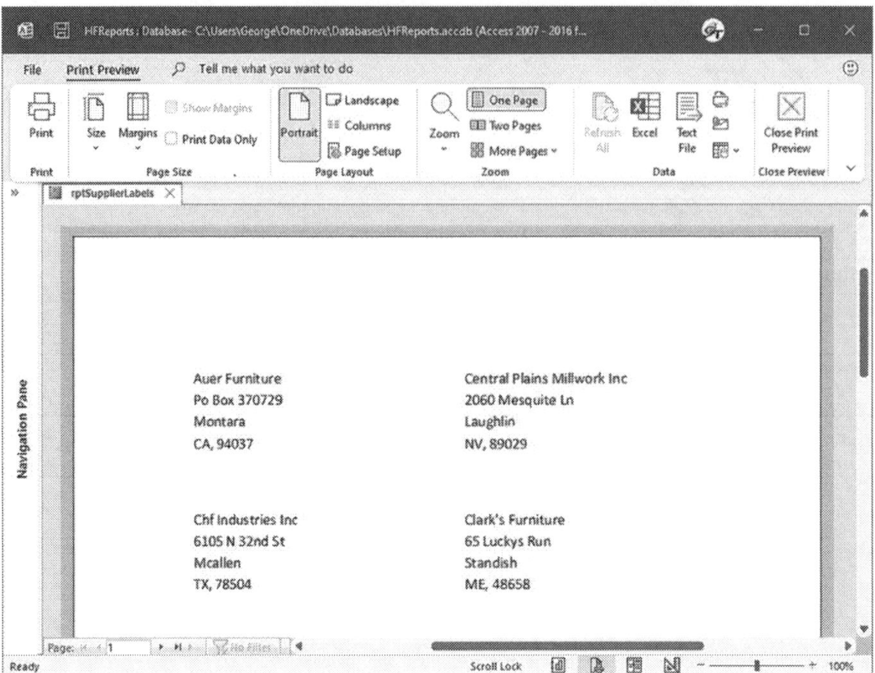

If you want to make design changes to the report, you can edit the label in Design view. You can manually resize and reposition fields or increase the height of a section. If significant changes are needed, it may be faster to run the wizard again and choose different settings.

Printing Your Report

The Print Preview mode of a report displays the report exactly as it would look when a hardcopy is printed. When you view a report in Print Preview mode, Access displays the Print Preview tab on the Ribbon. This tab provides a series of commands and options for changing the page size, changing the page layout, printing a hardcopy, or exporting the report to another file type.

Below are command options you'll find on the Print Preview tab:

- **Print**: Opens the **Print** dialog box where you can configure some print settings before printing the report.
- **Size**: This allows you to select the paper size from a list of options.
- **Margins**: Enables you to select from three pre-set margins or use custom margins.
- **Columns**: Opens the Columns tab on the Page Setup dialog box. The Columns tab enables you to define the number of columns you want for the report if different from the default.
- **Page Setup**: Opens the Page Setup dialog box, which provides more settings for commands in the Page Layout group.
- **Zoom**: Commands in this group enable you to zoom in and out of the report or change the number of pages displayed on the screen at a time.
- **Data**: Commands in the Data group enable you to export a report to Excel, Text, PDF/XPS, Email, Word, and other file types.
- **Close Print Preview**: As the button says, it closes the Print Preview window and returns the report to Design view.

Note You can also make changes to the paper size and page layout from the **Page Setup** tab in Design view or Layout view. However, to display the Print Preview tab on the Ribbon, you need to view the report in Print Preview mode.

Another way you can view a report in Print Preview mode is to select the report in the Navigation Pane, and from the Ribbon, click **File** > **Print** > **Print Preview**.

Page Setup

The Page Setup dialog box allows you to configure several print options before printing your report.

Print Options

To set the margins of the report, do the following:

1. Open the report in Print Preview mode.
2. On the Ribbon, in the **Page Layout** group, click the **Page Setup** button.
3. Access opens the **Page Setup** dialog box.

4. On the **Print Options** tab of the Page Setup dialog box, you can adjust the margins for the top, bottom, left, and right of the page. As you adjust the margins, on the right side of the dialog box, you will see a sample of how the reports will look when printed.

Page

The **Page** tab enables you to choose between Portrait and Landscape for the orientation. You can change the paper size from several options in the **Size** drop-down list. You can also change the paper source and printer if different from the default settings.

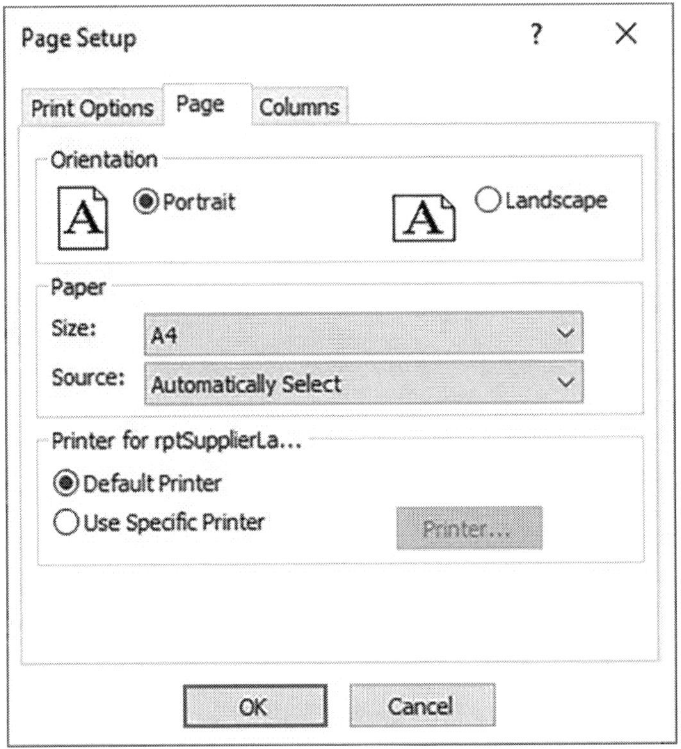
Page Setup
?
Print Options
Page
Columns
Orientation
Portrait
Landscape
Paper
Size:
A4
Source:
Automatically Select
Printer for rptSupplierLa...
Default Printer
Use Specific Printer
Printer...
OK
Cancel

Columns

You would normally leave the default settings in the Columns tab as they are set by Access. However, for labels, you may need to make some adjustments to change how the report is rendered if the default settings are not suitable for your report.

There are three sections in the columns tab:

- **Grid Settings**: This has the number of columns your report uses and how far apart they are on the page.

> **Note** The default number of columns in a report is usually one unless it is a mailing label, in which case the number of columns will be the number of labels you have across. The number of columns is not related to the number of fields you have on the report. If you increase the number of columns, your reports may show less information for each record.

- **Column Size**: You can adjust the height and width of the columns on the report here.

- **Column Layout**: Only enabled if your report has more than one column, for example, a mailing label. This option defines how Access renders the data on the page when your report has more than one column (usually for Labels). The default is **Across, then Down**. The graphic on the right provides a good depiction of how the data is rendered across the columns.

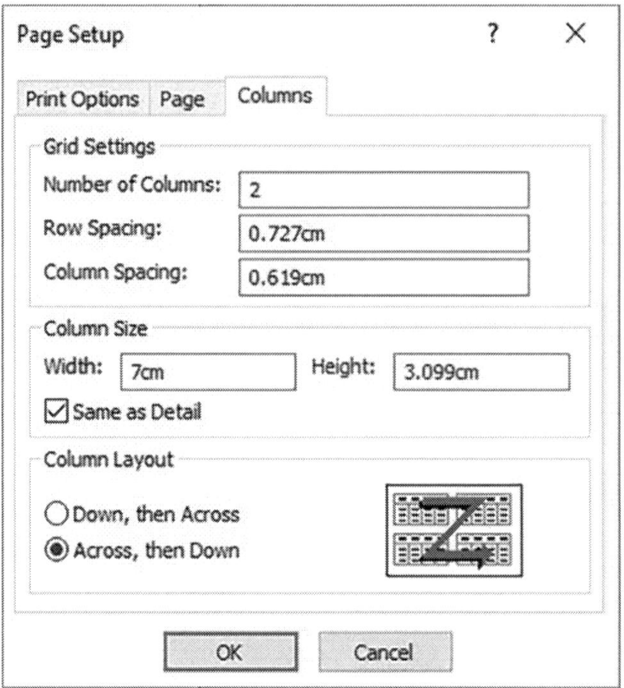
Page Setup
?
Print Options
Page
Columns
Grid Settings
Number of Columns:
2
Row Spacing:
0.727cm
Column Spacing:
0.619cm
Column Size
Width:
7cm
Height:
3.099cm
Same as Detail
Column Layout
Down, then Across
Across, then Down
OK
Cancel

Part 7

Database Maintenance

In Part 7

Creating and implementing an Access database is an important first step in the application's life cycle. However, there are often other tasks you may need to perform occasionally to maintain the system.

In part 7, we cover three topics that fall roughly under the area of organizing and maintaining your database. The chapters in this part cover backing up your database, splitting an Access database, and securing your database with a password. These tasks can be seen as optional, depending on how you're using your database. For example, if your database has production data that is regularly updated, you should create a backup routine to ensure data is not lost in the case of any problems with the working copy.

Contents at a Glance

Chapter 19: Backing Up Your Database

If your Access database is being used in a production environment, then it is essential to have a backup routine so that you can restore the database if it were to get corrupt. Regular backups are even more critical if several users use your database simultaneously in a multi-user environment.

Access supports up to 255 concurrent users, but it is most stable when there are no more than 10 simultaneous users. Above that number, there is an increased chance of something going wrong that causes the database to be damaged. A database can become corrupt for many different reasons. For example, a computer crash for one user in the middle of an update may lead to inconsistent data or a locked record.

If your database becomes corrupted or damaged, and you can no longer open it, you can restore the database from a backup version you have kept. One of the maintenance tasks you can perform to protect your data is to back it up regularly.

In this chapter, we will cover the following:

- Backing up and restoring your Access database.
- Restoring some objects in your database from a backup copy.

Backing up an Access Database

To back up your Access database, do the following:

1. On the Ribbon, click the **File** tab to go to the Backstage view.

2. In the Backstage view, click **Save As**.

3. Click Save Database As, and under Advanced, select **Back Up Database**.

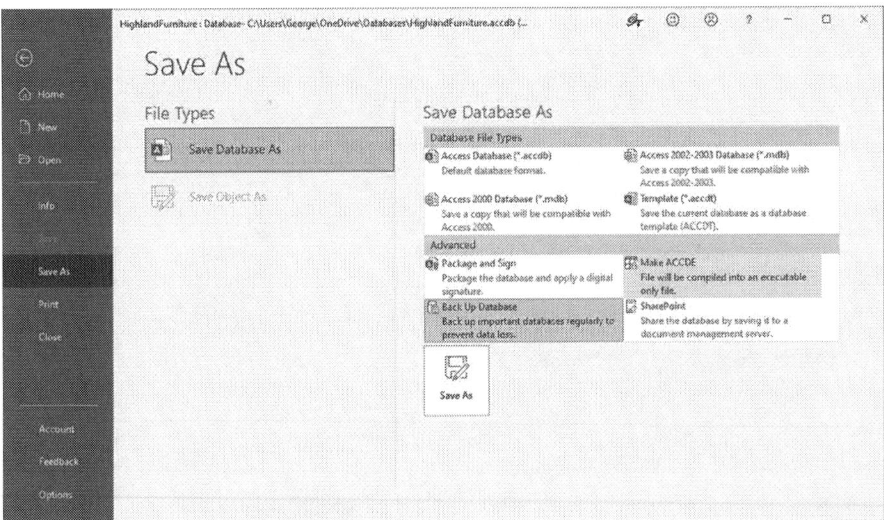

4. Click the **Save As** button.

   Access opens the Save As dialog box.

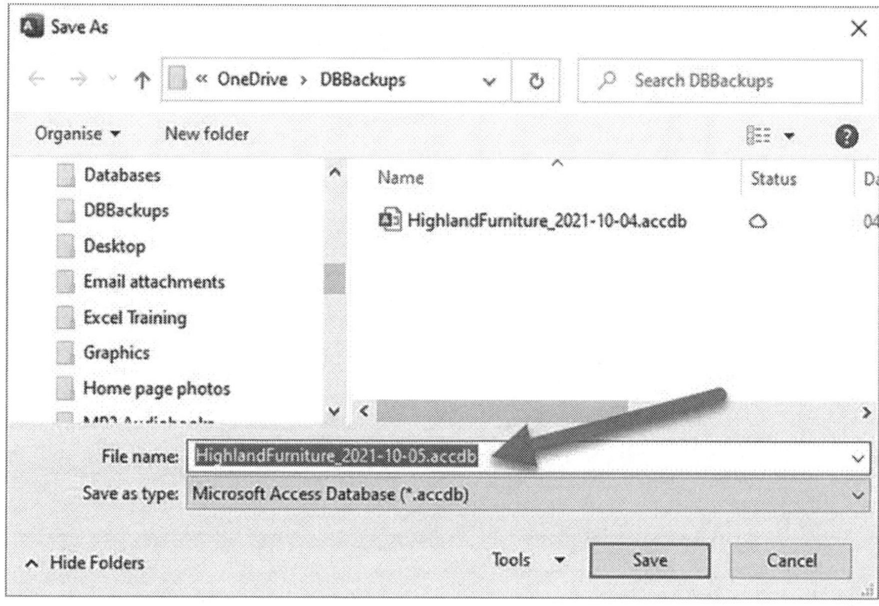

5. **Enter the name for the backup file.**

   In the **File name** box of the **Save As** dialog box, notice that Access appends the current date to the name of the database. You can use this name, which means any new backups will not overwrite a previous day's backup. Alternatively, you could choose to use your own naming format.

6. Navigate to the folder where you want to store the file and click **Save** to save a backup copy of the database to that location.

   Ensure the backup is not saved to the same folder as the working database. Ideally, the backup file should be on a cloud or network drive that is in a different location from where the working database is stored. This ensures that, for whatever reasons, if the physical machine storing the working database goes down, you can still access a backup copy.

And that is it! You now have a backup. If you're using the default name provided by Access, the database file name will tell you when a particular backup was taken.

How often you make a backup of your database will depend on how often the data changes. If the database is being updated daily, then you ideally want to take a daily backup.

Restoring an Access Database from Backup

If your database gets damaged or corrupt, you may be able to repair it with the **Compact and Repair Database** command on the **Database Tools** tab. If the Compact and Repair Database option doesn't fix the problem, you can restore a copy from backup if you have kept backups.

To restore a corrupt or damaged database, do the following:

1. Close the working database and ensure no one else has it open.
2. In File Explorer, rename the database with a name indicating its status, for example, MyDb_Damaged.accdb.
3. Using File Explorer, navigate to the folder with the backup database, then copy it and paste it into the folder where you have the working database.
4. Rename the backup database to the working database.
5. Check that the database is in full working order and all issues identified in the damaged copy have been resolved by the restore process.
6. You can either delete the damaged database or move it to an archive folder.

That's it! You can now continue working with a working copy of your Access database.

Importing Objects from a Backup Database

On some occasions, you may not necessarily need to restore the full database when something goes wrong with one of your database objects. For example, let's say one of the reports gets corrupted, or perhaps a couple of records were deleted from a table by mistake, and there is no way to undo the deletes. You can import a backup version of the object from a backup you have taken.

To replace a damaged object in your database, do the following.

1. Rename the current version.

   In the Navigation Pane of the database, rename the object that you want to replace. For instance, if you have a table with corrupt or missing data, right-click the table, and select **Rename** from the pop-up menu. You can append some text to the name to indicate its status, for example, tblMyTable_OLD.

2. On the Ribbon, click the **External Data** tab, and in the **Import & Link** group, select **New Data Source** > **From Database** > **Access**.

   Access opens the **Get External Data** dialog box.

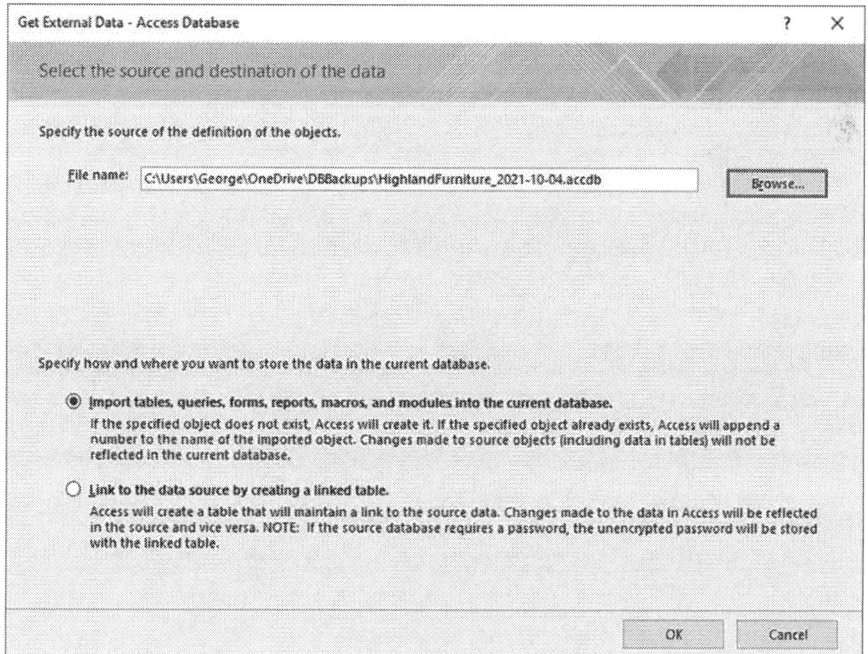

3. On the Get External Data dialog box, click the **Browse** button to navigate to the folder with the backup database and select it.

4. In the bottom half of the dialog box, select the first option, that is, to import the object, and click **OK**.

   Access displays the **Import Objects** dialog box. This dialog box enables you to select different objects from the source database and import them into the current database.

5. Select the objects you want to import and click **OK**.

   You have different tabs for tables, queries, forms, reports, macros, and modules. Click an object on the list to select it. To deselect an item, click it again. This is a multi-select list. Hence you can select multiple objects by clicking additional items on the list (or on different tabs) to select them.

Note If you've selected an object with the same name as an existing object in the destination database, a number will be appended to the name of the imported object to distinguish it from the existing object.

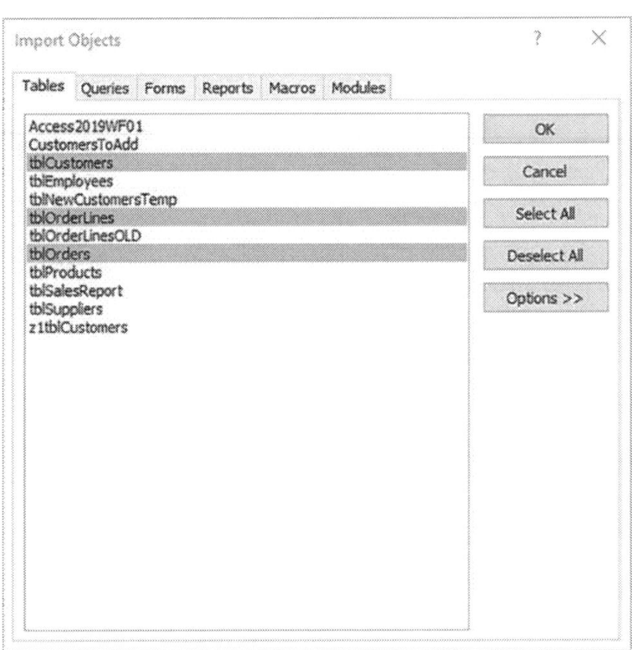

6. Click **Close** at the next dialog box.

Your imported objects will be available from the Navigation Pane and ready for use.

Chapter 20: Splitting an Access Database

If your database is being used by several concurrent users on different workstations over a network, you may consider splitting it into back-end and front-end files. Splitting a multi-user database can improve its performance and reduce the chances of corruption. You can split a database manually or use the Database Splitter Wizard in Access.

This chapter will cover:

- The advantages of splitting an Access database.
- Splitting your database into front-end and back-end database files.
- Managing linked tables in your front-end database.

Overview of Splitting an Access Database

Ideally, you only want to split an Access database if it is a shared application used over a network by several concurrent users. Splitting an Access database does come with some costs in terms of requiring more effort to manage and maintain.

When you split an Access database, you create two database files:

- **Back-end database**: Contains just the tables. This file is placed on the file server in a shared network.
- **Front-end database**: Contains all the other objects - queries, forms, reports, macros, and modules. A copy of the front-end database is placed on each workstation accessing the file server.

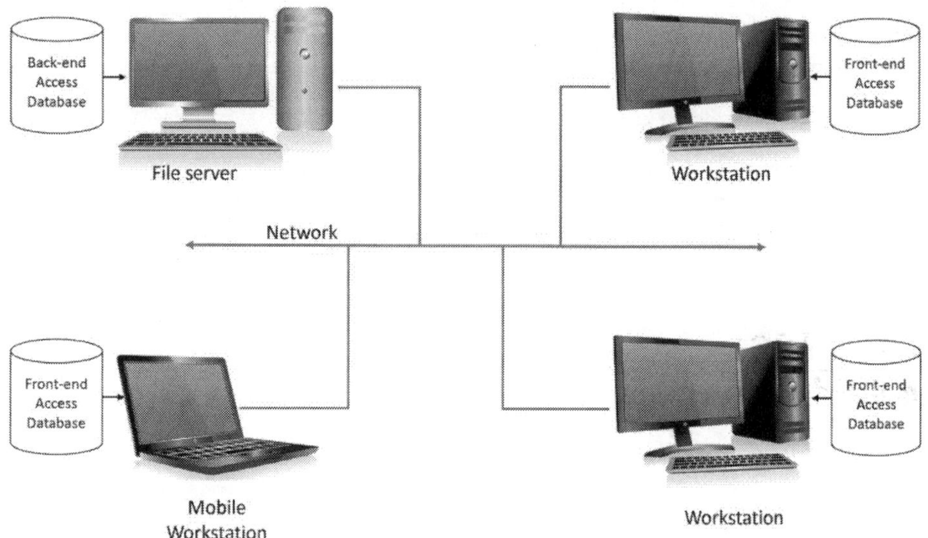

Benefits of Splitting a Database

Below are a few benefits of splitting your Access database:

- **Improved performance**: If your database is on a network, splitting the database into a back-end file and a front-end file could significantly improve its performance. With the front-end on the local computer, only requested data is transmitted across the network as opposed to all the objects being transmitted across the network for a single shared Access database.

- **Greater availability**: As only the data is being accessed in the back-end file, there will be fewer locks on the database, making edits and transactions faster in a multi-user environment.

- **Improved security**: Splitting the database into two means you can put the back-end file with the data in a more secure network drive with a different level of access control. Users can't make unauthorized design changes to the database tables if they don't have direct access to the shared folder with the backend file.

  You can also create front-end files that provide users with only the database objects they need for their role. For example, let's say you hire a temporary employee as a data entry clerk to update a particular table in your database. You could provide the employee with a front-end database that only contains the data entry form they need for their job to reduce the likelihood of them accessing other data.

- **Improved reliability**: As users only directly interact with the front-end file, if a problem occurs that causes the database to be damaged or corrupt, for example, a computer crash, the back-end file will be unaffected. Other users can continue to use the database if they are using a different copy of the front-end file.

- **Flexible maintenance**: Splitting the database enables you to carry out development changes or maintenance work on individual front-end copies without taking the back-end offline. This leaves the database available to other people using a different front-end.

Precautions to Take Before Splitting a Database

Before you split your database, consider the following points:

- Always make a copy of the database before you split it. If anything goes wrong with the splitting process, you can always restore your working copy with the backup.

- Depending on how many objects and tables you have in your database, splitting it may take some time. Thus, you need to take the database offline and notify users that they cannot use the database during the process.

Note If a user performs data updates while you are splitting up the database, the changes will not be reflected in the back-end database.

- End-users of the database must have a version of Access on their desktop that is compatible with the back-end file format. For example, a user with Access 2003 cannot use a back-end database with the .accdb file format (Access 2007 and above).

Split the Database

Note Using File Explorer, make a copy of the database that you intend to split. Put the backup copy in a different folder in case you will need it in the future.

To split your database using the Database Splitter Wizard, do the following:

1. Open the database you want to split.

2. On the Ribbon, click the **Database Tools** tab, and in the **Move Data** group, click **Access Database**.

   Access displays the Database Splitter Wizard.

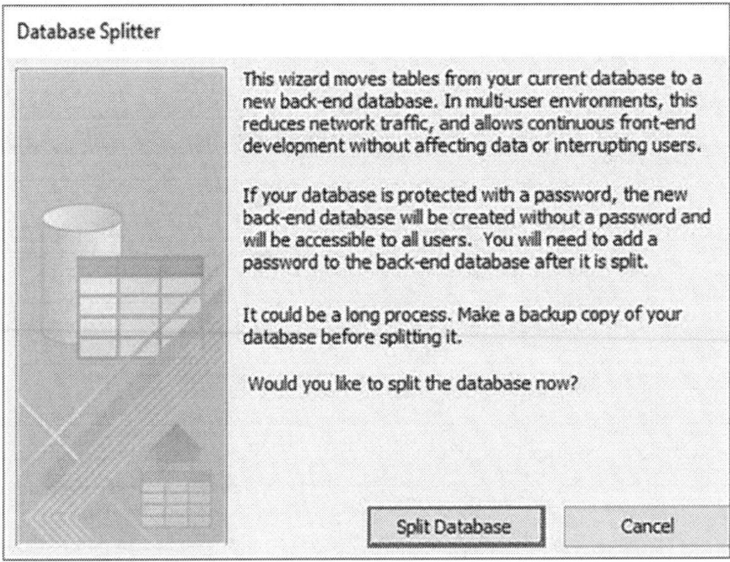

3. Click **Split Database**.

4. In the **Create Back-end Database** dialog box, Access appends **_be** to your database name. You can use this name or change the file name to your desired name for the back-end database.

5. Navigate to the folder where you'll be storing the back-end file and click **Split**.

Note If your database is on a network drive, you should enter the Universal Naming Convention (UNC) path in the **File name** box in front of the name rather than using a mapped drive letter.

For example, a UNC path should look like this:
\\server1\share1\Accounting\MyDB_be.accdb

Rather than looking like this:
G:\ Accounting\MyDB_be.accdb.

A shared drive can be mapped to different drive letters on different workstations, but a UNC path will remain the same for all workstations.

6. When the wizard has finished splitting the file, Access displays a confirmation message.

You now have a front-end and back-end database system. When you open the front-end database, you will see that the tables are now all linked tables. All the forms, queries, reports, and modules are still stored in the front-end. When you examine the back-end database, you will see that it only has tables.

Distributing the front-end database

After you split a database with the wizard, place the back-end database on a file server and then place a local copy of the front-end database on the workstation of every end-user.

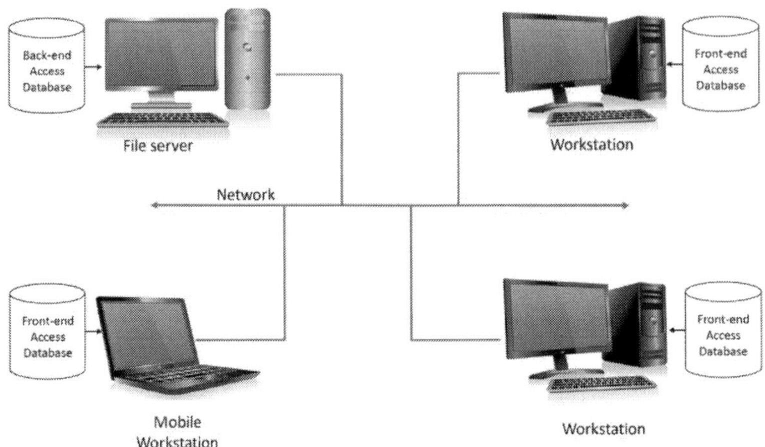

Important To ensure your data is protected, Microsoft recommends that you do not share copies of a database containing **links to SharePoint lists**. The connection information for links is not encrypted in Access. Hence, a link to a SharePoint list can make it possible for a malicious user to modify the SharePoint link, change its target, and gain unauthorized access to other data.

Managing Linked Tables

You manage the connection between the front-end and back-end database files using the **Linked Table Manager**. The Linked Table Manager is a central location for viewing and managing all linked tables and other linked data sources in your Access database.

Occasionally, you may need to refresh linked tables because of changes to the back-end database. For example, you may move the back-end file to a different folder, rename the back-end file, or make changes to the tables. Whenever you make any one of these changes, you must refresh the links using commands in the Linked Table Manager.

Note At the time of this writing, the Linked Table Manager is different in the standalone version of Access compared to the Microsoft 365 version of Access. The dialog box is simpler in the standalone version of Access, and you can export data to Excel.

Conversely, the newer Linked Table Manager in Microsoft 365 allows you to refresh, relink, add, delete, and edit linked tables, but you can't export data to Excel. The Linked Table Manager used in the examples in this book is the version available in Microsoft 365.

To relink to a back-end database that has been renamed or moved, do the following:

1. Open the front-end database.
2. On the Ribbon, click the **External Data** tab, and in the **Import & Link** group, click the **Linked Table Manager** button.
3. In the Linked Table Manager, there will be an entry for the data source that has been moved. Select the data source by clicking the checkbox next to the **Data Source Name**.

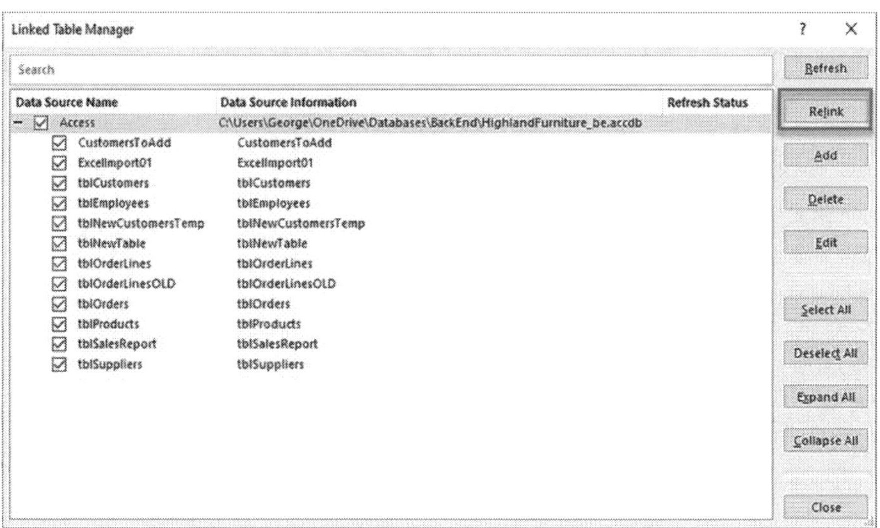

4. On the right side of the dialog box, click the **Relink** button.

5. In the dialog box, select the renamed database (or navigate to the folder containing the moved database) and select the database file. Then click **Open**.

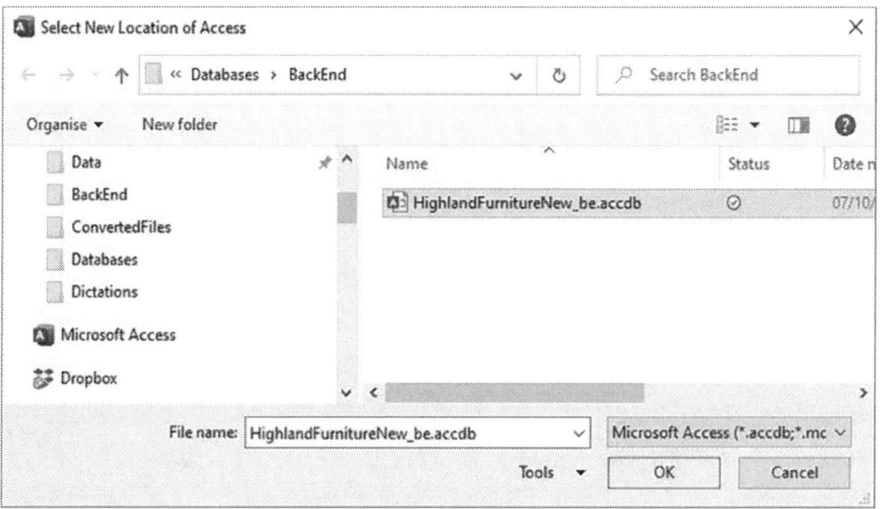

Note If you are using a UNC path to a shared network directory, enter it in the **File name** box.

6. Access displays a message asking if you want to choose new table names or retain the existing linked table names. To keep the existing names, click **No** at the message prompt.

7. If the relink was successful, the Refresh Status would show as **Succeeded** against each linked table.

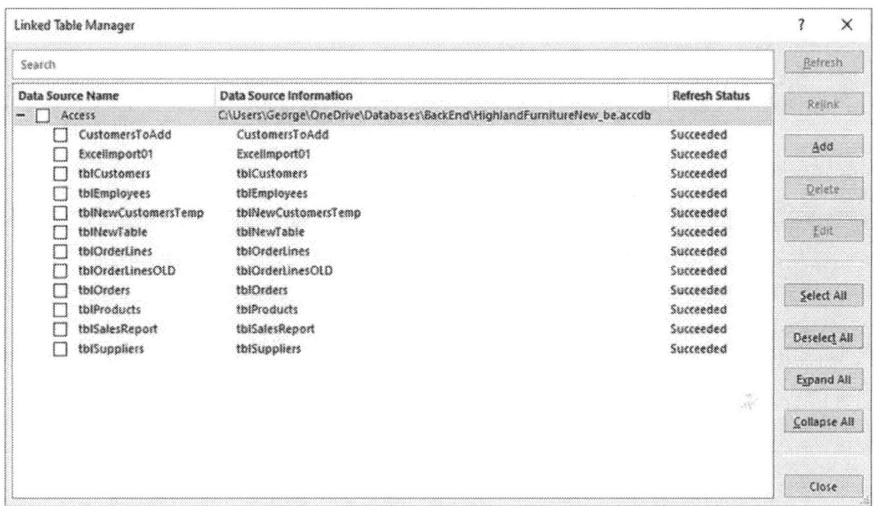

If you see a 'Failed' refresh status against any of the tables in the Linked Table Manager, it means the table has either been renamed or deleted. If the table has been renamed, you will need to relink it manually using the **New Data Source** command in the **Import & Link** group on the **External Data** tab.

If the table has been deleted from the back-end database, you can delete the linked table by selecting its checkbox and clicking the **Delete** button.

Adding a New Linked Table

After splitting your database, you may occasionally add new tables to the back-end database as requirements change over time. Access does not automatically link new tables added to the back-end database in the front-end database. In the front-end database, you'll need to add a link to the new back-end table using the Linked Table Manager.

To link to a new table in an existing linked data source, do the following:

1. Open the front-end database.

2. In the Navigation Pane, right-click any existing linked table and select **Linked Table Manager** from the pop-up menu.

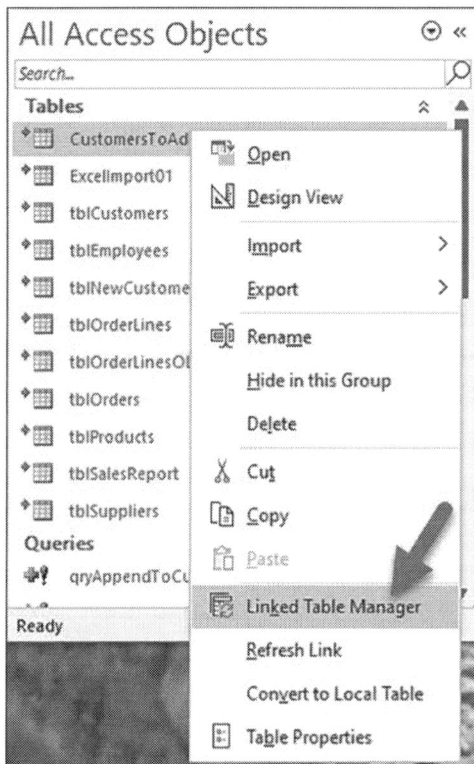

Access displays the **Linked Table Manager**.

3. In the Linked Table Manager, click **Add** to display the **Add New Link** dialog box.

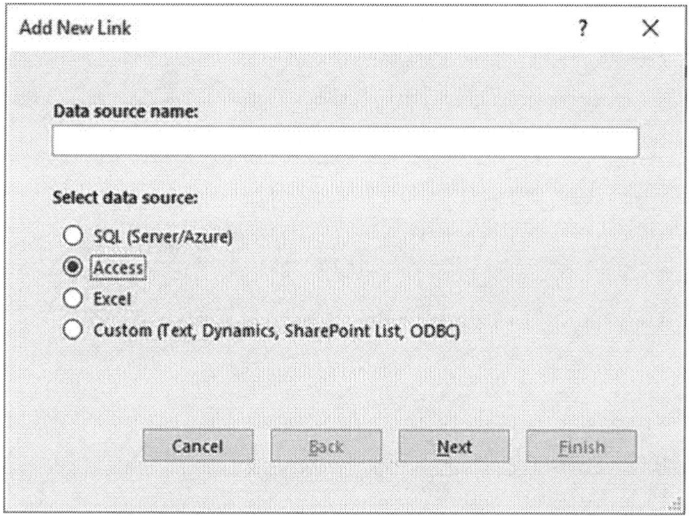

4. In the **Add New Link** dialog box, select **Access**, and click **Next**.

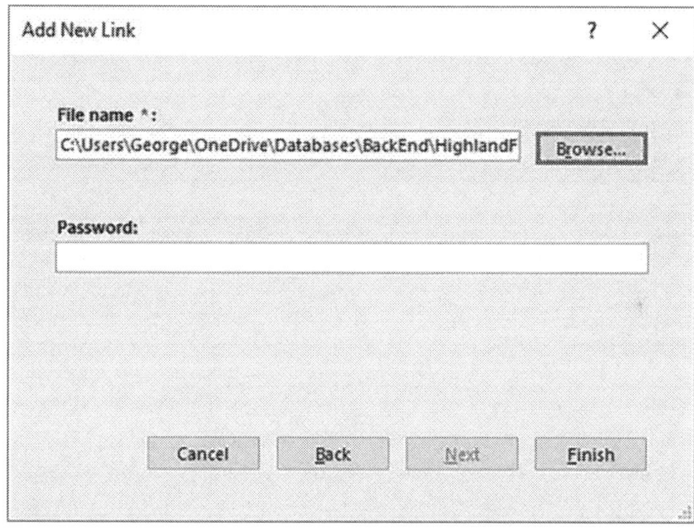

5. In the **File name** box, use the **Browse** button to locate the back-end database or enter the UNC path to the file (if it's on a shared network drive).

   If you've encrypted your back-end database with a password, enter the password in the Password box.

   Click **Finish** to display the Link Tables dialog box.

6. In the **Link Tables** dialog box, select the new table(s) you want to link and click **OK**.

That's it! Access adds the new table to the linked tables in the front-end database.

Chapter 21: Securing Your Database with a Password

Depending on how sensitive your data is and its location, you may decide to encrypt your database with a password. You can protect your Access database with a password in situations when you want to prevent unauthorized access to your data. The process encrypts the database and makes the data unreadable to other software tools. Whenever you log on with your password, Access decrypts the database, enabling you to work with your data.

In this chapter, we will cover how to:

- Encrypt your Access database with a password.
- Encrypt a split Access database.
- Decrypt an Access database.

Encrypting an Access Database

In versions of Access before 2007, you could create user accounts with different permissions to different sets of objects, which was called multi-user security. That feature is no longer available in the .accdb versions (2007 and later). In the current version of Access, each user will use the same password to access the database in a multi-user environment.

Note This new encryption feature is only applicable to databases in the .accdb file format. The encryption algorithm used is more robust than in versions before Access 2007. If you want to password a version of Access in the .mdb file format, the Encoding and Passwords features from Access 2003 are used.

If you encrypt a database and lose the password, you will be unable to open the database. You can't decrypt the database without your password. Hence, it would help if you were careful when creating a password for your database. You don't want a situation where you cannot access important data because the password has been lost. For that reason, only set a password if it is necessary for your working circumstances.

Important It is critical that you don't forget your password. To be on the safe side, before you protect your database with a password, ensure you've written down the password and stored it in a safe place where it can be retrieved if necessary. Microsoft does not provide any methods to access a password-protected Access file where the password has been lost.

To encrypt an Access database with a password, follow the steps below:

Step 1: Open the database in Exclusive mode.

1. Open Access.
2. Access opens to the Backstage view.

Note If you already have another database open, click the **File** tab to display the Backstage view.

---

3. In the Backstage view, click **Open > Browse**.
4. In the **Open** dialog box, navigate to the database you want to open, and then select the file.
5. Click the drop-down arrow next to the **Open** button, and then select **Open Exclusive** from the pop-up menu.

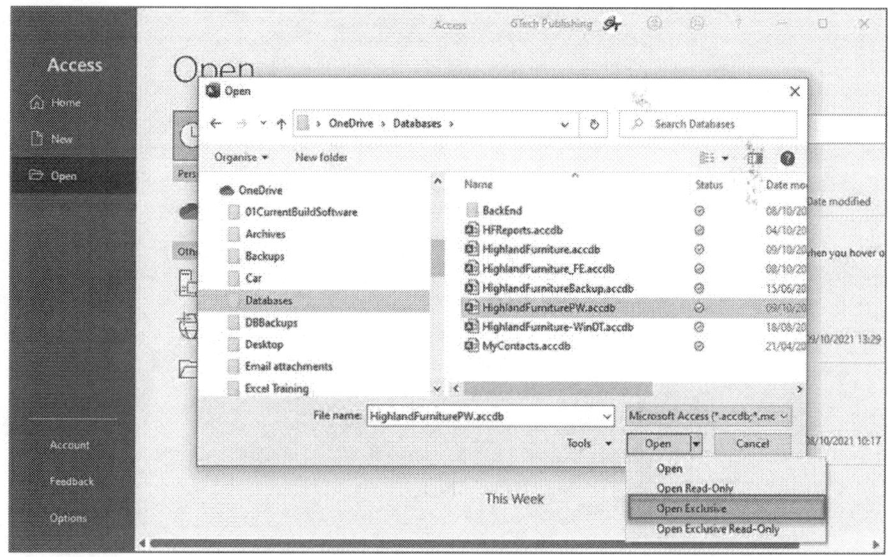

Step 2: Encrypt the Database with a password.

1. With the database now open in Exclusive mode, click the **File** tab to return to the Backstage view and click **Info** > **Encrypt with Password**.

   Access displays the **Set Database Password** dialog box.

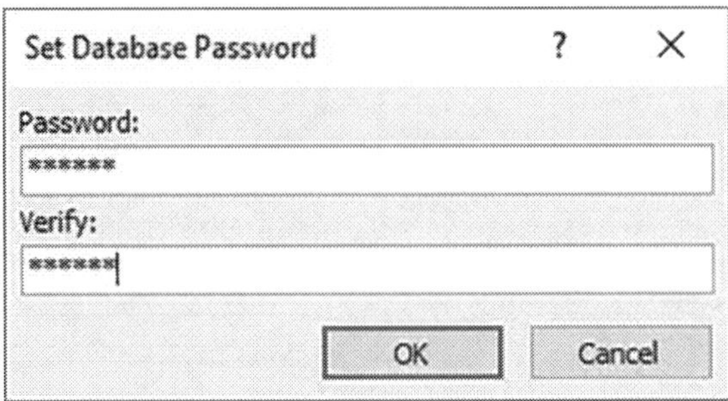

2. Enter your password in the **Password** box and again in the **Verify** box to confirm it, and then click **OK.**

3. Click **OK** at the next prompt to encrypt the database with a password.

4. Close the database and then reopen it.

   Access will display the **Password Required** dialog box.

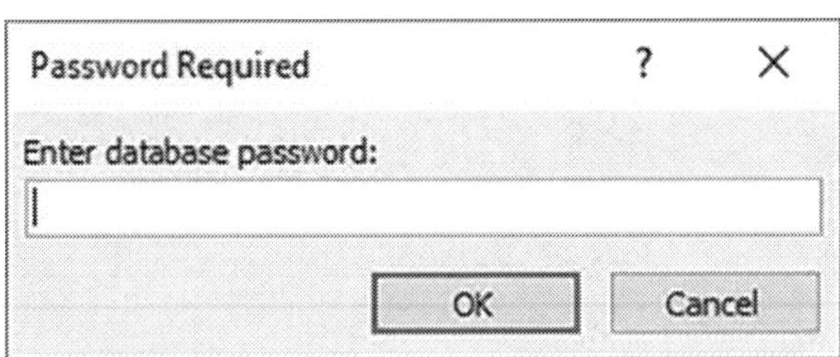

5. Enter your password in the box, and then click **OK**.

   Access will decrypt and open the database.

Encrypting a Split Database

To set a password for a split database, you need to encrypt both the front-end database and the back-end database. You need to first encrypt the back-end database, relink the tables in the front-end, and then encrypt the front-end database.

Important It is critical that you don't forget the password to both databases. To be on the safe side, before you protect your database with a password, ensure you've written down the password and stored it in a safe place where it can be retrieved if necessary. Microsoft does not provide any methods to access a password-protected Access file where the password has been lost.

Follow the steps below to encrypt a split database:

1. Follow the steps in the previous section to set a password for the back-end database.

2. In the front-end database, delete the links to the tables in the back-end database using the Navigation Pane or Linked Table Manager.

3. Relink the tables again using the **New Data Source** command on the **External Data** tab. Access will prompt you for the back-end database password this time.

4. After relinking the tables, set a password for the front-end database by following the steps provided in the previous section.

Note Ideally, you want to use the same password for both databases to keep things simple, but this is not mandatory. For example, you may have situations in a multi-user environment where, for greater security, you want to use different passwords for the back-end database and front-end database. Just ensure both passwords are written down and stored in a safe place where they can be retrieved if necessary.

Removing a Password

Occasionally, you may need to remove the password from an encrypted database to return it to its original unencrypted status.

To remove the password from an Access database, do the following:

1. Open the database in Exclusive mode as described in the section on securing a database with a password.

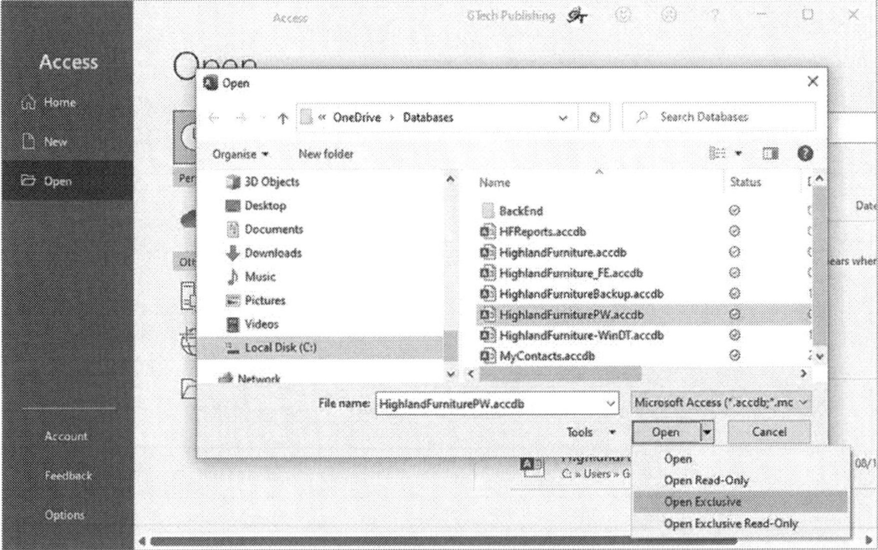

2. Enter your password at the **Required Password** prompt, and then click **OK**.

3. On the Ribbon, click the **File** tab to go to the Backstage view, and then click **Info** > **Decrypt Database**.

   Access displays the **Unset Database Password** dialog box.

Unset Database Password ? X
Password:
******
OK Cancel

4. Enter the password in the **Password** box, and then click OK.

5. Close the database and reopen it.

   This time Access will not prompt you for a password.

More Help

Thank you for buying and reading this book. If you have any questions or comments, please feel free to contact me at support@excelbytes.com.

For more help with Access, you can visit Microsoft's online help for Access and search for a topic:

https://support.microsoft.com/en-us/access

Leave a Review

If you found this book helpful, I would be very grateful if you can spend just 5 minutes leaving a customer review. You can go to the link below to leave a customer review.

https://www.excelbytes.com/access_review/

Thank you very much!

Appendix: Access Keyboard Shortcuts

Keyboard shortcuts for Access can help you work more efficiently. The following are the most common shortcuts used in Access in Windows.

Keypress	Action
F1	Opens the Access Help window.
F11	Toggle to show or hide the Navigation Pane.
F4	Toggle to show or hide the Property Sheet.
Alt+F4	Quit Access.
Ctrl+F	Opens the Find dialog box (in Find and Replace) when in Datasheet view or Form view.
Ctrl+H	Opens the Replace dialog box when in Datasheet view or Form view.
Alt+H	Goes to the Home tab on the Ribbon.
F6	Moves the focus and cursor to a different pane of the Access window.
Ctrl+O	Displays the Open screen of the Backstage view where you can open an existing database.

Ctrl+N	Displays the New screen of the Backstage view where you can create a new database.
F5	Changes a form from Design view to Form view.
Tab key (or Shift+Tab)	Tab moves to the next field while Shit+Tab goes to the previous field in Datasheet view and Form view.
Ctrl+P	Opens the Print dialog box while viewing a datasheet, form, or report.
Ctrl+Plus Sign (+)	Adds a new record when in Datasheet view or Form view.
Ctrl+F1	Shows or hides the Ribbon.
Ctrl+S	Save the currently active database object.
F12	Opens the Save As dialog box when viewing a database object.
Esc (in backstage view)	Returns to the database from the Backstage view.
F9	Refresh the contents of a Lookup field list box or combo box.
Ctrl+Z	Undo typing in Datasheet view or Form view.
Esc (in Form view)	Undo any changes in the current field or current record. Press Esc twice to undo the changes if both the current field and record have been changed.

Index

D

E

F

G

H

I

J

L

M

N

O

P

Q

R

S

T

About the Author

Nathan George is a computer science graduate with several years' experience in the IT services industry in different roles which included Access development, Excel VBA programming, end-user support of Access power users, and Access training. One of his main interests is using computers to automate tasks and increase productivity. As an author, he has written several technical and non-technical books.

Leave a Review

If you found this book helpful, I would be very grateful if you can spend just 5 minutes leaving a customer review. You can go to the link below to leave a customer review.

https://www.excelbytes.com/access_review/

Thank you very much!

Other Books by Author

Take Your Excel Skills to the Next Level!

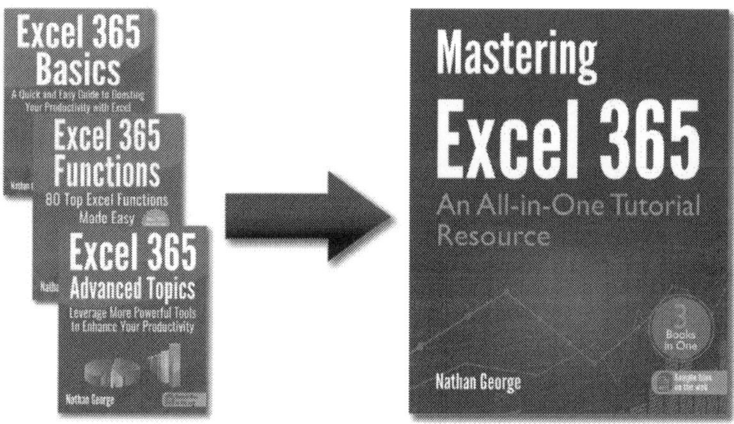

Mastering Excel 365 is your all-in-one guide to Excel. This guide contains everything you need to know to master the basics of Excel for Microsoft 365 and a selection of advanced topics relevant to real-world productivity tasks.

This guide has been designed as a resource for you whether you're an Excel beginner or a power user. You will learn how to use specific features and in what context to use them.

Available at Amazon:

https://www.amazon.com/dp/1915476119

Visit our website for more:

https://www.excelbytes.com/excel-books